ON OUR WAY

LIFE PASSAGES

Ronald L. Grimes and Robbie-Davis Floyd, Editors

1 *Deeply into the Bone: Re-Inventing Rites of Passage,*
by Ronald L. Grimes

2 *Cinderella Dreams: The Allure of the Lavish Wedding,*
by Cele C. Otnes and Elizabeth H. Pleck

3 *On Our Way: The Final Passage through Life and Death,*
by Robert Kastenbaum

ON OUR WAY

THE FINAL PASSAGE
THROUGH LIFE AND DEATH

Robert Kastenbaum

UNIVERSITY OF CALIFORNIA PRESS

BERKELEY   LOS ANGELES   LONDON

#57868176

*The publisher gratefully acknowledges
the generous contribution to this book provided
by the General Endowment Fund of the University
of California Press Associates.*

University of California Press
Berkeley and Los Angeles, California

University of California Press, Ltd.
London, England

Library of Congress Cataloging-in-Publication Data

Kastenbaum, Robert.
  On our way : the final passage through life
and death / Robert Kastenbaum.
      p.   cm.—(Life passages)
    Includes bibliographical references (p.) and index.
    ISBN 0-520-21880-9
    1. Death—Psychological aspects.   2. Death—
Social aspects.   3. Future life.   I. Title.   II. Series.
   BF789.D4 .K365   2004
    306.9—dc21   2003005044

Manufactured in the United States of America
13   12   11   10   09   08   07   06   05   04
10   9   8   7   6   5   4   3   2   1

The paper used in this publication meets the minimum
requirements of ANSI-NISO Z39.48-1992 (R 1997)
(Permanence of Paper).⊗

CONTENTS

LIST OF ILLUSTRATIONS   *vii*

1   Here (?) We Are   *1*

2   Practicing Death:
Some Rituals of Everyday Life   *25*

3   Good Death, Bad Death (I):
In Other Times and Places   *43*

4   Good Death, Bad Death (II):
Here and Now   *93*

5   Corpsed Persons   *138*

6   Abusing and Eating the Dead   *176*

7   Too Many Dead: The Plague
and Other Mass Deaths   *218*

8   Down to Earth and Up in Flames   *262*

9   Journey of the Dead   *311*

10   Living Through   *355*

NOTES   *415*

SOURCES CITED   *429*

INDEX   *441*

ILLUSTRATIONS

1 Resurrection *16*

2 The 120-meter midlife hurdles *20*

3 The Angel of Death taking a soul *22*

4 Little Red Riding Hood and the wolf *28*

5 Baby and skull *34*

6 Triumph over temptation *75*

7 The angry are dismembered *76*

8 The lustful are smothered in fire
   and brimstone *77*

9 Funeral for a lottery winner *114*

10 "Last tag" *127*

11 Heads hanging in the gallery of a
   Kayan house *147*

12 Kayan woman dancing and holding
   a head *148*

13 Plastinated section of human brain *174*

14 Attending dead women on Slovenia's
   Women's Day *190*

15 Goya's Saturnus gobbles his son *200*

16 Death hunts the hunters *220*

17 Three revelers meet three corpses *239*

18 Black Death victims emerge from
   the grave *240*

19 Dance of the dead *246*

20 Tolkotin cremation *264*

21 Deceased displayed in a mummy coffin *290*

22 Headstone with lamb on child's grave *290*

23 Plain fieldstone used as grave marker *291*

24 Metal grave marker in the shape of a
    mummy coffin *291*

25 Vultures *307*

26 Portal of death, on Paris monument *313*

27 Charon accepts a dead person to row
    across the Styx *316*

28 Charon tries to rent a rowboat *317*

29 Egyptian funeral boat *335*

30 *War Refugees* *357*

31 Portrait of Erik and Joan Erikson in
    old age *385*

32 *Procession* *407*

ONE

HERE (?) WE ARE

A book concerned with how we move through life and death might use-fully begin with who and where we are at this moment in the co-biography of ourselves and the universe. Scientists tell us that the universe started with a Big Bang, or that maybe it didn't. Life evolved to fulfill a cosmic plan, or maybe it popped up as a fleeting aberration. In our tiny zone of the universe, life will perish in some millions of years, but, then again, it might become a casualty of "Doom Soon," as others have calculated.[1] From a more poetic and spiritual perspective, it has been said that there is profound meaning in the fall of a sparrow—yet others hold that the stupendous surges, flame-outs, dark collapses, and vast scatterings of all that exists mean precisely nothing. And nothing itself is either a prime condition for everything or simply the product of overactive imaginings by scientists and mathematicians at play.[2] But more to the point: What's for dinner? Who's pitching for our team tonight? Is last night's fortune cookie reliable in its promise that love, success, honor, and enlightenment will be ours within the next phase of the teasing moon? We have our mo-ments of contemplation about what all of this means and where we're going. More often, though, we are likely to be engrossed in the scrim-mage of everyday life. There's been a past, and there will be a future. But here we are now. This is our life pulsing in the moment, and it commands our full attention. Just when we are most secure in our assumptions, though, the alarm sounds. Everything familiar and comforting threatens to give way. Our next step might spill us into the void. What comfort, *what rules, what guidelines, what meanings then? Some people in some societies seem to have developed firm answers to these questions; other people, including many in our own times, find themselves with shards of traditional beliefs and remnants of redeeming rituals. And so we preface our journey with a brief reflection on how matters stand with us before time and circumstance have further say.*

RITUAL, ROUTINE, OR OBSESSION?

Is it ritual or just routine to start the day with a cup of coffee? Routines are sequences that we have gone through before and most likely will go through again. A familiar routine is so well practiced that it hardly needs us at all. We can daydream or sing a television jingle as we dress in the morning (always slipping a foot into the left shoe first—or is it the right?). These routines can be solitary or interactive. Two individuals, each enacting personal routines, exchange the expected greetings as they meet once more in the workplace. The power of routines is in their unobtrusiveness. Like sophisticated engines, they perform their services smoothly and quietly, permitting us to conserve our vital energies for more challenging events or opportunities.

Fortunately, society does not consist entirely of routines. We are saved from so monotonous an existence by the creative energies released through the collision of differing routines, by generational change, and by a genial perversity in the human spirit that thrives on mocking and rocking its own established order. Nevertheless, routinization is among the processes that bind together individual and society. One of the first tasks of the new employee, student, or rookie member of the team is to "learn the ropes," a phrase that pays tribute to the crucial skills that were required in the days of tall ships. A novice who fails to master the ropes can sink the ship in a storm. Further, we must demonstrate not only our mastery of the relevant skills but also our acceptance of the reigning styles and beliefs. We can retain a smidgen of our own charming or snarling personality, but in the main we must act like everybody else and thereby keep the good ship *Society* true to its course, with sails puffed by a favoring wind. Routines make the journey of life seem safe and predictable, and it is a nasty whelp indeed who does not buy into this game and insists on reminding us otherwise.

Routines also do much to make a home a home. My family's first dog was all eyes and ears when he joined us from a stressful residence in the animal-control facility. He studied our routines and soon knew more about them than we did. Toby wanted to know who was supposed to be where when and doing what. Shortly thereafter, Toby created for himself the role of enforcer, providing cues and corrections when we strayed too much from the Way Things Are Supposed to Be. Honey and then Angel proved equally adept when their turns came, becoming custodians of our routines, hounding us for infractions and rejoicing in the comforting rightness when we met their expectations. When Toby, Honey, or Angel sighed peacefully after their hard work, it was a signal that things were as they were supposed to be. My family's cats, of course, have always been masters of their own routines. We hesitate to do anything that might interfere with the cats' intricate passages, settlings, and demands for attention on their own terms. We suffer their scorn when the daily performance of our interactive routines is occasionally interrupted by events or caprice.

Rituals, like routines, also involve repeated sequences. But there is good reason to distinguish between them in theory, even though this is sometimes difficult in practice. We apply the term *ritual* most often to formal sequences that have names (such as *graduation, wedding, funeral,* or *human sacrifice*) and that require the cooperation of many people who have well-defined roles in the process. As a rough guide, I am observing a ritual if at least one of the participants is considered to have become different by the time the sequence has concluded. That core participant might have become elevated to a status of higher privilege and responsibility or sent off properly on the next step of life's journey.[3] It helps if the events occur within a space made special for that purpose and if the participants are wearing special clothes, intoning traditional texts, making symbolic gestures, singing or chanting, and engaging in physical actions that affirm the ritualistic transformation. Let's scatter a handful of rice or dirt on the loving couple or the shrouded corpse. Let's add another star to the shoulder of the newly promoted general or the bedpost of the intrepid child who has graduated from diapers. Rituals can also make themselves special with wine or blood spilled or sipped; clothes cut and torn; faces smeared with mud or tints; participants swooning in ecstasy or despair or dancing until exhaustion . . . all of which just might be followed by tasty little cakes, serious drinks, and memorable partying.

Even a solemn ritual can have its festive overtones. The very fact that people have been able to enact a powerful ritual can evoke a sense of triumph and release, even though the occasion itself might have been gloomy. Similarly, the ritual might be festive yet have solemn overtones. People have been reminded of their loyalties and obligations. The graduate, for example, might as well enjoy the moment, because soon enough the bubble might be pierced by the challenges of student loan payments, the job market, and the need to test one's career hopes and fantasies against reality.

The ritual can be brief or extended over days. Noisy or subdued. Loaded with performance tests (e.g., memorized arcane phrases, feats of physical agility or endurance) or pretty much a done deal in which the participants need only to be there. It may be understood that all who have made it this far will become successfully transformed through the ritual, or there might be a daunting possibility of failure, humiliation, and even worse. Whatever the scope, difficulty level, and texture, the ritual will still be ritual because it has the purpose of achieving an action through the strength of communal belief and the implicit or explicit connection of that belief to a higher power.

SOMEBODY OR SOMETHING IS WATCHING

Sacred magic buzzes like a high-tension wire. Doing the right ritual right can persuade potent forces to rescue, renew, protect, and bless us. Doing it wrong exposes us to the whirlwinds of fate or the fiery rage of the gods. The closer to its primal sources that a ritual is, and the more life that is inherent in it, the more risk there is for catastrophe and the more hope there is for survival.

There are also individual actions that have something of the ritual spirit. These generally draw upon established religious and ethnic traditions even though they are conducted in privacy. A solitary prayer on behalf of the dead might use words and cadences from an ancient tradition. One might also pause to improvise a prayer before entering a challenging situation. Hospice volunteers, for example, have said that they often pray, not with terminally ill patients and families, but in their own hearts. For example:

I ask my Lord for the strength and wisdom to comfort them, to be at my best for them. I don't ask for miracle cures. I ask for only what is within my own limited reach, you know, let me be able to help somebody today and then, if I can, somebody tomorrow.

People of all religious faiths may perform small ritual actions as part of their daily lives. I see these as maintenance rituals. They keep the faith. They ask the Almighty to protect them from harm. Although performed individually, each small act of worship affirms the bond with other believers throughout the world as well as demonstrating love and respect for God. Observant Jews, for example, touch their fingers to their lips and then to the mezuzah when they enter or leave their home. This small, oblong metal box is fastened near the door. It contains a devotional passage from Deuteronomy ("Hear O Israel, the Lord our God is one . . . ," 6:4) that places the house and its people under divine protection.

OBSESSIVE-COMPULSIVE SEQUENCES

But what of obsessive-compulsive actions? Some people devise idiosyncratic sequences intended to protect them from harm. A bit of obsessive-compulsive behavior and a privately performed religious ritual could be hard to distinguish were we unfamiliar with the particular traditions involved. But personal performances of prayer and other established rituals do differ significantly from obsessive-compulsive reactions. Prayer is a communicative action empowered within a belief system that has served many people over many years. The obsessive-compulsive is engaged in a lone struggle to enforce order within a personal life that is threatened with collapse. The hospice volunteer who improvises a prayer and the Jew who symbolically kisses the mezuzah may otherwise live in a confident and spontaneous manner. They are not hobbled by the need to restrict their lives and invest their energies in complex routines.

There is a point of commonality, though. Both the performer of ritual acts and the obsessive-compulsive are believers in the possible efficacy of their actions. Things will get better (or, at least, not get worse) as a result. These favorable outcomes will not be achieved by ordinary cause-and-effect mechanisms. For example, even if the prayer-sayer enhances the offering by lighting a votive candle, there is no way of demonstrating that this act has actually provided illumination and comfort to the deceased spirit. Ritual usually—or, as Émile Durkheim insisted, *always*—involves a combination of magic and faith.[4] The obsessive-compulsive also would find it difficult to demonstrate that the forces of destruction are foiled by putting laundry away inside out; this is a magical trick discovered through personal desperation. The faith component is not clearly articulated, but by implication there is a demigod of inside-outness with the power to perform miracles when invoked by this apparently senseless action. Through ritual we convert our beliefs into outcomes through magic. Or something like that.

A religious person can be afflicted with obsessive-compulsive disorder, and a person with obsessive-compulsive disorder can seize upon religious practice for the wealth of thought and behavior sequences that might serve to control personal anxiety and rage. It would be careless of us, though, to equate religiosity with an obsessive-compulsive disorder.

LARGER AND GREATER THAN OURSELVES

The borderline between routine and ritual is permeable and shifting. For example, a patriotic occasion that was once imbued with deep meaning might become an empty routine, sustained only by faltering habit, as generations and circumstances change. And then perhaps something happens, something that shakes us to our foundations. Our secular routines and devices no longer seem adequate. We need something more—and so we open our lives again to the power of ritual.

How can we know when we are in ritual? We are engaged in a ritual event when we feel ourselves to be part of something larger and greater than ourselves. It is no longer you, and it is no longer me: it is *us*. We are a superorganism for the moment, an entity with innumerable voices to chant or shout and innumerable hands to open in supplication or close in fists. The clan and the god that has possessed them are now capable of so much more than any of the clan's individuals. If this gathering has a sense of direction, if it seems to be following rules, if we have become inflamed with feelings and beliefs long neglected, and, especially, if it appears somehow to be reenacting a momentous occasion that is remembered in the deepest fibers of our being, then we are indeed involved in a ritual.

A CUP OF COFFEE TO START THE DAY

So here is an office worker starting another day with a comforting routine in a familiar setting. There is none of the fear, intensity, and urgency that would call for invocation of sacred powers. Such manifestations would seem inappropriate, even bizarre. Routine, then, not ritual.

A sip or two of coffee, and now a telephone chat with a friend as the day's work lies just ahead. An unusual sound. The worker's eyes turn toward a window. "Look," he says, "a plane!"

The terrorist attacks of September 11, 2001, on New York City and Washington, D.C., stunned the survivors and much of the world. Even those in the immediate vicinity of the World Trade Center had difficulty believing their eyes. Many firsthand observers seemed to experience two contradictory but coexisting responses: "This can't be happening; this *is* happening."

There is a rational basis for the existence of these apparently discordant responses. Like other creatures, we are equipped with psychobiological response systems intended to improve our chances of survival. Perceiving a possible threat, we immediately go on full alert. Failure to switch to an emergency footing can be fatal.[5] On the other hand, we would become exhausted if we interpret ourselves as being continuously at risk. As Hans Selye demonstrated through years of research, our physiological response to stress can itself become a severe source of stress.[6] Faced with a possible threat, then, we might reduce our chances of survival by ignoring or trivializing it, or we might lock ourselves into such an intense and enduring state of alarm that the clarity and flexibility of our thoughts, the effectiveness of our interpersonal relationships, and the functioning of vital organ systems all become compromised. Long-term survival requires an adept balancing act between two states of being: the normalizing and the emergency.

Those endangered by the World Trade Center attack had to deal with the sudden and the unexpected. People had to make judgments about reality and meaning before individual and group emergency response potentials could be activated. They would have recognized other types of threat immediately—but *this?* Bad things can happen in the world. Every-body knows that. Here, though, was something catastrophic happening *to* the world as we understood it. The familiar frame of reference crum-pled in an instant.[7]

The terrorist attacks produced many casualties and deprived many fam-ilies of their loved ones. Additionally, though, a great many people ex-pressed the feeling that the world itself had changed. Things would never be the same again. How *would* things be? That question could not be an-swered immediately and is still a long way from being answered today.

Emergency and Routine

Front-line professionals such as police, firefighters, and paramedics have honed their capacity for immediate recognition and response. The rest of us tend to display a robust dedication to the predictable ongoingness of life. Things should continue to be the way they are because that's the way they are. *We* should continue as we are. There is an indirect survival link to this mode of functioning as well, even though it can be detrimental in emergency situations. We develop the skills necessary to thrive in our niche of the world. These skills are demonstrated in many small ways: for example, by learning the best and second-best ways of commuting between home and office and what to say and not to say at staff meet-ings. We master the routines and chart the highways and byways of our home territory.

Alternative and often competing ideas about the world are associated with each of these response sets. Our built-in emergency response sys-tem is rationalized by the Proceed at Your Own Risk model: "The world is a dangerous place. Bad things can happen. Don't get too comfortable; don't be too trusting. Stay on guard!" By contrast, our immersion in the routine and familiar is in keeping with the Now and Forever model: "Things must continue as they are because things are not different from what they are and cannot be imagined otherwise. We can surely trust the sun to rise, the birds to sing, and the coffee to brew."

Ideally we should be able to call upon the frame of reference and re-sponse set that are most appropriate for the occasion. The sun has risen as it should, in an innocent blue sky. What a nervous and gloomy wretch I would be to command those damn birds to cease their twittering so I could listen for sounds of danger. And I am the village paranoid if I keep a loaded shotgun at home and have nearly blasted away one of my neighbors when I thought I saw somebody suspicious. To expect the worst all the time not only makes us unpleasant to live with but also undermines our ability to detect and respond to actual threat. Similarly, we reduce our survivability prospects if we enrobe ourselves in the belief that no harm can come to us in this well-ordered and well-mannered universe.

We know something of how people perceived and responded to the September 11 terrorist attacks from the voices of the survivors and from phone calls made by passengers during the hijackings. Danger awareness had to pierce the enactment of routines and the assumption of Now and Forever ongoingness. The office worker who saw the plane incredibly approach his building had only enough time to convey his surprise to his friend on the telephone. Those who had a little more time to respond did recognize their peril and the need for rapid and intelligent action. There were several reports, for example, of people descending many flights of smoke-filled staircases without panic and then exploring alternative escape routes when the primary escape passage was blocked. Panic did not seem to be the most common response, despite the real and present danger.

Improvisation took the place of either routine or ritual. The passengers who rebelled against their hijackers had no script to follow. They forged themselves into an instant strike force. During the desperate moments in the air and on the ground, many people did all that could be done, not only as individuals but also as hastily coordinated groups. By contrast, the emergency personnel rushed to the scene with well-practiced sequences of action to perform. It is not oxymoronic to speak of their actions as "emergency routines." The events were chaotic, but preparation and training had instilled a coherent and functional approach. Emergency was routine—up to a point. A major disaster challenged all their skills and stamina but—up to a point—not their worldview.

Furthermore, their actions were not ritualistic, although they were carefully coordinated and well prepared by disciplined practice. The outcome they sought—rescue—could not be achieved through magic or divine intervention, but only through their own expert and determined efforts. The magic, the spirit, was *within* the people.

Later. A day or two, or even just an hour or two later. The horrific events have occurred. The situation now requires a variety of new intensive efforts: search and rescue; treatment of survivors; organization of human and physical resources; isolation of the disaster sites; vigorous actions to protect against other possible attacks; investigation and pursuit of perpetrators. Soon another concern will become salient: informing and comforting those whose family members and friends might have been killed or injured. Those involved are no longer strangers, only people trying to help one another.

Real-ization

We focus here on a response that started to emerge just after the first impact of the disaster was felt. There were other responses no less powerful, including grief, fear, and rage. But it is the quieter response that most concerns us here, a response that arises from sound and competent minds that have become for the moment dazed and uncomprehending. What is happening? What, what, *what?*

That such a catastrophic event could occur—literally out of a clear blue sky—confounds our expectations, shakes our belief in a coherent and predictable world. Is this real? What kind of life in what kind of a world had we been imagining all this time? What are we to believe from this moment forward?

It was difficult to integrate both the everyday frame of reference and the interruption that witnesses described as surrealistic. "It was like a movie!" was a common response. Some witnesses were even more specific, identifying disaster scenes in various popular films. The rules had been broken, though—the rules that separate fantasy from reality. Terror had leaked into "real life" from the silver screen. Americans had long enjoyed the option of entering the alternative world of cinema. There also had been many interpenetrations between the two realms. These horrifying episodes were different. Disaster had escaped its cinematic bounds. Bizarre special effects seemed to have replaced the world we thought we knew.

Smooth television commentators, seldom at a loss for words, were swept up by the wave of disbelief. "I can't put it into words," a reporter would admit, standing at ground zero, the extensive ruins of the World Trade Center. Witnesses and visitors to the site could not make sense of what had happened: "It's beyond anything." "There is nothing I can com-

pare it to." "I could never have imagined anything like this. Even being
here, I can't really believe it."

Avery D. Weisman, M.D., started his medical career as a pathologist.
He quickly observed that many people—including fellow physicians—
shied away from touching or even looking at a dead person. He transformed himself into a pioneering existential psychoanalyst who had become convinced that

> every question affecting mankind involves death. Our cultural heritage has
> largely given us only methods to deny, romanticize, and placate death. . . .
> The very facts that have brought healing into being—facts of life and
> death—have prevented the healing professions from responding to deep
> yearning to know more about death and deadliness in human nature.[8]

He identified *realization* as a subtle but critical process in our efforts
to understand "death and deadliness":

> Realization has two meanings: to perceive a reality, and to make it real. . . .
> Most people concede that death is inevitable, a fact of nature. But they are
> not prepared to realize. We postpone, put aside, disavow, and deny its rel-
> evance to us.[9]

There was little difficulty in realizing the destructive consequences of
the attack. Acknowledgment of the events was often embedded within
a haze of shock and confusion, but the events themselves were nevertheless acknowledged. There was little outright denial. A massive and
unexpected catastrophe would seem to be an ideal occasion to arouse
the desperation response of denial. Disaster researchers have often reported survivors who were dissociated and disoriented: for example, the
woman industriously sweeping the floor of her home, which no longer
had roof or walls, in the wake of a tornado.

Few World Trade Center survivors, witnesses, or bereaved family members entered into full denial, however. Instead there was a groping toward realization. For example, one early responder to the attack knew
precisely what had happened and why she was there. In a TV news inter-
view, she explained that perhaps there were still people to be rescued,
lives to be saved, within the vast rubble of twisted metal and concrete
fragments. She was literally in touch with reality and engrossed in her

difficult work. And then she turned for another look at a small object that had come into her hand. It was a hand.

> There was a wedding ring on her hand. She was a person. She was a person who loved somebody and whom somebody loved. This was a real person who was—no more.

Realization would come at various times and in various ways for the people on the scene. They quickly recognized that something momentous had happened and that their lives would never again be the same. But this was not yet full acceptance. It would take time and emotional effort to integrate these events into their preexisting view of the world. The *making-real* of the deaths and the terrorist danger would, in fact, require significant revisions to their worldview and its familiar routines. These revisions would include such new rules as

- we are vulnerable—all the time;
- even our powerful society cannot protect us completely;
- the solid and the enduring are not actually so: even the landmark World Trade Center towers were perishable;
- we cannot assume that life will just go on as it has been; secure expectations must be replaced by heightened alertness;
- we need to feel a greater sense of community in everyday life, to be appreciative of and helpful to each other.

At the same time, family and friends of the terrorist victims also had to contend with incompleteness. Was my friend perhaps one of the fortunate survivors? When will I know? How long should I keep hope alive? Few bodies had been recovered. Identification was often difficult even with some of the shattered bodies that were recovered. Both the person and the body were absent. This imposed an extended period of uncertainty on family and friends. The stress of grief was already upon them, but the long process of working through loss could not begin while doubt remained. A person did not have to be "in denial." One could simply exercise the right to remain hopeful. Emotional reality was the tension between clinging to the remote possibility of a loved one's survival and beginning the painful but essential process of getting on with one's own life.

For many families the turning point was a bureaucratic function: the certification of death. New York officials waived the usual extended waiting period to certify terrorist attack deaths in the absence of identified bodies. The certification enabled families to apply for needed insurance benefits and make other financial and legal adjustments. In approving the issuance of a death certificate, the next of kin also relinquished all but a very stubborn and private sense of hope.

Resonating Violence

Another unsettling element was still largely unrecognized months after the attacks. We are, most of us, a peaceable people. Violent acts usually are committed by sociopathic criminals, confused youths, the drug-buzzed, or the deranged. These exceptions only underscore the generally pacific nature of our lifestyles. We walk our dogs, contribute to charitable causes, and devote ourselves to self-improvement endeavors. We have plenty of outlets for frustration that stop short of murder. We can squawk about our politicians, write letters to the utility companies, emit bloody roars at sporting events, and, of course, sue each other, to the delight of the lawyers we also enjoy deriding. Furthermore, we try to keep our children not only safe from harm but also safe from developing a taste for violence.

And yet—violence is what fills the seats in movie theaters and the television screens at home. Our appetite for vicarious killing has demonstrated itself in childhood games (the cops-and-robbers shoot-outs of my dead-end-street Bronx neighborhood and today's computer simulations) and in the popular transformation of ruthless gangsters into romantic icons. Disasters have been equally popular, especially with cinematic special effects to heighten the impact. The ideal movie would give us homicides by a variety of methods, all lovingly presented through inventive camera and postproduction techniques—and capped with a lot of stuff exploding and bursting into flame.

The assault on our collective sense of reality includes this leaking of violence and terror from one realm to the other, the resonations of brutal death-from-a-distance with our own subdued, murky, but unvanquished impulses toward violence. In the old days we might have spoken of mythical spirits and monsters taking on flesh or of nightmares invading daily life. These images still hold some power, but more salient today are the realer-than-real cinematic disasters and killings that escape their boundaries. The common element is as uncomfortable as it is difficult to ignore: *there is something about the killing fields of the human mind that has shaped both realms.*

The abrupt and tragic events of September 11 stimulated a renewed quest for comprehension and meaning, as well as the reconfiguration of practical coping efforts. This was an extreme case, though. By contrast, let's take one example of the journey of life when it is completed more or less as expected and well within a shared framework of meaning and ritual.

A VIEW FROM THE END ZONE

Willkommen! Alt Wien (Old Vienna) radiates in every direction with its visible and invisible history. St. Stephansdom looms before and above us. If we were to clamber five hundred steps and then some to its ornate roof, we could see much of Vienna's life and architecture. That twisted, rather tortured-looking tower thrusting from one of the plazas is a hymn of praise set in stone: "Thanks be to God, who in His infinite mercy banished the plague from our ravaged and repentant city." This inscription appears on the ornate baroque column erected to praise God for ending a visitation from the plague in 1679 and to memorialize the estimated hundred thousand victims. It became the model for other plague memorial columns throughout the Habsburg Empire. The monument rises within a prime shopping district in the old city, close by the Kohlmarkt on a cobbled street called Graben (grave).

Inside the great cathedral we experience a vaulted space as long as a football field, end zones and all. Mere humans look overmatched within this soaring architecture, but their voices, when raised in song, can surely be heard in heaven. For a moment at least we all become acutely religious.

Now we descend a flight of steps into the actual end zones. We move through what could serve as the passage to an ancient underworld. Perhaps we shiver involuntarily. (I did.) There is not the slightest amenity to gloss the transition from all the life above to all the death below. Bones there are, though, and in abundance. These catacombs are not as old or as extensive as some others. Christians appropriated the catacombs of Rome in the third century, and those are said to have eventually extended approximately 750 miles and 80 feet deep. Less ancient but even more populated are the gypsum quarries of Paris that became the final residence of an estimated six million people.

The remains beneath St. Stephansdom were removed from Vienna's thirty scattered graveyards night after night, starting in 1786.[10] Here there is not only a sufficiency of dry bones but also the strong impression that they have no prospects for strolling again in the sun to enjoy a Sacher torte and a small cup of intense coffee.

We visit without knowing quite how to behave. What is the proper way to show our respect, give no offense, and yet satisfy the curiosity that brought us here? Perhaps the residents can provide us with subtle cues.

A few hooded skeletons are sufficiently intact to evoke the image of a pious monk or compassionate priest who moved his lips in silent prayer as the last moment approached. Try as we might, though, we cannot read faith, expectations, transcendence, or even disappointment in these barren skulls. The silence. The emptiness. Above all: the *absence*. Here we are beyond sadness and beyond either doubt or certainty. And yet we wait patiently for a resonation, a quiver, a message. Nothing.

Most of the bones lack any semblance of connection with a person, let alone with one another. They lie in untidy stacks or scattered about, pieces of a construction toy in which the child has lost interest. Like some other catacombs throughout the world, this one fits the description of an *ossuary*—a place for bones, not necessarily for the honored or venerated remains of a person. A tourist guidebook reports that the bones of more than fifteen thousand are stacked like kindling wood. Actually, though, kindling wood is usually stacked with greater care and has a brighter future.

The guidebook neglects to mention that these abandoned bones are actually among the more favored: they are mostly the remains of men. Women were less likely to be accorded even the humble status of kindling wood in the church basement.

Like the other visitors, we discipline ourselves not to break into a gallop as we head toward the light at the beginning of the tunnel. In fact,

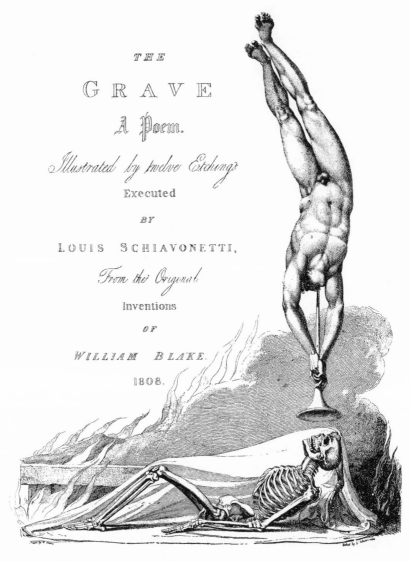

THE

GRAVE

A Poem.

Illustrated by twelve Etchings
Executed

BY

LOUIS SCHIAVONETTI,

From the Original
Inventions

OF

WILLIAM BLAKE.

1808.

Figure 1 Allegoric representation of resurrection: the skeleton arises from the grave.
Engraved by Louis Schiavonetti after William Blake. From Robert Blair, *The Grave*
(London: printed by T. Bensley).

we are impelled to pause for a moment with one of the monks who seemed—almost—to communicate something. We wonder: "What did the moment of death engrave deep into your bones? And what is it you've been feeling all this time?"

A response does filter through the musty air, across the tenuous distance between the living and the dead: "*Stunned. I was and I am— stunned.*" Fixed in death was the experience of terminal astonishment. Words form themselves within the silence: "So, this is death! Not what it was said to be. Not what was written. Not what we had decided to believe. Not what I would ever have allowed myself to imagine. Not what *you* imagine. Death is nobody's idea of it. I am as stunned as I was the moment I died."

The thousands whose bones lie beneath the feet of cathedral visitors in Vienna had names that are mostly forgotten, even to the keepers of records. Along with their names has perished the texture of their lives. What about the significance of their lives? No doubt many were active in the tumultuous events of their times. Some distinguished themselves and were mourned by those who cherished them and who then took these memories with them as their own lives came to an end. We also have no difficulty in supposing that, like most other good Christians, they believed that respect for the body they left behind was part of the process that would assure passage to the promised spiritual estate. So much of their lives had been given meaning and direction through this belief. Gathered unto the bosom of the magnificent cathedral, they would wait patiently until the moment of transfiguration. The sacred words and music rising above the vaulted ceilings were eternity's own soundtrack.

But experience taught otherwise. Below the inspiring cathedral was but a charnel house where they would lie exposed and abandoned. Their names, pious thoughts, and deeds would be forgotten even by the church they had served. Would God also forget? Or could one even remember God? All of this would take some getting used to. Was the spirit to be left stunned and confused, kin to all the uneasy ghosts who have made uneasy the people of numerous world cultures? How safe can a society feel when its ancestors are troubled and discontent? The attenuated bone-spirits beneath St. Stephansdom, though, do not seem to pose a direct threat to the living. They are still trying to keep the faith, and they are, in fact, secure within sacred space. It's just not what was expected.

There is also that touchy theological matter to consider: the true life was beyond flesh and bone, beyond the grave. The corruptible body in a flawed world was of little worth when compared with eternal spiritual blessing. And yet! Respect and care for the corpse was also of great concern. For example, the church and many of the laity, both Catholic and Protestant, long opposed with horror the emerging practice of post-mortem examinations. Could the soul really complete its journey if the body had been defiled? And would consignment to a grim bone house free or dishonor the spirit seeking redemption and its share of the sacred estate? One couldn't be too sure, one way or another. Taking one more fleeting look at the catacombs and inhaling one more breath, though, I found it difficult to feel optimistic.

We have explored two situations that were not part of our own everyday experience, with the exception of those who lost loved ones or were otherwise directly affected by the September 11 events. The first situation confronted us with a rupture in our received view of the world. This was not the way that either life or death was supposed to go. The second situation, by contrast, represented the completion of a life's journey within the rules and protection of the religious establishment. One floor above the catacombs the establishment continues to offer itself in all its physical and historical grandeur. Downstairs are "the remains of the day," a scene of morbid disorder after the ceremonies have been performed and the participants forgotten.

We would be phlegmatic folk for sure if we did not sense some connection to who we are now and to where we expect to go for the rest of our way. The people high up in a WTC tower had no time for consoling ritual or reflection on meaning. The dead in the catacombs have had more time than they need to wonder why their lives of faith have left their earthly remains in such a dismal state. We probably expect a different path through lives for ourselves and for those we hold most dear.

"WHO I AM"

Here is a simple thought exercise. Identify on paper or in conversation a set of specifications for who you are. There are no confining rules. Any statement you consider true and significant about yourself belongs on this list. Here is just one obvious example from my list: grandfather.

I am a grandfather here and now. But I could not have become a grand-father without first becoming a father, and that would not have happened without a certain degree of cooperation with a woman, and that arrange-ment would not have occurred without courtship, and so on. A descrip-tor of myself in the present tense implies and evokes a rich, complex, and only partly comprehended skein of past events, relationships, and expe-riences. So, too, with the future. As father and grandfather I have a stake in the future. Being a grandparent, spouse, sibling, child, or friend is not a static position. All these relationships have altered with time and cir-cumstance and will continue to do so. Who—and where in my life—I am now is framed by memories and expectations.

Work this out for yourself if you'd like. See if any of your here-and-now self-descriptors can be deprived of their temporal context. See if even the most constant descriptors are not, for that very reason, possessive of time past and future. "I am a person whose beliefs have always been con-stant and will never waver," for example, draws its power for the present from its time-bridging structure.

The end of our days is therefore an influence on who and where we suppose ourselves to be now. I'm not speaking of the actual end of our days here, of course, but of attitudes, expectations, and behaviors that could influence the manner and timing of our deaths. When pressed to define *thanatology*, I have suggested it be regarded as the study of life—with death left in. This might also be a useful guide in contemplating our own biographies. To understand the shape and direction of our lives, we might be well advised to include not only the next fork in the road but also the distant mist in which finitude awaits. Similarly, fascination with funerals and other rituals can be only a diversion if we fail to consider their connections to the heartbeat of daily life.

And where do thanatologists come from? During World War II, Her-man Feifel was assigned to the island of Tinian, where he watched the *Enola Gay* depart for Hiroshima with the first atomic bomb. This ex-perience continued to resonate within him while he conducted pioneer-ing studies in the psychology of death and made the forceful case that America is a death-denying society. I know another man who, as a teenager, opened the apartment door one day when his father returned from work. Just barely inside the room, his father collapsed and died in his arms. This young man would also become a psychologist, and one of the first to offer therapy to people with a life-threatening illness. Noth-

IN THE BLEACHERS By Steve Moore

The 120-meter midlife hurdles.

Figure 2 IN THE BLEACHERS © 1997 Steve Moore. Reprinted
with permission of UNIVERSAL PRESS SYNDICATE. All rights
reserved.

ing like this happened in my own early experiences as I played stickball in
a dead-end street in the South Bronx and wondered early in the morning
and late at night what it is all about. The story of my thanatologizing
has been told elsewhere.[11] Essentially, I have felt that life cannot be fully
appreciated or understood without somehow taking death and loss into
account. Along the way, I have worked as a psychologist with people
who were terminally ill, grieving, and suicidal; I have engaged in both
empirical and scholarly research; I have taught death seminars for—
what's it been? forty years?—and have served first as a psychologist,
then as director of a geriatric hospital. Over the years some of the people
most dear to me have ceased to be, and their absence remains a kind of
presence.

THE MORTAL JOURNEY

Life has often been envisioned as a journey. We move through time, or time moves through us. In Western society it has often been agreeable to tell one another that this is an orderly procession, as in a seventeenth-century German depiction of the Ten Steps of Life.[12] An infant cradled in its mother's arms occupies the first of the ascending steps. At the apex stand a couple enjoying the physical prime of life. Now the steps start to descend, until we see an aged and feeble couple tapping along companionably with their walking sticks. A social and moral sequence accompanies the physical. Different role obligations and privileges are associated with each step of the procession. In many world societies there is also a less visible but perhaps even more significant journey in progress—the quest for spiritual discovery, purification, and renewal.

The beauty of the spiritual concept is displayed in several ways. People know who they are, who they were, and who they will be. They also have a guide for interacting with those who are younger ("I was like that once") and those who are older ("I'll be like that some day if I make it that far"). Further, it serves to bind anxiety. Life as raw experience can seem chaotic and vulnerable. But there's a plan. There's a way things should go. This sublime progression is under the general direction of a Supreme Being who cares about the creatures made in his likeness.

The beginning of the journey has allowed for a variety of interpretations. Life starts at conception or birth, or souls preexist, awaiting the opportunity to be born or reborn. The idea of one life and one death has long had to contend with the rival conception of lives recycled through death. The journey may seem to be a linear progression only because of our limited perspective and dichotomizing habit of thought.

Where and how does the journey end? It makes a difference if we focus on the individual or the people. We might believe that *the people* continue on their journey through time, like waves that roll across the sea even though composed of ever-changing drops of briny water. History has been both kind and unkind to this belief. Some peoples appear to have vanished from the earth both in ancient and more recent times; but, then again, a scientific case has been made for the possibility that we all carry forth a genetic inheritance passed along by a few remote and common ancestors.

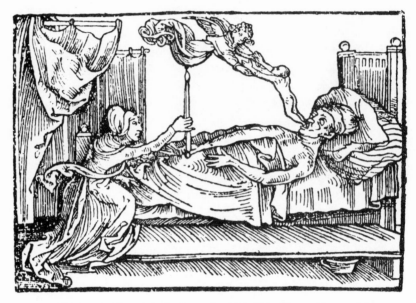

Figure 3 The Angel of Death, in the form of a child, taking the soul from a dying man. From Reiter, *Mortilogus* (Augsburg: printed by Oegeling and Nadler, 1508).

By contrast, the individual's journey seems to come to an end sooner or (not all that much) later. Confine ourselves to a moderate time scale and we might find comfort in the assumption that people have always found a way to go on and always will. Share the worldview of specialists on human extinction and the question becomes not if but when both we and our mortal coil will shuffle off (us first). Life will have become an improbable little episode in a history of the universe that will have neither author nor reader and, therefore, not so much of a history either.

It is the death of individuals that most concerns us here. Even the most elaborate theories and beguiling fantasies have not been able to overcome the fact that life's journey on earth does come to an end. What individual passion and societal construction have added are glosses on life and death, meanings whispered in the lonely wind or proclaimed in proud temples. Death is the natural outcome of life. But what we call death might also be much more, according to many belief systems. Our journey continues not only through life but also through death. There is destination as well as outcome.

And so the shape of our lives cannot be fully known until the entire journey has run its course—assuming we share the tenets of a traditional belief system. This system also gives us shelter along the way: the intergenerational flow of stories and memories, the symbols, the daily practices and the grand rituals, all working hard to hold back the anxieties, the doubts, and, of course, the irrational forces that seize and destroy even our finest achievements, even our most innocent or gifted comrades. The belief system. The ritual. The passion for order and meaning. These creations of the human mind have proven more durable than any individual or society.

The terrorist attacks of September 11 brought sudden death to thousands and grief and a heightened sense of vulnerability to many others. The expected, the assumed, journey through life had been ambushed. What is life if it can be destroyed so brutally, spilled so wantonly? What is death if it comes so prematurely, allows no opportunity for preparation, even for a farewell word and touch? The perspective from the end zone can also be demoralizing. What was it all about? Was it a fatal flaw in our belief systems or the eruptions and dislocations so pervasive throughout history that failed the employees of the World Trade Center towers and the priests of Vienna? And is it still reasonable, still useful, to believe in an orderly life within an orderly universe?

ABOUT THIS BOOK

This book provides a fresh opportunity to consider what it means to journey through life and possibly through death. Perhaps we might emerge with a heightened appreciation of who and where we are now. We draw upon the thoughts, passions, and actions of many people who took on the challenges of life within a variety of sociohistorical contexts. Anthropology, psychology, and sociology come to our aid, as do history, the arts, and the life sciences.

I begin with what is most familiar to us: our own daily lives. "Practicing Death" offers the opportunity to explore some rituals of everyday life. A pair of broad-ranging chapters, "Good Death, Bad Death" (I and II), examines death, first in other times and places and then in our own. What is the relationship between how we live, how we die, and how we fare after death? And what, if anything, can be regarded as a "good death"?

The passage from life to death is a spiritual mystery, a biological event, and a societal transaction with many implications for the survivors. In "Corpsed Persons" I explore some of the ways in which a person is transformed into a corpse. "Abusing and Eating the Dead" is perhaps not for the faint of heart. World societies have often given high priority to respectful treatment of the dead. Nevertheless, we have sometimes been on our worst behavior as well. This visit to the dark side of corpse management has its own lessons to offer. "Too Many Dead" is an apt follow-up. What happens when there are so many dead that the living are hard-pressed to perform the traditional caregiving practices and rituals? And what is it like to live within a once-familiar environment that has been turned into a necroscape?

We now follow the person beyond the point of death, identifying some of the major pathways into whatever might be waiting on the other side. "Down to Earth and Up in Flames" explores the options of earth burial and cremation within a historical framework. We are reminded once again that our hopes, fears, fantasies, and status distinctions all influence the way in which we carry out our obligations to the dead. "Journey of the Dead" takes us even further. With all due trepidation, we accompany the soul on its mysterious after-journey as it has been envisioned throughout history. Finally, in "Living Through," we come to terms with the mortal journey in our own glittering, tawdry, powerful, and vulnerable times. What can we rescue from the past and bring through us to future generations, and what might we more wisely let go? And what comfort and what joys can mortals offer to one another in a universe whose strangeness exceeds our most extravagant imaginings?

TWO

PRACTICING DEATH

Some Rituals of Everyday Life

The unknown often arouses an uneasy blend of excitement, hope, and dread. "Be gentle with me. It's my first time" can apply to situations other than a farewell to virginity. What will it be like to move away from the old neighborhood? To leave the familiar companions and routines of home? To leave school for the workplace? To retire after so many years of work? Life is replete with endings and beginnings that could provide partial rehearsals for the final passage to Hamlet's "unknown territory." Here I explore a few of the experiences with life that foreshadow our encounters with loss, separation, and death. The examples include bedtime rituals, religious and philosophical conceptions of the relationship between the quotidian and the cosmic, and the symbolism found in funeral and memorial rituals. Perhaps we will discover hints from everyday life that the final passage and its rituals are not entirely without precedent.

NOW I LAY ME DOWN TO SLEEP

Now I lay me down to sleep
I pray the Lord my soul to keep
And if I die before I wake . . .

"And if I die before I wake"? What an idea to plant in a child's mind! How comforting to suggest that one might not wake up! No breakfast, no hugs, no teasing sister or brother, no playing with pooch or kitty, and, worst of all, no television! What can be said in support of this once ubiquitous bedtime prayer?

First, it affirms the comforting idea of a god who watches over us night and day and will be there for us should all else fail. In addition, children do think of loss, separation, abandonment, and death a lot more than most adults realize. Trying to make sense out of death is a significant part of mental and emotional development from early childhood onward.[1] The "Now I lay me down" formula recognizes the child's vulnerability to separation anxiety and thereby offers some comfort. Anxiety about abandonment shows itself almost immediately and can be triggered by even such small happenings as Mother leaving the room for a few minutes.[2] The little ones are not being spoiled or neurotic when they seek the reassurance of an adult presence: their survival pretty much depends on it.

Historically, children have been at high risk for death. Contagious diseases, uncontrolled infections, accidents, and lack of adequate food and shelter have combined to make the children's hour a perilous time. Infant and child mortality has declined markedly for advantaged citizens of technologically developed nations as a result of public health education and preventive measures and medical advances. This is a fairly recent development, though. Centuries of filling the family plot with the mortal remains of infants and children are not easily forgotten. "And if I die before I wake" was all too often spoken within the context of family grief and concern.

Even today, and even for adults, going to sleep requires closing our eyes to the solid and familiar world around us and yielding our conscious awareness and control. Sleep is a night journey on which the structure and rules of the day are not serviceable. As we embark on this journey, it is comforting to trust that the world we have temporarily surrendered will be restored to us.

Finally, perhaps parents need the "Now I lay me down" chant just as much as their children do. Adults who try so hard to maintain control in a difficult world all day long must also surrender this effort as they hit the pillow, trusting that the Lord or a reasonable facsimile will look after things for a few hours. Comforting the child may help to comfort ourselves.

Considering this, I asked myself: what rituals of everyday life might influence our feelings about the final passage? "Bedtime rituals" is the answer that flashed back without hesitation. And so, let's yawn, stretch, brush our teeth, and get ourselves ready for bed.

BEDTIME RITUALS

My earliest remembered experiences took place in a South Bronx tenement on a dead-end street that doesn't seem to be there anymore. It was a noisy and chaotic neighborhood, I suppose, and the tumult carried over into our own ground-floor apartment. Often there was a crescendo of sound, action, and emotion a little before bedtime. My brother and I would have been outside playing with our friends. Chases through the dark alleys strung with clotheslines would become the sport when there was no longer enough light to play stickball. Meanwhile, our parents would be inside discussing such matters as bills and lack of money for paying same. We kids would have to do a lot of shouting in order to compete.

Bedtime, though, was accompanied by a sea change. Things quieted down. People seemed to look at one another again and remember who they were. The routine for kids like us included a sequence of practical actions: wash-up, toothbrush, 'jamas. Then would come story time. One parent—usually Mother—would read us a story. I remember mostly tales from the Old Testament and Oscar Wilde fables such as the Selfish Giant. This was a satisfying time of day. Our parents were as relaxed as they were going to be and focused on their two wonderful sons rather than their troubles (some of which had to do with their two wonderful sons).

The stories gave our overheated little minds something to work on as we phased toward sleep. These occasions provided the opportunity to raise our own questions even if the answers sometimes eluded our comprehension. After listening to one of the more epic biblical stories, I asked what or who God is. In answer I heard: "God is a Great Bean." Almost certainly, my father said, "God is a Great Being," but when I dozed off that night it was with the image of God as a Great Bean floating down Fifth Avenue as part of a Macy's parade. Thus did peaceful, structured, and predictable bedtime rituals both escort me to sleep and provide seeds—or beans—for further thought.

I have since asked many adults about their childhood bedtime rituals

Figure 4 Little Red Riding Hood and the wolf, a Victorian-era illustration of a bedtime scene that perhaps tells us more about the Victorian imagination than we want to know.

and the possible connection with their present lives. The respondents were mostly students, staff, and colleagues in a university environment, so the way is clear for others to expand the study with a more representative sample. I would certainly like to hear of your bedtime experience. Here are some of the memories and observations, written and reflected upon by students of my seminar "Death, Society, and Human Experience."

A woman completing her graduate studies in social work had this to say:

> In reflection, my childhood rituals were the foundations of my spirituality. For a child, evening rituals and prayers shared with Mom and Dad gave me the opportunity to squelch the fears and anxiety some children face in going to sleep at night. I had fears myself when my kindergarten classmate Reggie died during the night. In my prayers I would ask God to keep me safe and not let me die in the night. My Mom would check in on us before she went to bed for the night. Sharing a room with my sisters, until I went away to college, was very comforting.
>
> Sleep is a time of separation from wakefulness and is frightening to some children. The fears we face as children overflow into adulthood if not addressed. If I had been able to process Reggie's death by talking with my

parents and having their reassurance that I wouldn't die in my sleep, per-haps I wouldn't have been afraid that I might die, too. Instead, I prayed to God that He wouldn't let me die during the night.

A comforting ritual, such as a bedtime story read by parents, and some quiet time to spend a few moments talking together would allow for a child to express any thoughts, fears, and concerns. Sharing the child's prayer time could transform anxiety into peacefulness and comfort before going to sleep. A warm hug and kisses from Mom and Dad can heal so very much in the life of a child.

This woman clearly sees a pattern of continuity between early repeated everyday experiences and how we deal with our fears of separation, loss, and death in adulthood. Her narrative also mentions affectionate touch during the bedtime ritual. A comforting ritual that takes a child up to the point at which she must proceed alone—this progression toward a little sleep might be one of our most influential everyday models in prepa-ration for a rather longer sleep. This woman now has a family of her own and, with her husband, provides warm, supportive bedtime rituals.

Others also have emphasized the importance of comforting commu-nication and touch through a predictable bedtime ritual. One recently retired woman speculates that her motivation to become a hospice vol-unteer might have arisen from the way her parents helped to see her through the dark aloneness of the night:

> A person can be comforted. A person does not have to go off from this world alone, either in sleep or death. I seem to feel that in my bones, and I think I learned it over and over again at happy bedtimes.

Comments from another graduate student add further insights:

> There is an absolute connection between saying good night as a child and how I have constructed the way one should say goodbye, whether it is the goodbyes of returning home after a visit, or the goodbyes as one leaves this life. The most important thing is that the immediate family must be present—at car-side for the leave-taking, or at bed-side for dying. The im-portant events of the day—or the visit—or life—need to be reviewed as one readies for bed, or leaving, or death. Saying goodbye to the day (as a child), the family, and this world all require an accounting of what went on before and what is to come, and the presence of significant others in order to be done properly. That is the lasting message.

One could hardly improve on her insight into the connection between the apparently small events of everyday life and our most momentous partings. How we support each other through these little separations could have powerful consequences for our ability to cope with the final passage.

Troubling Memories

Some respondents had troubling memories to report. One woman, for example, had been adopted into a family that took good care of her but, in her words, were

> rigid and distant and not very demonstrative of affection. . . . Later, when I had my own children, I realized that I had to force myself to hug them and kiss them good night. . . . As I reflect on separation and parting issues with people throughout my life, it does not surprise me that I have not responded with strong emotions in most cases. . . . It surprised me even now to think that when grandmother died, I cried but at the same time it never crossed my mind to take that special trip to see her before she died. At the time of her death, I cried but at the same time I felt a sense of detachment and went on with my life and my daily routine, and till now I never analyzed it. I see a definite connection between the lack of attachment I have felt with most people in my life, and this awareness helps me reflect on the relationships while on this journey here on earth.

Some people do feel unable to show emotion during funerals, and avoid attending them. There is more than one possible reason for this, but the one that is suggested here also deserves consideration: people who were deprived of comforting bedtime rituals and support during other little life passages may be unprepared to feel deeply and wholly when exposed to a final passage.

A business major observes:

> I think the bedtime rituals I used as a child were a startup to other rituals I have now. It wasn't completely ritualized like a Roman Catholic funeral or the singing of the national anthem before a sports event, but it was ritualized to the degree of the same procedure a cop uses to pull somebody over or the same way a pilot may do a systems check on an airliner.
> When I was growing up the bedtime ritual to me was no big deal, but

now I see it as a tool that was used to help me in life. It enables me to have something consistent in my life and create a daily routine, which a lot of my friends lack these days. Though a lot of rituals are done without any thought, and indeed were taught to you at a young age by your parents or society, they enable one to cope with many of life's expectancies and un-expectancies.

Recently one of this man's best friends had died. It was the first such loss he had had to deal with. But then he discovered that those old bed-time rituals were there for him:

[P]raising God every night from as far back as I can remember to now helped me cope with my friend's loss because I had built up a trust with God. Pray before bed and be alive and in good health is plenty evidence for me to know my friend will be going to a better place.

And there were respondents who could not recall anything that an-swered to the name of bedtime ritual. "Anything happened any which way at home," remembers a communication major. "Anybody might be there or not. I usually put myself to sleep or, really, just fell asleep, some-times on the couch in front of the TV. We were not the most organized family." He has been to graduations, weddings, and funerals, but none has made a big impression on him. "I think because there's always so much coming and going. Those ceremonies just drip right off me, like rain off a duck's back." This young man was now thinking seriously of getting married.

I want my children when I have them to have a more organized life, but I have to get myself organized first. One thing I know: I will read them sto-ries at bedtime, or my wife will or we both will. We will have meals to-gether and bedtimes and maybe things will go better.

This man's experiences are typical of a number of others who have not had much sequencing, predictability, and guidance in their lives. They may also be at a loss for habit, structure, and guidance when faced with separation and death. Ritualized preparation is just not there for them. This raises a larger question. What is the connection between our house-hold rituals and our feeling about formal public rituals? Bedtime rituals flourished in the days of stable two-parent, one-marriage families. There are fewer such domestic situations today. Single-parent homes, divorces, remarriages, splittings, and mergings have made it more difficult to establish and maintain household rituals.

The two-paycheck configuration reduces togetherness time. The single parent may find it difficult to muster the energy for leisurely and dependable bedtime scenes. The extended family is still a valuable resource, but face-to-face communication can become a casualty of mobility and distance. Does this mean that we will be less prepared for and less inclined to participate in formal public rituals such as funerals? Or, quite the contrary, does it mean that we will seize upon formal ritualistic opportunities because of an unfulfilled need for structured communal interaction? Do we crave ritual more than we realize, and does this make us more vulnerable to cults and the spastic, proxy-priest gestures of rock stars? Consider still another possibility: perhaps we will become primed to create our own rituals when the big events of life are upon us. Perhaps our aching toward ritual sometimes devolves into obsessive-compulsive quirks when we fail to establish a cadre of the like-minded. Whatever the particular answers, it is likely that connections will be discovered between the little rituals of everyday life and how we participate in or withdraw from major public rituals.

AT DAY'S END:
TWO CHRISTIAN MODELS OF DYING AND DEATH

Bedtime rituals have a place within two contrasting models that arose within the Christian tradition, each of which gave profound significance to the moment of death.

Jeremy Taylor was a soldier turned doctor of divinity and, by all accounts, a remarkable person whose inspiration and counsel were widely sought. He authored a book on how to live and another on how to die. *Holy Dying* was published in 1651.[3] It is now recognized as the classic presentation of the *Ars moriendi* (dying well) tradition and therefore deserves to have its full title bannered out:

The
Rule and Exercises of
HOLY DYING:

in which are described
THE MEANS AND INSTRUMENTS
of
Preparing ourselves and others respectively for a
BLESSED DEATH;
and the remedies against the evils and temptations proper to
THE STATE OF SICKNESS
together with
PRAYERS AND ACTS OF VIRTUE
to be used by
SICK AND DYING PERSONS
or by others standing in their attendance.
To which are added,
RULES FOR THE VISITATION OF THE SICK,
and
offices proper for that ministry

Now that's a title! Treatises on the art of dying or how to die well started to appear early in the fifteenth century. These took the form of brief instructions for clergy who would be called upon to assist dying people and their families. We will have more to say about the *Ars moriendi* tradition in the next chapter. Taylor, chaplain to King Charles I, offered an approach both broader and deeper than any that had gone before. The deathbed was a crucible, a final test of one's faith and moral substance. What was foremost here was his relentless insistence on individual responsibility.

Taylor does not emphasize deathbed miracles and conversions and, in fact, encourages us not to expect last-minute reprieves. Instead, we should devote our entire lives to preparing ourselves for a good death. Life is preparation for a test, and it's all going to be on the final exam. How matters conclude depends on how we live each day—and no hour is more important than the one in which we impersonate our future corpse by horizontalizing ourselves on the bed. Settle back, if you will, and heed this eloquent discourse on the relationship between the moments before sleep and the moments before death. Even better—read it aloud in your best PBS or BBC narrative voice.

He that will die well and happily, must dress his soul by a diligent and frequent scrutiny: he must perfectly understand and watch the state of his soul; he must set his house in order before he be fit to die. And for this there is great reason, and great necessity.

Figure 5 The fifteenth-century artist who created this bronze statuette gave us two chances to understand that even the infant is already enrolled in the lists of death. He not only contemplates the skull situated on his leg but also rests an elbow on an hourglass. From Frederick Parkes Weber, *Aspects of Death and Correlated Aspects of Life in Art, Epigram and Poetry* (1910; College Park, Md.: McGrath, 1971).

Reasons for a Daily Examination

1. For, if we consider the disorders of every day, the multitude of impertinent words, the great portions of time spent in vanity, the daily omissions of duty, the coldness of our prayers, the indifferences of our spirit in holy things, the uncertainty of our secret purposes, our infinite deceptions and hypocrisies, sometimes not known, very often not observed by ourselves, our want of charity, our not knowing in how many degrees of action and purpose every virtue is to be exercised, the secret adherences of pride, and too forward complacency in our best actions, our failings in all our relations, the niceties of difference between some virtues and some vices, the secret indiscernible passages from lawful to unlawful, the perpetual mistakings of permissions for duty, and licentious practices for permissions, our daily abusing the liberty that God gives us . . . our little greedinesses in eating, our surprises in the proportions of our drinkings, our too

great freedoms and fondnesses in lawful loves, our aptness for things sensual, and our deadness and tediousness of spirit in spiritual employments . . .[4]

How are you doing? Still with Jeremy? Good! We will fast-forward just a bit:

> . . . from all this we shall find, that the computations of a man's life are as busy as the tables of sines and tangents, and intricate as the accounts of eastern merchants: and therefore it were but reason we should sum up our accounts at the foot of every page; I mean, that *we call ourselves to scrutiny every night when we compose ourselves to the little images of death.* [italics added]

Taylor was a practical as well as a spiritual person:

> For, if we make but one general account, and never reckon till we die, either we shall only reckon by great sums, and remember nothing but clamorous and crying sins, and never consider particulars or forget very many; or if we could consider all that we ought, we must needs be confounded with the multitude and variety. But if we observe all the little passages of our life . . .

The bottom line is as plain as can be:

> As therefore every night we must make our bed the memorial of our grave, so let our evening thoughts be an image of the day of judgment.

Bed = grave. The final scene of life is prepared for as many times as we lay ourselves (or our children) down for sleep. How well we make use of these opportunities is up to us, but Jeremy Taylor does not want us to suffer spiritual agonies at the end because we have been ignorant of these crucial opportunities.

Reconstructing the Image of Death

Our second example comes from a more recent development within the Christian tradition. The Roman Catholic belief system has fathered a number of orders with their own emphases and specific missions. Jesuits,

Franciscans, and Benedictines are among the best known. The Marist Brothers came into existence in the aftermath of the French Revolution. The "Marist" appellation is related to their esteem for Mary, Mother of Jesus. Marcellin Champagnat (1789–1840), the founder, stimulated the development of a cult of "the good death." He had been called upon to instruct a dying peasant youth in the fundamentals of Christianity. This was a revelatory experience for Champagnat, who would then succeed in attracting followers throughout the world.

There had been flares of interest in "the good death" in the past, as we have seen with Jeremy Taylor and the *Ars moriendi* tradition. The Marists sounded a different note, however, in response to the outrageous modern times of the nineteenth century. Technological, economic, and political forces were altering the fabric of society and the shape of individual lives. The cry for independence and nationalism, for example, enlisted some of the ardor that had more customarily flowed into religious causes. As Matthew Arnold wrote in "Dover Beach," "The Sea of Faith / Was once, too, at the full. . . ." Not quite so full by now. The engines of progress were steaming mightily ahead (or at least in the assumed direction of "ahead"). Religion was having a hard time, trying to maintain its grasp on the past while securing a place in the future.

And what of death? The march of material progress did not pause for those who fell by the wayside. The disabled, the aged, and the dying were taking on the aspect of failed machines. For many, their exit from life was just one more station of suffering and despair, usually of little interest to society. Charitable activity was limited. The poor had a short track ahead of them, doomed to perish of hunger, disease, and violence, and suffering oppression and degradation throughout their brief lives. It looked different, though, in upper reaches of the social hierarchy. There, death was starting to be seen as more of an unfortunate interruption to achievement, power, and pleasure. Life was good; death spoiled the party. The best thing was to ignore death, deny it access to thought or conversation. In contrast to people's compulsive fascination with death during the Middle Ages, the privileged of the nineteenth century practiced at dancing through life as though the sweet music would never end.

Into this early modern stew stepped the newborn Marist order. They held the radical conviction that death was both a very important and a very good thing. So focused were they on our mortal move that William J. K. Keenan speaks of the Marists as a death cult.[5] The Marists could be bold and courageous in acting on their beliefs, so their example attracted some who had been disappointed by more established religious orders.

The Marists reconstructed the image of death by word and action. The end of life is not the final clunk of an obsolete machine or a mere inconvenience that deprives one of continued pleasure. Furthermore, the day of judgment is not to be so dreaded that we must review and purge our sins one morbid night after another, from childhood's hour to the last tick of the tock. Jeremy Taylor had it wrong. Rather, death should and could be joyful. Death is not so much a departure as it is an arrival. Under Marist auspices, the deathbed scene again became the moment of moments. Fellow believers would companion the dying person all the way. People whose lives had been obscure and humble could die as well as the most illustrious: Jesus and Mary welcomed them all.

The quality of deathbed visions was also much improved.

> In 1838, Brother Justin . . . fell ill with tuberculosis and was soon at death's door. . . . [He] spent the last days of his life in constant communing with Jesus and Mary. . . . The Brothers at his bedside inquired what he wanted and why he smiled. "I smile," he told them, "because I see the Blessed Virgin; she is there; she is coming to get me." The next moment he fell asleep peacefully in the Lord, the smile still on his lips and his eyes still fixed on the spot where he had claimed to see the Blessed Virgin.[6]

He fell asleep peacefully in the Lord. We think immediately of the bedtime prayer: "Now I lay me down to sleep. I pray the Lord my soul to keep." Every bedtime prayer, every trusting voyage into sleep, prepares us for eternal rest with the Lord. Try to tell the Marists that those trivial little bedtime rituals have nothing to do with preparing ourselves for the final passage!

THE DOOR AND OTHER EVERYDAY SYMBOLS THAT TRY TO MAKE VISIBLE THE UNKNOWN

The cliché is so familiar that it may have lost its ability to make an impression on us. Brother Justin was "at death's door." This is another everyday proxy for separation and death. We pass through doors all the time. Is that such a big deal? Sometimes it is; supposing, for example, that the other side of that door is a doctor's office, a hospital bed, or a funeral home, in which cases the connection between any door and death's door becomes fairly evident. But think also of all those other moments when you felt your heart pounding, your breath paused, and your mind saturated with hope or fear as you hesitated before opening a door. We are practicing just a little for the same exit that was so close to Brother Justin whenever we experience emotional arousal and a rush of mingled thoughts before opening a door. (It's probably safe to admit now that I listened covertly, i.e., under the bedcovers, to the strictly forbidden radio show *Inner Sanctum,* with its creaking door of delicious menace.)

Sometimes the scene is played in reverse. We are safe in our own abode, or so we think. But there's somebody at the door—

Death began to hammer on the door. HOO HOO HOO! it yelled. LET ME IN.

Go away, said Kleinzeit. Not your time yet.

HOO HOO! yelled Death. I'LL BLOODY TEAR YOU APART. ANY TIME'S MY TIME; I WANT YOU NOW, AND I'M GOING TO HAVE YOU NOW NOW NOW!

Kleinzeit went to the door, double-locked it, fastened the chain. Go away, he said. You're not real, you're just in my mind.

IS YOUR MIND REAL? said Death.

Of course my mind's real, said Kleinzeit.

THEN SO AM I, said Death. THERE I HAVE YOU, EH?[7]

This brilliant passage from Russell Hoban's *Kleinzeit* illustrates the tensions and ambiguities of the door. What will happen if I go out? Who might be out there waiting to come in? Am I safe on this side of the door— or anywhere? Where is it safe? Nowhere? The door itself is but a familiar example of a potent distinction made since ancient times. For example, a circle etched in the earth with a pointed stick can also separate the mundane from the sacred, the safe from the dangerous.

What this passage also illustrates is our dependence on everyday objects and events in order to conceive of death as a "concrete universal," that is, an abstraction we have brought down to ground level and human scale. In our imagery, symbols, and rituals, we use what is familiar as a link to the unknown and perhaps unknowable. Most of us find it just too difficult to think long and hard about death. It is easier to focus on visual images and familiar objects and activities. The door is only one of many concretisms that provide us with at least a precarious grip on that mysterious universal, death. (So much the better if the door boasts a tiny keyhole through which we can peep through to the other side without being seen—HOO! HOO! Fat chance of that!). A much more powerful imagining is to conceive of death as Death—a person. Kleinzeit probably didn't have much to say about death, but he jousted zestfully in conversation with Death. Do we feel stronger and more pleased with ourselves when we can go a round or two with Death? To answer a question with a question again: why else would we take so many extra risks with our lives?

POPPING OUT OF CLOSETS

We sometimes practice death with each other in creative or sneaky little ways. Children love to pop out of closets and other dark hiding places to get a good scare out of somebody. (One of my sons was a virtuoso in this art form.) The dark is a natural proxy for death. Lying motionless is another. Children's games in the pre-Nintendo centuries often featured dark hidings and sleep and death-feigning acts. What fun it was to be dead for a little while, then spring into action and become shrieking Death oneself. Terror of the dark forces is transformed into joyous terrorism, often contained within the rules of a game such as hide-and-seek.

Ethnographers have noted the popularity of death themes in children's games throughout the centuries, going back at least to the early Roman Empire. Here is a prime example of a game that was still played in the early years of the twentieth century and may still be going on today. It's called Dead Man Arise! and was performed under that name in Sicily and the Czech Republic, where dead men have seldom been known to arise:

> One child lay down pretending to be dead while his companions sang a dirge, occasionally going up to the body and lifting an arm or a leg to make sure the player was dead, and nearly stifling the child with parting kisses. Suddenly he would jump up, chase his mourners, and try to mount the back of one of them. . . . In Czechoslovakia the recumbent player was covered with leaves, or had her frock held over her face. The players then made a circle and counted the chimes of the clock, but each time "Death" replied, "I must still sleep." This continued until the clock struck twelve when, as

in some other European games, the sleeping player sprang to life, and tried to catch someone.[8]

Adults as well as children sometimes play sneaky games with death. We may assign another person the responsibility of standing in for Death. The rest of us are then free to mock, trick, evade, or even attack this harmless substitute. A normative example in our society is the funeral director. Not all funeral directors are cast as Death by all members of the community. There is a reservoir of respect and affection for funeral directors and their families who have served a town well in helping people through several generations. Nevertheless, funeral directors are among the most identifiable, therefore most readily available, targets for our death-related angers, confusions, and fears. Impressionable people evade contact with funeral directors because they are imagined to be in cahoots with Death. Sneaky people say anxiously nasty things about funeral directors behind their backs and make (usually not very funny) jokes.

Objects associated with funerals and funeral directors also are tainted by death. We sometimes practice for death, then, in our interactions with and conversations about funeral directors as well as in our dealings with the objects of their trade. The first class of students at Bell Gardens High School were more fortunate than most in our introduction to the grim specter of death that was embodied in the funeral director. The family that operated the local funeral home often came to our rescue when school financial resources were not adequate. Furthermore, the sons were among the most stalwart of classmates, friendly, confident, and reliable. If the Allen boys were OK, then, why, death might not be so awful either. The deal was sealed for many of us when the basketball team patched together for this new school found itself short of transportation (not to mention talent). On a road trip to Citrus or Puente we would spring out of J. G. Allen's sleek black hearse, ready for action. There was something to be said for repeatedly clambering into a hearse and each time escaping back to life.

Many of us also practice our death strategies on people who have had the misfortune to suffer a recent bereavement. Children and teens are often spooked by the proximity of survivors. Part of this response comes from uncertainty. They have had little opportunity to learn how to act and what to say when confronted with a person who has suffered a loss. The other part comes from the hesitation to relate to a person upon whom

Death's touch may still linger. This fear of death contamination may continue into adulthood. We want to comfort our friends, neighbors, and colleagues in their loss. But that would bring us uncomfortably close to Death ourselves. As each of us sorts through our feelings and response options, we are practicing for death encounters that will come even closer to our own skins.

People themselves, then, may become symbols of or proxies for death. When this happens, we practice on them, or they on us. By the time we face our most personal encounters with mortality we will have already practiced our strategies for dealing with or avoiding death many times over.

A CONCLUDING WORD

We practice again and again as we linger at the bus stop, train depot, or airport, reluctant to allow our loved ones to depart even though the horn is honking, the lights flashing, the public address announcement becoming ever more insistent.

And we practice when we forget to pack the camera/sunglasses/hair dryer and therefore have to delay our departure, our separation, just a little longer. And we practice when you-know-who experiences an upset stomach or goes into a sputtering fury over an insignificant matter around the time of departure. And we practice when that-other-you-know-who becomes impatient and rushes off without saying good-bye.

We practice death in many small ways throughout our lives. The strategies we use are generally selected from the models, values, and expectations in our society, although we may also improvise at times. Our strategies might be coherent or contradictory. Our strategies might be encased in rituals or cobbled together from our unique individual experiences. And, when the time comes, we might discover that the way we have practiced death is either a boon to ourselves and others or a source of heightened anxiety. Some of us attempt to smooth out, neutralize, and tame our leave-takings. Others become engrossed in the critical moments of leave-taking and separation, experiencing keenly both the hurt and the hope.

In one way or another, our many small dealings with loss, separation, and change will have something to say about the challenges that lie ahead for us all.

SEPTEMBER 13, 2001:
A POSTSCRIPT

She had been a wife. Now she was into her second day as widow, one of many who were directly affected by the World Trade Center attacks. She had seen her husband off to work as usual, and they had looked forward to their upcoming family events and plans. That was all gone now. Through the window of television we could see her picking her way through the ruins of her life even as an impromptu army of other citizens labored among the physical rubble. She chose her words carefully. What came keenly to mind at the moment was a memory and its enduring effect on her life. "After my father died, I tried to think, 'What was the last thing I said to him?' We think this way when we have lost somebody we didn't expect to lose so suddenly. So I try always to say, 'I love you,' as though every parting might be the last."

The loss was devastating. No amount of "practicing death" could have protected against the anguish. The pain of self-torment would not be added to her burden, however. She had bridged their "little" parting with loving touch and words. Paradoxically, perhaps, practicing death can help us to appreciate life and the living.

THREE

GOOD DEATH, BAD DEATH (I)

In Other Times and Places

Does it make any sense to think of a person as having either a "good" or a "bad" death? History suggests that it does. People in many times and places have developed strong preferences about ways to live and die that are deeply rooted in religious beliefs and cultural values. "The good (or bad) death" actually refers to the end phase of life. The latter term usually describes what medical people call terminal illness and the rest of us call dying. Death may also come suddenly, though: alive one moment, dead the next. Is it good or bad to die in a twinkling? Not everybody has the same opinion. But an even larger question seeks our attention: what is the relationship between how we die and (1) how we have lived and (2) how we fare after death? In this chapter we explore the anguish, inspiration, wisdom, and, perhaps, foolishness of societies in times and places other than today's mainstream North America. Particular attention will be given to the concepts of the deathbed scene and the moment of death. In the next chapter we work up the courage to look in the mirror to view the "good death" in our own lives.

I had spoken with Mr. Carter the previous morning. He didn't have much to say and not much breath to say it with. We didn't have to talk about death. That had become a worn-out topic. Life had been pretty much worn out, too, as can happen after more than ten years as a bed-and-chair resident in geriatric facilities. "Another day, another dollar," he had wheezed. Now I was standing in a cool, sparkling-clean room two doors down from the converted broom closet that had become my office as psychologist. The consulting pathologist was completing the postmortem exam. He commented that Mr. Carter probably had engaged in vigorous physical activity in his earlier years; he was still a strong and healthy man, allowing for his age and deadness. "The ward says he died in his sleep," I dutifully noted. Dr. Rimini produced one of his elegant snorts. "Or he died in the nurses' sleep. No matter. He died."

I felt sad that Mr. Carter had died, that Mr. Carter had to die, that anybody did. I also wondered what I would find in my studies of death and dying—did most people *want* to pass on in their sleep, or what? Later, another thought hit me as I met with students who had signed up for my strange new kind of class on death and dying at Clark University (in Worcester, Massachusetts) in the 1960s. Few had had direct experiences with the dying or the dead. Not many of these college students had lost a family member or close friend, and the deaths themselves had been processed and packaged by professionals. I might also have been isolated from the dying and the dead had I not embarked on what was then a beyond-the-fringe career of working with the aged and the life-threatened. Mr. Carter's life and death had been more instructive to me than any textbook on death (which did not exist at that time). If my office had not been so close to the morgue (a little joke on the part of the hospital administration), I would not have been acquainted with the unprocessed body of a person I had known.

My experiences with the dying and the dead did not come through everyday life in our society. We have succeeded more than most societies in reducing the presence of the dead. In part this has been accomplished by keeping people alive longer. In part, though, we have cultivated techniques for keeping not only the dead but also the dying from general view. For most people in other times and places, death and the dead were more a part of everyday life.

We begin with a visit to the Lugbara of Uganda and Zaire (now the Democratic Republic of the Congo). Our guide is anthropologist John Middleton, who studied the Lugbara during the 1960s.[1] The world has much changed since these observations, but they offer insights into a culture much different from the Euro-American mainstream. We step now into that time and place.

A MAN SHOULD DIE IN HIS HUT

Not much is hidden from view among the Lugbara. There are a lot of Lugbara families within small neighborhood areas. Everybody knows pretty much what's happening with everybody else. Death is the most important thing that happens, from the Lugbara standpoint, and it happens all too often. Illness and death become known quickly, and most of the community participates in funeral rites whether or not they are related to the deceased.

> The Lugbara have few rites to do with birth, puberty or marriage. But the rites of death are important, elaborate, and often long-lasting, and lead to the reorganization of local social relations of many kinds. A death is more than that of an individual family member: the dead person has also been a member of a lineage which is assumed to be perpetual . . . [the death] disturbs the continuity of the lineage and mortuary rites are performed in order to restore this continuity.[2]

There is something else to know about the meaning of death for the Lugbara before we focus on the deathbed scene itself. The dead continue to exist in some mysterious way, but no mortal can understand how and why. What the people can understand is that there is safety in the *akua* (the home, the village compound) and danger in the *amve* (the outside, literally "in the grass"). The forces of good are concentrated in the home compound; evil lurks outside.

Death raids the compound from the outside. Gods in a nasty mood or witch-women are responsible for each death: *nobody just dies.* The sexist nature of Lugbara belief cannot be ignored. Males are fully human. Females can be almost human if they accept male governance and make no trouble, but females have the potential to become witches and disrupt the order of things. Much of Lugbara life consists of trying to control or placate evil forces. Death, then, not only threatens social structure and continuity but also represents a victory for the forces of evil.

How can there be a good death within this belief system? And what, precisely, would be a bad death?

The Lugbara have a clear understanding of physical death. The person stops breathing; the body grows cold, and after a while it starts to smell. Like many other people, they believe the soul or spirit departs the body after the last breath but may still hover around for a while, making everyone feel uneasy. The newly dead are neither here nor there. Or, perhaps more accurately, they are both here with us, drifting and lurking, and there, seeking admittance to the spirit realm.

There is something else to consider as well: the person dies to society. The loyal dying person will accept disengagement from all the obligations and powers possessed during life. These obligations and powers will then be redistributed among the living according to established principles. Here we start to get an inkling of what a good death might entail. Middleton makes it clearer:

> A man should die in his hut, lying on his bed, with his brothers and sons around him to hear his last words; he should die with his mind still alert and should be able to speak clearly even if only softly; he should die peacefully and with dignity, without bodily discomfort or disturbance.

The when of dying is also important:

> He should die at the time that he has for some days foreseen as the time of his death so that his sons and brothers will be present; he should die loved and respected by his family. He should die physically when all these conditions have been or can be fulfilled and when he is expected to do so because he has said his last words and had them accepted by his kin, and especially by his successor to his lineage status.[3]

Obviously, the Lugbara have given a lot of thought to the deathbed scene. The dying person is not viewed primarily as a "medical case" or a "patient" or as a passive entity. The dying person has lines to speak and actions to perform. Dying happens to a person, but it is also something a person has to do—and do right.

The scene climaxes with the moment of death. Ideally, the dying person will have shed his social identity, powers, and responsibilities. The successor observes the final breath and then steps outside the hut to sound the dead man's *cere*.

> The *cere* is a falsetto whooping cry whose "melody" is that of certain words that make a phrase "belonging" to the "owner" and which is unique to a particular man or woman. It may never be called by anyone else than his successor on this single occasion. It then marks the death, physical and social, and the actual moment of succession.[4]

The moment of death, then, is the signal for a firm and public reorganization of social structure in the community. A person dies, and at the very next instant the community starts to make its adjustments (though preliminary adjustments have already been in progress).

That was a good death for the Lugbara. A person has died well when the community can persuade itself that the performance did not stray too much from the ideal. There was a little room for the fudge factor. A person might not be ready to die on schedule. The successor and others most closely affected are kept waiting. What to do? The community has the option to go ahead with the rites of mourning even though the recalcitrant fellow in his hut is still clinging to life. He becomes socially dead, and that helps to move things along. It will be concluded that he had a good death even though the schedule was a little off.

There is an important contingency here, though. The dying person should feel well disposed toward kin and community, well respected, well treated. The whole community will be at risk should the person die in bitter resentment. Spirits of the discontented or disconsolate dead are terribly malevolent. It is therefore in everybody's interest to provide the dying person with every comfort, whether physical or socio-ritual. We will want to look at this mutual obligation system again when we look at deathbed scenes in our own society.

The bad death for the Lugbara is very bad indeed. It's more than bad—it's downright dangerous. Sudden and unexpected deaths are bad; so are deaths that occur in the wrong place, such as far from home. What makes these deaths bad is that the deceased does not have the opportunity to prepare and enact a final scene. There may be nobody (or only inappropriate people) to hear the last words. The end of life is not firmly punctuated by the *cere* call, which restores social order while also respecting the death of the individual. Furthermore, the person who has died in the "out there" may yield up a confused spirit that has difficulty finding its way home. The wandering spirit is frantic. Wild with fear and rage, such a spirit is not pleasant to encounter when it tries to find its way home or to its next destination. A woman who dies in childbirth poses a special risk to others because this event has fractured the relationship between sexuality and fertility.

Whatever interferes with an orderly deathbed scene within the bosom of the community is likely to produce a dangerous ghost and at the same time interfere with social reorganization. It's pretty clear that how—

and how well—a person dies has postmortem implications for kin and community.

SETTING SAIL FOR DEATH

We are now far from the Lugbara of Uganda and Zaire. We set down in the rugged landscape of Papua New Guinea. Kaliai is a political district in West New Britain Province. The thousand or so Lusi-speaking villagers who live along the northwest coast are known locally as *the* Kaliai. These interesting people are slash-and-burn farmers who also hunt and fish. They had little or no contact with the outside world until the turn of the twentieth century. Most converted to Roman Catholicism but continued to keep pretty much to themselves. Our guides are anthropologists David R. Counts and Dorothy Ayers Counts, who explored Kaliai ways in the 1960s and 1970s.[5] Again, we will want to acquaint ourselves with the structure and strictures of a society's life before focusing on dying and death.

Theoretically, all are equal among the Kaliai. In practice, though, there is a decided advantage to being male, first-born, and of the senior generation. One thinks of George Orwell's four-footed character in *Animal Farm* who observes that all are equal, but some are more equal than others. Furthermore, not everybody is a person. To become a full-fledged person one must be integrated into the community. Young children are not yet part of the core social structure because they do not have command of the language and ways and are unable to distinguish between dreams and reality. Strangers and enemies (to the extent that these categories are differentiated) will never be enfranchised persons in the Kaliai scheme of things. Personhood among the Kaliai entails a complex network of perks and obligations. Count and Count tell us that "everyone in Kaliai society is debtor to some, creditor to others."[6] As with the Lugbara, death upsets the ongoing pattern of obligations, resources, and relationships. As death approaches, then, attention focuses on the resolution and distribution of the dying person's accounts. Ideally, an aging person of wealth and status in the community is expected to disengage somewhat from economic and social activity. In theory, this gradual withdrawal makes it easier to detach the person from society at death. In practice, though, few are so willing to step into the shadows any sooner than need be.

What of dying and death? To minds saturated in Western thought and traditions, there is a sharp divide between life and death. Indeed, "the moment of death" is salient in Euro-American culture, and we even expect time of death to be recorded fastidiously (if often erroneously). For the Kaliai and many other world cultures, though, death is a process. The Buddhist stages of death, for example, include four phases that occur while the person is still among the living and up to four additional phases beyond the point at which physical death is certified.[7] For the Kaliai, death is a process of separation that can—and should—begin while the person is still able to make decisions and perform socially significant actions. Separation continues through the dying process and as long afterward as might be necessary to free the deceased person and society from each other.

What is the good death, then? It is the death that the dying person has accepted, and it results in the proper and thorough severance of social relationships within a reasonable period of time. Again, as with the Lugbara, the bad death is the unprepared and the unresolved. The spirit of the deceased still has social power and obligations clutched in his hands. The complex network of social exchange cannot function effectively while the dead are still caught in the system. And, of course, the spirit cannot proceed toward its mysterious destiny while still entangled. The *incomplete death* is the worst kind because it disrupts basic patterns of interaction and obligation in the community and threatens to turn loose an unappeased ghost.

Assuring the good death is by no means simple. Furthermore, the Kaliai perspective can be quite different from our own. The following are examples of end-of-life scenes among the Kaliai.

An aged bigman dies. After a time, his widow asks other males in her family to kill her. The kin confer. If all agree, the widow will kneel on a mat. Her oldest son will strangle her with a garrote or break her neck at the base of her skull with a wooden club that was carved especially for that purpose. This is a good death. We see that it is prepared and acquiescent. The widow's request is rational: she enjoyed the prestige and comfortable life of a bigman's wife, and now she does not want to become a burden on others. Because the couple enjoyed an affectionate relationship, it is obvious that they will be rejoined in a spirit village. Suicide, it should be noted, usually is a bad death, because it is unnatural and leaves things in a jumble of unresolved obligations. Furthermore, a death by one's own hand is interpreted as homicide-at-a-distance, so the search begins for the "real" killer. A bereaved woman's assisted suicide is the exception; and most widows do not elect to end their lives in this way, nor are they under social pressure to do so.

Twins are born. This is unnatural. The infants are exposed to the elements until they die. This is neither a good nor a bad death: the babies have not become Kaliai persons.

An aged man falls ill and is taken to the mission clinic for treatment but soon judges that he will not recover. Despite protests from clinic staff and family, he insists on being moved to the beach not far from his home. There a sail is set up as a tent to provide protection from the elements, and word is sent to his relatives that Avel, the old man, is preparing to die. Because he has long been disengaged from the normal turmoil of shell money finance, the people who gather do so to comfort him and to say their farewells. He himself remains composed, his deepest concern being to cling to life until he can say good-bye to his children. Avel waits until all his children can arrive. Villagers and nurses expect him to die at any minute, but he holds on for two weeks, until his eldest daughter (a novitiate nun) reaches him via a small coastal vessel. Kumui is brought immediately to the tent where her father lies. Avel speaks only once, saying, "Ah, now that you are here I can die easily." He then closes his eyes, and within two hours he is dead.[8]

A sail fashioned into a tent, rippling slightly in the coastal breeze. Family in attendance. The dying person well reconciled and having no grievance or claim on the survivors. This was definitely a good death: it came at just the right time and had been so well prepared that all significant economic and social relationships had been resolved, save for that final visit from Kumui.

Another sail on the beach. Another person has returned from the hospital as quickly as possible, coming home to die. This return is the signal for erection of the sail shelter and the onset of mourning by relatives. The dying person is placed under the sail. Relatives minister to his or her needs. Others from the community also crowd around. What are they all buzzing about? They want to know who killed this person and why. What rules has this person transgressed, what enemies has he or she made? All deaths, after all, are homicides, even though they may take such varied forms as illness or shark attack. Attention is also given to the financial implications: for example, has a widow been left wealthy or impoverished? Note that the gathering is carrying on lively discussions *about,* not *with,* the dying person. It is the significance of death for the community that matters most. (Incidentally, some of these "dying" people recover from their apparent fatal condition, and everybody goes about their business, unperturbed about the reversal of fortune. They have all acted prudently.)

REFLECTIONS ON GOOD AND BAD DEATHS IN BAND-AND-VILLAGE SOCIETIES

Time for an intermission. What we have learned about the Lugbara and the Kaliai has much in common with deathways in many other face-to-face societies around the world.[9] These are people who know they belong—belong to a culture with definite opinions about the world and their place in it, and belong to one another. When all goes as it should, they grow up within a framework of established rules and conduct their lives with familiar people in familiar surroundings. Not much is kept from others, and even that for not very long. People among us today who grew up in small towns beyond the reach of superhighways may feel a kinship with this kind of experience. Death, like life, is everybody's business, and it is a business that must be conducted properly. Private grief and loss are respected. In band-and-village cultures, the parents of twins or a deformed infant will experience personal pain and loss when they fulfill their communal obligation by exposing these "unnatural" births to death. Whatever one feels in private, though, is secondary to protecting the community against the ever-present risk from demonic powers.

There are examples of cross-cultural influence, but it is difficult to escape the conclusion that many peoples seem to have arrived independently at the same basic ideas about dying and death. The commonalties I see as most prevalent are as follows: All or most deaths are caused by hostile agencies, whether human, spirit, or god/demon. Death is a process that includes, but goes beyond, what we call dying. *How* this process occurs can be either good or bad—for the individual and for the community. The "dying process," "deathbed scene," and "moment of death"—

important concepts in Western thought—must be considered within the totality of the flow of life for individual and community. The judgment that this is either a good or a bad death, then, cannot be limited to the experiences of the person in the last days and hours of life. The ideal death (1) requires some advance planning or awareness on the part of the individual and, if possible, kin; (2) requires acceptance by the individual; (3) takes long enough for kin and community to engage in both personal comforting and ritual observance but (4) does not take so much time that the waiting and rituals interfere with other community needs; and (5) has full and proper funerary and mourning rituals afterward to make sure the soul of the dead has headed off to its next destination instead of becoming a discontented or even a dangerous spirit. Finally, the ideal is just that. In practice, perfect deaths are rare, perhaps almost as rare as perfect lives. Nevertheless, the vision of the good death provides guidelines and inspiration.

THREE EXEMPLARY DEATHS: SOCRATES, JESUS, AND MARY

Not everybody today accepts the idea that there are better and worse ways to die. A fellow a few seats away at the ballpark replied to some comment by his friends that he did not care how or when he died. My ears automatically dialed up to eavesdrop (the baseball game itself seeming beyond rescue for the home team). He was going to eat what he liked to eat, drink what he liked to drink, and smoke what he liked to smoke. To make himself absolutely clear, he concluded: "When you're dead, you're dead. How you get dead—who the hell cares!" I will assume that others through the ages have held a similar opinion. Resistance to the idea of good and bad deaths is worth consideration, but not right here.

Our immediate concern is with deaths that have been taken as models for how we should live and die. The two most widely known and influential exemplary deaths come from antiquity: Socrates, the aged gadfly philosopher of Athens, and Jesus, an unknown miracle worker from a small town who had become disturbingly popular. It is not easy to find even a third example of a death with resonations so deep and wide. But the pages of history reveal that the mother of Jesus was once revered through all of Christianity for her death as well as her life. Much about Socrates, Jesus, and Mary will be left unsaid here in order to keep our focus on models for the good or ideal death.

The Fatal Cup

We know this of Socrates. At age seventy (and for many previous years) he was a luminary of intellectual life in Athens, attracting bright and inquisitive minds. He earned fame in his own time and for centuries thereafter through his introduction of what became known as the Socratic method. This is a form of adroit questioning and listening that lures knowledge from the inexperienced, hesitant, and inarticulate. So powerful was his impact on Western thought that the history of philosophy remains divided between the Pre-Socratic and the Socratic.

He entered the world theater of imagination, however, through the manner of his death. Athens had recently lost the Peloponnesian War, and the various political factions were in an ugly, blame-pinning mood. Socrates' conscience got him in trouble. He was chosen by lot to be presiding officer of a senate committee that proceeded to condemn eight commanders to death for having lost a critical naval battle. Socrates thought this condemnation was unjust and the punishment extreme: he did not sign off on it. Nevertheless, the commanders were condemned and executed. As Athenian power continued to deteriorate, Socrates became one of the more conspicuous scapegoats, although he had done nothing wrong. The story of the charges brought against him, his trial, and his defense has been told many times. We proceed directly to the execution of his death sentence in the year 399 B.C.

What we think we know about Socrates' death comes from the words of a man who wasn't there. Plato, one of the great names in the history of thought, was a disciple and friend of the condemned man and had visited him faithfully during his incarceration. On the appointed day, though, Plato said he was too ill to go—perhaps he meant too sick at heart. Plato did hear reports from his fellow disciples who had been with Socrates to the end. It was Plato who brought Socrates to future generations in a series of dialogues. In *Phaedo* he gives us the final scene, the last words of Socrates, spoken even as death crept through his body.[10]

There is a facade we have to get past to comprehend Socrates' death and its influence on posterity. Plato's description is almost certainly not an objective report of what actually happened. This was clearly understood in its own time. Readers would have expected Plato to cast the events as a moral lesson in the form of a dialogue. They would not have expected verbatim reportage. Instead they would have expected a coherent account with a satisfying beginning, a middle, and an end, an account that perfectly captures the mood and message without sweating the details. Socrates did end his life more or less as described by Plato, but it is probable that the surviving account also includes literary construction, selection, and invention.

What we have, then, is a moral story built around fact. We do not know precisely how fact and invention play together. Nevertheless, it is this literary take on the death of the great philosopher that has come down through the years to perplex and inspire: perplex because we are free to ponder why Socrates did not save his life while he had that option, and inspire because here was a man who remained true to his principles and looked Death in the eye.

The scene divides naturally into three sections. First is the period of his incarceration, when Socrates and his friends had wide-ranging discussions but always with his impending death well in mind. The jailer was friendly and respectful. He and the guards could have been bribed; they were not keen at being party to the execution of this wise and entertaining old man. Socrates was the one who wouldn't go along with such a plan. He would continue to be the law-abiding person even though dealt an injustice by the court. Socrates also knew that his escape would mean big trouble for his friends and was not about to let that happen. And so they waited together. Specifically, they waited for a ceremonial ship to return from its mission to Delos. This was an annual voyage that played a role in citywide purification rituals. No prisoner could be executed while the ship was away on its mission. Here was one of those little quirks of history that may have made all the difference in the turning of significant events. If the ship had still been in harbor, Socrates would have been given the fatal cup on the day he had been condemned. Now, however, there was time—time for Socrates to respond to all the questions and arguments his young friends could generate and, in so doing, to express for the last time his thoughts about death.

His friends believed the individual soul is immortal and that therefore everlasting happiness awaited them after death. Socrates did not rubberstamp these assumptions. Instead, he did what he did best. He drew out their assumptions and subjected them to the light of critical reason. After exercising them through the labyrinth of thought, Socrates did affirm his belief in immortality. His reasoning is as ticklish as ever: the idea of life is imperishable, and since this idea dwells within us, we must be imperishable as well. His reasoning on the subject of immortality takes several other turns intended to pique and instruct his disciplines but not crucial to us here (a sigh of relief is permissible). His famous conclusion is that death should not be feared. It is the gateway to immortality, or, if not, then it is a kind of sleep, and who doesn't enjoy a nice long nap?

Peter J. Ahrensdorf believes that all this talk about death was intended as an instructional unit for Socrates' disciples.[11] Through contemplation of death we can best realize the importance of the examined life. And the world takes notice when a philosopher can philosophize lucidly on the verge of his own death.

This brings us to the remaining two scenes in the drama of Socrates' death: receiving the fatal cup and uttering the last words. By tradition, it was a cup of hemlock that the jailer reluctantly placed in Socrates' hands. This was a fraught moment: the hesitant executioner, the hushed and appalled friends, the philosopher still quite vigorously alive. Socrates tried to make it easier on everybody. He had already bathed "rather than give the women the trouble of washing me when I am dead."[12] Socrates also politely declined the invitation to give directions for what should be done after his death. Everybody wanted to please him. Socrates turned the decision back upon his friends. "Nothing new," he told Crito, "just what I am always telling you. If you look after yourselves, whatever you do will please me and mine and you too, even if you don't agree with me now. But if you neglect yourselves and fail to follow the [philosophical] line of life as I have laid it out for you both now and in the past, however fervently you agree with me now, it will do no good at all."

Crito agreed to this challenge, yet asked, "But how shall we bury you?"

"Any way you like," replied Socrates, "that is, if you can catch me and I don't slip through your fingers."

Now the time had come. Socrates accepted the cup without fuss or ostentation. A question for the jailer: was it permitted to offer a few drops as a libation to the gods? Sorry, but there was just enough for a lethal dose. Very well. Another question: what should he do after he had drained the cup? "Just walk about," replied the jailer, "until you feel your legs grow heavy, then lie down."

Socrates drained the cup. His friends, despite their resolve, broke into weeping. Socrates scolded them gently: we should end our lives in a peaceful state of mind. His listeners made a renewed effort to restrain their tears.

He did as instructed by the jailer, walking about until his legs felt heavy, then lay down on his back and covered his face. The jailer placed his hand on Socrates and a few minutes later examined his feet and legs. He asked Socrates if he had felt his foot being pinched. No, he hadn't felt a thing. The jailer's touch ascended upward, following the path of cold numbness. As the coldness moved above his waist, Socrates uncovered his face. He had one more thing to say:

Crito, we ought to offer a cock to Asclepius. See to it, and don't forget.

With these words—asking his friends to offer a fee to the god of health, possibly a final quip—Socrates died.

But not of hemlock poisoning. Or, that was pure hemlock in the cup, but the description of his last moments has been scrubbed clean. The latter alternative seems most likely. The progressive numbness from lower to upper regions of the body is characteristic of hemlock poisoning. But where is the agonized gulping for air, the burning sensation in the mouth, the blue tinge of the skin, the tremors, the cramps, the convulsions? Hemlock is nasty stuff. It does not make for a tranquil deathbed scene. The dying person suffers, as would any compassionate witnesses. Medical historian William B. Ober asks and answers the logical question:

What could have been Plato's motive for such a *suppressio veri?* The simplest answer is that he wanted to preserve the noble image of his friend and teacher, "the wisest and justest and best," and that he wanted no undignified details to obscure the heroic manner of his death.[13]

This celebrated philosophical death, then, depends at least as much on its telling as on its doing. We do not have to be ancient Athenians or trained philosophers to appreciate the way that Socrates mastered his final scene: the acceptance of an unjust verdict, the compassion shown to jailer as well as friends, the fearlessness in the face of death, and, above all, the very model of a person remaining true to his principles right up to the moment of death. This scene—as shaped by Plato—was so impressive that centuries later believers in a newly emerged religion could also admire Socrates and judge that he had died in grace even though never baptized into Christianity.

Jesus: The Death of the Messiah

It happened a long time ago. A well-known man was unjustly condemned to death. The final scene in his earthly life resonated not only among his contemporaries but also through the corridors of time to this day. How we think of this man and his message has much to do with the way he died.

This general description applies to the deaths of both Jesus and Socrates. There are other similarities. Although both were executions, neither death was instantaneous. There was time for the condemned man to reflect on his situation and time for witnesses to observe. And there was suffering. The agonies of the crucified Jesus have been at the center of Christian faith since the beginning. Now we know that in all probability Socrates also suffered in his last moments even though this was concealed by Plato. On the surface of things, then, neither of these endings would seem promising candidates for the exemplary death, the good death that should inspire us throughout our lives. Obviously, there is a lot under the surface, something that has stirred us deeply.

One more similarity, and this is critical: how we know what we think we know about these deaths. Father Raymond Brown has placed us all in his debt with his magisterial studies *The Birth of the Messiah* and *The Death of the Messiah* (this in two lengthy and tightly packed volumes).[14] His command of scope and detail is crowned by a sophisticated perspective. Father Brown lays the situation out for us early on:

> Understandably there is a desire to know what Jesus himself said, thought, and did in the final hours of his life. Yet Jesus did not write an account of his passion; nor did anyone who had been present write an eyewitness account. Available to us are four *different* accounts written some thirty to seventy years later in the Gospels of Mark, Matthew, Luke, and John, all of which were dependent on tradition that had come down from an intervening generation or generations.[15]

Whatever eyewitnesses saw and heard and however they spoke about the death of Jesus have been lost to history. Brown notes that the pre-

Gospel tradition has not been preserved. The earliest sources accepted by the church, then, are at some distance from the actual events. There are additional cautions that Father Brown urges we keep in mind:

The evangelists had their own purposes, their own agendas, in preparing and disseminating the Gospel accounts of the passion of Jesus. Brown devotes much attention to elucidating these intentions because we are otherwise vulnerable to misunderstanding their messages.

The Gospels were intended for the audiences of the day. These listeners and readers would know some things that are unfamiliar to later generations, and they would have their own distinctive experiences, hopes, fears, and vested interests.

Even within these limits of knowledge and interpretation, there is much we do not, and in all probability will never, know about the circumstances of Jesus' death. Brown leads us through the available sources to note again and again that there are significant questions that simply cannot be answered.

Brown would also have us realize that we cannot well understand this "social and thought world quite different from our own."[16] It would be naive to assume that Jesus and his contemporaries thought about the world as we do today and that Jesus was speaking to us like some talking head on television. There is an enormous linguistic, cultural, and historical gap between us and the three crosses raised high on Calvary.

We don't like to hear things like this. We don't like to be told that what we think we know is not precisely and firmly what happened. Most often, we also don't like to have somebody coming along to shake our beliefs and assumptions—especially if that somebody is himself a man of faith who knows a lot more than we do about his subject matter.

With these qualifiers in mind, then, we focus on the received image of Christ on the cross and what centuries of believers have taken from this image. Jesus probably died on the day before the Sabbath, which would be a Friday, and probably in the middle of the month of Nisan in the religious calendar. This would have been either just before, or during, or just after the hours when thousands of lambs were being slaughtered for Passover. Years later a Gospel writer would speak of "the precious blood of Christ as of a lamb without blemish or spot" (1 Peter 1:19). We are reminded immediately that blood and slaughter were in the air. And we see that the image of Jesus as the paschal lamb is rooted in traditional events of the day.

I catch myself about to characterize this vein of thought as mystical. The man and the lamb are somehow one. Blood seems to be both actual and symbolic, a sanguine exchange between the sacred and the profane. And circling around the lamb and the man is the theme of sacrifice. I close my eyes and can envision Greeks of remote antiquity sacrificing grain and wine but also, most dearly, blood to their gods. I blink again and see Isaac on the verge of becoming a sacrifice to Jehovah. In my mind's eye I see a gallery of blood sacrifices by many people to many gods. The death of Jesus seems to ride on a long wave of mystical thought in which blood unites and lubricates the troubled relationship between gods and men. But then I do catch myself, with Brown's cautions in mind. Did Jesus as the sacrificial lamb seem at all mystical to the people of his own time? Or was it an auspicious event, but one which seemed quite in accord with their prevailing view of the world?

Do astounding events occur as Jesus dies? Yes and no, depending on sources. In Matthew, Jesus screams, *"Eli, Eli, lema sabachthani?"* "My God, my God, why have you forsaken me?" (Matthew 27:46). A moment or two later he screams again. Just then,

> . . . the earth was shaken, and the rocks were rent, and the tombs were opened, and many bodies of the fallen-asleep holy ones were raised. And having come out from the tombs after his raising they entered into the holy city; and they were made visible to many. (Matthew 27:51–53)

This miraculous event would surely have made the death of Jesus portentous. The earth itself trembled and marked his passage, the tombs opening to release their hostages.

Luke's version is different. Jesus cries out loudly but once and does not question God's intentions from the depth of despair. Instead: "Father into your hands I place my spirit" (Luke 23:46). The special effects in this version are limited to a solar eclipse (also mentioned by Matthew) and rending of "the veil of the sanctuary," presumably also by earthquake, but the tombs do not release their dead to mingle with the living.

Still different is John's account. Here there are no special effects in the form of eclipse, earthquake, or the dead emerging from shattered tombs. Instead, John offers one of the very few glimpses of Jesus as a son to his mother. He sees her in the crowd before the cross. "Woman, look: your son" (John 19:26–27). He then saw to it that his mother adopted one of his disciples, saying to him, "Look: your mother." In this version Jesus does not cry out in agony, although surely he is suffering, nor does he either question God or ask for safe passage. He simply bows his head and says, "It is finished" (John 19:30).

Mark gives us a version much like Matthew's, but here Jesus cries out only once and the tombs do not yield up their dead.

These descriptions agree on the basics: Jesus died on the cross after prolonged suffering. The Gospels are not quite in harmony about the occurrence of striking natural or supernatural events. There are also lingering and unresolved questions about two other salient matters. What should we believe Jesus actually said on the cross—and to whom? And what was the cause of death? No attempt will be made to answer these questions here. We simply note that scholars have been perplexed by these questions for a long time and have offered a variety of theories.

The most obvious discrepancy is between the last words of Jesus as given in three different versions. But there is also ambiguity regarding the listener to whom Jesus addressed his final utterances. If Jesus said, "It is finished," and only that, he might have been speaking to the witnesses and to himself. It is generally taken, however, that Jesus was either questioning or petitioning God. This interpretation is consistent with the subsequent belief that Jesus was the son of God. Yet the possibility has been raised that Jesus was addressing his final words not to God but to the prophet Elijah, who some people at that time expected to return soon to announce the end of days. Did Jesus actually call out to Eloi, Eli, Elias, Elahi, Eliyahu, or Eliya? We don't know, of course, and we don't know for sure how his original utterance might have been altered when his Aramaic language was translated into Hebrew, Greek, and Latin. The argument here is that Jesus considered either Elijah or John the Baptist (held by some to be the embodiment of Elijah) to be the representative of God on earth, not himself. This interpretation could make it a little more difficult to see Jesus as the Messiah.

The cause of death is a question that did not become of much concern until medical science in the twentieth century decided to try its hand at remote postmortem examination. Jesus died of asphyxiation, the lungs having filled with carbon dioxide, or of a lance thrust that pierced the right auricle of the heart, or of circulatory failure and loss of blood, or perhaps of a previously diseased condition of the heart muscle, or perhaps even of despair. Some medical theorists have suggested that several of these causes were involved. Father Brown comments that all these explanations are based on a misplaced confidence in the descriptions offered by evangelists and Gospel writers, none of whom had any personal knowledge of the actual details.

Where does all of this leave us? Most believers through the centuries have focused on the basics: the suffering man on the cross. This is a vivid and affecting image. Discrepancies and ambiguities have been left to the disputing partisans and scholars. There has been an important divide, however, between those who build their faith around the passion of Jesus and those who make much of the natural and supernatural events said by some Gospel accounts to have accompanied his death.

Would the death of Jesus have become so engraved in hearts and minds if he had not been resurrected (as some believe)? This is another question for which we have no firm answer, but it is clear that the resurrection lit the torch for the dissemination and survival of Christianity in its early years and has remained at the center of the faith ever since. Jesus' death became increasingly compelling as it was woven into a larger fabric of belief over the years, much of it generated by Paul.

What became the traditional version was a triumphant message: "Death, where is thy sting?" (1 Corinthians 15:55). The man who died on the cross had now become a sacrifice. Through the death of Jesus others might live forever. Other religious cults had rituals in which a person became a sort of temporary god and was then sacrificed. Jesus' death has often been compared to these. In the public mind, though, God is often seen as having offered his own son in sacrifice, thereby forging a closer link with humanity. Victory over death was welcome news indeed. Historians conclude that death anxiety was rampant throughout the Roman Empire during those turbulent years. The new religion that called itself Christianity just might have provided the way out.

But—what precisely was the way? Should we follow to the letter the precepts of Jesus' own religion—the Hebrew? Should we emulate the compassion and mercy shown by Jesus, performing an "imitation of Christ"? Should we withdraw from the family circle and societal obligations to live a detached spiritual life, as Jesus had specified? Should we punish and mortify the flesh to overcome our inherent sinfulness and thereby gain entry into heaven—and escape the horrors of damnation? Should we live in a frenzy of anticipation because the end of days is at hand, the fiery apocalypse and the final reckoning as the Messiah returns?

Should we die as Jesus did and thereby prove our devotion and depart from our corrupt mortal shell to pure and everlasting glory?

People who regard themselves as Christians have sometimes taken one of these paths, sometimes another. The image of the suffering man on the cross and the assurance of everlasting life for true believers became the font of diverse rituals and ways of life. In the early years the suffering and death of Jesus held a fatal attraction. Roman authorities made martyrs of some Christians but soon found themselves annoyed by those who insisted on being put to death. The line between martyrdom and suicide became difficult to discern. Eventually church authorities would condemn suicide and attempt to restrain their more susceptible believers from imitating Christ by seeking painful deaths instead of living devout lives.

That people *should* suffer terribly and therefore identify with Jesus on the cross and expiate their own sins has remained a persistent theme even when overtaken by sociotechnological change. Progressive physicians in nineteenth-century Scotland introduced anesthesia and other measures to protect women in childbirth. This movement was hotly resisted by men of the cloth, who insisted that women were meant to suffer and, if needs be, die because of the carnal act that led to reproduction. In the twenty-first century there are still clergy and some physicians who believe that terminal agony is a test of character that should not be remedied. Not many dying people agree, however. Few of the terminally ill cancer patients interviewed in the National Hospice Demonstration Study considered suffering to be a spiritual value.[17]

Through succeeding centuries the image of the man on the cross would continue to inspire not only devotion but also a variety of responses to the challenges of living and dying.

The Beautiful Sleep of the Virgin

In the first thousand years that passed after Christ's death, Christianity expanded its domain, although not without both martial and spiritual combat. The Catholic Church still reigned, though convulsed by serious difficulties of its own. In later medieval years there was a persistent need that could no longer be denied. The people had Jesus, the pope (or, for a while, the popes), and the church fathers. But where was woman? Who could truly understand the prayers and tears of a mother with a sick child? Who could comfort the widow? Who among those most sacred to God embodied the female principle?

The Virgin Mary, Mother of God, was the obvious person to fill this void. Cults of the Virgin continued to develop. She became a popular figure in literature and song, the worship-worthy mother of the Holy Infant. She knew what it was like to bear a child and then to see this child die. Mary understood sorrow. Mary was the brave and loving mother— and she was the personal link to comfort and salvation for every anxious woman in Christendom. People wanted to know more about Mary's life than the sparse information offered in Scripture. How had she lived after the infancy of Christ—and how had she died? Philosopher Donald F. Duclow explains how a woman finally became an exemplar of the good death.[18] By the seventh century the Roman church had entered the Feast of the Assumption into its calendar, celebrating the ascension of Mary to heaven (despite the lack of support for this event in the writings accepted for inclusion in the Bible). Artists started to depict the Dormition (literally "sleep," but here referring to Mary's death) in the tenth century. Gothic churches were dedicated to Mary, and her imagined likeness appeared in stained glass, paintings, and manuscript illuminations.

The story of Mary's death and ascension was greatly enhanced in the thirteenth century when Jacobus de Vorgaine wove apocryphal materials into *The Golden Legend*.[19] This account provided the basis not only for art and literature but also for the intensified worship of Mary. Actually, two narratives are given by de Vorgaine, and, as with the Gospel accounts of Jesus' death, they differ in some details. What do they agree on? Mary has been revisiting the places where Jesus was baptized, suffered, died, was resurrected, and ascended. She weeps with longing to be with her son. One day an angel appears: "Hail, blessed Mary!" He presents her with a palm branch from paradise. She is told she will die within three (or forty) days. Several miracles occur involving apostles and unbelievers. In the more popular version, Mary arrays herself in funeral clothes, bids farewell, takes to bed, and dies peacefully—then ascends to heaven in soul and body.

This story inspired a great many works of art, often depicting the deathbed scene and the flight of her soul to Christ at her death. Visitors to Massachusetts can view a late-thirteenth- or early-fourteenth-century panel at Harvard University's Fogg Museum, and other examples have survived from this period when Mary's deathbed scene first became a powerful image throughout at least Western Christianity. Dormition iconography is all about a woman, a mother, a bereaved mother. Other women can relate. It's also a reconciliation—the lost son who abandoned his family and hometown people in favor of an extremist mission has now opened his arms to his mother. Mothers can be appreciated. They are not used up, worn out, and thrown away after they have served their men. Death, in fact, is renewal, rejuvenation: the iconography often depicts the soul of Mary as an innocent babe rising to heaven. The deathbed scene is really important. It is the crucible for miracles, where the last mortal breath becomes the first taste of immortality. The ideal deathbed scene is serene and confident, well prepared by knowledge and acceptance of the mortal move. And there is something more: blessed Mary, ascended to heaven, might also bless our own lives and deaths. In our fear and doubt we can pray to her for merciful deliverance.

Duclow reports that the popular books of the hours often included *obsecro te,* a prayer addressed to the Virgin:

> At the end of my life show me your face, and reveal to me the day and hour of my death. Please hear and receive this humble prayer and grant me eternal life.

Duclow comments:

> Like the dormition itself, this prayer suggests the ideal death as one foreseen, consecrated, and leading to salvation. That the Virgin's intercession may confer such a death is a medieval commonplace . . . a model for dying.[20]

Prayers, works of art, and theatrical enactments of the last beautiful sleep of the Virgin combined to make this the most influential example of the good death in the later medieval years.

What Was Good about These Deaths?

Socrates died while he was still at the top of his game. Philosophers often have lived a long time, continuing to cerebrate impressively. Jesus was at that glorious season of life where youth and maturity complement each other. A charismatic person who seemed to have already done wonders, Jesus might have graduated to the rank of exalted elder, a treasured resource to his people. Mary had other children to cherish and protect. She could also have become a person venerated in life, an embodiment of the wise and loving crone. None of these people really had to die when they did. They were not physically or mentally deteriorated. From this standpoint their deaths were not so good, since they were deprived of further experiences, and the world of their continuing contributions.

Socrates died in pain (if we believe medicine rather than myth), and Jesus much more so. According to one Gospel account, he also died in doubt and despair. Most people regard suffering as a bad thing. Indeed, some choose death to avoid further suffering. It goes against common experience to praise or emulate a death that is ravaged by pain. Socrates and Jesus also died in disgrace with the establishment, although supported by others. Other things being equal, the prospect of meeting one's death as punishment and rejection is not what most of us would consider ideal.

Whatever was good about the deaths of Socrates and Jesus had to be powerful enough to overcome the formidable negatives. And apparently this is just what happened. The gadfly philosopher and the man hailed as prophet or messiah ended their lives in ways that spoke deeply to others. There was a message too important to ignore—even if we would not necessarily agree on the specifics of that message. Their deaths were *meaningful*. Therefore, should our deaths not also be meaningful? They died *for* something, something they had also lived for. Should we not also live and die for something? And both showed us it was possible to look death in the face, to accept and perhaps to transcend it. Should we not also embrace death as part of life?

It was different with Mary. Good men die heroically in military or spiritual battles. Good women lie down, close their eyes, and sleep the sleep of the innocent. Mary's successors include Briar Rose, Sleeping Beauty, and the many other representations of the beautiful, innocent, and passive woman who must be animated by the warming breath of a gallant man (dark, handsome lover or gentle comforter).

We know that these great exemplary deaths owe much to literary license and invention (which can be said without denying those historical facts that have been reasonably well established). We also know that such deaths have been out of range for most people, whether in ancient or in modern times. Not that many of us will be condemned to death, nor do we have Mary's privileged access to angelic intercession. We must step closer now to visions of the good and the bad death in the hopes and fears of ordinary people, and to the church's response to their final passage.

ORDO DEFUNCTORUM:
DEATH BECOMES CHRISTIAN

The Christian leadership in the first millennium A.D. had its hands full. Evangelists sallied forth to spread the good word throughout the world. This was a daunting task, considering the hazards of travel, the multitude of languages, the competition from entrenched local religions, and the bellicose response to strangers. Furthermore, not everybody agreed on the precise nature of the good word. The Christian message diversified as it melded with local cultures. Attempting to forge the one true canon of belief was a difficult and fractious effort. There was a lack of consensus on who was the authentic standard bearer and who the dangerous heretic. This engendered confusion in the regulation of life and death. What rituals are appropriate when? And just what do these rituals mean? To understand the rituals surrounding death, we will also need to become familiar with other ceremonies and customs, especially communion or the Eucharist.

We now have a better idea about the Christian approach to dying and death in the first millennium, thanks to advances made by recent scholarship. Our primary guide here is Frederick S. Paxton. *Christianizing Death* is the apt title of his integrative contribution.[21] There had been rites devoted to the dying and the dead before Christianity split itself off from Judaic tradition. The "Christianizing" of these rites started right away, and not surprisingly so. Salvation and eternal reward were the lure of Christianity for most of the new disciples. Tracing the development of death rituals over a millennium has produced a lot more information than can or should be stuffed into these pages. The following are what's really important to us:

The early Christian church responded to sickness with prayer and ritual. A passage from James (5:14–15):

> Is any among you sick? Let him call for the elders of the church, and let them pray over him, anointing him with oil in the name of the Lord; and

the prayer of faith will save the sick man; and the Lord will raise him up; and if he has committed sins, he will be forgiven.

Prayer and ritual enhance each other. Anointing with oil for both medical and ritual reasons was already a long-established tradition in the Mediterranean. Not mentioned by James in this passage was another important ritual: the laying on of hands. These basic elements of prayer and ritual have continued to be called upon to the present day.

The primary purpose of prayer and ritual was to cure the sick and return them to the community. These performances were not specific for the dying. Instead, they were inspired by the cures that Jesus had wrought when he was among the living.

Yes, as implied by James, there was a connection between sickness and sinfulness. Purification rituals could rinse away the sin, hence restore health. This belief had been held by many religious communities prior to Christianity and was criticized by Jesus. Nevertheless, as Paxton notes, Jesus himself performed healing miracles that included forgiveness of sins. So, then—sickness is caused by sin and cured by forgiveness and ritual purification. Why wouldn't that also work for dying and death?

Feasting for the dead continued as a popular, though non-Christian, practice. Pagans excelled in commemorative services for their dead. The phrase "Roman banquet" has come down to us through the years for good reason. They liked to eat and to eat again. Paxton tells it thusly:

> The first of many meals served in honor of the dead was eaten at the grave on the day of the funeral. Others were eaten on the ninth and fortieth days, on the anniversary of the dead person's birth, and during the festivals of the dead, especially the Parentalia. The centrality of eating in these commemorative acts links them with similar rites of incorporation observed in many societies around the world, for eating symbolizes the re-establishment of the integrity of the family in the wake of the death of one of its members as well as the incorporation of the dead into their new home in the tomb or into the society of the other world.[22]

Fill the platters again! The more we eat, the more we help the dead (a possible marketing ploy not yet discovered by McDonald's). It was also useful to illuminate funerals with torches so the dead could find their way. (Abandoned lovers today who "carry the torch" for their fickle flame might be emulating this tradition. Or maybe not.) Roman Christians continued to participate in these torchlight banquets for the dead with the tacit approval of the church until about halfway through the first millennium, when Augustine of Hippo proved the spoilsport. Douse those torches, curb that appetite! Augustine sounded a modern note in saying that making such a do was simply a way for the living to satisfy themselves; it didn't do a thing for the dead—better that the funereal bread and meats be given to the poor.

The road to distinctively Christian death rites was paved by the establishment of special cemeteries for the special dead. Little attention had been given to the earthly remains of the average person. The martyred dead, though, deserved something better. Cemeteries for the sainted dead were established throughout Christian lands. Did this really matter? Yes, very much so. These holy sites are credited with stimulating an enhanced sense of community. The powerless and the poor, who were otherwise excluded from ritual care, could feel embraced by the loving strength of the sleeping martyrs.

The final Eucharist enabled the dying Christian to journey from this world to the next in a state of grace. It was, in effect, a second baptism. Ritual had welcomed the infant into the Christian community, and ritual would again confirm this membership at exit. This practice had been foreshadowed by the Greek practice of placing a coin in the mouth of the dead as payment to Charon, the ferryman on the River Styx. The dying Christian—or, sometimes, his corpse—would receive instead the body and blood of Christ. The Roman Christian *ordo defunctorum* encompassed rituals for both the dying person and the corpse. Here is what was done for the dying:

> As soon as they see him approaching dying he is to be given communion even if he has eaten that day, because the communion will be his defender and advocate at the resurrection of the just. It will resuscitate him. After the reception of communion the Gospel accounts of the passion of the Lord are to be read to the sick person by priests or deacons until his soul departs from his body.[23]

The good death, then, was one that passed through Christian ritual. A crucial facet of that ritual was the identification of the dying person with Jesus in the form of the Eucharist and the Gospel readings. One died with Christ.

In this ritual we see purification, blessing, and safe conduct from life through death. Although there are parallels with other religious customs of the time, the passion of Jesus the Redeemer provided the dying Christian with a special state of grace.

One problem, though: precisely what happened after death? Salvation, of course, if all had gone well. But salvation *when?* Not just yet. Not until the end of time, when the graves yawn open and final judgment is meted. In the meantime, defunct Christians subsisted in the *refigerium interim,* cooling their heels while many another generation birthed, bred, and died. Dying and death were just not that simple. And another problem: as already noted, the blessings of deathbed communion were not equally accessible throughout the population during the early Christian years or thereafter. Diligent priests would attempt to comfort the most humble members of society and even to convert pagans to the true faith before the last breath. Nevertheless, it would be a continuing challenge for the Christian message of brotherhood to overcome entrenched prejudices based on social status, hierarchy, and discrimination against out-grouped peoples.

The foundational *ordo defunctorum* would lend itself to variations and refinements throughout the first millennium of the Christian era. Setting aside the differences, though, we can see that the human race had divided itself on the deathbed: there were those who died in Christian grace, swathed in reassuring ritual, and those who went to earth without the benefit of baptism into the truth faith.

What happened as we moved well into the second millennium?

ARS MORIENDI:
THE ART OF DYING WELL

We may find it difficult today to imagine a time when death was the prevailing object of thought and emotion. But by the fifteenth century the religious establishment was relentlessly directing attention to the day of our demise. We wake but to sleep. We live but to die. And what is the bed but a grave? Money, power, fame, even mortal love are vanities. All will perish. Who embraces the hollow things and empty pleasures of earthly life also embraces damnation. Even children were taught to prepare themselves for death. We must live in keen anticipation of our death. The prize we can wrest from the snares and deceits of earthly life—and it is the only prize worth having—is to die well.

The deathbed is more than the last stop on the mortal journey: it is the beginning of either surpassing joy or agony everlasting. Death is with us every step of the way from the toddler to the striding knight, from the dignified cleric to the shuffling elder. Unlike early Christians buoyed by hope, the later Christians were expected to realize that they lived every moment in death.

This was the message of the *Ars moriendi* movement at its high tide. Images and representations of death were everywhere—in art, theater, song, dance, literature, and, perhaps most chillingly, in stone. Sculptures had taken to showing the illustrious dead suffering graphic postmortem decay. Somehow the joyful message of Christian triumph over death had taken a dark turn. Why? Recall the origins of Christianity. Jesus had lived, had died, had lived again. Big things were sure to happen right away. The Messiah would return. Sinners would be punished. The righteous would be rewarded. The dead would rise from their tombs and the valley of bones. What hope! What excitement!

Disappointment! Dismay! Doubt! The world continued much as it had been. The nascent theologians now had a lot of explaining to do. Many persevered in the belief that the big bang was still coming any time now and that we should continue to look for the signs and portents. Others held that the master plan was still unfolding. We had not understood perfectly. We must be patient. Still others proclaimed that we had been misled by the deceits and dissemblings of Satan, that we miserable sinners did not yet deserve the Messiah. Argumentation became more subtle, disputes more arcane.

The common people did not find solace in the ever-growing thicket of theological speculation and assertion. What they observed was that people kept dying and the dead stayed dead. Absent the foretold transformations, faith had to rely ever more on faith.

And so it continued year after year, century after century. Hope flickered, nursed along by exhortation and ritual and nourished by the occasional beatific vision. Miracles were eagerly seized upon as proof that the Lord had not forsaken them: the deal was still on. A thousand years and more had passed since Jesus had walked on this earth, and there was still unfulfilled yearning in Christian hearts.

The heritage did furnish striking images of the tormented death of Jesus and the newly invented peaceful Dormition of the Virgin. Perhaps if one could die in a state of grace? Perhaps if one could die as a true Christian even if one had lived as a sinner? Perhaps salvation depended on one's own state of soul at the last moment of life? Perhaps it was really up to each of us as individuals?

The game plan for a Christian life and death was changing. There would still be an end of days, a final reckoning for all. But now the fate of the individual had become more salient. *I* will be saved, or *I* will be damned. This exposure of the individual was in consequence of a long, slow wave of social and economic transformations. Most people still perceived themselves primarily as members of a kinship network and a small community. Individuality was starting to break loose from its moorings, however. History started to have more names and faces. People were going to more places and doing more new things. As lives became more conspicuously individual, so did deaths. And with the liberating winds of individualism came also the intensified anxieties of choice and personal responsibilities. *I* must learn how to live well, and *I* must learn how to die well.

Learning how to die was the essential goal of the *Ars moriendi* movement. Instructional tracts were created for this purpose and snatched up by those who could read. (Many tracts were flamboyantly illustrated for the benefit of the illiterate majority.) These books, in turn, were influenced by the popularity of mystery plays—theological dramas, not whodunits. Deathbed scenes were enacted in which the dying person was either raised to heaven or dumped into hell as angels and demons fought over the departing soul. We have already touched on the crowning literary achievement, Jeremy Taylor's *Rules and Exercises of Holy Dying*. Now we take an instructive sample from the first generation of tracts that appeared around the turn of the fifteenth century. These were brief books that much resembled one another in content and tone. The passages quoted here come from a rare-document collection edited by Frances M. M. Comper.

SAMPLE A

As then the bodily death is the most fearful thing of all other things, so yet is the death of the soul as much more terrible and reproachable, as the soul is more precious and noble than the body.[24]

This is not good! Dualism was supposed to give us two lives; here it makes us vulnerable to two deaths. Furthermore, anxiety is heightened by passages such as this because we in the medieval period know plenty about the loss of the body, especially through memories of the recent Black Death. We are invited to become nervous wrecks, then, when informed that the death of the ever-elusive soul is even more catastrophic. And we can hardly miss the reminder that body and soul are somehow in competition with each other, and it is up to us to favor the latter over the former.

SAMPLE A, CONTINUED

And the death of sinners is right cursed and evil; but the death of just and true people is precious before God for the dead men be well happy that die in our Lord.[25]

Just as body and soul are sharply divided, so are the ranks of sinners and the righteous. Dying is not just the natural end of life. The Old Testament expected people to come to terms with the withering away: "For all flesh is as grass" (Isaiah 40:6); "To all things there is a season" (Ecclesiastes 3:1). But now dying is presented as *judicial*—punishment for the guilty sinner. And as *paternal rejection*—kicked out of the house with Father's curses stinging like a swarm of hornets. Perhaps it is almost as much a strain to envision the radiant alternative. Men (and it's men, men, men; rarely if ever a mention of women in these tracts) should joyfully anticipate becoming dead men. Death is supposed to make men, well, happy. This is a mental strain because it is so difficult to associate the miseries of dying and the silence of death with great happiness. We may ardently wish to immerse ourselves in the vision of happy death, but it does rub against the grain of everyday experience.

So—what to do? This question is answered by passages such as the following.

SAMPLE B

I purpose me to learn to die. And I hope by God's grace to amend my life . . . for I am made so sore afeared. Wherefore now do away for me the softness of bedding, and the preciosity of clothing, and the sloth of sleep, and all that letteth me from my Lord Jesu Christ.[26]

Good dying must be learned. The motivation here swings to the side of being "so sore afeared" rather than the spiritual ecstasy of salvation. There are occasional passages in which the joys of dying have the upper hand, but as the *Ars moriendi* gained its footing we more often encountered fear-driven impetus. We also see that the snug routines of life, all that comforts body and mind, must be cast aside. Interestingly, Heinrich Suso (quoted above by Comper), who wrote a very early tract in the fourteenth century, has chosen sleep as his main example. A person following this example to the letter would become sleep deprived and, eventually, mentally and emotionally unhinged. This would enhance a mind-set that tunes out everyday life. It is difficult to see how society could function if all or even most or many people deliberately deprived themselves of "the sloth of sleep" and withdrew from their tasks and obligations.

Must learning to die be reserved for the elite? Should everybody else toil in the fields and raise the children, only to die a miserably ignorant death while the spiritually elite prepare their souls for that auspicious moment?

The following sample, by a Rycharde Hampole, has a statistically tinged cost-effectiveness message.

SAMPLE C

[Consider] the measure of thy life here; that is so short that unnethes it is nought; for we live in a point—that is the least thing that may be—soothly our life is less than a point if we liken it to the life that lasteth forever.

Another is the uncertainty of our ending; for we wit never when we shall die, nor how we shall die, nor wither we shall go when we be dead; and that *God will that it be uncertain to us, for He will that we always be ready to die.* [italics added][27]

Let's use our heads: why cherish this mere point in time that we call our earthly lives when all of eternity balances on our righteousness? And why delude ourselves into thinking that death will come in some distant time and circumstance when the next moment could be our last? We must always be on the ready to trade this life for the next. How foolish it would be to imagine that we can predict, let alone control, the future. It's God's game, and he holds all the cards.

Now—to the deathbed scene itself.

SAMPLE D:
THE COMPLAINT OF THE DYING CREATURE TO THE GOOD ANGEL

O my Good Angel, to whom our Lord took me to keep, where be thee now? Me thinketh ye should be here, and answer for me; for the dread of

death distroubleth me, so that I cannot answer for myself. Here is my bad
angel ready, and is one of my chief accusers, with legions of fiends with
him. I have no creature to answer for me. Alas it is an heavy case![28]

Perhaps the most vivid expression of the *Ars moriendi* centered on the
cosmic struggle around the deathbed. Bad angels (Satan, his demons,
imps, and familiars) contested with angels for the dying Christian's soul.
How many people of the time believed this to be a literal and how many
a symbolic or allegorical conflict? This we do not know. But we do know
that theology was transformed into high drama (which did not exclude
low comedy) with the soul of the Dying Creature at stake.

The bad angels or demons usually represent temptations. The good
angels represent inspirations that strengthen us against yielding to temptation. Although wicked to the core, the temptations present themselves
in an orderly manner. First, the Evil One attempts to lure the dying Christian into doubt and heresy. The resolute Christian will recite or listen to
Scripture in order to affirm faith. Next comes one of Satan's most powerful temptations—despair. The dying person has been such a sinner that
there can be no last-minute rescue. The Evil One presents a list of the dying person's sins so there can be no doubt about them. "You did forni-
cate with that woman!" accuses the devil, having at that moment produced that woman at the head of the bed. "You did stab that man!" he
continues (a splash of red blood might be added to the pages of the tract
at that point). Even more tellingly, "You ignored those in need. Because
you gave no mercy, you will receive no mercy!" If the devil has his way,
the dying person will collapse in despair, having lost faith and confidence
in God.

But—inspiration to the rescue! Recite or listen to a penitential psalm:
for example, "O Lord, deliver my soul: oh save me for thy mercies' sake.
For in death there is no remembrance of thee: in the grave who shall give
thee thanks?" (Psalm 6:4–5).

The Seven Deadly Sins were whipped into an official list in the sixth
century. Pride, Envy, Avarice, Wrath, Lust, Gluttony, and Sloth would
trigger the finger of divinity to strike the eject button and hurl the mis-
creant into the bottomless pit of despair (later, purgatory became an option). Furthermore, each sin carried its specific torment. Pride, the root
of all other sins, was punished by the sinner's being broken on the wheel.
Envy? Encased in freezing water. Avarice? Boiled in oil. Wrath? Torn

Figure 6 The triumph of the virtuous Christian over temptation was a dominant theme, as depicted in this image from a German edition of the *Ars moriendi* (Augsburg: 1471).

Figure 7 The angry are dismembered in this scene of infernal punishment for the Seven Deadly Sins. Woodblock print from *Le grant kalendrier et compost des Bergiers* (Troyes: printed by Nicolas Le Rouge, 1496).

apart, limb from bloody limb. Lust? Roasted by fire and brimstone. Gluttony? Forced to eat live rats, snakes, spiders, and toads. Sloth? Into the snake pits! These sins were deadly not because they might be responsible for termination of earthly life, but because they endanger the soul after death.[29]

And so the battle rages. The bad angel tries to provoke the dying per-

Figure 8 The lustful are smothered in fire and brimstone in another scene of punishment for a deadly sin. Woodblock print from *Le grant kalendrier et compost des Bergiers* (Troyes: printed by Nicolas Le Rouge, 1496).

son into impatience, pride, and avarice. Prayer and ritual are available to overcome each of these temptations. If all goes well, the Dying Creature passes this final test and confirms trust in "none other thing [than] His passion and in His death wrap all myself fully."[30] Meanwhile there should be abundant witnesses to the scene, pulling as hard as they can for the imperiled soul. The deathbed scene is not a passive tableau: everybody has work to do. Furthermore, this cosmic drama is public. Every person's death concerns everybody else, as John Donne would later say more elegantly in one of his devotions.[31] In one popular illustrated *Ars moriendi* instruction, ten prayers are sent to heaven by the witnesses. This sequence is crowned by an image of the good death itself. A priest offers the dying man a candle, and an angel receives his soul in the form of a child. Off to the side is a Crucifixion scene featuring Mary and a selection of notable saints. Bad losers that they are, demons at the foot of the bed fuss and fume.

Aries makes a telling point about this new intensified way of conceiving the deathbed scene:

> All that used to take place at the end of time now happens at the hour of death, in conjunction with the traditional rites—no longer in the explosive world of the Apocalypse, but instead . . . in the bedchamber, at the bedside.[32]

The death of the individual and the ultimate day of judgment for humankind become merged at the final moment.

Another significant observation is offered by Paul Binski.[33] He reminds us that the dead body was an object of dread for most people in the Holy Land prior to Christianity. (This fear was also shared by many other societies throughout the world. Into modern times anthropologists have found many examples of the fear of contamination by contact with the dead.) Christian belief went counter to these deeply entrenched beliefs. The last rites, then, have a function that has sometimes escaped notice: purifying the corpse, making it not only safe but sacred. Those busy little demons hopping around the deathbed scene might be regarded as the evil spirits of folk cultures who have been deprived of their prize by the more powerful force of Christian piety.

Binski also notes that the good death has a significant structural value for society. The Dying Creature is at the center of things in this drama, but the survivors benefit greatly, too. Discontinuity and disorder threaten society when a full-fledged member of the community dies. We have already seen this problem and how it is addressed among the Kaliai of Papua New Guinea. It is, in fact, a common source of concern practically everywhere. The good death does a lot to keep the game going, to lessen conflict and dysfunction at the loss of an important person. Relieved that this person has died in spiritual grace and that they have all done their part, the survivors can start the process of grief recovery and restored function with a clear conscience. There can be little doubt that how we die (or how we are *perceived* to have died) has significant implications for the living.

Nevertheless, some people had still another temptation to deal with— to play the deathbed scene for even more than what it was worth. Bernardino of Siena (1380–1444) caught them at it. Bernardino was a celebrated Franciscan priest who attracted many disciples and left enough of his own words to fill nearly twenty volumes of sermons. Franco Mormando distilled and commented on Bernardino's message. Most relevant here was Bernardino's critique of slothful and wobbling Christians who believed that all would be forgiven and the gates of heaven open to them if they pulled off a convincing deathbed scene.[34]

Don't count on it! First, there is the practical matter of being sufficiently in possession of one's physical and mental faculties as the fatal moment nears. Racked with pain and anxiety, the sinner may be in no condition to repent. Second, fear is not enough to win salvation. Of course, one might become sincerely afraid as the Infernal Pit yawns open for an eternity of torment. At this moment the wayward Christian finally gets the message—but it's too late. A charitable word or gesture is also insufficient. Heaven doesn't come that cheap. Bernardino takes the trouble to specifically undermine an ace-up-the-sleeve that many people of his time assumed they could bring to the deathbed scene. Yes, the "Good Thief" crucified next to Jesus did win his way to heaven because he spoke a word of compassion to his companion in suffering. But, no, such an easy redemption is not in the cards for the everyday sinner. In fact, the Good Thief is the only fellow who got away with it.

We must bring a credible track record to the deathbed scene. Prayer, ritual, and the mercy of Mary and Jesus can pull through the truly repentant Christian who has made a few errors along the way. But a desperate deathbed conversion may not cancel out a life etched in sloth and sin. Live the good life and we have a fighting chance for a good death, even though we have stumbled now and then.

We cannot close even this brief book on the *Ars moriendi* without acknowledging a sisterhood whose humane ministrations to the dying not only provided comfort in their own time but also set an example for palliative care today. The Beguines first appeared more than half a century before the Black Death. There was already more than enough dying and death and not nearly enough hands to offer personal services. Christine Guidera tells us that the Beguines came forth from France, Germany, and the Low Countries.[35] They were pious women who had no official status in the church hierarchy. Their good works reached into many spheres of life but were perhaps most distinctive and welcome in care of the ill, the dying, and the dead. Unfortunately, little is known about the specifics of their practice with the dying. It is reported, though, that the Beguines incurred suspicion and hostility from some quarters because they provided intimate care to the dying. Were they seducers? Sorcerers? In all probability the Beguines were just what they seemed to be: compassionate women who ventured across the threshold to provide care for the dying that others were unable or unwilling to provide.

DEATHBED SCENES
AFTER THE DEPARTURE OF ANGELS AND DEMONS

Angels and demons left the deathbed scene only with considerable reluctance and have returned for numerous encore appearances since the heyday of the *Ars moriendi*. But, just as people in the late medieval period reconstructed the mysteries of dying to accord with their changed circumstances, so subsequent generations have experienced deaths as influenced by their own altered circumstances. History in general has unearthed more information (and misinformation) about the lives of movers and shakers than the lives of other individuals. This bias holds true with their deaths as well. We will join this parade by reviewing the fairly well-reported exits of several eminent people that bear on our exploration of good and bad deaths. The royal deaths we visit here have been collected by historian Olivia Bland.[36]

Queen Elizabeth I had been in robust health most of her seventy years. What proved to be her fatal illness, in 1603, was preceded by two and possibly three stressful events. Upon her inauguration forty-five years earlier, the queen had announced that her marriage would be to the kingdom. As a token of this union, she had placed her coronation ring on her finger in lieu of a wedding band and had never removed it. But now it had grown painfully into the flesh, and she had to have it filed off. Afterward the queen brooded—did this presage her complete severance from the mystical union with her kingdom? Two months later her closest friend, Lady Nottingham, died. The queen responded with despair. Her legendary energies had evaporated. Only Elizabeth's habit of resolve kept her going at all. Later a story circulated that has never been either confirmed or dismissed conclusively. Supposedly, Lady Nottingham made a deathbed confession that devastated Elizabeth: Elizabeth had given her true love, Essex, a ring in their younger days, and he had later given it to Lady Nottingham with an urgent request to rescue him from the Tower of London and his imminent execution. Instead, Lady Nottingham had hidden the ring, and Elizabeth—after self-tormenting hesitations—had signed the execution order. (The lovers' ring sent by Essex should not be confused with the coronation ring that had burrowed itself into the queen's finger.) Favoring the authenticity of this dramatic episode was the intensity of the queen's despair during the interim between robust health and terminal illness. If the story was true, Lady Nottingham could not die in grace with the weight of that terrible betrayal of her friend Elizabeth. To spare herself a disgraceful death, she had to confess—but this, in effect, passed the trauma on to the queen.

Reports agree that Elizabeth was in low spirits before showing signs of physical illness. As her health failed she complained mostly of her sad and heavy heart. She refused nourishment and medicine. Only the closest and most persuasive people in the royal circle could persuade her to take a few sips of broth. Those who assured her she would live many more years were waved off; more of this life was not appealing. Respiratory infection and pneumonia were bringing her down.

When the aged archbishop and his retinue attended her for the last time, the queen answered all his ritualistic questions promptly and firmly. She was in the faith, had always been in the faith.

After he had continued long in prayer, 'till the old man's knees were weary, hee blessed her, and meant to rise and leave her. The Queene made a sign with her hand [desiring] he would pray still. He did so for a long halfe houre after, and then thought to leave her. The second time she made signes to have him continue in prayer. He did so for halfe an houre more, with earnest cries to God for her soul's health, which he uttered with that fervency of sprit, as the Queene to all her sight much rejoiced therat, and gave testimony to us all of her christian and comfortable end.[37]

The queen fell asleep. A few hours later she was dead.

Was this a stereotypical good death? Not quite. Actually, not close. The central element was there: passing in a state of grace embroidered by extended prayers from the archbishop himself. She had also carried out her final obligation, signifying that the crown should be given to King James VI of Scotland. There was something missing, though: the resistance, the fear. It was almost a conspiracy, as though Elizabeth had opened the door a bit so Death, like a secret lover, could slip in. A state of depression robs this world of its joys. It could hardly be a good death, pure and simple, if one were sad and heavy of heart, no longer desirous of life. Earthly temptations to overcome, there were none. Faith was supposed to overcome fear. But should one actually invite death?

This question became salient when, as we recall, some early Christians rushed to martyrdom. The church came down on both sides of the issue. On the one hand, suicide was a grave sin: the dead sinner could not then repent of any sins and thereby earn salvation. On the other hand, martyrs often became revered saints. Circumstances are often more subtle and ambiguous than this, however. Elizabeth did not arrange for her own execution, nor did she lift a hand against herself. At that point in her long and eventful life, though, she seemed ready enough for death that she yielded almost gratefully when the opportunity presented itself. In general, deathbed scenes after the *Ars moriendi* seemed to become less formulaic and more tinged with ambiguities and conflicts. The goodness of a death became more relative to circumstances.

Consider, for example, the Stuart monarch Charles II. It is the evening of February 1, 1685. Here is an abridged version of Bland's account:

> The King had dined heartily that night, but unusually included two goose eggs in his menu which may have accounted for the restless night he passed. . . . the King, who always slept like the dead, tossed and muttered all night. . . . When the King woke . . . he felt very ill. . . . His countenance was pale as ashes. [His doctors] persuaded the king back to his bedchamber where it became apparent his speech was affected. Then . . . he was seized with a violent convulsion and fell back with a terrible cry into the arms of Bruce.[38]

Charles II recovered! A robust man, he seemed on the road to full recovery, but the doctors insisted on doing their bit. He was pierced with lancets, the better to bleed. "Physicks" purged his bowels repeatedly. Additionally he was administered tinctures of white vitriol in peony water, juleps of prepared pearls, sneezing powders of white hellebore root, emetics of orange, infusions of metals in white wine, blistering agents, and spirits of sal ammoniac in antidotal milk water. But the doctors, in their onslaught of remedies, had by no means exhausted their bag of tricks. Now it was time for the more exotic: Peruvian bark, and Oriental bezoar stone from the stomach of an eastern goat, augmented by spirits of human skull, and more herbs and spices than anyone was able to catalog. Nobody could accuse the royal physicians of standing by and doing nothing—even though doing nothing might have been a much better plan, leaving recovery to nature and the king's hearty constitution.

The more odious or painful the procedure, the more it was deemed likely to work a cure. A dose of catharides, a pseudoaphrodisiac irritant, made his urine scalding hot. Speaking of heat, the king's head was shaved and red-hot irons and plasters applied to his scalp and to the soles of his feet. The king endured these medical assaults with remarkable patience. When, despite everything, Charles II again showed signs of recovery, the physicians renewed their attacks on the royal personage with purges, enemas, emetics, cuppings, and bleedings. Even a strong man with an ardent will to live could not long withstand so much medical assistance.

Now occurs not only the drama of a king's death but a bizarre sideshow as well. His passing would reflect the crises of the times, particularly the sharp division of faith between Catholic and Protestant claims on the immortal soul. Prayers for the sick were offered in both chapels day and night, followed by the bedside services for the dying. This was just as it should be in the Protestant kingdom ruled by Charles II. The king did not follow the approved script, however. He was not comforted by prayer and, worse, refused to take the Sacrament. At this point, then, both the soul of the sovereign and the safety of his realm were compromised by the prospect of a bad death. If the king should die unrepentant (not that he had been a wicked fellow), this could only make the kingdom increasingly vulnerable to the forces of disorder. What to do?

Imagine this sequence, if you will. First we have the duchess of Portsmouth whispering in the ear of the French ambassador. In turn he quietly seeks audience with the duke of York and whispers in the ducal ear. York now betakes himself to the king's bedside, and a whispered message is again imparted. The plot is now on the kettle. A Catholic priest is smuggled into the palace (a risky covert operation for all concerned). The disguised priest enters through a secret door. He performs the *ordo defunctorum* for the grateful king, who declares his sins and tries to rise in order to receive the Holy Communion. The dying monarch is much relieved when the priest assures him that Almighty God will accept his good intentions. Now the priest slips away through the secret passage. The king? He has become calm and serene. When he lasts through the night, he apologizes to his attendants for having imposed on them by "so long a-dying." Assured of forgiveness and salvation, he is ready for death.

The story should end here. But both bishops and doctors keep after him. He is repeatedly besieged by clergy to receive the Protestant version of the Sacrament (they don't know about the priest). The physicians— by now numbering fourteen!—are still concocting treatments. Despite all these impositions, Charles II remains tranquil and focused. He bids a tender farewell to Catherine; they had been a rare example of a truly loving regal couple. He then embraces all his legitimate children and sees to their continued education and well-being. Later he asks for the curtains to be opened so he may once more see the day—and reminds his attendants that the eight-day clock needs to be rewound. About an hour later he experiences difficulties in breathing and struggles unsuccessfully to arise. This gives his crowd of physicians another opportunity to bleed the king and force stimulants into his mouth. This time the king foils them. He dies. Unable to try any further remedies on the royal personage, the physicians return to their lengthy and learned discussions: "You should have given the Whatchamacallit before the Whoknowswhat!" "You failed to diagnosis the Blippitybop properly!" "You should have allowed me to use more hot plasters!" and so on.

This eventful, moving, and flawed deathbed sequence tells us much about the conditions of life in late-seventeenth-century England and, to some extent, elsewhere in Europe as well. The good death envisioned in the past had emerged within a monolithic religious structure. For most Christians, there had been only one church and one set of doctrines and rituals (heretics were inviting violent death). The black comedy of disguised priest and secret passage was a product of the schism within Christianity and, at that time, one fraught with peril for those who were perceived as being on the wrong side. Charles II could not

accept the wrong good death, but there would be hellacious consequences for the regime and his family if his Catholic allegiance were to
become known.

Another source of stress had also become increasingly pernicious.
Physicians were less humble, though not spectacularly more effective, than
their medieval predecessors. Physicians were advancing their own claims
for power and prestige. Many brought ignorance, arrogance, and rivalry
to the deathbed scene, more often adding to the torment than working
a cure. It was Charles II's misfortune to suffer from three demonstra-
tions of medical ineptitude. First, excessive, unnecessary, and wrong-
headed interventions deprived the king of his best opportunity to recover
naturally from his illness. Second, the royal physician refused to acknowledge later that the king was on the brink of death, resulting in additional exhausting and painful measures. *He,* reassured by ritual and
aware of his condition, could accept death. *They* could not or would not.
There had always been circumstances in which the impulse to rescue a
person from death had conflicted with the impulse to provide comfort
in the last hours. Now, however, physicians were feeling sufficiently empowered to fight the battle to the very last breath, if not beyond. Ritual
and comfort for the dying—or a full-court press to restore life? The
deathbed scene was becoming more complicated. And third, only the
wealthy few were so tormented. The numerous and anonymous poor died
too soon after too deprived and stressful a life, but at least their demises
were not aggravated by the painful and useless interventions of a swarm
of physicians. Overall, there were advantages to medical care, which is
one of the reasons the wealthy enjoyed a significant edge in life expectancy. But, then as now, many physicians hated to say die.

The deathbed was becoming a contested zone between the claims of
the church and those of the physician, while political considerations (such
as succession to the Crown) also were influential for "important" people.
But what about deaths without beds? We will take just one example here.
Back we go some years to 1649 and another British monarch, Charles I.
He had been convicted of high treason and murder and denied the opportunity to address the court after his death sentence had been passed.
When the time came, the king said his farewells and gave various per-
sonal objects to his children and faithful attendants. The drums rolled.
The crowds gathered for the execution. He marched faster than the drum-
beat in the procession to the palace and then, after an interval, to the

scaffold. According to reports, he conversed cheerfully with the bishop and guard by his side.

At this point, can we speak of his impending death as good or bad? Today we might think of a death as bad—or, at least, unfortunate—if it comes while the person would still have had many years ahead. This, however, was not the decisive consideration in the time of Charles I. A lot of people died young; this had come to be expected. Furthermore, in some quarters the death of the very young did not count for much from a societal standpoint: infants and children consumed resources and contributed little. The king, however, was a mature adult; he had had a life. Next, we recall that tribal peoples have emphasized the importance of being well prepared for death. The person who dies by sudden violence becomes a risk to the community as a disconsolate spirit. Readiness for death was a core element in the *Ars moriendi* and, indeed, in the sacraments for the sick and the dying. Purification from sin should precede death.

In this regard Charles I was well served. He accepted Holy Communion from the bishop and announced that he was relieved of sin and prepared for all that he would have to undergo. Charles I knew that his head would be severed from his body within about an hour. To this fate he was philosophically resigned and at peace with himself and his God. Perhaps this was a good death emerging from difficult circumstances. The victim was prepared, and the nation had decided upon regicide after what it considered to be due process in court, so the death itself should affirm rather than weaken the spirit of the land. "We chopped off the bloody head of the bloody king, but we did it the right way!"

Nevertheless, the scene would not play out quite as devised. The king, the executioner, and the mob had to wait hour after hour. The stroke of the ax could not be delivered until the stroke of the pen on the death warrant, and the commissioners were dillydallying. It was one thing to grandly condemn a king to death in the name of the people; it was something else actually to sign one's name to the document just before the blood began to flow. The impending death no longer seemed so justified, so desirable to those who had condemned the king. Finally, the administrative deed was done.

We come to the final scene. The king is quite in command of himself and cooperative with the proceedings. A cloak accidentally flaps against the blade of the ax. Cautions Charles I: "Hurt not the ax that may hurt me." He has a few words to say to his people:

Sirs, it was for the liberties of the people that I am come here. If I would have assented to an arbitrary sway, to have all things changed according to the power of the sword, I needed not to have come hither; and therefore I tell you (and I pray God it be not laid to your charge) that I am the martyr of the people. I die a Christian according to the profession of the Church of England, as I found it left me by my father.[39]

Charles I removes his coat and presents it to an attendant, saying, "Remember." He adds, "I go from a corruptible to an incorruptible crown, where no disturbance can take place." Still in command, the king instructs the executioner: "I shall say a short prayer, and when I hold out my hands thus—strike." The hooded ax man replies: "I shall wait for it, sir, with the good pleasure of Your Majesty!" He intends no irony.

The ax is raised. A thud is heard. The severed head, held aloft by the regal hair, is shown to the crowd.

At this moment the crowd is given its opportunity to judge. It was something amazing—to see a king get his head lopped off. Every grudge against the Crown could now be given voice in a thunder of vengeful roar and mockery. That response would have stamped the decapitation of Charles I as a good death for the people, if not for the victim. Instead: a rumble, a groan, a cry of grief from the crowd. No, this was a wrongful death. During the last moments they had seen in their monarch a brave and reasonable man who was perhaps the best Christian of all. They surged forward to dip their handkerchiefs in his precious blood but were driven back by mounted troops.

Many an ax had fallen on many a neck in not-entirely-merry Olde England. These had been entertaining spectacles as well as warnings to other potential miscreants. The crowds had jeered, not wept. This was different. This was a death that hit home to them, a death that made them feel more than a little guilty themselves.

The Puritan Struggle

Charles I had a good death *if*—if being prepared is good, if receiving safe passage through ritual is good, if continuing to act as a responsible member of the community until the last breath is good, and if touching the hearts of others is good. And he also had a good death in a more distinctive way. Unlike many others, the king had the opportunity to speak his mind to attentive listeners, his last words being duly recorded for posterity. The drama was further intensified because these words were uttered against the stark stage set of a scaffold with a small crowd of guards, dignitaries, and, of course, that hooded fellow with the ax. Somehow he had managed to make this death his own. Three centuries later there would arise a movement in England that was quickly taken up in North America, and later throughout the world. This movement was predicated on the value that the good death should be one's own, not the standardized demise doled out by the establishment. We will consider "the appropriate death" and the hospice/palliative care movement in the next chapter. For now we allow ourselves one more memory image of Charles I as he bows his head for the blow. He is still a king, still a Christian, and still very much himself. In fullness of life he is ready for death.

We cross the Atlantic now, taking the seventeenth century with us. Here, too, salvation was an urgent issue. The Puritans, struggling to survive in a literal wilderness, also faced a wilderness within, a tangle of fears, desires, and imperatives. One must live the good life. This must be accomplished over and again each day, fighting off temptation, pride, and sloth. Even so, the good life does not necessarily beget the good death. In other words, the Puritans were imbued with the Calvinistic philosophy of predetermination. God has already selected the Select. But who has been chosen, who rejected? Only God knows. All we can know is that doubt is necessary. Why? Because we should live in faith, not require proof, not demand guarantee. Eschew false hope and test thyself severely lest thee discover the hypocrite beneath thy respectable visage. Puritans therefore became their own inquisitors. Daily the diligent Puritans examined themselves for evidence of impurity while lamenting the inherent depravity of the entire deplorable human race.

Historian David E. Stannard tells us that people could and did crack under this pressure. For example, the notable John Winthrop spoke of a Boston woman who was so desperate about her spiritual estate that

> one day she took her little infant and threw it into a well, and then came into the house and said, now she was sure she would be damned, for she had drowned her child.[40]

Doing good did not necessarily win heaven, but doing evil assured hell: the certainty of a dismal fate might be preferred over prolonged uncertainty.

To the deathbed now. The fleeting pilgrimage through the imperfections of earthly life would now be transformed into a beautiful flight to heaven. All one had to do was die. A passage from 2 Corinthians (5:6–8) was frequently cited:

> Being therefore always of good courage, and knowing that, whilst we are at home in the body, we are absent from the Lord (for we walk by faith, not by sight); we are of good courage, I say, and we are willing rather to be absent from the body, and to be at home with the Lord.

Life without or death with the Lord? The true believing Puritan would not hesitate. And yet—dying was an ordeal, a severe test for body and soul. Furthermore, death was punishment because it had entered into the world by sin. Talk about ambivalence! Death was agony and punishment but also the gateway to redemption and heaven. Furthermore, unlike Elizabeth and the two Charleses, the Puritan could not be assured of salvation by ritual and prayer. Absolute faith was demanded, but doubt ever gnawed at even the most stalwart.

Consider, for example, two of the most devout of the devout Puritans. Increase Mather and his son Cotton have remained durable exemplars of the creed. The long tide of the *Ars moriendi* had very nearly subsided, but the Mathers told all who would listen that we should die daily and always have foremost in our minds that each strike of the clock brings us an hour closer to our blessed release. Cotton even wrote several books on the subject, including *Death Made Easie & Happy*. Increase declared, "How glad should I be, if I might dye before I stir out of this pulpit!"[41]

In practice, though, it was the doubt, the dread, and the horror that had a death grip on the Puritan soul. Stannard concludes:

> The Puritans were gripped individually and collectively by an intense and unremitting fear of death, while *simultaneously* clinging to the traditional Christian rhetoric of viewing death as a release and relief for the earthbound soul.[42]

When the desired and dreaded moment came, Increase was wracked by doubt. Cotton, at his bedside, heard his father speak about the Dark

Vapors that assaulted him, the Great Wrath that might be unleashed at the Last Judgment. Perhaps despite everything, despite his severe self-criticisms, despite his relentless effort to live the saintly life, the dying man had been deceiving himself all along, a gullible fool misled by the Serpent. The phrase "fear and trembling" occurs repeatedly in Cotton's report of his father's death. A devout life could still end in a state of doubt and anxiety.

CONCLUDING THOUGHTS

What precisely is the connection between how we live, how we die, and how we fare after death? Can we get away with a dissolute life if we manage a deathbed conversion? Does even the most devout life end in anguish and uncertainty on the deathbed? Are prayer and ritual enough to see us through, or can other circumstances alter the outcome? Does the deathbed scene belong to God (perhaps in competition with the demons) or to the physician fascinated by an "interesting" case? These are among the questions that remain ponderable after two millennia of Christianized death.

What *can* be said with confidence? We can say this: the passage from life to death became central to the Christian experience by the end of the first millennium. The good death required dying in a state of grace, and this in turn required preparation, ritual, and, when possible, community participation. We can also say that the good death was a powerful tool for arousing the complacent: "This is how it should be done. Can you do the same?"

The bad death was experienced by those who departed unprepared. This included unrepentant sinners and heretics and also those who had procrastinated. It was the responsibility of every devout person, then, to remind others of their mortality, to guide them along the path of redemption before it was too late. Nevertheless, many people perished without either pastoral or medical care. These were mostly the anonymous, the poor, the marginal. John McManners speaks, for example, of the gap between theory and practice in eighteenth-century France.[43] Here there was an unusually strong emphasis on paying last respects to dying people and their families: this was a demonstration of piety and charity. It was good to be seen at a deathbed as a sympathetic and consoling citizen. Even here, though, people died alone, untended, unconfessed, and unsanctified. Devout and socially responsible citizens suffered from their inability to prepare every Christian soul for the passage.

The *ordo defunctorum*, with all its ancient associations and resonances, would find itself in a strange new context as industrialism took hold in the nineteenth century. There were increasing signs that both the dying and the dead were losing their special status, perhaps even within the church. Slowly but steadily arising was the image of the aged and dying person as a failed machine. What, then, of the soul? Christianity responded, but with various voices. The Marists formed themselves and, as noted in chapter 2, renewed the gravity and intensity of the deathbed scene. For those touched by the Marist endeavor, the dying person was once again engaged in a cosmic struggle. The inspirational death had returned—but this time it was available to peasants as well as to the high and mighty.

Others, though, practiced a degraded form of deathbed ministry. Elsewhere I have offered a sample of the spiritual comfort meted out by a nineteenth-century English doctor of divinity. The Reverend Dr. Warton specialized in hectoring and humiliating dying people and their families, all supposedly in the service of redeeming their immortal souls.[44] It is clear, though, that he thoroughly enjoyed the opportunity to bully the lower class at their most vulnerable moments and to score points through his clever rhetoric. The deathbed scene attracted both the most ardent and the most self-serving ministers as Christianity rallied against the machine and the pitiless cities.

A formidable new challenge would appear a generation later: Darwin, with his specimen and his theory. Science now threatened to demote mankind to the animal kingdom. The special arrangement with God was called into doubt. And, perhaps worst of all, humans seemed consigned to die like other creatures rather than rejoice in salvation. As the century lengthened, the prime battleground shifted from the deathbed scene per se to the defense of immortality. Ghosts, phantasms, and other spirit visitors were frequently called upon to testify. Rituals for safe passage of the dying became less salient than the emerging shadow rituals for contacting the dead through seances and other mysterious procedures.

Meanwhile, in Uganda, Papua New Guinea, and very many other places, the traditional beliefs were proving resilient. Even as missionaries accomplished their work, the native peoples for the most part con tinued to think of life and death as part of a flow rather than as the radical dichotomy that had become installed in Western thought. Some were learning—with difficulty—to think of death as punishment for original sin. It was even more difficult to think of the dying person and especially the corpse as sacred: everybody knew how dangerous the dead could be!

A general pattern can be discerned through the many variations: the passage from life was deeply embedded in beliefs and practices regarding how one should live and what occurs after death.

So—how about us? What is the good death for us today, and how does this accord with our media-massaged lifestyles and our expectations for what happens after the doctor signs our death certificate? Next chapter, please.

FOUR

GOOD DEATH, BAD DEATH (II)

Here and Now

More people are alive today than at any time in history. How will all these lives end? In the past, acute infections and contagious diseases were the leading causes of death. Infants and children were at especially high risk, as were women during and after childbirth. Famine, accidents, and violence also claimed many lives. It is different today in countries with effective public health systems. People are much more likely to escape deadly epidemics and survive into adulthood. Death is now more patient, waiting for us not only to sow our wild oats but also to see them raise their own lively crops. When it is time for Death's harvest, the work is often accomplished through conditions that we have lived with for a while, such as heart disease and cancer, but also through lifestyle influences, such as heavy drinking and smoking. We are also about four times more likely to die in a hospital than in all other places combined. How well all these lives end depends somewhat on the nature of our terminal condition but also on issues of value and meaning that influence the way we treat one another. Through all these changes, the quest for a "good death" continues.

NOTHING HAS HAPPENED TO NOBODY

Humane and effective care of dying people has become a higher priority in recent years. The emergence of the hospice/palliative care movement, death education courses, peer support groups, and a useful clinical and scientific literature are all contributing to this welcome change. Unfortunately, though, many people still do not receive the benefits of comprehensive and skillful assistance and so experience stress and suffering that could have been prevented. In this chapter I focus on the aspects most relevant to our concern about the good death in our own times. I also discuss the deritualization and reritualization of the dying process and identify value conflicts and ambiguities.

Into the Valley of Death with Stetho- and Ophthalmoscope

Dying was momentous in band-and-village societies such as the Lugbara and Kaliai and also throughout Christendom from its formative years onward. How a person died and how society responded were intense concerns. Dying had to be done right if the departing soul was to prosper and society to regroup and remain viable. There were practical matters, such as redistribution of assets, but at the core was the sacred, a subtle exchange with the gods, a mysterious contact between the mortal and the immortal. These consequential dealings could not be left to chance. The passage from life was therefore swaddled in ritual.

This hardy and resilient tradition still exists today, sometimes above and sometimes below the surface. The modern health care system, though, has fostered quite a different attitude toward the dying person.

> Every scientific or clinical advance carries with it a cultural implication, and often a symbolic one. The invention of the stethoscope in 1816, for example, can be viewed as having set in motion the process by which physicians come to distance themselves from their patients.

Our informant here is Sherwin B. Nuland, M.D., surgeon and medical historian. He continues:

> Seen from the strictly clinical perspective, a stethoscope is nothing more than a device to transmit sounds; by the same kind of reasoning, an intensive care unit is merely a secluded treasure room of high-tech hope within the citadel in which we segregate the sick so that we may better care for them.

And now he reaches the point of main interest to us here:

> Those tucked-away sanctums symbolize the purest form of our society's denial of the naturalness, and even the necessity, of death. For many of the dying, intensive care, with its isolation among strangers, extinguished their hope of not being abandoned in the last hours. In fact, they *are* abandoned to the good intentions of highly skilled professional personnel who barely know them.[1]

The tucked-away sanctums, though, are not sacred places where comforting and purifying rituals are performed by religious adepts. The imam, minister, priest, rabbi, or shaman who ventures into the intensive care unit often encounters a less than hospitable environment. Nuland criticizes the high-tech approach to the dying person as a denial of the naturalness of death. The intensive care unit is also subject to criticism as a chamber nearly inimical to the performance of sacred rites of passage. But I have observed for myself that ritual is not completely absent. In fact, ritual is dominant—the sleek, institutionalized professionalism that Nuland has symbolized through the stethoscope—so useful for hearing the heart, so useful for not having to listen to the heart.

Take another example, if you will. Hospital nurses are generally kept busy seeing to their patients, carrying out physicians' orders, and charting from the beginning to the end of their shifts. Often they have several things to do at the same time. The psychologist Larry LeShan wondered how terminally ill people fit into this priority system. He did a simple study. Patients ring for attention by using a bedside button. Nurses respond when they can. LeShan found that nurses took a lot longer to respond to calls by terminally ill patients.[2] The more interesting part came when he shared his findings. The nurses were startled and disappointed in themselves. They had not intended to neglect the most vulnerable patients. The nurses decided to take corrective action; they would overcome this unfortunate tendency. But they were unable to do so. Despite their firm intentions, the follow-up study found that the nurses were still taking longer to respond to the terminally ill.

One function of ritual, surely, is to bind anxiety. The avoidance of dying people by this set of nurses was a pattern, not necessarily a ritual. However, it was not just one set of nurses or a few physicians in the intensive care unit. The pattern of avoidance had become pervasive in modern health care systems throughout the world. It was carefully taught to initiates in professional schools and on the job. The occasional physician or nurse who resisted was subject to punitive measures including expulsion from tribal membership (e.g., he or she became the person nobody would have lunch with). Like others who have worked in the hospital setting, I have seen again and again how rituals to control staff anxiety have not only contributed to the social isolation of the patient but also created barriers to the performance of religious and family rituals.

"Who's in control around here?" is an issue with which all organizations must contend. A clear and effective answer to this question is vital when lives are at stake, as in military and medical situations. It is not surprising that hospitals and skilled nursing homes are subject to multiple echelons of rules and regulations. The people who must operate within this framework often complain about the complex, rigid, and cumbersome regulations to which they are subject. Nevertheless, it is generally acknowledged that rules of the game are essential. Professional and institutional rituals overlay the formal regulations with a more subtle system of control that attempts to keep a lid on anxiety at the expense of spontaneous feeling and situational judgment.

Avoidance rituals often persist even when the rules change to encourage more personal and flexible interactions. Here are two examples. The medical director of a New England hospital has become impressed with the hospice approach to terminal care (more about hospice later in this chapter). How might he introduce this approach to his institution? He starts with a small but significant modification: relatives are now permitted to visit with terminally ill patients at whatever time is convenient to them. Furthermore, it also becomes permissible to include children and have more than one visitor at a time, depending on staff judgment of the situation. This new policy does not require staff members themselves to interact longer or more intimately with dying patients; it just makes it possible for family to do so. Nevertheless, the staff perceives danger: family may "hang around" and ask unwelcome questions; staff sense of control may be compromised.

The staff is divided by the new open-door policy. Some welcome the change as long overdue; others regard it as opening the way to messy situations and who knows what complications. The tension between these factions works against everybody, patients and families included. Families receive inconsistent and confusing responses from staff. The expanded time for patient-family contact is tainted by the stress and conflict that torment the staff. In this case, ritual triumphs. Although the open-door policy is supposedly still in effect, the interstaff conflict is resolved by restoring the more traditional policy of very limited visitations.[3] Control and avoidance rituals help the staff to face another day at work with less fear of being confronted with unpredictable events.

Is Anybody Listening?

The other example is one that recently shocked and distressed the medical community. A major study had found that physicians seldom responded to the wishes of terminally ill patients who sought pain relief and who did not want to be "coded."[4] Had the doctors not listened to these patients, not taken their pain seriously, or what? Nobody knew for sure. Perhaps with a little help and encouragement the doctors would feel comfortable enough to sit down and actually converse with their patients and come to a mutual understanding. An intervention phase was carried out with just that intention. Steps were taken to reduce barriers to effective physician-patient communication, all of this under the direction of experienced clinical researchers. Unfortunately, this well-intentioned intervention failed. Patients still died in pain. Resuscitation procedures were still carried out for people who had specifically asked that this not be done. There was no evidence that physicians had made any additional effort to know and respect their dying patients.

This was a stunning and disappointing finding that is still being discussed. It was assumed that by the 1990s the health care professions had become familiar with such developments as informed consent, palliative care, and shared responsibilities with patients and families. No doubt they had. But anxiety still reigned, and chaos threatened. It was still too dangerous to be a person with a dying person, still too dangerous to go where the situation suggests rather than to follow standard operating procedure. "Don't get involved" remained a mantra. "We know what's best for the patient" was sacrosanct. And, beneath that: "The patient's death is failure—cut your losses!"

And beneath it all: "I am not ready to think about my own death, and I don't have to, because I am a doctor."

This last creed is not accepted by all physicians. In fact, some of its severest critics are members of the medical profession who interact closely with their patients and are attentive to their needs and values. Nevertheless, avoidance rituals can be seen every day and night in medical and nursing care facilities. We see it in the brevity and emotional distance of physician visits. We see it in word magic as patients are not quite told the truth. And we see it when the physician will not even speak with the patient but chooses the more protective option of filtering information through a (preferably placid) relative.

RITUALS—OR WHAT?

Are we discussing actual rituals here? Or are we stretching and distorting that term as some others have? Well, let's think about it. Here are several characteristics of ritual behavior.

- *Rituals are performed by people who are bonded together.*
  It can also be said that performing rituals has the effect of bonding people together. "We are the people who perform these rituals—you are not one of us."
- *Rituals are carefully taught and scrupulously performed.* These are not individual behaviors that have somehow been strung together, but established patterns, more like a ceremonial dance with fixed movements than individual expressiveness.
- *Rituals involve a "knowing."* The participants know something that others do not.
- *Rituals are concerned with the most significant human challenges and experiences.*
- *Rituals transform.*
- *Rituals are the expression or performance of religion.*
- *Rituals invoke the past for control of the future.*

Physicians often avoid contact with dying persons. This pattern has been confirmed by many independent observations. But is this a ritualistic pattern? Yes, in the following ways: medical students are not only instructed in subject matter and skills but also socialized into their profession. This includes proving themselves capable of inhabiting the role of an unmortal. Others die, and others become upset over these deaths, but the initiates into the medical guild wear the mask of the unmortal. Intrinsic to the ritual performance are *face control* (don't show your feelings), *eye control* (don't risk involvement), *no-nonsense intonation* (don't invite conversation), and *time-space management* (stay no longer and come no closer than needed). Initiates belong when they prove able to behave consistently in this manner, when they do not give in to a layperson's sentimentality or otherwise compromise their professional role. Furthermore, adepts learn to perform these rituals in step with other adepts. (Catch the action when a senior physician leads a troop of students into a hospital room and conducts the exam and lecture with barely a word to the patient.)

Moreover, hospital practice is rich in secrets known only to the initiated. There are "in" words for practically everything. Staff discourse is conducted on two levels: the terms and explanations given to patients and families, and the words and gestures that the knowing exchange with each other.

The passage from life to death has long inspired powerful rituals worldwide. The comfort, the predictability, the companionship of ritual are also much appreciated here, a hedge against terror and despair. Robbie Davis-Floyd has analyzed the parallel ritualistic sequences that surround "giving birth the American way" (that would be, of course, in the hospital).[5] She observes that some of these processes and behaviors are unnecessary and even deleterious to the mother's well-being (e.g., being immediately converted to a dependency status by being placed in a wheelchair on admission). The hospital-managed birthing process is rationalized as efficient and scientific, but it can also be seen as a ritual that asserts the control of society over both the mother and the newborn. "Deathing" and birthing rituals in the institutional setting have more than a little in common. Later we will consider the social control issue in a little more detail. There is often a ritualistic quality to verbal and nonverbal sequences in the hospital setting, especially as called forth by the mysteries of birthing and dying.

It has been said that rituals transform. But what, if anything, is transformed by the distancing and objectifying behaviors that we have been considering here? What does the dying person become? Often rituals produce a clear change in status. Initiation rituals provide clear examples of transformation. The initiate enters as a child or outsider and emerges as a full-fledged adult or insider. There is a risky and eventful process between entry and emergence, a process that involves tests of knowledge, faith, and courage. The initiated may be only a few days older than the initiate, but a symbolic transformation has occurred, a journey has been completed.

It is also said that rituals are the expressions or performances of religion. But where is religion here? Religion—and magic—figure heavily into initiation rites in most world cultures. The modern medical system, by contrast, does not transform the final illness into a sacred passage. No proper transformation. No proper religion. But there are transformations aplenty. At the outset the person is reconstructed as a patient. This is highly consequential because it excises most of that person's thoughts, feelings, achievements, and interpersonal connections. The medical establishment (including its labyrinthine financial bureaucracy) now can focus on a downsized specimen shaped to fit its categories. Many of us go through this process several times as we experience hospital stays. We endure a temporary suspension of our personhood in return for medical care, knowing that we can get back to being our usual boisterous or cranky selves. Even so, being a "good patient" has more than a passing resemblance to being a good (passive) little boy or girl.

It is far more daunting when we are converted from patient to *continuing patient* status. That's *all* we will be from now on. There is an exchange here, as with all status shifts. As continuing (or permanent) patients we are usually released from most other obligations. We do not have to do our part in the larger community. We just have to be "good patients." In this situation, many feel that a part of themselves has already died or been erased.

Shock, numbness, despair. I have seen these expressions often on the faces of men and women who have been newly admitted to a geriatric facility. This is especially common among those who have lived in the community all their lives and have no previous experience with institutionalization except for perhaps one or two brief hospital stays. The disconnect from the community—from all their previous life—is experienced as a kind of dying. It is not unusual for the new admissions to withdraw into themselves, even spurning food and drink, as well as social interaction. "Why should I?" one woman asked me. "I am dead to the world. The world is dead to me. *I* am dead to me."

Some of these despairing people later prove resilient as they realize that there is life within the institution and within themselves. They make the transition from person to continuing patient and find a little consolation in exchange for the devastating loss.

Becoming a Dying Person

There is still another transformation to come. The continuing (or will-not-recover) patient eventually becomes the dying patient. The dying—excuse me, the *terminally ill*—patient now is switched to the exit track. Another protocol is put into operation for managing the end-of-life situation. Diet, medication, ward placement, and paperwork are adjusted. A more predictable and powerful change occurs in staff attitude. The upper-echelon staff wash their hands of the patient. This is ritual purification, but of the doctors, not of the dying person. An implicit zone of contamination arises around the patient. There may have been limited visitation in the past because this was a will-not-recover patient. Now, as a dying patient, contact may be even further limited (as the call-bell study demonstrates). Physicians tend to vanish. Registered nurses fulfill their obligations to check status but are encouraged not to neglect their other chores by spending time with what used to be called the incurables. That leaves a minimum of personal contact from the lowest-paid and lowest-status staff members—those who have to be in the vicinity, at least from time to time.

The contamination zone has its roots in the physicality of the dying person, just as it always has, from ancient times to the present. This body will soon be a corpse. There is that sickly sweet smell of bodily corruption in the air. There is the aura of death. Superimposed on this universal scenario, though, is another level of contamination. Here lies a person who has already passed beyond the pale. He or she is no longer one of us. Furthermore, he or she is no longer of use to us. There is no power or prestige in this laboring frame. Nothing to demand or reward our attention. Therefore, *we* ourselves lose status, *we* become less valuable if we become too closely associated with the dying.

Status contamination has often been endemic in institutions and units that serve the frail and vulnerable aged.[6] It works this way: a staff member may feel in her heart that she is doing God's work by showing care and compassion to people who would otherwise end their lives in neglect. Society, however—and the health care system in particular—doesn't see it that way. The aged are not worth much; therefore, neither are those who apparently have such meager skills that they cannot find more exciting and prestigious employment. Now add dying. Why should really competent professionals work with the dying? What do they accomplish? And it certainly isn't cost efficient. The old will get older, and the dying will get dead whatever we do. The caregiver's impulse to bring everything she can to the bedside of a dying person has often conflicted with the prevailing attitude that the aging and dying (separately and together) are sources of contamination. It is better by far to isolate them in Nuland's "tucked-away sanctums" and carry out ritualistic purification techniques so that we can stroll in the sunlight.

Ritual is best served when there has been an obedient stop at all the stations: person → patient → continuing patient → dying patient. This provides time to flesh out the medical chart, time for all health care services to perform their services, time for the erstwhile person to become socialized into the final role. There is less opportunity but perhaps more need for ritual when a person dies precipitously, as in the quick trajectory described by Glaser and Strauss.[7] A hospital team works intensely in an effort to resuscitate a person who, unfortunately, is much like themselves: a prime-of-life, educated, successful adult who had been a picture of health until becoming a trauma victim. Look at this scene in one way: highly trained professionals are using state-of-the-art techniques to save a life. Look at this scene in another way: every member of the team knows that the odds are much against the survival of a person in this condition. But the personal resonances are driving them to the edge. This person is so much like themselves, and this person is or soon will be dead! How much they need a comforting ritual. The slow, stately, always accessible ritual of avoiding the dying person does not cover this situation. What to do? Answer: what they are doing. What started as a skilled technical procedure subtly transforms itself into ritual. See them perform their beliefs! See their physical and spiritual involvement in the process! Their efforts probably will fail to restore life—but ceremonies, prayers, supplications, and sacrifices must be offered even if they do not always persuade the gods. The ritual itself, well performed, is a kind of blessing.

From Dying Person to Corpse

One more transformation is to come: from dying patient to corpse (see also my next chapter, "Corpsed Persons"). Hospital staff know what to do when a patient dies; so do paramedics and police officers who come upon a corpse. There is no lack of procedures and guidelines. These procedures are carried out in accordance with the distancing strategy so evident in the death-avoidance rituals we have been discussing. David Sudnow, a pioneer in the sociological study of the hospital culture, gives us an example:

> In nearly all DOA cases, the pronouncing physician, commonly that physician who is the first to answer the clerk's page or spot the incoming ambulance shows . . . little more than passing interest in the event's possible occurrence and the patient's biographical and medical circumstances. He responds to the clerk's call, conducts his examination and leaves the room once he has made the necessary official gesture to an attending nurse (the term "kaput," murmured in differing degrees of audibility depending upon the hour and his state of awakeness, is a frequently employed announcement).[8]

The death is now official. A doctor has said so. The death has not evoked sorrow, compassion, anger, or any other conspicuous emotion. Furthermore, it has not called forth a response in keeping with religious ritual. The physician says and does nothing to suggest that he considers the corpse to be sacred. These days, these times, we would be surprised if he did.

This cool disavowal of personal feeling and religious ritual is flawed, though. It can be penetrated. Sudnow reports, for example, that two patients arrived in the ER with similar physical characteristics during the same shift. Neither showed the vital signs of heartbeat, respiration, or pulse. The doctor later confirmed that both could have been pronounced dead, or both could have been given resuscitation efforts. In the event, one (an elderly woman) was certified, the other (a young child) treated. The staff extended itself to eleven hours of intensive effort for the young child. There was mouth-to-mouth rescue breathing and direct stimulation of the heart. The elderly woman was wheeled away. The physician said afterward that he could never bring himself to put his mouth to "an old lady like that."[9] The prevailing medical distancing ritual functioned smoothly in the case of the elderly woman, but they just could not let that young child stay dead.

There have been continuing developments in life-support systems and new treatment modalities since Sudnow's study, which was done in the mid-1960s. More options, more decisions. More ambiguity. A nonresponsive body may be considered as

- a corpse, pure and simple;
- a permanently disabled biological configuration whose vegetative functioning can be prolonged;
- a disabled biological configuration whose functioning might possibly be restored;
- a source of tissues and organs for the living.[10]

Two questions demand prompt resolution: what medical procedures should be performed, and what religious, ethnic, or family rituals? These questions have been proving divisive within the medical and family circles as well as in the interactions between these two groups. Tension, uncertainty, and conflict occur when people do not share the same interpretation of the somewhat dead person. It is difficult enough to deal with failure (physician) and loss (family). The death becomes even more troubling if people have different interpretations of the situation. Within this context, then, we might consider the good death to be one that everybody understands in the same way. This is not the only criterion for a good death, but it has become increasingly salient since the advent of high-tech medicine. Odd though it may seem, the element of competition can also influence the perceived goodness of a death. Suppose we are both physicians with different responsibilities in the same hospital. You believe this person is alive enough to be maintained indefinitely on a life-support system; I believe this person is dead enough that we can harvest tissues and organs while they are still useful. The administrators wish you and I would simply agree and not cause trouble: that would be a good death.

Biomedical and sociophilosophical considerations influence judgment. We have already been reminded by Sudnow that our society generally places a higher priority on children than on elders. Our other value priorities also affect judgment about the condition of a somewhat dead person and what, if anything, should be done. Whom should we consider still somewhat alive and viable at the critical moment: the wealthy person or the indigent? the person we know or the stranger? the person of our race and ethnicity or the outsider? Add to this list whatever additional discriminants come to mind: the person with first-rate health insurance or the uninsured? the man or the woman? the heterosexual or the homosexual? the churched or the unchurched? the routine or the interesting case?

New advances, exigencies, and fashions continue to work against establishing stability and coherence. The concepts of clinical death and brain death, for example, have become increasingly important in recent decades. There are limits within which these concepts can be used responsibly. But within these limits physicians sometimes have a zone of discretion and decision. The decision may be that, for all reasonable intents and purposes, this person is dead. Or the decision may be that sufficient integrity of the body remains to try longer and give both medicine and nature another chance.

Back in 1819, Rev. Walter Whiter proposed that death is not quite what it seems to be.[11] He was speaking as an imaginative and speculative naturalist, not as a religious mystic. Whiter described situations in which the apparently dead have returned to life, and lamented what he considered to be the many who were buried prematurely. Some of what he proposed to a dubious readership has become standard practice today. People who have lost consciousness and vital signs as a result of seizure or drugs, victims of drowning and lightning, and others apparently frozen to death have shown the resiliency to recover—sometimes. Since Whiter's time, the boundary between dead and alive has become even more ambiguous and permeable. Situations arise, then, in which one might reasonably judge that a person is dead or might almost as reasonably cling to the hope of recovery. Much depends on the availability of techniques for preservation of the current physical status and restoration of suspended functions. How dead the person is, therefore, can have a significant relationship to the medical options available at that particular time and place (and so, of course, can the money to pay for these options and the will to employ them).

Meanwhile, the newly dead person has also become more complicated on the socio-symbolic level. Getting dead leads to a decline in status, especially since religious meanings have been excluded from the medical process. Yet there is now a status redemption for eligible corpses—the cornea, the heart valve, the pancreas that is being donated as, sometimes literally, a gift from the heart. The medical system whose rituals desanctify the dead also applauds those willing and able to share their physical remains. (The aged and the "sick dead" are not given this opportunity.) This is not the first time that the passage from life to death has been tainted by utilitarian considerations. In the chapter "Corpsed Persons" we will see how the poor of London, already treated like dirt, experienced further anguish when they learned their corpses would be slabbed beneath the anatomist's knife. They could nurture a fervent if forlorn hope for comfort after death as more or less pious Christians. But anything resembling a good death now seemed beyond possibility, because as newly dead they would be nothing but meat.

One additional characteristic of rituals was mentioned earlier: rituals invoke the past for control of the future. We honor, worship, and, in some rituals, become the brave, powerful, mystic, and wise ancestors. We salute the founding fathers or mothers. We call upon their secret knowledge and influential connections to protect and enhance us now. On this count, medical rituals fall short. There are illustrious names from the past—the gods of healing in many world cultures, the Hellenic pioneers Hippocrates and Galen, the Islamic masters Rhazes and Avicenna—to the moderns. Aside from the medical historians, though, there is not much notice taken of either the gods or the mortals who brought the healing arts forward from ancient times. In this respect the practice of medicine is similar to many other professions today: up-to-date but rather dismissive of the past.

Religious ritual (e.g., the *ordo defunctorum*) remains available for those who feel that the passage from life requires the protection of sacrament and ceremony. Some hospitals encourage the attendance of clergy and the performance of rites; others just barely tolerate them. Hospice programs do stand ready to support the religious dimension for those who choose this path. The general sidestepping of religious ceremony, though, has not resulted in the absence of ritual. The gap is being filled by professional and institutional practices that, as we have seen, have many of the characteristics associated with ritual.

Next, we note that changes are occurring even as we attempt to understand the current situation. A movement toward reritualization exists both within the health care sphere and in society at large. Some schools of medicine and nursing have developed simple but effective rituals for helping their students to come to terms emotionally with the dying and the dead they encounter. They hold their own memorial services in which they express their own sense of loss for the terminally ill patients they have seen. There are also group ceremonies to honor the people whose bodies they dissect for learning purposes. Rituals such as these are as religious as the participants choose. Slowly but, we may hope, steadily, a new generation of health care professionals is coming along with more support for their interactions with the dying and therefore less need for avoidance rituals.

Who Benefits from the Rituals?

Final rites have been practiced in such varying contexts as band-and-village communities, such as the Kaliai and Lugbara, and the widespread "Christianification of death," in Paxton's phrase. Through final rites, the dying person was thought to be better prepared for the postmortem journey. Society was spared malicious visitations from the dead, property and power redistribution conflicts, and retribution from the Almighty. Both individual and community received benefit.

The present-day rituals described here primarily serve to reduce the anxiety of medical personnel. Individuals are benefited, but these are usually physicians, not patients or family members. Avoidance rituals also prop up the medical system as a whole in its efforts to retain control or, failing that, to retain the illusion of control. Physicians are themselves products of society, so as they mask-dance around the dying, it is to the tune they have heard since childhood. They have been twice-socialized into evasion of death and dying. (Death-evasion rituals are also common in other nations whose physicians have become part of the North American death system.)

But we have missed something—an exception that, yes, does prove the rule. Consider a typical metropolitan hospital in the United States just a little past the mid-twentieth century. Let's say it's in a city that bears a fair resemblance to Detroit. The patient population includes people with a wide variety of conditions, most of whom return to their normal lives before very long. There are also a few people whose lives will soon elapse. They are monitored by the nursing staff and served with professional diligence. Although the failing bodies are not neglected, person-to-

person interactions are only occasional. It does become increasingly difficult to interact with people as they move further along toward the end
phase of life. Medication can interfere with mental clarity. Weakness can
diminish the ability to speak audibly. Pain, if not well managed, can distract from relating to others. And yet, many terminally ill people have
both the desire and the ability to communicate. It just takes somebody
being there, somebody with the time, the sensitivity, the motivation. Ward
staff may well include people with the sensitivity and the motivation but
not likely the time or the institutional support for bedside interactions.
And back in the mid-twentieth century, family and friends often felt in-
timidated and unwelcome in the hospital environment.

It is within this context that one physician deviates from the mainstream. He is interested in the dying patients. *Very* interested. He inquires
regularly into their condition and insists on being informed when their
last moment is approaching. Here he comes now, in the dead of night.
A nurse has fulfilled her promise to call him. The doctor arrives bedside.
Is he in time?

The patient's eyes are closed. The doctor raises the eyelids and holds
them open. He stares eye-to-eye with the aid of an ophthalmoscope. Look
at that retina—it is already segmented; blood circulation has ceased; no
tears either; the cornea is hazy; as a whole, there is cooling and paleness.
A useful set of observations, then, but not bingo! Dr. Jack Kevorkian has
again been unable to catch this person at the ideal time, the instant at
which death absorbs life. In the late 1950s and early 1960s, this pathologist was already treading his lonely path within the medical establishment. In one significant respect he was no different from the general run
of physicians: he seldom spent time with dying patients. But the time he
did spend was as close to the moment of death as possible. While death
was a topic scrupulously avoided by most health care workers, Kevorkian's avid curiosity led him repeatedly to the life/death edge.

There was a good and sufficient reason for this mission. The status of
the eye at death had been neglected by medical research. Furthermore,
Kevorkian believed that the eye offers the most reliable basis for determining that death has occurred. He was aware that medical advances
such as life support systems and organ harvesting were making the determination of death a salient issue. It would therefore be a useful contribution to add to knowledge about the status of the eye at death, and
Kevorkian published two papers on the subject.[12]

But there was another and perhaps even better reason for Kevorkian's mission. He had been fascinated by death since childhood. His fellow medical students affectionately and nervously dubbed him "Doctor Death." Was this an obsession related to the death of family members during the genocidal atrocities committed against Armenians during World War I? Whatever the reason, here was a man with an intense personal agenda, and, as a physician, he was in a position to pursue this agenda.

Kevorkian's eyeing of death was not ritualistic in the technical sense of this term. He was a solitary individual who had developed his own pattern of behavior, not a participant in established group traditions. And yet his aim was to bridge and possibly transcend the mysterious divide between life and death. *Kevorkian's proud isolation and solitary pursuit would not have been possible without the mass avoidance of dying and death by his colleagues.* He was the enigmatic inside-outsider. Clearly, his style of relating to the dying and dead was an exception to the rule. How did it prove the rule, though? The man who did the opposite, who sought out the dying patient whom other physicians were avoiding, nevertheless did so for his personal agenda. He did it for research. He did it for his own compulsion to get close to death. He did not do it for the dying patients, who interested him only as eyeballs as they passed from the light to the darkness.

WHOSE GOOD DEATH?
THE HOSPICE APPROACH ARRIVES

The situation I have been describing would soon change, though not everywhere, not at once. The signal event was the establishment of St. Christopher's Hospice (London) in 1967.[13] A tradition of comforting the dying person had wended its way through history from Roman times, if not before. Religious conflict, especially the Catholic/Protestant schism, later created an inhospitable environment for enlightened terminal care. The emergence of raw, competitive industrialization had also battered this tradition. Nevertheless, the flame had been kept alive and was brought forward into our own times by the efforts of Dr. Cicely Saunders and her United Kingdom colleagues.[14]

Hospice became a beacon of hope, with St. Christopher's Hospice providing the model. Many questions arose soon after the establishment of St. Christopher's and the initiation of new programs, mostly in North America and the United Kingdom. A basic concern was the development of standards for hospice care: what precisely did hospice intend to accomplish, and how would it do so? This was not an attempt to overregulate hospice programs. Then, as now, there was encouragement for innovative approaches. Furthermore, there was no attempt to prescribe a particular form of the "good death." Hospice patients and their families were not to be placed on a conveyer belt for the assembling of a standard-issue death. Both the dogma of religion and the efficient production model of industry were eschewed by the founders of the modern hospice movement. Nevertheless, the need for standards was felt.

Standards of Care

And so it was that in the mid-1970s an international panel of caregivers and researchers met to hammer out standards and, if necessary, one another. My colleagues and I found common ground by first identifying what would no longer be considered acceptable. We came up with a set of hidden or implicit standards of care that had long constituted "the book" of terminal care, but the book had never actually been written down until then.[15] Here are a few of the hidden standards that were identified by the international task force:

1. A successful death is quiet and uneventful. The death slips by with as little notice as possible; nobody is disturbed.
2. Few people are on the scene. There is, in effect, no scene. Staff is spared the discomfort of interacting with family and other visitors whose needs might upset the well-routined equilibrium.
3. Leave-taking is at a minimum: no awkward, painful, or emotional good-byes to raise the staff's anxiety level.
4. Physicians do not have to involve themselves intimately in terminal care, especially as the end approaches.
5. The staff makes few technical errors throughout the terminal care process and few mistakes in medical etiquette.

6. Attention is focused on the body during the caregiving process. Little effort is wasted on the unique personality of the terminally ill individual.

7. The person dies at the right time, that is, after the full range of medical interventions has been tried out and before the onset of a long period of lingering.

8. The staff is able to conclude, "We did everything we could for this patient."

9. Physical remains of the patient are made available to the hospital for clinical, research, or administrative purposes (via autopsy permission or organ donation).

10. The cost of the terminal care process is determined to have been low or moderate; money was not wasted on a person whose life was beyond saving, so reimbursements at least balance expenses.

In other words, the "good death" was implicitly defined in terms of the needs of the medical system. It was the mission of hospice to offer a distinct alternative. New standards were proposed and subsequently became the basis for federal legislation in support of hospice programs. These standards begin with two general propositions:

- *Patients, family, and staff all have legitimate needs and interests.*
- *The terminally ill person's own preferences and lifestyle must be taken into account in all decision making.*[16]

These guidelines address the balance of control issue. Decisions should not be meted out by authority systems bound to their own habits and agendas. The final phase of life belongs to the dying person, the circle of family and friends, and those who are providing terminal care. What are the implications here for the good death? First, there is process. A good death benefits from a process in which the uniqueness of the individual's life and situation is respected. Closely associated with this is a kind of "retribalization." Power remains with a few immediately and intensely committed people rather than residing in such large and abstract entities as the medical and religious systems. (Physicians, nurses, social workers, and clergy may all play significant roles, but as service providers rather than enforcers.) Next are the flexibility and diversity of outcome. One person's good death is not necessarily the same as another's. Perhaps we might think of a skillful gardener who understands the conditions that favor optimal growth. These principles are applied with diligence and sensitivity. When the time comes, there is blossoming everywhere— but the garden is graced with flowers of many varying colors, shapes, and fragrances. Each seeks the opportunity to fulfill its own nature. Human nature is even more complex and variable, and so the hospice emphasis on a caring and responsible process might be expected to result in an even broader range of outcomes.

Process and outcome merge together, though, in two other standards that are high priorities in the hospice approach. *Control of pain and other symptoms has been a primary goal of hospice care from the beginning.* This approach has also become known as *palliative,* whether employed in hospice programs or in other care settings. (*Palliate* derives from the Latin *pallium,* or "cloak." It later came to mean the mitigation of suffering and was introduced into medical lingo by Canadian specialist Dr. Balfour Mount when he discovered that "hospice" had negative associations in some cultures.)[17] A palliative care program is effective if pain, nausea, respiratory distress, and other symptoms are prevented or significantly ameliorated. This is good process that contributes to good outcome. The two are not quite the same, though. A person might continue to suffer pain and other symptoms, yet feel secure in both the life that is being completed and the death that is approaching. Similarly, a dying person may be in despair for other reasons even though physical distress is held to a minimum.

This brings us to the other high-priority standard: *the person should have a sense of basic security in his or her environment.* Psychiatrist Avery D. Weisman has described this facet of care as "safe conduct."[18] Both the caregivers and the environment are so reassuring that the patient has the sense of being companioned through the perilous journey. This sense of trust can come from many sources, such as the presence of familiar faces, the dependability of medications and other comforting actions, the open lines of communication, and the protection against unexpected and unexplained interventions. Within this zone of comfort the dying person has the opportunity to draw upon personal values and meanings and share intimate thoughts with people of like mind.

A Better Death?

Freedom from agony and overwhelming physical distress and the presence of a safe and caring environment are certainly remarkable improvements from the ordeals that many have experienced in the past. Hospice/palliative care programs developed in response to the pain and social isolation that have too often been the fate of terminally ill people. Expectations have risen, however. Some of us seek not only a good but a better death. I have referred to this as the healthy dying movement. It took a while before contemporary society overcame its reluctance to discuss dying and death (and there are still many holdouts). Let's see how this happened, and then look specifically at the question of an even better death. The forces identified below overlapped and interacted with one another.

Consumerism Flexes Its Muscles   The consumerism movement started in a tenement building in the South Bronx of the 1930s when my mother shamed a major bakery company into atoning for an error (a sliver of sharp green glass in a slice of white bread: we received free loaves of bread every day for a month, so were able to supply many of our neighbors as well). But some credit is also due Ralph Nader and associates, who later took on automobile manufacturers on the safety issue and awakened the public to the potential of consumer power. Soon this awareness carried over to services as well as products. Patients started to realize that they were consumers of medical services and might even be able to ask questions and demand answers. It would take even longer to feel halfway comfortable about discussing dying and death with physicians, but there was at least an awareness that patients could be more active in their own health care decisions.

Question Authority   Teachers, clergy, police officers, and other people in a position of authority once were automatically respected unless undermined by individual failings. The medical profession was prominent among pillars of society but represented only one area of authority. Traditional respect for authority weakened, however, as we moved deeper into the twentieth century. There had always been corruption, but widespread distrust of authority was a relatively new development and was brought to prominence by reverberations of the Vietnam War. It was not

Figure 9 From *I Need Help*, by Vic Lee. © 2002. Reprinted
with special permission of King Features Syndicate.

just that all-trusting patients were becoming tough consumers; it was that
open season had been declared on authority personages in general, who
were wearing targets on their chests and had their backs to the walls.

Funeral Directors: A Safe Target   By and large, funeral directors (or morticians, as some preferred to be called) cultivated a sober, conservative,
responsible lifestyle. They did not seem to be a particularly promising
target for invective. But times were rapidly changing. Three books did a
lot to hasten these changes. Evelyn Waugh's satirical novel *The Loved
One* offered an unthreatening way for readers to enter into the mysterious and dreaded ways of the funeral director.[19] We could smile at the
ridiculous characters and situations while still catching a whiff of form-
aldehyde and eyeballing some corpses. Jessica Mitford's *The American
Way of Death* provided the opportunity for us to examine our funeral
and burial customs from a critical and supposedly objective distance.[20]
This was also amusing, though not to the funeral industry. Again, we
could start to deal with some facets of death without too much personal

involvement and threat. Ruth Harmer's *High Cost of Dying* officially kicked in the consumerism component.[21] It was—and is—easier to discuss money and rip-offs than to probe feeling and meaning. These books and other publications that followed set up the funeral industry as a safe target for our anxieties. It was not unusual at this time to hear people purpled in rage against those terrible funeral directors and Park Lawn–type operatives. Most of us were still not ready to deal openly with the dying person and our personal mortality, but at least now we had one eye open.

Long Time Living; Long Time Dying   Society took a deep breath after World War II and slowly started to look around to see where it was. One discovery was that people had suddenly grown older. Actually, this had been going on for a while, of course, but it also took a while to comprehend that life expectancy had been increasing throughout much of the world. This was mostly to the good but also had the effect of intensifying the relationship between aging and death. It went like this: *fewer die young, so → death is concentrating among the elderly, so → there are more people around to remind us of death: scary!* Furthermore, once people started dying, they kept at it for a lot longer. This period of limbo kept family and caregivers in sustained tension, like a string stretched to its maximum.

Worse than that: many other people existed in a condition that could not be described as dying but could not be described as flourishing life either. Medical advances kept people going longer before their conditions became clearly terminal and kept them longer in the terminal condition as well. "Life support systems" and "persistent vegetative states" entered our vocabularies and sometimes our nightmares.[22] Increasingly, people were appalled at the idea of a long period of preterminal decline and suffering, with the dread prospect of indefinitely floating somewhere between life and death as the ventilator hissed its hideous song. It was becoming ever more difficult to avoid end-of-life realities.

Doctor Miracle   Advances in medical care and public health had accomplished so much in so short a time: scourges such as malaria, yellow fever, scarlet fever, and smallpox were brought under control. Cholera, typhoid, and typhus also gave way as improved prevention techniques and heightened public awareness took hold. Childbirth and surgery became less dangerous as the risk of infection decreased. Trauma victims had a better chance of survival through transfusions, intravenous hydration and nutrition, and the development of paramedics and emergency rooms. More sophisticated diagnostic procedures contributed to saving lives throughout the broad spectrum of illness and trauma. There was more reason than ever to believe that people with life-threatening conditions might pull through. The United States and other nations with advanced technologies at their disposal acquired special expertise in acute care. For centuries there were self-proclaimed miracle doctors to prey upon the hopes and fears of desperate people. Now the real miracle workers had arrived.

There was another side to this golden coin, though: more coin for the heroes. The medical establishment and society in general rewarded those who could rescue the imperiled from the jaws of death: money, prestige, and power were theirs. By contrast, there were few if any incentives for becoming adept at managing the complex symptomatology of elders or people of any age with long-term conditions. Even today there is a marked shortage of physicians with expertise in geriatric care. Understanding and managing the problems besetting dying patients had even less priority. By and large the public consented to these medical priorities. Why even think of dying when there might be a cure just around the corner? People at serious risk for death were routinely advised to "think positive" and seldom given the opportunity to think through the implications of the terminal phase of life. As Doctor Miracle's bubble continued to expand, there was little willingness to prepare for the possibility that, no matter who does what, sometimes people really do die. As time went on, though, the limits of the medical arts and sciences became more apparent, as did the number of people with complex, long-term conditions and those whose death was clearly in prospect. The public had to grow up, and, to an appreciable extent, it has.

Order Restored: Dying in Stages   It was becoming more difficult to avoid the subject of death and dying by the mid-twentieth century. There were still few clues, though, on how to approach the subject. By the 1960s some illuminating research had been conducted on attitudes toward dying, and a few counselors and therapists were already helping terminally ill people to navigate their final journey. The public at large was conflicted about interacting with their own terminally ill family members and friends. Yes, they wanted to provide comfort and maintain their valued relationship as long as possible, but, no, they could not face the anxiety, the uncertainty, the not knowing just what to say and just what to do. This fear exacted a high toll on emotional well-being. People communicated less than adequately, and intimate relationships became more stressful at the very time that their affirmation and human contact were so desperately needed.

By the middle 1960s people were at least able to disclose their anxieties. Most often I heard that it was so difficult to be with a dying person because one didn't know what to expect and how to act. ("Being natural" was perhaps the most challenging role to play.) Then, in 1969, Elisabeth Kübler-Ross's *On Death and Dying* provided The Answer. People die in stages, she said. There are five stages, and each has its name: shock and denial; anger; bargaining; depression; acceptance. What a relief! Dying is not a confused, chaotic mass of unlimited suffering and anxiety. First one thing happens, then another.

There were definitely some positives in this conception. The dying person was still a person, experiencing and adapting—not just a bundle of distressing symptoms. This reminder provided a useful counterbalance to the prevailing overemphasis on the physicality of terminal illness. Kübler-Ross was also demonstrating in her public appearances that one could actually sit down and talk with a dying person. If she could do it, perhaps others could as well. What many people took from Kübler-Ross's lectures, interviews, and writings was a selective and simplistic version of what she actually said. Attention fastened on the stages. Identify the stages as they occur. Chart their progress. Assist the dying in moving on to that next stage—and give them a little push if they are stuck too long in denial or anger. This was not precisely what Kübler-Ross had in mind, but it is what the media and even many human service professionals latched on to. Feeling more secure with this guideline in place, more people spent a little more time with their dying friends, relations, or patients. Order had been restored to the dying process. The ancient *ordo defunctorum* had been enhanced with this new scientifically established format.

Except that the stages had *not* been established scientifically and have subsequently been found seriously flawed. Except that immersion in the supposed stages actually inhibited and distorted authentic interactions in many instances. Except that a quasi-religious cult developed around the assumption that people *should* pass through all these stages—not to achieve "acceptance" would be a spiritual shortcoming, so we should all give the dying person a gentle but determined push through the sequence. Except that biography and situation were too often neglected. Who is this dying person and what experiences, values, obligations, and purposes does he or she bring to the last phase of life? What is the sociophysical environment in which the last phase of life is taking place? For example, is this person really "in denial" or trying to conform to the implicit rules about avoiding communications that are too direct, too intense, too honest? Research and theory were stultified for years by the assumption that in reciting the sequence of stages, one had said all that need be said about the travails of the dying person.

Eventually many professional caregivers and a growing number of volunteers and members of the general public would realize that the five stages did not provide an adequate guide for being with terminally ill people. But, at the very least, this *Novum ordo defunctorum* had contributed to reducing the isolation of the dying person and the taboo against speaking of death.

Healthy Dying and the Wondrous Journey   Two other related developments can be considered together. Some imaginative minds ventured far beyond recognition of dying and death. Skillful and compassionate care could reduce the suffering, and stalwart companions could support the sense of security and continuity. But that was hardly enough. Dying had to be healthy and, while we were at it, dying should also be inspirational. This view was most often nurtured by people who had either become unchurched or felt they were not receiving enough to sustain them when they read scriptures or listened to sermons.[23]

In their own discourse there was little mention of the physical symptoms that often accompany the terminal process. Depression and anxiety about the loss of physical function and social role occurred only among the unfortunates who failed to realize that death was but the doorway to the next adventure. "It's just a change of clothes," more than one person informed me. "It's a joyful time," another assured me. "There is no dying and there is no death. It is all part of the wondrous journey." (These informants did not include any of the people who were actually experiencing the "wondrous journey," complete with pain, weakness, nausea, constipation or diarrhea, and concerns about the future well-being of their families.)

Dying had now become acceptable to some people, but only if one were fit as a fiddle and hot for the miraculous transformation. This type of expectation was hard on the caregivers, even in hospice-type programs. Teams of physicians, nurses, respiratory therapists, social workers, and other skilled professionals, along with well-trained volunteers and sensitive clergy, were using every available resource to reduce suffering. It was a collective achievement if a dying person could spend a peaceful day with family in familiar surroundings. To ignore the physical realities seemed an exercise in self-deception and denial. To expect the dying person to provide an inspiring example was to place a cruel and unrealistic burden on everybody in the situation. There would, in fact, be peaceful deaths, and there would be memorable moments that might be taken as miracles. By and large, though, the determined effort to convert the ordeal of dying into a picture of brimming health and joy was singularly unconvincing to those most immediately involved.

People were coming around to the recognition of dying and death. In various ways, though, many of us were saying that we wanted a better death—better than what was offered by hospitals and nursing homes, better even than pro forma rituals that did not actually touch the spirit. In other words, we've still been looking for the good death. Some observers believe we are searching for nothing less than a new *Ars moriendi*. Others, more skeptical, warn that we are already becoming entrapped in a subtle ideological and political web in which the manner of our deaths is being manipulated by power brokers with hidden agendas.

WHAT CHOICES DO WE HAVE?

Perhaps we really do not have much choice among possible versions of the good death. Some philosophers have claimed that choice is mere illusion; nevertheless they were usually quite firm about whether they wanted their tea with or without. It is a refreshing exercise to argue against the assumption of choice. But every day we do face what seems like choices, and the consequences of deciding or not deciding. A reasonable working assumption is that we do have something that answers to the name of "choice," though not necessarily free and comprehensive choice. Were we given the choice of being born? And born mortal? Not all imaginable options are available to us, but we still have significant choices to make, including some with life-or-death consequences.

Fatalism takes the extreme position: doesn't matter what we think or what we do, does it? The future is written in the stars, the tea leaves, or our genome. Add nihilism: nothing is better or truer than anything else, and nothing means anything. These philosophical positions have something in common with a behavior pattern known as *learned helplessness*.[24] A resolute passivity, a surrender to an oppressive and noxious situation, may develop after the organism has had prolonged failure experiences. An unfortunate laboratory animal will cower in its cage and accept still another electric shock rather than walk through the now-open door to freedom; a person with a sense of low self-esteem will shrink from ready opportunities for pleasure and success. Horrendous life experiences can do that to mice and men. We may generalize our own stress and frustration to the universe and conclude that choice is illusion and striving would merely invite more pain. Fatalism tends to produce self-fulfilling prophecies, subtly speaking for the power of choice. And even the cowering is a kind of choice, because not all mice and men allow themselves to be trapped in this modality. Furthermore, determinism and fatalism are neither subject to verification nor conducive to zestful and responsible living. Here I will proceed with the heartening illusion that, as the species that was able to conceive of choice, we actually do have some ability to choose.

There is a natural starting place for our inquiry. Why don't we just ask people?

Imagined Deaths

Suppose that Hollywood has finally realized that a major motion picture should be made of your life. The script is coming along well, and the studio has signed the star you suggested to play the leading role. Now your assistance is requested for scripting the deathbed scene. The helicopter has landed on your roof or front lawn, and the producer herself, accompanied by several flunkies, specifies what is needed. "I'm a stickler for authenticity," she reminds you. "This film will be as faithful to your death as to your life. Follow? OK. So we need from you a description of your deathbed scene just as it will be. The death you expect. Still follow? OK. Where will this happen, and when? What are you thinking and feeling? Who will be with you? What will be going on? All that stuff—OK? The camera has to know what it's going to look at. Don't forget—what we want to know is how you *expect* to die. We'll do the rest. Get all of this down, Herb."

The foregoing is a relaxed version of instructions I have used with hundreds of college students, most of them in graduate programs such as nursing and social work. Some of the respondents already had appreciable experience in health care situations: they had witnessed and even provided care for people with terminal illness. So—what did they envision as their deathbed scenes? The typical respondents expected to end life at home in ripe old age with the companionship of the people most important to them. Women often described the scene in detail: for example, a breeze gently riffling the curtain, the scent of flowers, a favorite song playing. Right to the end they would be mentally alert and then just slip off quickly into their final sleep.[25]

Did you notice something missing in this scenario? Hint: it's the same thing that was missing in most motion picture depictions of deathbed scenes until recent years. Yes, you're right: the symptoms are missing. It's all healthy dying. The people are dying but otherwise healthy and robust.

Studies of actual end-of-life experiences tell a different story. We are not usually that healthy as body systems struggle and fail. The list of possible symptoms include pain, nausea, vomiting, dyspnea (respiratory difficulties), pressure sores, insomnia, incontinence, weakness, fatigue, confusion, and depression. In describing their expected deathbed scenes, very few respondents mentioned pain, and it was rare indeed to hear of pressure sores, incontinence, and other problems that caregivers are challenged to prevent or control.

Most respondents had transformed "expect" to "desire." They understood the instructions. They started out to describe their deathbed scenes as expected but soon found themselves writing about their hopes and fantasies. We checked on this transformation by asking the respondents to alter the scene they had described in a negative direction—change it in some way so that it would be less desirable. They were also asked to change it in a positive direction, to make the expected closer to the ideal. These follow-up exercises often evoked astonishment and smiles. Everybody could make his or her original deathbed scene worse (e.g., "My children wouldn't be able to get there in time"). But hardly anybody could improve on their "expected" death. "I already died the best way I know how!" exclaimed a master's degree candidate in nursing. "I know you said 'expect,' and I even wrote down, 'expect,' but it came out all fairy tale!"[26]

How difficult it is to acknowledge the physicality of dying! How tempting to comfort ourselves with idyllic scenes! Even first-hand knowledge of the last phase of life can be shunted aside in favor of a more satisfying, even a more romantic, vision. Here is a little vignette I should probably not share with you. Let's say that somebody's bed partner was quietly weeping. She had just finished reading one of the most popular books of the day: *Love Story* (soon to become a major motion picture that would have the same effect). We—I mean somebody and his bed companion— talked about the book and its effect. A few days later many of her fellow oncology nurses were over at the house for a dinner party. At that point it was not much of a party because all were emotionally exhausted from their experiences with dying cancer patients. All had read *Love Story*, and all had wept because "it was so beautiful." The one nonnurse in the group asked: "But was any of it true to life? Have you ever seen a person actually die like this?" No, they hadn't. And that was just the point. The nurses knew very well about terminal ordeals, but there had to be, there just had to be, a better death, if only in a book. This now being understood by all, the group dashed outside and played a vigorous, smash-mouth game of half-court basketball under a cheddar moon that was both real and fantastical.

We see that there are several modalities of the good death. The palliative care movement envisions terminally ill people whose symptoms are well under control within a familiar and comforting environment. This is *a good death through subtraction:* pain and other distressing negatives have been eliminated. It is an image of the good death that challenges the state of the art in symptom relief and requires the dedication of quality staff, but an image that has often proven within the capacity of hospice and family support. Rather different is the image of the *good death as a sublime and inspirational experience.*

Some partisans have misappropriated Kübler-Ross's fifth stage for this purpose. Acceptance of death is the way to go. People should be helped, even prodded, to achieve this elevated spiritual state. What Kübler-Ross actually describes, though, is a state of depletion and resignation: the struggle is over. There may be a welcome sense of relief. But it is questionable to transform fatigue, depletion, and relief into a transcendental state of being to which we should all aspire. Making death seem so good requires overlooking a lot of reality, raises questions about agenda and motivation, and—most unfortunate—impairs effective caregiving.

A third implicit version of the good death also seized upon the stages for legitimization. *The good death is one that achieves.* The dying person should complete a psychological or spiritual journey. Dying is the final exam, and acceptance the top grade. Echoes of medieval deathbed scrimmages between angels and devils? Perhaps—but now encased in the individualism and achievement motivation more typical of our own times.

Previously we also observed that the goodness of a death has often been defined in terms of its effect on the community: discontented ghosts do not take revenge; status and property redistribution does not incite destabilizing conflict; medical personnel are not exposed as failures, nor is their immortality shield penetrated by the pinprick of too close an encounter with the dying. There is still more, however, to our quest for the good death.

VOICES OF THE DYING

Before the hospice care and death awareness movement, people whose deaths were in close prospect seldom had the opportunity to speak their minds, because few were available to listen. The communication context has improved for many people as a result of hospice care and the death awareness movement in general. Furthermore, improved management of pain and other symptoms has enabled more people to communicate effectively in the final phases of their lives. Too often in the past (and still too often today) pain and social isolation so dominated the dying person's experience that it was difficult for individuality to shine forth. Stereotypes about "the" dying person were formed from the cauldron of insufficiently relieved suffering and our own anxious reluctance to be part of the scene.

We probably should not have been surprised to learn that dying people speak in many voices, each reflecting unique life histories and ongoing situations. You may already have had experiences that confirm the various ways in which people cope with the terminal phase of their lives; if not, there are now moving and illuminating experiences conveyed in print and video. Here we take a few examples from personal observation and research that may contribute to understanding the good death in today's world.

I had the privilege of participating in the National Hospice Demonstration Study (NHDS; 1978–1985), a major attempt to evaluate the effectiveness of palliative care when this was still a new venture in the U.S. health system. The study focused mostly on medical and economic matters, but we were able to ask some terminally ill cancer patients two questions about their own views of the situation:

1. Describe the last three days of your life as you would like them to be.
2. What will be your greatest sources of strength and support during these last days of your life?

These direct and personal questions are scaled-down versions of abstract issues, values, and beliefs made practical. The cancer patients replied in their own words. Here are the most common types of response concerning the last three days of life, starting with the most frequent:

- I want certain people to be with me.
- I want to be physically able to do things.
- I want to feel at peace.
- I want to be free from pain.
- I want the last three days of my life to be like any other days.

Some people expressed several of these hopes. Their sources of strength through the ordeal included:

- supportive family or friends
- religion
- being needed
- confidence in self
- being satisfied with the help received[27]

We see that relationships crown both response lists. More than anything, these terminally ill people drew strength from their closest life companions and most desired their continued companionship up to the end. This finding rings true with what many other people with life-threatening illnesses have told family, friends, and caregivers. In and beyond the NHDS, most terminally ill people hope for continuity in their most treasured relationships. This does not mean that they want everybody to be with them all the time. Usually there are definite preferences: one or two people they really want to see every day, others on occasion, and some not at all. *The good death is the continuation of a good life until it is no more.*

Past constructions of the good death neglected the sustaining human relationship. Ghosts, property, and the fate of the immortal soul commanded attention. Yes, many people then as now either drew solace from loving companions or despaired because of their abandonment. Nevertheless, the intimate human connection was generally ignored in the most influential versions of the good death. The terminally ill cancer patients were trying to tell us that the good death can be a simple matter: being in the company of a few very important people, being free enough from pain and other symptoms to cherish their company, and still having some ability to do things, to be useful to others. "You see, I can still make tea for visitors," said one woman in the NHDS. "As long as I can still do some little something for people I care about, I will be all right."

The Value of Relationships

The core value of relationships also came through clearly in studies conducted by Australian sociologist and palliative care expert Allan Kellehear.[28] And again it was not just a matter of "the more people the better." Some dying patients complained that they had become too popular, the doorbell and the phone ringing all the time. They appreciated the wealth of well-wishers but nevertheless felt stressed and tired out by so much call upon their limited reserves of strength. By and large, the patients did welcome continued attention from their friends. It was best, though, when they could exercise some control over who, when, and for how long. Other studies have also confirmed that people confined by advanced age or illness benefit from having some say about visitors.

The importance of farewelling also became evident in Kellehear's studies. People found their own ways to say good-bye. One memorable example is that of an elderly woman who arranged for final visits with each of her friends and presented them with a small doll that she had just made with her own hands. Taking leave of our companions in a way that is meaningful to us and them is often an important component of a good death defined in relationship terms.

Individual differences often assert themselves, however. Some people in Kellehear's study and many in other settings have chosen to withdraw from relationships. They would rather be alone. Why? Sometimes because they don't want to be seen in a deteriorated condition. They'd rather be remembered as the person they used to be. Sometimes they feel tainted by their condition as well. They hold themselves responsible for their impending death or fear that others will. Sometimes there are unsettled grievances. They'd rather not experience the conflict and tension that have built up between a family member or friend and themselves. And sometimes there is something they have to work out inside their own minds and doubt that others can be helpful. In still other situations, the person may have experienced an abrupt change from reasonably good health to a terminal condition. Attempting to absorb and deal with this transformation, the dying person may feel that others will just add more confusion and distraction. One thing more: the dying person may have come to the conclusion that family and friends are not prepared for meaningful and supportive interactions; perhaps they do not even seem to realize or accept that death is in close prospect. Artificial and superficial interactions would only add to the distress.

There are drifters. There are people with such emotion-starved childhoods that they have never been able to establish intimate human relationships. There are emotionally scarred people who have not been able to open themselves up again to the risk of close relationships. All these people can still benefit from compassionate care, and a few will even transcend their biographies to establish meaningful relationships near the end of life. For example, some of the most suspicious, cynical, and crusty residents in Cushing Hospital, a geriatric facility where I worked, formed surprisingly open and affectionate relationships with staff members during their final weeks of life. Despite their habits and misgivings, they reached out and found somebody who accepted and comforted them without question, demand, or judgment.[29]

Figure 10 From *MAD Magazine* #75. © E. C. Publications, Inc. All Rights Reserved.
Used with permission.

People with a history of vibrant and meaningful relationships are more likely to attract and maintain social support during their terminal illness. This does not mean that there is a single, uniform pattern of relationships. One dying woman continues to be bossy, telling everybody around her what to do and how to do it. Another sweetly accepts the situation and is content just to see and hear the bustle of everyday family life around her. A professional entertainer stages several deathbed scenes to bid farewell in turn to his audiences, his family, his mistress, and his god— each scene with its own distinctive character. A patriarch beloved for his kindness and wisdom quietly arranges for "a few days at a respite center" and then promptly dies: the family immediately recognizes that he was trying to spare them any further suffering in watching him suffer. An unmarried aunt—renowned for her unpleasant, "you-can-never-please-me" disposition—is transformed by the warmth and charm of the young niece who voluntarily comes to care for her. Cherishing this unexpected gift of friendship, the aunt reciprocates by insisting the niece now return to meet the needs of her own family. With a sense of repose she had not known for years, the aunt decides it is the right time to die, and she does.[30] Many other people on the verge of death hold on until they can see a favorite person for the last time: how this can happen is not clear, but it does happen more often than we might have thought.

The good death, then, may depend primarily on the feelings that flow back and forth between the dying person and the most treasured family and friends. By implication: whatever safeguards the continuity of relationships through the end of life also contributes to the good death. This would always include pain and other symptom relief without clouding consciousness and would usually include the opportunity to remain in a familiar and comforting environment.

TAKING DEATH INTO OUR OWN HANDS

There is quite a different approach to the good death that also must be recognized. Each year about thirty thousand people commit suicide in the United States (an underestimate, if anything). Many others contribute mightily to their own deaths by risk-taking behaviors with suicidal motivation. For instance, I've heard people say such things as, "I got myself good and smashed [with booze], then I went out to really get good and smashed. Why do you think I never got my brakes fixed?" Some try to enlist another person's help in ending their lives, for example, suicide-by-cop. Less obvious to the outside world are the nursing home residents who refuse to take nourishment and the people with life-threatening conditions who do not follow the medical regimes that could prolong their lives.

Furthermore, there are also traditions of noble and heroic deaths. The person had a choice, although not always much of a choice. The Roman emperor or the mob boss sends a little message. You don't absolutely have to open your veins in the bathtub. It is the honorable thing to do, though, and you an honorable person, right? (Also, if you decide not to behave like a person of honor, you're going to get made dead soon anyhow, and your family will also suffer cruelly.) Suppose instead that you are the honorable wife, sister, or daughter in an (of course) honorable family. A treacherous lout has raped you—or maybe he hasn't, but people think so. Suicide is also the good death for you. It is not good for, say, the children who lose a mother, but better that than disgrace. Now you are a general, a person of power and respect. One problem: you have just lost a battle, whether through your incompetence or forces beyond your control. There's your sword. Fall on it. You have perhaps strayed just a little from the path of righteousness—or others accuse you of same. There is a swordlike instrument designed just for that purpose: open your insides and let the spirit breath of life escape. Or you have been abused hatefully, say by a mother-in-law who treats you worse than dirt. Killing yourself is a courageous act that will tell the world how mean she is—and, besides, you can also turn into an angry ghost and torment her for the rest of her miserable life.

Suicide solves problems. Or so people believe at the time. Suicide is therefore *a good death because it is a quick and decisive resolution of a difficult situation.* It is an especially good death when it is seen by society as honorable or noble. One dies not as a failure or outcast but as an upholder of moral principles. Viewed within this perspective, suicide is more than a merely acceptable way of death.

The same often has been held true for heroic death in battle. Die as a coward or as a hero? That is not so difficult a choice. But: hurl our lives into almost certain death, or escape to live another day? This is not entirely the moral dilemma it might seem. Under battle conditions people may respond to their immediate situations without time for reflection.

The difference between "coward" and "hero" might turn on small incidents or fleeting perceptions. Society, though, can make the difference if it chooses to come down heavily on the themes of glory and sacrifice. Vilification of the enemy also contributes to reckless disregard for one's own survival. Some of the most effective belief systems have played the immortal rewards card. During the Crusades, for example, the vision of a Christian heaven or an Islamic paradise was a powerful motivating force.[31] Those formidable horned ladies in Wagner's *Der Valkyrie* embodied the Nordic myth of a never-ending happy hour in Valhalla for brave warriors slain in battle. Getting killed in battle was not enough, and being brave and surviving was not enough. The trick was to be brave *and* get killed.

There is plenty of precedent for current ideology about taking death into our own hands. Glorious death in battle, though, is not nearly as popular a theme. The realities of war have become too well documented for any but the terminally naive to organize their lives around the quest for a hero's death in battle (and, of course, battles and war deaths are not what they used to be, either). We remain deeply divided about the moral status of suicide, assisted suicide, euthanasia, and that entire spectrum of deaths that occur through various behaviors that shorten life. The Catholic Church remains firmly opposed to suicide, as it has since Saint Augustine articulated this position in the fifth century. Not all of Christianity agrees that suicide is always a sinful death. In the New Testament, for example, Judas Iscariot was not scorned for hanging himself after betraying Jesus; it was regarded as an appropriate act of repentance. In the Old Testament as well, suicide was regarded more as a reasonable response to an unfortunate situation than as a big moral issue. Ahithophel, usually a responsible person, set his house in order before he hanged himself after having deserted King David and failing to impress Absalom. Ahithophel was given a ritual burial in the family tomb, signifying that his act had disgraced neither himself nor his lineage.

It is not my mission here to discuss the ongoing controversies about assisted suicide, euthanasia, and related topics. What is of concern is the divisive, unsettled, and still evolving attitude of society toward the option of taking life into our own hands. A rock star whose death is suicidal or near-suicidal may seem a hero to some people, while others think, "This person really needed help."

Overall there has been a growing tendency to regard suicide as a desperate action taken by people who feel they have tried everything else and can find no other way to escape from an intolerable situation. Sociologists look for ways to ameliorate the conditions (such as unemployment) that increase suicide risk; the psychologically inclined try to understand the thought processes and interpersonal relationships that are often associated with suicide. Society as a whole is less apt to brand suicide as either a sinful or a heroic action. What, then, is a suicidal death? Maybe good. Maybe bad. Certainly sad. And, almost invariably, a source of long-term distress for friends and family.

IF WE COULD CHOOSE OUR OWN DEATH . . .

Sure, it can be said that we *do* choose our own death by all the other choices we make throughout our lives. We enjoy taking risks, or we are ruled by safety concerns, or, like most people, we're somewhere in between and not entirely consistent. There's something to that. I will focus here, though, upon feelings, thoughts, and values that are more closely directed to the end of our lives. These are influenced by many experiences and events, such as our exposure to religious beliefs and customs in childhood, the deaths that have entered our lives, and the special anxiety we may associate with a particular form of dying. We may also find ourselves with uncertainty and conflict because we are among the many people with multiple cultural heritages. For example, should I quietly take to bed and die without making a fuss, or seek every advantage and possibility offered by the modern health care system? Should my death be accompanied by the extensive traditional rites of my heritage or be as pragmatic and functional as the contemporary life I have lived?

We might be ill-advised, then, to insist on a single ideal death, especially in so diverse a society as ours. But it might be possible to offer a few useful propositions.

Proposition 1: *Some forms of death are terrible.* We might never agree on the ideal death, but perhaps we can agree that people should be spared extreme physical, mental, and spiritual suffering at the end of their lives. Terrible deaths are dominated by suffering. What Dan Leviton calls *horrendous* deaths also include torment and humiliation inflicted by others (as, for example, during the viciously misnamed process of "ethnic cleansing").[32] There is still a residual tradition in which suffering is regarded as somehow good for us. Maybe it is in some ways, in some circumstances. But people facing death—including people of strong religious faith—seldom regard suffering as a benefit. For many years this suffering-is-good-for-us tradition contributed to the agony and risk of women during childbirth; advocates of pain relief had to struggle against the belief that pain is not only natural but also somehow a fit punishment for having become pregnant or just for being a woman. We should be more than ready today to reject the view that we should die in physical pain. The same, I would urge, holds true for mental and spiritual pain. "Should people live in despair?" The question is almost too ridiculous to ask. "Should people die in despair?" Same thing.

Proposition 2: *A good death should enact the highest values held by society.* This proposition does not specify one particular set of values or attempt to judge one society's beliefs as superior to another's. Throughout history most people have been firmly entrenched within their cultural traditions. Today many are still strongly integrated into a society with firm and clear rules of operation. These people are likely to derive a sense of security and achievement by dying, as well as having lived, as model citizens. They followed the path of righteousness all the way. Furthermore, society also benefits. Communal values are affirmed when people end their lives in a congruent manner.

Fulfillment of cultural ideals can involve extraordinary actions, such as the Japanese Zen master or the Tibetan holy man who creates a spontaneous poem a moment before dying. Often the poem expresses a sense of liberation without fear of death. Unlike advocates of prevailing Western conceptions, the spiritually enlightened Buddhist does not see life and death as dichotomous and oppositional. "I am at one with all" is the kind of theme that is likely to be spoken with the last breath. But fulfillment of cultural ideals can also include having that last round of drinks around the deathbed with a favorite raunchy toast on everybody's lips. It can center around dying within one's most defining role, for example, as a mother or soldier. Big-band leader and clarinetist Woody Herman clearly articulated his preference: "I want to go down swinging." He did.

Proposition 3: *The good death affirms our most significant personal relationships.* We have already seen that close and caring relationships are of prime importance to many terminally ill people. Superficial and conflicted relationships may crumble under the pressure. Some relationships, though, may prove themselves even stronger than previously realized as the occasion calls forth the deepest levels of response. In fact, one of the most gratifying outcomes of hospice care is often the family's realization that they were able to experience such closeness with the dying person and appreciate how much they had meant to each other. "We did it together—we did it!" is not a wild shout of triumph but a quiet affirmation of the human bonds that had proven their worth to the very end. Grief counselors are quite aware of the less fortunate outcome: when people for whatever reason have been unable to extend their relationship to the final phase of life. The terminally ill person may have felt this absence keenly, even if not put into words, and the survivors may also be left wondering what they had really meant to each other through the years. Survivors may grieve not only for the loss but for the missed opportunity to affirm their relationship.

Proposition 4: *The good death is transfiguring.* One experiences an epiphany—a profound sense of beauty, love, or understanding. "So, this is what it's all about!" "How wonderful!" "The heavens have opened!" "Now my real life begins!" The moment of death becomes the peak experience of life. The ideal of a transfiguring death was prominent in the heyday of religious deathbed scenes. The bright wings of salvation were even more prominent when the foul-breathed demons were clawing at the deathbed. The protection of ritual, the sanctification, the conversion, the miracle, the Hail Mary touchdown just before the clock runs out! The person who throughout life had been a nondescript performer or sinful loser could become a big winner at the end; in fact, that was the only best chance.

Variations on the theme of transfigured death have occurred throughout history. For example, feverish youths dying of tuberculosis in the eighteenth and nineteenth centuries had moments of brilliance in the midst of the tragedy of their foreshortened lives. In one of his last and most gripping poems, Keats allowed that he was "half in love with easeful Death."[33] A cultlike following developed around the theme of youth flaming into death with white-hot genius. Suicide—in fantasy and sometimes in reality—became viewed by some youths as a dramatic means to fulfillment. Along came Wagner with his yearning chromatic harmonies in music dramas that glorified the love-death *(Liebestod).* Find your destined lover and consummate your passion through ecstatic death! Death was so great that it improved even love and sex. Richard Strauss brought the theme to the concert hall with his tone poem *Death and Transfiguration,* in which the musical pulse is marked by a persistent heartbeat.

In our own time, drug-induced altered states of consciousness have achieved a kind of renown for evoking experiences of leaving the quotidian world and giving the experiencer a sample of paradise (when they do not deliver hell instead).

Proposition 5: *The good death is simply the final phase of the good life.* People should die as they have lived. This could be the most feasible, realistic, and comfortable way to go. Why try to reshape a person's life at the last moment? We know how difficult it is to get people to change their ways even under ordinary conditions—try getting a smile out of your grouchy neighbor; try getting your brother-in-law to take anything seriously. The dying person has been formed by the entire life he or she has lived. There is for each person a natural conclusion, but not the same natural conclusion for each person. We think of the concept of an appropriate death, as introduced by existential psychiatrist Avery D. Weisman.[34] Basically, this is the death a person would choose if given the choice. Most often this choice turns out to be going out the way one has been going along (minus suffering, plus compassionate support). We think also of the afterlife beliefs held by many band-and-village societies. We die. Then we live. How do we live after death? Pretty much as we have been living all along, in a world similar to the one we have left, the only world any of us have ever known. The afterlife will be different from, but in significant ways still continuous with, the life one has already experienced.

The good death, then, is another step in the individual's unique journey through time, space, person, and symbol.

Proposition 6: *The good death is coherent.* It is a story, a drama that makes sense, that satisfies our need for closure. We can recognize the story line, the plot turns, the conflicts, and finally the resolution. This need for a death that can be told (to ourselves as well as to others) is important to both the dying person and the circle of family, friends, and caregivers. For example, dying persons may feel a sense of relief in learning that they did not hasten death by some foolish thing they either did or neglected to do. This smoothes out the story and removes a discordant element. A family member may regain composure after speculation and confusion are replaced by accurate information about the illness and its management. If the perceived story is not sufficiently coherent or acceptable, all parties concerned may devise their own customized versions: death has got to make sense, somehow.

There is another facet to the coherence theme. Dying is a process of progressive limitations. Our immediate world shrinks: we just can't get around so well anymore. Our ability to accomplish things through our own actions diminishes. This is challenge enough. But we are also apt to intensify the stress through our lack of preparation to cope with limits. The United States has an expansionist history, "from sea to shining sea." Immigrant generations worked hard to help their children have a better life. This is the culture of more, bigger, newer, younger, and, in recent decades, "We're Number One!" What the national culture does not especially cherish and develop is the ability to live within limits. Some people become depressed, even suicidal, at the prospect of looking "not young" (even if not "old") or losing any of their peak physical abilities. Healthy and financially secure middle-aged people have told me of their plans to end their lives before they "get to be like that" (elderly). Aging often is associated with a loss of status and attractiveness.

Within this cultural milieu, dying can be perceived as almost an insult, a put-down. It is not just that life is coming to an end but also that one now has to function within an increasingly limited orbit. The wonder is that many people do find the resources within themselves and their families to make the transition. This contributes to a splitting of the ways with regard to the good death. Some people invest their energies and self-esteem in resisting both aging and death. The story of these deaths is one of determination, persistence, and the refusal to say die. Age and death are enemies to be resisted as long as possible. "Death knows where to find me," a woman in her nineties told me, "but I'm not going to hold still for him." Others decide instead that "the time has come." Their stories center around the slow and often subtle dance of withdrawal from the scrimmage of life. "My body's been telling me something. I know what it is. I have to listen to it," another aged woman informed me. This realization did not plunge her into the depths of despair. Instead she established a quiet little realm within which limits she experienced security and treated others with such graciousness that she continued to have as much company as she might desire. *How we integrate the concept of limits into our personal and cultural worldview has much to do with the story of our deaths as well as our lives.*

A CONCLUDING WORD

Control issues have dominated public and professional discourse ever since dying and death became something we could talk about again. Who makes the decisions? Who should make the decisions? Usually the controversy swirls around what are framed as right-to-die issues, including informed consent, advance directives, euthanasia, and physician-assisted death. Social critics have started to warn about what we might call institutional creep—the tendency for medical, religious, political, and economic establishments to seek hegemony over deaths as well as our lives.

I agree up to a point. Half a century ago dying and death were personal concerns that often were kept private. Major societal institutions did not see themselves as having much at stake in this realm. A high priority mission of the early wave of "deathniks," as we sometimes dubbed ourselves, was to increase awareness and dialogue, to get more people interested in dealing with dying and death issues from whatever standpoint. As time went by we saw the institutions gradually wake up and take notice. There was more at stake, more possibilities for profit and control now that the public was reclaiming end-of-life issues. The question was—and remains—whose version of the good death will prevail? What model of dying will be most persuasive?

I think there is reason for concern that society's striving for a *nova ars moriendi* might be channeled into directions that serve the purpose of institutional agendas rather than personal and communal needs. I don't think we have nearly reached that point yet, but it is in our own interest to be aware of efforts to manipulate the death awareness movement (including palliative, educational, and legislative components) for the sheer joy of power and profit.

We have been exploring issues of broader scope, which have entered little into the sound bites of media discourse. The good death—if we may use this phrase just a moment longer—is linked with our overall worldview as shaped by culture and our own thoughts and experiences. Consider again all those propositions offered above. What precisely are the highest values held by our society? This abstract question takes on a more practical aspect when we consider the good death. For example, is competitive success our highest value? And would this mean that we should strive to be Number One—to flash that triumphant index finger—on our deathbeds? It is difficult to affirm either the highest societal values or the highest personal values if we are not clear and convinced about them, so here again life and death interact vigorously. Or consider the proposition that death should be transfiguring. Does it matter if this transfiguration is fantastical or psychotic? Should everything be directed toward the hoped-for transfiguration—the decisions made during life, the type of care received near the end? Or consider all the propositions taken together: Can these variations on the good death theme be served by a single set of rituals? Or do we need to innovate—perhaps continually—fresh rituals to accommodate the diverse forms of passage? And, if so, what are the background stories we can call upon to bolster these rituals?

Who can best answer these questions for us? Perhaps, just perhaps, ourselves!

FIVE

CORPSED PERSONS

"Funerals are for the living, not the dead." This glib statement is often heard and is often incomplete and dismissive. In many instances, funerals have been for the dead as well as the living. Many peoples have developed core religious beliefs and practices around the fate and well-being of the dead. What does it mean to be a corpse? Where has the person gone? How should we deal with the physical remains? What special precautions should we take—for the sake of both the dead and ourselves? In this chapter I focus on the corpsed person, the central figure in funeral and memorialization rituals. We will see that human remains are variously treated as trophies, identity markers, and devices for communicating with the gods or working magic spells. We will meet corpsed people who can cure and others who can kill us. Through it all, through all the changes that have been wrought in the history of the human race, we will keep our eyes on what the corpsed person is still becoming as we move further into the third millennium.

This person is dead. By that, I mean the person we have known. The person who walked and talked, who toiled and loafed, quarreled and loved, suffered and enjoyed. The motionless, unresponsive body that remains seems but an empty shell. Where is our friend now? We are left with the same questions that survivors have always faced: What should be done with the physical remains? How should we interpret this death—and all deaths? How should we remember this person, and how should we go on now that this person is no longer with us?

Most cultures have come up with answers to these questions. Rituals were developed to affirm, perform, and perpetuate these answers. Anthropologists have been trying to puzzle out the resemblances and differences among peoples living in different parts of the world. In the meantime, traditional societies have been swept up in massive social, technological, and ecological change. The old ways may continue to have much of their appeal and some of their power, but it is becoming increasingly difficult to keep a people united in their deathways when all about them is melting away. As elders chant an ancient funerary prayer, the young may be listening to hip-hop on headphones; as the women of one family assemble to wash and dress a corpse with their own hands, those of another family watch stoically as a van drives off to the commercial funeral establishment.

The winds of change are blowing across the graveyard. Ambiguity, uncertainty, and conflict increase as cultures collide, split, merge, and split again. We take up one important element in this process: the corpsed person. This will not tell the whole story, but it will help to develop an informed perspective on the final passage.

ABOUT BONES

When those bones were walking around, they made up only about a tenth of the total body weight. Nevertheless, bones are mostly what endures after the early phases of corpsehood. There are a few striking exceptions. Extreme cold slows bacterial action and thereby delays or even inhibits putrefaction. Occasionally an intact body is found many years after death. We have had recent examples. Medical researchers worked hard at trying to find intact corpses of victims of the killer influenza pandemic that raged in 1918.[1] Despite strenuous efforts, the results were disappointing. It does not take much earth warming for a body to deteriorate quickly, even in the tundra. Nevertheless, it was clear that some bodies were relatively intact while others had pretty much been reduced to bones.

"Iceman" and the "Ice Maiden" are among the most remarkable people to have emerged from the frigid grasp of death.[2] He was a thirty-year-old hunter whose frozen body was discovered after five thousand years of residence on an Alpine slope. Cause of death is not on record, but the arrowhead found in his body has raised suspicions in some quarters. "Otzi"'s body was well preserved, down to the elaborate tattoos. Also in good shape were his leather clothes, copper ax, and quiver of arrows. The Ice Maiden was a girl found on a mountain peak in Peru, where she had apparently been offered as a sacrificial victim, accompanied by gold and silver dolls. Her body had been well preserved by the freezing temperature.

Volcanic ash can also act as an effective preservative. The sudden and intense heat of the volcanic eruption probably plays a significant role. Once in a great while a corpse is unearthed in an extraordinary condition that cannot be readily explained. One such event occurred in 1485, when Rome was being torn up and rebuilt on a massive scale.[3] Such unusual events are certain to attract keen attention. Pope Innocent III wanted to see the great city renewed in splendor after so many years of neglect. Not everybody was pleased with this endeavor: many ancient treasures were destroyed in this urban renewal project and individual property rights were overturned. And then one day—amazement.

Workmen uncover an ancient Roman sarcophagus. The real find, however, leaves people nearly speechless. There she lies, stretched out upon the white marble. She is young, hardly more than a girl. The fair youth is dead, of course, but so intact that we might imagine she fell asleep one night and perhaps could be induced to awaken to the pomp of the new papal Rome. But no, there is something else about her, something that puts all other thoughts out of mind, that dismisses the idea that she had been sleeping for more than a millennium. *Her eyes are open. Her eyes are open and staring. Who is she? What happened to her? And who—or what—is she staring at?*

After the first shock had subsided we probably would have marveled and muttered along with the Romans. This has to mean something. A maiden from an ancient time who has somehow lived in death all these centuries, transfixed by a vision, and here to tell us—what? Excitement! Confusion! And hordes of people hurrying to this remarkable scene.

The Incorruptibles

There have been other reports within the Catholic sphere of a corpse declining to strip to its bones. Catherine of Bologna proved to be one of those whose flesh remained uncorrupted and presumably incorruptible.

In life she was a member of the Poor Clares, nuns who devoted themselves to the care and comfort of the poverty-stricken. In death she seems miraculously to have been spared the depredations of the grave. Her funeral in 1462 was simple, as was customary with her convent. She was carried to the graveyard without a casket and lowered into an open grave.

> The nuns were startled at a sweet scent that seemed to issue from the flesh. No flowers or trees grew nearby, nor could anything else account for the fragrance. After earth had been shoveled into the grave and Catherine's corpse buried completely, the scent persisted. As the nuns made their way home, it followed them, wafting across the graveyard and then perfuming the entire district.[4]

The heavenly fragrance continued to caress the convent for days afterward. The nuns became convinced that it was emanating from Catherine's grave. At this point something else happened to intensify the mystery. Pilgrims attracted to the grave by reports of the fragrance claimed they had been healed of their ills. Curiosity prevailed. Catherine was unearthed. She looked terrific. There was no evidence of decay, and the wondrous fragrance ("the odor of sanctity") seemed to breathe forth from her. A medical examination confirmed Catherine's status as dead but healthy. Catherine was fortunate in not being consigned again to the earth (a further trial that several other incorruptibles were assigned). After a brief spell in a crypt she was placed on a platform out in the fresh air, where she could be venerated by pilgrims and her awestruck sisters of the faith. Years later it was decided she would be still more impressive if less horizontal. Catherine was offered a chair. Generally speaking, a corpse of several years' standing (or, more accurately, reclining) would not be able to comply easily with the request to fold herself gracefully onto a chair. Catherine, however, was up to the challenge; her body had remained supple.

We are told that Catherine subsequently took an even more active role in her own disposition. Apparently she had been thinking about this for a while, because it was not until more than two hundred years after her death that she presented herself in a vision to another nun and described in detail the chapel in which she wished to be enshrined. Catherine had been a skilled artist in life, so nobody was that surprised at her suggestion. This chapel now survives in Corpus Domini, a small and otherwise unexceptional church in Bologna. Anneli Rufus visited Catherine not long ago:

Posed upright in a glass-enclosed golden chair, with a big crimson cush-
ion behind, Catherine of Bologna's body sits erect with its head tilted
slightly to one side, as if listening. The generous folds of a black and white
habit all but hide bare feet as dark as Hostess cupcakes. In its lap, the corpse
cradles a book. A gold ring shimmers on its finger. . . . Catherine's face
has kept its soft curved contours. But the flesh has turned so dark that from
across the room you can discern neither nostrils nor lips.[5]

Nevertheless, it is exceptional for a corpse to remain even remotely
lifelike over an extended period of time unless it was the recipient of expert embalming or mummification. The usual expectation has been for
flesh and bone to part as well as spirit and body. Corpses that confound
these expectations often evoke a special response. Catherine was rewarded with sainthood and a chapel. But what of that nameless Roman
maiden found on the white marble sarcophagus? Where is she? Nobody
knows. And those who did know were not telling. Unfortunately, she
made an immediate enemy in a high place. Pope Innocent III had problems of his own. The pagan spirit in Rome had not yet been extinguished
despite centuries of persuasion and power moves. Furthermore, other
influential families had their eyes on the papacy and would have relished
an opportunity to undermine His Holiness. Best not to give this pagan
maiden her chance. Best not to stir up the populace. Best not to give an
opening to his enemies. The pope nodded (or perhaps winked), and it
was done. The mysterious youth who had surfaced after so many years,
whose wide, staring eyes could arouse so much confusion and mischief,
was whisked away as quickly as she had appeared.

Veneration and a one-way ride to obscurity are radically different responses to a corpse that seems to have achieved immunity against natural law. Scientific study is another response, as Iceman is discovering.
There is still another response, as we will see. Perhaps what is so special
about the corpse can be used for our own benefit. What God may have
decided to leave intact is still available to be dismembered by zealots and
opportunists.

RESPECT OR FEAR?

The exceptions are instructive because they help to reveal our attitudes
toward the usual. How *do* we respond to human remains? As a child I

was apprehensive about visits to the doctor's office: he might jab me with a needle, and I would have to act brave. Dr. Paleg was a kind and sensitive person, though, and often took the time to whet my curiosity about matters medical. The attraction of all attractions in his office was the skull. It was just out there where you could touch if you liked and if you dared. The skull seemed to inhabit its own world more than our own. Although mute, it spoke of mysteries. Although motionless, it beckoned. "Learn me," seemed to be its message. "Know me and you will understand what they never will teach you in school." It seemed, well, not exactly friendly, but real and as true as true can be. The skull was noble, dignified, and totally cool.

One day Dr. Paleg took me aside and spoke quietly, man to man. "I will give you the skull if you become a doctor." Wow! In the meantime he slipped me a handful of tongue depressors as a sort of down payment. Fortunately for public health, I did not become a physician. The skull gradually submerged in my consciousness as other interests arose (Sylvia Barish, Alberta Williams, and Florette Ruben, for example). This little unfulfilled romance with Dr. Paleg's desk ornament (and with Sylvia, Alberta, and Florette) did make it easier for me to understand how a great many peoples throughout the world have respected and even venerated the skull.

Respect, then, for human remains? No, only for the remains that remain, not for the gushy-ushy stuff inside! Graphic depictions of violence to the human body were rare during my childhood, though commonplace today. Even the horror movies were plenty scary enough without severed necks pumping out gore. Nevertheless, I did have a stolen glimpse of the human body in grotesque disorder. Way up high on the home bookshelf were items that we children were not supposed to read. Naturally, I cultivated covert climbing skills and hacked into many books placed there by Uncle Abe, who appeared and disappeared in our lives like a phantom. *The Horror of It* was a photographic essay of World War I battlefield casualties. The photographs were black and white, but all the more drenched blood-red. So—that's war. And that's what happens to people in war. What I recall is the stillness of the bodies. What I recall is the grotesque distortion of their positions, like an agonizing dance paused forever in time. What I recall are the insides of people exploded to the outside.

There was another memorable lesson. This verse, then new to me, appeared across from a severed hand:

The Moving Finger writes; and, having writ,
Moves on: nor all your Piety nor Wit
Shall lure it back to cancel half a Line
Nor all your Tears wash out a Word of it.[6]

Granted, this was probably not the best possible introduction to the insides of the human frame, and perhaps not to Omar Khayyam either. Chances are, though, that I would have come to share the common attitude toward the innards by one path or another. Many a manly man has been known to become acutely distressed when confronted with what throbs beneath the skin even in the living. Some prospective nurses and physicians have a hard time of it before they can adjust to the streaming flesh as it struggles for life. Health care experts have the inestimable advantage of knowing what they are about (or so we hope). Most others tend to be grossed out when in exposed to a plenitude of open wounds and leaking fluids.

Discomfort with the soft and perishable bulk of the human frame extends to the corpse. Our preference is clear: we often respect the skull and other bone remains but experience disgust and fear toward the decaying flesh. This is such a strong pattern that it deserves more detailed attention.

SAVE THE BONES FOR HENRY JONES

Read anthropologists' accounts by the score and you are likely to be impressed by the frequency with which bone cleansing appears in a culture's deathways. The dead are not quite dead and done enough as long as flesh cleaves to their bones. In the United States today we are expected to believe that the corpse is the inert residue of a life. Furthermore, the person is as dead after a day as she or he will be a week, month, or year later. "Wrong!" most world cultures would have told us up to and even somewhat into modern times. There is important work ahead for both the newly dead and society to accomplish after the last breath is drawn. A corpse must be deconstructed into its elements. The flesh must melt, the spirit escape.

The Trobriand Islanders hold a special place in anthropologists' affection, being among the first among native peoples to be studied systematically. They are often cited as an example of an *exchange society.* Many of these exchanges occur at the surface of things: people giving each other gifts. We exchange gifts with each other, too, of course, but for the Trobrianders the act of exchange serves as a major cultural function that affirms and negotiates status, acquires property, keeps rivalries and jealousies in check, and binds people together. Beneath the surface is a belief system rooted in the idea that all the universe operates on the principle of exchange. The rules of Trobriand exchange are complex. I don't understand them at all. However, it is clear that there are firm gender-related rules and clear also that the dead as well as the living have their deals to make, their obligations to fulfill.

A corpse can be handled only by relatives through marriage. Nigel Barley explains:

> The flesh of the dead man would be lethal to his own "blood" so they pay others to deal with it.
>
> The sons have the important job of sucking the putrefaction from the bones of his exhumed corpse and washing them of rotting flesh in the sea so that his spirit can travel back across the water and ultimately be reincarnated. This disagreeable job is explained by Trobrianders as repaying the care the father showed in feeding his sons mashed yam and cleaning away feces and urine when they were babies. They were dismantling him, the way he constructed them, and converting him into dry bone as he made them into hard men.[7]

The exchange and distribution process continues after the sons have sucked off all the putrefaction. The corpse has been deconceived and deconstructed into bones. These are now distributed to marriage relatives who will shape the bones into ornaments for their own bodies. Blood relatives of the deceased are not on the distribution list; the bones would be harmful, perhaps lethal, to them. The hair and nails of the corpse will also be given for use as ornaments.

> A man's skull may be converted into a lime-pot for his widow and his long bones into lime spatulas to be licked when chewing betel nut. . . . The jawbone often becomes a necklace, recalling the way fathers gave necklaces and earrings to their children. The bones will be passed around from one relative to another over the years, be decorated, and change their form constantly.[8]

The King of Bones

The skull has been widely treasured as the king of bones. Often it is the entire intact skull that is preserved and honored; sometimes it is a more compact and portable fragment, such as the lower jaw. (The skull is broken when the deathways happen to call for quick removal of the brain.) Widows in the Huon Peninsula region of Papua New Guinea once wore their husbands' jaw bones in a band around their own heads. Families in New Caledonia once collected the skulls of their kin. It was the three-dimensional family photo album of pretechnology but also more than that. The skulls could also listen to one's prayers in troubled times. (I have known nominally sophisticated New Yorkers who have done the same with the likeness of ancestors preserved within a picture frame.)

The remains of important people receive special attention practically everywhere. Royal skulls are more likely to be decorated with elaborate designs or beads, as in Borneo, housed in a shrine, as in Uganda, or entombed with a bell, as among the Busoga. These distinguished skulls also are thought to have exceptional powers. The son of a Masai chief, for example, would draw strength and wisdom from his father's skull.

How deeply dead heads are integrated into a culture is well illustrated by practices that were still common in Borneo into the twentieth century. I draw here upon field observations made by Charles Hose and his colleague in this endeavor, William McDougall, better known subsequently as a founder of social psychology and one of the leading lights in the behavioral sciences.[9]

For the Kayan of Borneo, there are many spirits abroad in the land (actually, in the sea and sky as well). The Toh are the most feared spirits. They hang around with the dried human heads that can be seen dangling in every house. The Toh are easily ticked off if they feel that insufficient attention and respect is being given to the ubiquitous ancestral skulls adorned with their leathered and weathered skin and still sporting a reasonable complement of teeth. They are not the spirits of that particular head, nor do they dwell within, but they are just, well, hanging around and looking for an excuse to make trouble. You can tell when trouble is coming. The resident Toh will cause the skull's teeth to grind together in anger. If there is no satisfactory response to this warning, the head may

Figure 11 Heads hanging in the gallery of a Kayan house. From Charles Hose and William McDougall, *The Pagan Tribes of Borneo* (London: Macmillan and Co., 1912), plate 105.

fall to the earth in what can only be characterized as a postmortem sulk. Reanimated heads are a definite nuisance unless one can be sure they are in a gracious mood.

> This animation of the *Toh* is illustrated by the treatment accorded to the heads. Having been dried and smoked in a small hut made for the purpose, they are brought up to the house with loud rejoicings and singing of the war chorus. For this ceremony all members of the village are summoned from the fields and the jungle, and . . . every one puts off the mourning garments which have been worn by all since the death of the chief for whose funeral rites the heads have been sought.[10]

Here is a fairly common feature of the relationship between a corpsed person and the mourning practices of the survivors. People must lament as long as the death is somehow incomplete—the corpse still a mixture of bone and flesh, spirit and corruption. A signal is needed to convert the mourning to celebration and enable people to return to

Figure 12 Kayan woman dancing and holding a head that has been dressed in leaves. From Hose and McDougall, *The Pagan Tribes of Borneo*, plate 102.

their everyday lives. Producing the skull (or, as with the Kayan, the whole dried head) is a splendid signal indeed.

The ceremonies continue. Old men carry the heads into the house, accompanied by warriors in full regalia with shields and swords, singing their battle chants and performing a ritualistic dance:

> Each man keeps turning to face his neighbours, first on one side, then on the other, with regular steps in time with all the rest. This seems to symbolize the alertness of the warriors on the war-path, looking in every direction.

Now the heads are suspended on a beam over the hearth, joining a goodly collection of dried heads that had already been in residence. A rattan rope is passed through a hole cut in the top of each skull so that they can be strung together on high. Well done! The men now sit and drink, and the new chief praises the warriors for their prowess in collecting the new batch of heads. (As with their own venerated chief, the bodies of those slain to provide the heads are of little importance; they deal only in the head count.) The feasting begins. The drinking continues. Every now and again the boisterous war chant breaks out again. The heads are not neglected. A consecrated drink is offered to the heads

> by pouring it into small bamboo cups suspended beside them; and a bit of fat pork will be pushed into the mouth of each. The heads, or rather the Toh associated with them, are supposed to drink and eat these offerings. The fact that the bits of pork remain unconsumed does not seem to raise any difficulty in the minds of the Kayans . . . the essence of the food is consumed.

I would put a little more Borak in the cup and fat pork in the mouth of that third head from the left . . . his Toh is making me nervous.

> At all times the heads hanging in the house are treated respectfully and somewhat fearfully. When it is necessary to handle them, some old man undertakes the task, and children especially are prevented from touching them; for it is felt that to touch them involves the risk of madness, brought on by the offended Toh.

There can be too much of a good thing, though, as the Kayan realized.

> The Kayans do not care to have in the house more than twenty or thirty heads, and are at some pains occasionally to get rid of some superfluous heads—a fact which shows clearly that the heads are not mere trophies of valour and success in war.

Actually, all those imported heads have been assigned the job of servant or slave for the chief in his new regime in the land of the dead. The surplus heads are hung in a small hut and

> a good fire is made in it and kept up . . . for several days. It is supposed that, when the fire goes out, the Toh of the heads notice the fact, and begin to suspect that they are deserted by the people.

Fortunately, the head-burners will have escaped by the time the Toh fully realize what has happened. One has to be careful at all times, though, to avoid the wrath of the Toh, with madness the usual punishment for those who do fall victim. To make things even more complicated:

> These beings are not wholly malevolent. It is held that in some way their presence in the house brings prosperity to it, especially in the form of good crops; and so essential to the welfare of the house are the heads held to be that, if through fire a house has lost its heads and has not occasion for war, the people will beg a head, or even a fragment of one, from some friendly house, and will install it in their own with the usual ceremonies.

Perhaps no observer of island peoples was more acute than W. H. R. Rivers, a psychiatrist who developed a passion for field research.[11] Rivers became convinced by his experiences that the human skull was the most sacred and powerful object in the native religions, the centerpiece of most rituals. This was startlingly clear in such places as the Solomon Islands, where a cult of the dead remained dominant. But why the skull? Rivers suggested that the skull was taken as a symbolic representation of the whole person. It is as though all the special characteristics of that person had condensed to their essences in or around the skull. If you had the skull, you still, in a sense, had the person. Furthermore, the skull, along with other bones, also symbolized that-which-endures. Under ordinary conditions one could not see the spirit-self, and the fleshy parts of the body would quickly deteriorate. The bones were therefore a visible, cleaner, more stable, and less frightening symbol of a personhood that survives death.

Bones and the Winds of Change

There are also many charnel houses scattered through Europe, though some have given way to population growth and land development. These are ground-level structures, often simple edifices of brick or stone. Charnel houses, or ossuaries, provided a place where the corpsed person could deteriorate in privacy. The bodies held in these structures would also be less likely to cause harm to the public. Eventually, there would be only skulls and bones. These might be given permanent burial . . . or just forgotten and left to sit blindly in the dark until Judgment Day.

However, even the dead are not immune to social change. Skulls and bones might be survivors, left to their own discretion, but become either lucky beneficiaries or helpless victims of the caprices of the living. Ellen Badone gives us an example from Lower Brittany.[12] The local version of the charnel house had been common in this area from the late seventeenth to the early twentieth century. Here the direction of movement was from the graveyard to the charnel house. Eventually the local cemetery would become overcrowded. The bones were then exhumed and placed in the ossuary. An accompanying priestly ritual would remind the participants of anything they might have forgotten about death, judgment, and damnation.

Despite this polite attention, the bones would lose something in the move: their individual identity. Over the years, then, there would be many a harvest of individual skulls and bones that were henceforth consigned to the anonymity of a community ossuary. Occasionally bones were returned to earth when the ossuary became more crowded than the graveyard.

> By the late nineteenth century, however, a movement toward more individualistic treatment of the dead had started to develop in Brittany. Bones were still stored in ossuaries, but the skull was often kept separate and housed in a small wooden box with a heartshaped opening at the front and peaked covers like the roof of a house.[13]

Here was something that the death cult in a Pacific island or an ancestor-venerating people in Africa might well admire and emulate: a friendly little house for the skull to call its own. They might have wondered, though, about the individual attention to deceased who were not necessarily the most heroic or sacred of the group.

> Information about the deceased, such as names and dates of birth and death, was inscribed on the outside of the box. . . . Skull boxes were stored in the ossuary or the church. Even today visitors to the cathedral in Saint-Pol-de-Leon can see a number of such boxes, most dating from the nineteenth and early twentieth centuries.[14]

And then the customary shifting of bones between ossuary and earth slowed to a halt. The remains remained where ever they happened to be. What happened? The War to End All Wars. The massive impact of World War I changed much in Lower Brittany as well as many other places. The ossuaries were largely neglected thereafter. Reburial became rare. From this point on, those who died were given "modern" funerals. The skull box tradition perished after its relatively short run of a little more than two centuries, yielding both to the upheaval of war and to the upsurge of a "romantic response to death." People became less willing to accept separation from beloved relatives. It was more appealing to think of a family reuniting itself in the tomb, more comforting to erect imposing funerary architecture. Badone observes that the older, more direct way of relating to the dead is still part of the culture, but now inhibited by the mental and physical edifices that have arisen to protect one from unmediated contact with death.

Skulls in their cozy little houses, peering out through the heart-shaped openings! This respect and veneration for the king of the bones is one of many examples of widespread but creatively varied deathways that have held the skull in high esteem. It also stands, however, as an example of the vulnerability of traditional deathways to the accelerated change that has increasingly affected individual and social life since the early nineteenth century, to take a somewhat arbitrary marking place in time.

Dead Red

Just when did humankind develop this fascination with skulls and bones? Neanderthals used flint tools to dig graves and there deposited and covered up the bones of their dead. We can speculate, but we do not really know whether it was the whole corpse or just the bones that were buried. We also cannot speak with assurance about the religious beliefs that may have governed this practice. Perhaps ground burial represented a kind of underground spiritual journey to the next life; perhaps it was even imagined that the dead might sprout back to life after an interval in the ground, as plants did after a hard winter. Perhaps, though, it was a more pragmatic task: bury the dead so they will not be devoured by animals or discovered by enemies.

There are clearer indexes of the funerary practices of the people who are known as the Cro-Magnon. They obviously devoted considerable attention to the condition of their corpsed people. The skeletons were decorated with shells, bracelets, and headdresses. The bodies were oriented in a north-south direction. And to the bones themselves red ochre was applied. As more and more burials were unearthed from earlier and earlier periods of history, this curious feature was repeatedly noted.

> Sometimes a paste of red ochre seems to have been rubbed over the entire body; sometimes it would appear that the colour has been applied to the desiccated bones . . . often accompanied by the provision of supplies of red colouring matter, either in pinches or morsels placed in grooves in the earth or in the hand of deceased or in little pots. Moreover the objects found within the grave are occasionally stained red.[15]

C. E. Vulliamy is convinced that the red ochre, applied and supplied, was "the equivalent of the rouge and lipsticks of to-day." A cosmetic enhancement to look one's best on a long and consequential trip? Perhaps so. But why red?

It turns out that the practice of enhancing bones with red ochre, red clay, or other red substances has been carried out by many others since the Cro-Magnon. The Algonquian and Delaware peoples who were on hand when Europeans started to become rather too numerous reddened their dead with a fine powder that appears to have been red oxide of iron. The Choctaw, Vulliamy tells us, decorated the skulls of their dead with a mixture of bear oil and vermilion. A similar procedure was used by the Monacan after their corpsed people had been exposed to the drying action of the sun. Other (but not all) Native American peoples throughout the land also found ways to enhance the bones or whole bodies of their dead with a red hue. Today we might wince at the once popular expression "redskin." Nevertheless, this would have been an accurate way to describe the physical remains of many Native Americans as they proceeded through that dangerous interval between one life and another.

Dead red was the preburial status of the corpsed person (whole or boned) among peoples as varied as the Maori of New Zealand and Australia and the Ndolo of Africa. The former took care to separate bones from flesh and clean and scrape them thoroughly before painting them red; the latter covered the whole body with a paste made from red bark. More dramatically, the Torres Strait Islanders would saw the head off its body, then deliver it to a red-painted anthill to be picked clean. It was then "placed in an elegant basket."[16]

Vulliamy offers his informed opinion on the "why red?" question.

The finest and fiercest of colours has been associated throughout the world with the rites of the tomb. The Sphinx . . . had a red face. What is the significance of this association?[17]

He rejects the previous theory that red signified health and vigor, noting, among other objections, that swarthy and dark-skinned peoples were not likely to be interested in a ruddy complexion. Vulliamy reminds us that cultures may use similar practices for dissimilar reasons. Reddening the bones might have had some special meanings within one culture that should not be attributed to another. He attributes the popularity of red tinting to the brilliance of the color as a postmortem cosmetic enhancement. However, the symbolic link with blood should not be ignored. Red blood is, of course, universal, and perhaps universal also is the recognition that, as a celebrated though fictitious nineteenth-century Transylvanian count would later pronounce, "Blood is the life." These reasonable explanations are still a little vague, so we will want to revisit the blood-life-bones connection elsewhere in this book.

No visit to the king of bones would be complete without peering over the shoulders of an ancient scryer. He is totally engrossed in his mysterious art, whether his sacred chamber be hut, cave, tent, or priestly cell. His eyes are fixed on another visage whose return gaze is empty, yet charged with meaning. The skull was the first crystal ball. For a long time and for many peoples it remained the mediating object through which the future might be revealed, what with crystal balls not growing on shoulders or trees. Crystal ball gazers have been around for a while, but who is to say that those who used the real and original thing might not have been more successful?

In one way or another people have sought to preserve and interact with the skulls of their ancestors through the centuries. Not for us, though, right? By the way—going bowling tonight?

THE CORPSE MARKET

The separation of bone and flesh has provided comfort for at least four reasons. (1) Bone remains—the skull above all—are more presentable and less horrifying than the sight and stench of decaying flesh. (2) The corpsed person stripped down to the bone has become sufficiently dead to release the spirit and authorize ritual mourning behaviors. (3) An aura of the sacred is associated with skulls and bones, especially those of people who have been very important to family or society. Through these lived-in artifacts, survivors and descendants can attempt to maintain contact both with their own dead and with the spirit world in general. (4) It is a really good idea to do justice to physical remains, not only because we may have loved and respected the deceased person, but also because spirits of the dead can be grumpy if we fail to do so. The dead have their bad habits, too.

Now we go beyond the time-honored beliefs, practices, and rituals that have affirmed the personhood of the corpse. Let's go to market!

There has been some vigorous and profitable trafficking in human remains through the centuries. Relics of the saints were usually the items of interest. For every saint whose whole body has been more or less preserved there were many others who were available only piecemeal. Churches competed for heads, hair, hands, fingers, fingernails, and even etcetera.[18] One might find reliquaries in which several competing churches claimed to contain the same piece of the same saint. There was an undeniable financial consideration here. Pilgrims were more likely to line up and ante up to a church that could boast of body relics from a beloved saint.

Nevertheless, religious belief was still the fundamental consideration. The body relics would have had little significance were it not for their religious associations. It is true that many of the body relics were obtained in gross and brutal ways—just chopped off and spirited away, even if that meant disfiguring an otherwise intact corpse. Once in hand, though, these fragmentary remains were usually spared further indignities. After the rigors of a saintly life and perhaps some postmortem misadventures, what was left of the body was henceforth an object (or objects) of respect and veneration. Not to mention profit. The destination of many medieval pilgrimages was a church or a tomb where one might approach the (reputed) remains of a notable saint, or even Jesus himself.[19]

The body market did not really heat up until the late eighteenth and early nineteenth centuries, though. This story deserves to be told in some detail for the way in which it illuminates the relationship between society's treatment of the living and its treatment of the dead. In what follows we draw much from Ruth Richardson's masterly account *Death, Dissection, and the Destitute.*

Early in the nineteenth century, corpses were becoming a prized and profitable commodity.

> Corpses were bought and sold, they were touted, priced, haggled over, negotiated for, discussed in terms of supply and demand, delivered, imported, exported, transported. Human bodies were compressed into boxes, packed in sawdust, packed in hay, trussed up in sacks, roped up like hams, sewn in canvas, packed in cases, casks, barrels, crates and hampers; salted, pickled or injected with preservative. They were carried in carts and waggons, in barrows and steam-boats; manhandled, damaged in transit, and hidden under loads of vegetables. They were stored in cellars and on quays. Human bodies were dismantled and sold in pieces, or measured and sold by the inch.[20]

Human bodies . . . sold in pieces . . . and sold by the inch. The Solomon Islanders and Kayan might have paused from their skull-duggery to wonder at this madness: had the Toh unhinged the minds of all those strange people who steamed across the great sea in strange boats?

"Not really madness," the Brits and other Europeans might have replied. "Not really madness when you can pay for your room and board by selling a bit of flesh for which the owner has no further use. Not really madness when you teach physicians properly and help them learn more about keeping us alive."

Fueling the demand was medical and scientific zeal. Many doctors continued to putter around with a grab-bag of ill-sorted remedies, many of which were worse than the disease. The received knowledge about anatomy and biology included some useful home truths but also much assumption, speculation, and fantasy. Now, however, some physicians were advocating a radical agenda. Medical practice should be based on science. And medical science must be learned from the only authentic source—the human body, not the dusty tomes of antiquity and their dubious commentators.

This movement toward empirical investigation was an unwelcome and even frightening prospect for the traditionalists. Furthermore, it offended the church establishment and unnerved their flock. Nevertheless, it could not be denied that medical practice was marked more by failure than by success. People often avoided falling into doctors' hands except as a last resort or when they happened to have one of the few conditions that actually responded to the medical ministrations of the time. It would be a boon to have more knowledgeable and effective doctors. The cost of medical advances, however, seemed far too high to many people if it meant carving into cadavers.

There was already a history of supply and demand coming into the nineteenth century. Since the time of Henry VIII, there had been only one legal source for corpses: the bruised fruit plucked from the gallows. This was a limited crop that could not meet even what was at first a modest demand. Another problem lurked here as well, one that would become increasingly salient as demand increased: dissection had the aspect of punishment. Who was condemned to the gallows? Criminals, of course, the depraved and accursed. And if the gallowed were not every one of them violent monsters, at least they were not among the best of folk. For the worst of them, perhaps hanging wasn't punishment enough: let the morbid sort of surgeon ply his fearful craft in dark and foul dungeons. (Actually, many dissections did take place in dark and foul dungeons or their facsimiles, whether in England, Scotland, France, or the German-speaking lands. It was miserable work, performed, by and large, under miserable conditions.) Bottom line: dissection was a punishment heaped upon punishment.

As medical knowledge increased, so did demand for more cadavers. Who wanted the dead? Anatomists for their research and teaching. Their students. Physicians interested in furthering their own education. The occasional artist.

Who would supply the growing demand? The fellow next door, per-haps. You know who I mean. A nice-enough-seeming chap, but with not much to say, drunk or sober. More drunk than usual lately, come to think upon it. But also with more coins jingling in his pocket and, every now and then, a new pocket in a new jacket as well. Wonder how he does it in these hard times?

We have our answer if that nice-enough-seeming chap answers to the name Igor. It's all true, what we have seen in the many movie versions and variations of the Frankenstein theme. Well, at least the bare bones of the story are true. There were body snatchers. They did rob grave-yards. Moonless nights were the preferred time, though London fog and drizzle often could be counted upon to shroud their doings even if a stray moon loomed overhead. Up from the graveyards of London, then, the dead arose, but not to rapture toward heaven. Bumping against bowed backs, the exhumed were hurried to safe houses until they could be brought to market.

This illicit trade did not go unnoticed. A brilliant young woman in-troduced a body snatcher into her novel about the next step in medical science: reanimating the dead. Mary Wollstonecraft Shelley's monster was not the poor patchwork brute strapped to the table but the egoistic sci-entist who respected no legal or sacred limits, "a modern Prometheus," as she subtitled her novel *Frankenstein*.[21]

Civic authorities had also noticed the unsettling practice of body snatching. Measures had to be taken. What measures? Security patrols did what they could to deter transgressions, but they could not be every-where all the time. A more promising idea occurred to first one church organization, then to another and another. The bodies were of com-mercial value only when freshly buried. The new graves were the ones sought by Igor and his brethren. These would have been regarded by most native peoples as the incompletely dead, their spirits still trapped in the decaying flesh. Some churches took action. The just-deceased were hus-tled off into a charnel house and there kept under lock and key until they had deteriorated beyond commercial use. This was an irregular proce-dure and stirred controversy. On the whole, though, church members agreed it was better to delay ground burial than to risk dissection.

Guardians of the grave made other adjustments as well. Clever con-traptions were designed to thwart thieving hands. Corpses could be se-cured inside their coffins with iron straps or metal bands whose screws could not be removed by the devil himself. Other devices included coffins with hidden spring catches inside the lid that resisted levering and forcing. In Scotland some cemeteries provided cages to encase the coffin.

These countermeasures worked pretty well. Fewer graves were robbed. The dead could sleep more soundly and their grieving survivors as well. This, however, was not the end of the matter. In fact, measures to foil grave robbers prepared the way for even more disturbing developments.

But first, an intermission. We leave Igor holding his empty sack for a moment to reflect again on the fear of dissection. Do corpsed persons suffer on the autopsy (postmortem) table? Even today, more people torment themselves with this belief than might be supposed. We perhaps should not underestimate the anxiety associated with dissection, both then and now. People feared not only the imagined pain but also the sense of helplessness—lying there unable to defend oneself against the surgeon's brutal onslaught. In our own day, a related anxiety is fairly common: imagining what it must be like to be kept semi-alive in a persistent vegetative state.

In the nineteenth century, fears of dissection were crowned with the terror of catastrophe after death. Those unfortunate enough to fall into the dissectionist's hands would lose their heaven. It was a common belief that body and soul would be reunited in the Great Hereafter. Theologians and church officials might entertain each other with subtle arguments on this subject, but many of the faithful cleaved to this belief without question. Life was harsh and insecure enough in the early phase of industrialization with its unremitting stresses and dislocations. The downtrodden and bereft could hope only for something better in the next life, and the dissectionist's scalpel was poised to sever that slender thread.

The wealthy shared some of the same concerns. They shuddered at the idea of having their graves ransacked. Money bought protection through the comparative safety of entombment and paid security patrols.

Snatch as Snatch Can

Frustrated physicians. Frustrated medical students. Frustrated body snatchers. Who will lend a helping hand?

The problem was perhaps most acute in Edinburgh, which was a center of excellence in medical instruction and practice in the late eighteenth and early nineteenth centuries. The shortage of cadavers led to higher prices, and this inflationary trend was passed along to the students, who, less able to bear the expense, were becoming less numerous and thereby weakening the economic base of the whole enterprise. There was talk that students in Edinburgh and London were planning to hotfoot it to France, where cadavers were more available and therefore less expensive. The growing but still shaky edifice of scientific medicine was threatening to collapse for want of suitable instructional materials, that is, corpses of quality.

The Guild of Loyal, Hygienic, and Philanthropic Body Snatchers (had their been one) would have deplored the common appellation given to their trade. They preferred to be known as *resurrectionists,* although no deeds of resurrection, in the usual sense of the word, were achieved. The resurrectionists became willing to take more risks once they discovered that their elite clientele were desperate enough to shell out serious money. Richardson offers an example of what happened next:

> On Friday evening last [in 1831], about six o'clock, a party of resurrectionists rushed suddenly into a house in bow-lane, where the corpse of an aged female named Carrol was being "waked" by her friends and neighbors, in an upper apartment, and succeeded in possessing themselves of the body, which they bore off, before the persons present could offer any effectual resistance. The ruffians acted with the most revolting indecency, dragging the corpse in its death-clothes after them through the mud in the street, and most unfortunately baffled all pursuit. . . . Several of the fellows engaged in this outrage are well-known resurrectionists, but though the police are acquainted with their haunts, strange to say that none of them have been apprehended yet.[22]

Bodies were snatched wherever bold hands could reach. Actually, it was less harrowing work than digging up fresh graves. No more damp and chilly midnights inhaling the graveyard vapors. No more discovering that your prize had already been spirited away by swifter rivals. No more trying to stifle the secret fear of being seized by graveyard spirits or even by a reanimated corpse leaping out of the ground. And a little money proffered here and there could do wonders with workhouse staff. A beer and mutton supper just for happening to look one way while a scrawny corpse went the other way: who could resist that offer?

Resurrectionists also adjusted by colonizing graveyards in more remote areas and importing cadavers from other nations when conditions were favorable. Medical students adjusted, too. Some tried their own hand at body snatching, therefore bypassing the middleman. Two nearly paid for such a caper with their lives when they were arrested and then surrounded by hundreds of outraged citizens, whose brandished axes suggested that the miscreants might themselves be resurrectionist bait ere long. Charles Darwin happened to witness a crowd assault on two other grave robbers who were pulped rather severely before police could haul them away to the safety of prison.[23]

Depressed and disgusted with themselves, the medical clientele became increasingly tense. It was a frightful business, they felt, but justified by their mission. Some of the anatomists were deeply religious people who were intent on improving their understanding of the marvelous designs God had wrought in creation of the human frame. Physicians preferred to keep mum in public but in private wrestled intensely with their consciences and their colleagues. There was a pragmatic as well as a spiritual side to this conflict. Physicians were just now starting to achieve social status and prosperity. To solidify this gain and build upon it they needed a reliable supply of cadavers—yet their reputations would be destroyed if they were discovered to be in league with the repulsive body snatchers. They had to know that their payments at the back door were supporting the bribed theft of bodies of the poor from hospitals as well as from workhouses.

Poor or wealthy, physician or layperson, almost everybody shared the cultural consensus that the corpsed person should be respected. And almost everybody also shared the dread that scoundrels might unearth the bodies of their loved ones—and, on some mist-shrouded evening, perhaps their very own flesh and bones.

Let's Pass a Law!

The assumption that the dead are out of the loop in modern Western society was itself knocked for a loop in the furor that raged around the vulnerability of corpsed persons in the first quarter of the nineteenth century. The issue became so heated that the authorities felt they had to take decisive action. A curious story-within-a-story contributes to the outcome. Jeremy Bentham was a social philosopher whose ideas remain influential today. He gave us "the hedonic calculus," the moral position that society should seek to provide the greatest good to the greatest number of people. In an era of rapid technological change and social upheaval, Bentham labored to introduce a pragmatic sort of morality that might deter exploitation and alleviate distress. This approach became known as Utilitarianism. Bentham declared that the prevailing systems of philosophical thought were too vague, ponderous, and detached from everyday realities. Many agreed.

He recognized that authorities were in a hard place between public fear and outrage and the legitimate need for cadavers. Bentham offered his suggestions in hushed conversations and correspondence that remained hidden from view until recently. It would not be wise for such discussions to come to public attention while fears and passions were in the saddle. Bentham himself drafted the Body Providing Bill.[24] This measure would legalize and regularize one of the most common violations, the spiriting away of cadavers from hospitals, workhouses, and other charitable institutions. The universally loathed body snatchers would be out of business and the most proper corpsed persons off limits.

How would the plan work? Just as a pragmatic social philosophy should work: through a contractual arrangement in which both parties exchange "goods." Hospitals and work- or poorhouses would provide their charitable services to those in need. The recipients of this charity later would deliver their goods in the form of their dead bodies. This would be a perfectly legal agreement entered into voluntarily by both parties. Bentham also suggested that the public receive notification of deaths that occurred in the charitable institutions from which bodies were to be harvested. He added a clause that would have halted the practice of consigning the bodies of murderers to the dissection table. The general idea was not original with Bentham; something along these lines had already been introduced in France. Bentham's draft was bruited in private discussions among the decision makers of the realm, and a revised version, the Anatomy Act, was reported out of committee in 1828. Unfortunately, this measure proved to have serious defects and has been charged with actually worsening the situation.

Meanwhile, as sagacious heads conferred in London, something unknown to them was afoot in Edinburgh. The United Kingdom was about to be rocked by one of the most appalling—and therefore fascinating—crimes in its long and bloody history. Appalling, but not surprising. Bentham and others had already sensed that events were moving to such an extreme that it was only a matter of time until . . . miscreants would discover a new way to line their pockets.

The Last Boardinghouse You Will Ever Need

This heading gives the gist of the story away, but no matter. The cheap boardinghouse in question was run by a Mrs. Hare. An indigent old man died in this lodging, still owing money to the proprietor. Mr. Hare and his friend Mr. Burke looked at the corpse, then at each other, and soon returned from a little trip with money in their pockets (seven pounds and one shilling, to be precise, a very handsome reward that more than repaid Mrs. Hare). That was just the beginning.

Another lodger later became ill. Burke and Hare plied him with whiskey and smothered him. It was so easy! And so profitable! This time they returned with the munificent sum of ten pounds. From this point forward, Mr. Burke and Mr. Hare took a more proactive approach. They lured impoverished travelers and street people into their den for a hearty meal and a cozy place to rest. Eventually their execution list would include fifteen more people.

The serial murders were discovered in result of the following incident, reported in an Edinburgh newspaper on November 3, 1828:

> An old woman by the name of Campbell, from Ireland, came to Edinburgh some days ago. . . . She took up her lodgings on Friday, in the house of a man named Burt or Burke, in the West Port. It appears that there was a merry making in Burke's that night; at least the noise of music and dancing was heard, and it is believed the glass circulated pretty freely among the party. The old woman, it is said, with reluctance joined in the mirth, and also partook of the liquor, and was to sleep on straw alongside of Burke's bed. During the night shrieks were heard; but the neighbors paid no attention, as such sounds were not unusual in the house. In the morning, however, a female, on going into Burke's, observed the old woman lying as if dead, some of the straw being above her. She did not say anything, or raise any alarm; but in the evening circumstances transpired which led to a belief that all was not right, for, by this time the body had been removed out of the house, and, it was suspected, had been sold to a public lecturer. Information was conveyed to the police, and the whole party taken into custody.

Note the spin on the next revelation:

> After a search, the body was found yesterday morning in the lecture room
> of a respectable practitioner, who, the instant he was informed of the cir-
> cumstance, not only gave it up, but afforded every information in his
> power. The body is now in the police-office, and will be examined by med-
> ical gentlemen in the course of the day. There are some very strong and
> singular circumstances connected with the case, which have given rise to
> the suspicions.[25]

Fifteen murders and seventeen bodies delivered to the same respectable
practitioner—hmmm, could that be a tad suspicious, Inspector?

We are now ready to interweave the major themes and developments
in the marketing of corpsed persons as the nineteenth century roared into
modernity.

Bodies and Souls

The respectable practitioner was John Knox, one of the most distinguished physicians of his era and a force in the advancement of medical
instruction and science. He had surely known that most of the death-
fresh bodies he received bore the marks of violence. The police gentle-
men surely knew that he knew, and the public—oh, the public! They were
enraged that a doctor of such high standing had bankrolled the serial
murders, medical science or not. Public anger intensified when Knox was
not even called upon to testify during the proceedings against the Burke-
Hares ensemble. The lower classes, in an astounding departure from custom, mobbed in front of Knox's mansion and set him on fire—in effigy.
This action did not merely irk Knox. It sent a chilling message to the
Powers That Be'd. Had the public found its voice? Had the anonymous
mass shed its attitude of resignation in the face of rampant class discrimination? Worst of all, was the public now on the verge of discovering that there were more of them than there were of the elite? A roiling,
vengeance-seeking public could diminish one's enjoyment of pheasant,
plum pudding, and sherry.

Public fear and anger intensified as the Anatomy Act became law, and
its consequences evident. The populace was not comforted by the trade-
off between charitable services and body harvesting. The poor, aged, and

disabled sunk into deeper despair when confronted with the new contractual arrangement: their bodies and therefore their immortal souls were
doomed to be fed into the bloody and insatiable maws of technology. A
sad life was to be followed by a hopeless death. Their last shreds of self-
esteem were torn asunder by an amendment to Bentham's original draft.
Parliament had decided to keep dissecting the murderers. This had the
predictable effect of making hospital patients and other charity recipients feel that they were as subhuman and worthless as the most brutal
killer. To make matters worse, schools of anatomy ruthlessly competed
with each other for first pick in the corpse market. Hypocrisy, fraud, class
prejudice, and the profit motive continued to blight the passage from
corpse to spirit.

Eventually another dirty little secret came out. The public tumbled to
the fact that there were so many bodies available from the workhouses
because the mortality rate was so appallingly high. Predictably, this increased anxieties and outrage. The social reformers of the time were given
even more case examples and statistics to assault the complacency and
connivances of the establishment.

The Reform Act was passed a few years later with the intent of quelling
objections to the treatment of both the living and the dead poor. Protests
were feared because the new law actually had another round of adverse
consequences for society's unfortunates. Opposition was minimal and
muted, however, because the new measures were implemented in a low
key and piecemeal manner. It took a while before the realization set in
that the humanitarian reform was in fact "a class reprisal against the
poor." The humble had shown their teeth and brandished their axes for
a moment or two, but now the establishment had regrouped and designed
new methods to continue the old way.

We take our leave of this episode with an observation by one of the
most ardent of the true social reformers, as quoted by Richardson:

> George Godwin said that in the 1850's he had seen poor people "used as
> though they were not of the same species as those who crowded them into
> passages, and pushed and drove them like so many sheep and cattle."[26]

For many people, then, the character of their final passage was prepared in advance by the insensitive treatment they had received throughout their lives. Little respect during life, less upon death. A share of this

anguish was experienced by conscientious clergy and welfare workers and by all citizens capable of feeling another's pain and desperation. Were the doctors sinners, if not criminals, because they needed the dead to help the living? Were the police and the judiciary blameworthy for looking the other way? Were the big movers and shakers evil to the core because they sought the benefits of technological development for their own profit without having to deal with public pressure? Perhaps we should withhold our judgment until we consider the related questions that remain with us today as the corpsed person continues to figure in medical, economical, cultural, and spiritual conflicts.

BAD IN THEIR BONES?
WHEN THE CORPSED PERSON IS A SUICIDE

A new element enters our discussion now. We have had glimpses of cultures that revere and use their distinguished dead and also a glimpse of institutionalized disrespect toward entire classes of people within a society. Here we consider the corpsed person who opted out of society. Is there something so special and so contaminating about death by suicide that it somehow adheres to the mortal remains and must be dealt with in a special way?

Many societies have denied suicides the customary funerary rites and have also excluded them from the sacred burial ground. This practice suggests that (1) suicidal deaths are different from others; and (2) whatever it is that makes the act of suicide so unacceptable cleaves to the finished product, the corpsed person.

Two bodies equally dead are to be treated differently because one died of self-murder. Cultures, like individuals, may engage in similar actions for different reasons. I see six major reasons or motivations at work. Several of these factors may be present within a particular culture at a particular time and with varying degrees of prominence.

1. Danger. The suicide has died in a state of incompletion and impurity. It is therefore dangerous to be close to the body, because evil spirits thrive in just such a circumstance. By implication, a suicide's corpse might contaminate the bodies of people who were downright upright throughout their lives.

2. Punishment. The suicide cannot profitably be scolded, flogged, jailed, or executed. However, if we consider person-hood to persist after death and to be an attribute of the corpse, then there is still something to heap punishment upon, if only reputation and family survivors.

3. Dissuasion. Denying sacred ritual and burial to the suicide will frighten others away from taking their own lives.

4. Self-interest. This demonstration of condemnation by the authorities will affirm their power and thereby discourage rivals and revolutionaries.

5. Disgust and revulsion. The thought of suicide can cause these responses, which are primarily emotional, although they are probably conditioned by cultural values and beliefs.

6. The tinge of sin. Suicide is sinful. God is offended. The mortal remains of a suicide are contaminated by this sin and must so be regarded.

Not all cultures have made a big fuss about suicide.[27] The Greeks and Romans of antiquity often lamented the injustices, cruelties, and pains of existence. Suicide was considered a rational option when misery became unbearable and future prospects were even more dismal. Ending one's life was even an admirable action under some circumstances, such as the defeated military commander or the woman charged, rightly or wrongly, of adultery. People who surrendered their own lives to save others were considered heroes, not deviants or sinners. In fact, most of the specific suicides described by the Romans were of the heroic type. A person whose mode of death affirmed rather than challenged a culture's values was in no danger of having disrespect shown to the mortal remains.

The Bible also refrains from censuring suicide. Neither in the Old nor the New Testament is self-murder judged as sinful. There are no strictures about rites and burial. In the Old Testament, that great repository of stories, only four suicides are mentioned (Abimelech, Ahithophel, Saul, and Sampson), and these are brief, straightforward reports. Life was hard over the centuries that saw the development of Judaism and then Christianity, so few people would have been surprised when suicide occasionally was selected as the least terrible option available. The tenets of Hinduism, Buddhism, and Islam express little concern about suicide. There are good reasons not to end one's own life (e.g., that would not accomplish much in the weary rounds of reincarnation), but their sacred writings do not make a target of the suicide. Being tough on suicidally corpsed persons is a practice that developed outside the range of the emerging world-class religions and found its way into Western society after disputes and upheavals occurred within Christianity.

Suicide at the Crossroads

In premodern times, one way of dealing with the body of a suicide enjoyed popularity in many parts of the world, from tribal peoples in Africa and Polynesia to both rural and urban Europe. For example, the Baganda people in what later became Uganda knew what to do. They would haul the corpse away from the village, taking precautions against reprisals either by that person's ghost or by other malevolent spirits. The disposal party would trek to a crossroads. There they would burn the body. The best fuel consisted of wood from the tree or hut in which the deceased had hanged himself (hanging being the most common mode of suicide and men the more common perpetrators). If all went well, the ghost would realize that he was no longer wanted in that vicinity and hotfoot it away. The remains would be buried at the crossroads to make it that much more difficult for a bad-tempered spirit to return to the village. If the spirit was still within the cremains, it would have to scratch its dimensionless head in consternation, wondering which direction to choose at the crossroads. Just to be sure, women would come by later and cover the site with grass or twigs to make it even more difficult for a banished ghost to return and get himself reborn.

In all of these precautions the Baganda were not punishing sinners. They were just trying to protect themselves against the hovering threat of evil spirits. The deceased had perished in an agitated state of mind—not good! The ghost might well take out his frustration and anger on the living. It was even more dangerous if blood had been spilled; this would be considered the blood not only of the suicide but of the whole family clan.

Burying (and sometimes also burning or disfiguring) a suicide at a crossroads would become common practice throughout much of Europe from early medieval times and continue to exert its influence in the waning years of the nineteenth century. Some of the thinking behind this practice was similar to that of the Baganda and other tribal peoples. There is something contaminating about this corpse. It could be dangerous. Get it away. Try to prevent its revengeful depredations by burial at a crossroads. But this practice now had the additional authority of church dogma. Suicides were not just unhappy, desperate, and perhaps unhinged people: they were *sinners*. This was a departure from both the Judaic tradition and the formative years of Christianity. What had happened and why?

Martyrs happened.[28] Persecuted at times by Roman authorities, some Christians chose death over betrayal of their faith. In doing so they could call upon the example of Jesus on the cross. He had died that they might live. Jesus had shown the way to a new and incomparably better life *through* death. Those who died for their faith would leave their earthly life strong in conscience and prepared for spiritual and perhaps physical rebirth on a higher plane of existence.

Christian attitudes toward suicide might have continued in the tradition of sorrowful acceptance or toleration if just a few had martyred themselves to make their point. Martyrdom, though, was getting out of control. Too many zealots were impelled to achieve instant salvation. The Roman authorities were themselves put out by this deluge. Some were appalled at all this unnecessary killing (the popularity of lions vs. Christians notwithstanding). Christian leaders debated and disagreed among themselves. By the fifth century, one man at least had had quite enough. Augustine of Hippo, later to become one of the most illustrious of saints, condemned some of his fellow Christians for pursuing martyrdom as though a sport. More serious was the loss of useful church members and the distracting appeal of what today is called suicide-by-cop.

Augustine set forth arguments against suicide that were taken up by the church and bolstered by later contributions from Thomas Aquinas. These arguments still constitute the core of Catholic opposition to self-murder. Augustine was tough and uncompromising. No exceptions! Suicide is a sin under any condition. Life is a gift from God, said Augustine, as others had before him; it is a sin of pride to assume God's office. For example, even young virgins who chose death over rape were thereby to be condemned as sinners. (Actually he did make one exception: Samson was excused for his mass murder and suicide, although this generous concession might have puzzled the brawny man who slew Philistines long before the appearance of Jesus and the Catholic Church.) Augustine had additional reasons, but his cruncher was that suicide was the worst of all sins because it eliminates the opportunity for repentance. Hitler's great sin, then, would have resided in his suicide, not his massacre of millions. There was opposition to Augustine's views within Christendom, but his condemnation of suicide as sin became and has remained dogma.

And so for more than a millennium suicides (with the occasional sympathetic exception) were denied burial on sacred ground. Many corpses were hauled to a crossroads for the mortification and disarmament of their sinful souls. Historian Alexander Murray notes that crossroads also were a favorite locale for the performance of a variety of magical rites, even though these were not officially condoned by the church.[29] The "curse on self-murder" accorded well with popular European superstitions. The souls of the self-murderers would suffer in hell, or in purgatory, as this option later received grudging acceptance from the church. Meanwhile, in Japan and other cultures with other value systems, suicides were variously tolerated, admired, wept over, and deplored, depending on circumstances.

Fast-forward to nineteenth-century London (actually, I suppose, we are fast-backwarding, having visited London not many pages ago). Let's spin down in 1823, during the same years when body snatchers were lurking in the fog and anatomical lecturers were waiting impatiently for the goods. The mortal remains of a nobleman were to be interred in Westminster Abbey after a state funeral with all the trimmings. The public, usually respectful of such solemn ceremonies, was shocked and enraged. Crowds formed themselves in St. James Square with placards avowing that no suicide should be buried in the splendor of the abbey, not even the high and mighty marquis of Londonderry. Said person had slashed his throat in the privacy of his boudoir. The coroner and other officials had a difficult determination to make. If this were an out-and-out suicide, then His Lordship died as a felon. If, however, he was mentally distraught to the point of insanity, then madness made him innocent—but also brought rather too much satisfaction to critics of the ruling class who held that most of their betters were loons anyhow.

The more genteel option was taken: the marquis had self-destructed "under a state of mental delusion." This meant that his body could receive all of the deservings, considering his eminence and the sympathy felt for Lady Londonderry. Furthermore, this was, after all, the nineteenth century and London. Behaving shabbily toward a suicide corpse was no longer what civilized people did.

The law, however, was on the side of the protesters. Despite the somewhat wayward march of progress, suicides were still being denied sacred rite and decent burial wherever that practice was in tune with the local populace. Lord Byron would comment on this incident:

> Of the manner of his death little need be said, except that if a poor radical . . . had cut his throat, he would have been buried in a cross-road, with the usual appurtenances of the stake and mallet. But [he] was an elegant lunatic—a sentimental suicide—he merely cut the "carotid artery," (blessings on their learning!) and lo! the pageant, and the Abbey![30]

Lord Byron's harangue tells us three interesting things, all of which are confirmed by other reports: (1) here in the modern England of the 1820s it was still legal and customary to abuse corpsed persons who had suicided; (2) yet this practice was held in contempt by a growing number of social critics; (3) and the ruling class with its institutionalized hypocrisy could suspend the law at its pleasure. The public protest, it will be remembered, was not against savaging a suicide corpse and burying it at a crossroads but against circumventing the law. The funeral procession was reduced in scale in the hope of avoiding further public outbursts, but some protesters were on hand to express their anger as the pallbearers brought the body into Westminster Abbey.

That a corpse could become a sort of political football was demonstrated again a year later. A young law student had killed himself. His unwashed, still bloodied body was clad only in drawers, socks, and a winding sheet, then wrapped in a bit of cheap matting. The mortal remains of Abel Griffith had been adjudged tainted because he had killed himself in a sound state of mind. Actually, Griffith was mentally ill, as a reliable witness had reported. His true condition had been switched officially from insane to felonious self-murder, while Lord Londonderry's status had been altered in the opposite direction. Barbara T. Gates tells us:

> Constables and watchmen were stationed about the neighborhood of the deceased to keep an eye out for protesters. They would be the last such watchdogs ever needed, for Griffith was the last London suicide known to have been buried at a cross-roads. Glaring legal inequities, like those apparent in the Londonderry and Griffith cases, were to come to an end in mid-1823.[31]

Gates further informs us that the new law required that the suicide be interred in a churchyard or public burial place. Centuries of giving in to superstition, abusing suicide corpses, and playing class politics had come to an end. Only, not quite!

> Superstitions and the desire to punish self-murders remained, however. Suicides had been buried at cross-roads because these were signs of the cross; because steady traffic over the suicide's grave could help to keep the person's ghost down; and because ancient sacrificial victims had been slain at such sites. Since they were considered the ultimate sinners, suicides had been staked to prevent their restless wanderings as lost souls . . . [and even] the 1823 law contained punitive clauses. A *fell-de-se* must still be buried without Christian rites and at night, between the hours of nine and midnight, and his/her goods and chattels must still be turned over to the Crown.[32]

Prejudice against suicide corpses continued throughout the nineteenth century and was picked up in poetry, literature, and drama. Mere law and logic could not easily overcome so fear-ridden a tradition. And the Crown took its regal time before ending the practice of pocketing the goods of suicides, lest these resources be misused in paying for the surviving family's food and shelter.

People kill themselves for a variety of reasons and within a variety of situational contexts. Nevertheless, suicide almost always is an option taken by a person who feels that life has become unbearable and no hope remains. Society would seem to have the inherent purpose of preserving, protecting, and enhancing the lives of its members. Hardly seems fair, does it, that one's own society would continue the abuse after death as well as during life? But not all societies have demonized the suicide and run in terror from the corpse. We have a choice in the matter, a choice we are in a better position to exercise when we have recognized our own demons for what they are and are no longer willing to play politics with the dead. (That will be the day!)

A CONCLUDING WORD:
THE USEFUL DEAD

This chapter has focused less on the spirits of the dead than on the bodies they have left behind. The emphasis on other societies is appropriate because the United States is a fairly recent arrival, coming along after attitudes and practices were strongly established throughout much of the world. We should a least remind ourselves that there has also been "a traffic of dead bodies" in nineteenth-century America, as well researched by Michael Sappol, who reports:

> The upper classes were not obliged to contribute their bodies, only the indigent. Incarceration in the almshouse and burial in potter's field already signified social death. . . . The dissector was a butcher who reduced the human body to the status of thing, to the condition of "meat." . . . The contrast with the "beautiful deaths" depicted in sentimental fiction could not be greater. The utilitarian ethic of the anatomist ("the uses of the dead to the living"), like the commercial ethic of the body snatcher, violated the sacrosanct boundary separating death from life.[33]

Medical students sometimes made things even worse by drunkenly brandishing body parts (of the corpses) from their windows. It would take some years before medical schools could develop and live up to professional standards in the treatment of cadavers and gradually earn the public's respect.

We now cadge a bit from later chapters to offer a simple list of ways in which corpsed persons have been recruited to serve the needs, ambitions, or caprices of society. Some of these uses are perhaps on the way out while others may be coming on strongly. This list is, of course, provisional: who knows what new uses of the cadaver might catch our fancy?

1. the whole corpse for medical education (dissection)
2. the whole corpse or sections for public health and research
3. organs, tissues, and preparations to improve health or extend the lives of other people
4. fetal tissue for the markedly different purposes of basic research and commercial cosmetics
5. the whole corpse—or just the head—frozen for possible rejuvenation (cryonic suspension)
6. the whole body preserved for symbolic and political purposes

A relatively new technique is starting to gain popularity. Plastination involves dehydrating slices of brain, lung, or other cadaver tissues, replacing water and fats with silicone (more commonly known as implants

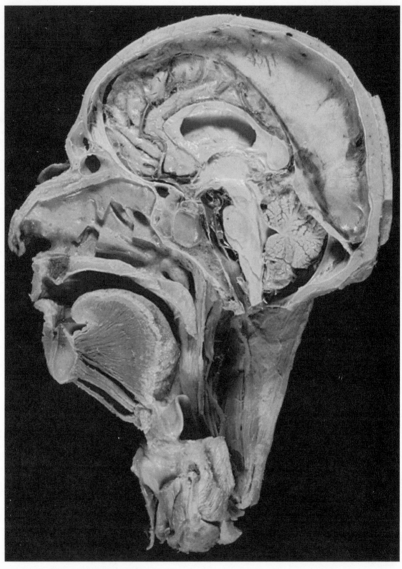

Figure 13 Plastinated section of human brain. Reproduced courtesy of Dr. Roy Glover, Plastination Laboratory, University of Michigan, Ann Arbor, Medical School.

for the living). The Plastination Laboratory of the University of Michigan is one of several that prepare specimens for education and research, and it reports:

> The tissue has no odor and it is extremely durable. Thus, the anatomical specimens are safer to use, more pleasant to use, and are much more durable and have a much longer shelf life.[34]

We seem to have tumbled from immortality to shelf life. This is perhaps as good a time as any to acknowledge that those treasured keepsakes so important in many world religious and funerary practices also have a limited shelf life. Bones deteriorate at various rates under various conditions, with exposure being especially hard on their survival. The effects of time and circumstance on bones are of keen interest to forensic detectives seeking to discover cause of death and perhaps a killer's identity.[35]

Any doubt we might have about the importance of the corpsed person should be dispelled when we consider the anguish experienced by survivors when the body is absent. Families of a victim of an air or sea accident or a person in the military who has remained "missing in action" are likely to suffer continued stress even if a memorial service is conducted without the body.

Yet somebody somewhere is probably designing a *virtual* corpsed person even as we speak. Why not place an even higher and thicker wall around the actual physical remains and replace them with a much improved digitized and customized version? In the meantime, though, we might want to give more attention to the way we think the mortal remains of a human life should be treated and why.

SIX

ABUSING AND EATING
THE DEAD

There are good reasons to behave well toward the dead. Usually we do so. Furthermore, there are many examples of people who have devoted themselves to correcting a perceived injustice to their own dead. Here, though, we explore the opposite response. Abuse of the dead has been widespread throughout the centuries, almost always coexisting with traditions of respect. To neglect this shadow side would restrict and distort our view of humankind's dealings with its dead. We would fail to learn from these stains on the moral fabric of society. Even worse, we would miss out on some interesting stories.

WHY SHOULD WE TREAT THE DEAD WELL?

Why do we usually treat the dead well? There are plenty of good reasons. Here are some of them. First, we usually treat each other well, don't we? Therefore, we are just being our polite, responsible, and caring selves when we do the same with those who are no longer with us in person. *Continuity,* then, is one plausible basis for treating the dead well.

The dead have been deprived of life and therefore of all the experiences, opportunities, and satisfactions that life can offer. This loss is felt even more deeply when people seem to have died before their time or have suffered greatly. We should therefore do what we can for them as they leave this life, and perhaps in their next life as well. *Compensation* for what the dead have lost, then, is another reason for treating them well.

Honoring the dead is a way to comfort the bereaved and help them to move through the grieving process with less pain. We participate in public and private rituals that are beneficial to the family survivors. *Consolation* for the living is, therefore, another reasonable reason for treating the dead well.

Failure to honor the dead could sully our reputations and damage our relationships. *Conformity,* then, may serve as a sufficient reason to show proper respect toward the dead.

Our turn will come. We know this very well even though we may seldom allow ourselves to think about it. A death that is close to us and the events that ensue after it remind us that others will one day observe our passing. We should therefore keep the Golden Rule shining brightly by setting a good example now. *Cycling* communal spirit by treating the dead well today might be a wise investment to assure that this spirit will still be flourishing when we make our exit.

Our religious faith and tradition may require us both to carry out specified actions with respect to the dead and to express a particular type of emotional response, be it extreme anguish or unbridled joy. How and why these traditions originated are a separate topic. Once established, though, ritualized responses toward the dead can possess a power of the sacred that goes far beyond social conformity. *Conviction* in our religious faith and tradition, then, may demand that we follow the well-established ways; furthermore, we will feel better for having done so.

Beware of the Discontented Dead

We have identified six pretty good reasons for treating the dead well without even mentioning what some observers would consider to be the most powerful of all: *fear of the dead.* Sir James George Frazer placed this phenomenon on center stage with an influential book entitled *The Fear of the Dead in Primitive Religion.* He offered many examples in support of his belief that this was both the most common and the most terrifying fear in "primitive" societies throughout the world. Frazer latterly received his comeuppance from anthropologists with more field experience and methodological savvy. He was the urban outsider describing and interpreting people whose ways of life were very different from his own. Frazer, like many other writers of his generation, tended to be judgmental and oblivious to his own biases. Furthermore, his own "field research" consisted of visiting British museums where the "natives" were obliging and a proper lunch (although, again, British) never in doubt. Nevertheless, Frazer digested firsthand reports by those who did have direct contact with a variety of world cultures. Report after report fell into a clear pattern: fear of the dead was both prevalent and salient. This basic finding has survived the critical storm.

Examples can be found in the present as well as past. Consider, if you will, two very different contexts within which fear of the dead has been expressed in our own times.

The majestic wilderness of the American Southwest has long been home to tribal communities with the skill and stamina to survive desert heat, hardship, and hazard. For a time, this forbidding ecology protected the native peoples from massive invasion by white settlers, who opted instead for rolling plains, green valleys, and enticing coasts. Inevitably, though, "the course of Western empire" reached into this remote domain as well. An expansionist national agenda, railroads, gold strikes, and other commercial prospects spurred a wave of gritty opportunists but did not have an immediate and decisive impact on the old ways. The Tohono O'odham in particular were not in the primary path of the westward drive, nor were they either a wealthy or a warlike people.[1] Fast-forward now to the sociotechnological changes that followed the conclusion of World War II. Air travel had conquered distance; air-conditioning had provided refuge from desert heat. Truck stops became cities. Rivers were emptied for large-scale agricultural, industrial, and residential purposes. The O'odham were not pursued by murderous cavalry. Nevertheless, they were to suffer immensely as they became outcasts in their own land. The consequence that speaks most directly to us here was a heightened fear of the dead. How can that be? What is the connection?

Anthropologist David Lee Kozak is our guide to the Tohono O'odham, now of the Sells Reservation in southern Arizona.[2] He leads us first to their alarming rise in youth mortality from the 1960s onward. Males are dying young and dying violently. Wave after wave of young men fall away. Perhaps surprisingly, the infant mortality rate has been decreasing markedly. More deaths and fewer deaths at the same time? The O'odham are benefiting from improved health care services, yet continue to be devastated economically by the loss of employment opportunities: victims of "progress." The mechanization of the local cotton industry cost many jobs. The global market for copper also declined, and there went many other jobs at the nearby mines. Few alternative sources of employment were available.

A distressing story—but where does fear of the dead come in?

Some young men became reluctant migrants in search of work. Others stayed on the reservation. They drew welfare payments but had no occupation or other manly role. Both choices often proved disastrous to self-esteem and emotional health. The migrants were deprived of their supportive community and adrift in the impersonal and alienating mainstream culture. Those who stayed had little incentive and little opportunity. Drinking problems increased and, all too predictably, so did vehicular fatalities. Young males died not only in accidents and brawls but also at their own hands. Suicide rates for men increase with age in the mainstream United States, peaking in the later adult years. The reverse has become true for the O'odham. Stress, deprivation, and anomie are most severe for the young, particularly for males.

These circumstances have had a profound effect on the older generations: parents and grandparents recognize the threat to the tribal future as well as to the continuity of their own line as young males perish. That is not all, however. *Most of these young men have died badly.* They have not become the *wickol* soul at the moment of death. In other words, they have not died in peace with themselves and with their people. Sudden and violent death has prevented them from entering the next world in a state of spiritual readiness. This troubled demise spells more trouble for the community as well. The young men have died unnatural and unpredictable deaths, upsetting the basic order of things. Furthermore, their spirits, their ghosts, are dangerous. Kozak explains:

> All O'odham are deeply affected by the violent death of these young adults. Death is of course emotionally charged on a personal level, but it is also emotionally charged on a social level. A violent death can precipitate other bad or dangerous situations. A "bad" death is "bad" because evil caused it, which leaves the soul of the dead unrestful, unfulfilled, and desirous of returning to the living out of a longing for what has been taken away. The soul returns to the living, although not out of malevolence, to visit loved ones. It is on these visits that the dead can bring a

form of *karcim mumkidag* (staying—Indian—sickness), to the living—
hence their dangerousness.[3]

It would be a mistake, though, to conclude that fear is the only attitude toward the dead in a particular society. Frazer seems to have emphasized fear to the neglect of other feelings. Sorrow, yearning, and respect are also common human responses to a death, and these responses
may continue over the long term as well as in the period of official mourning. The O'odham, for example, certainly grieve over the premature
deaths of their young. They also have devised a way to express their grief
while reducing the danger of fatal visitations from the deceased.

> To counteract this danger, the living erect death-memorials so that the soul
> of a "bad" death victim will return to the location of their demise, rather
> than returning to their previous, worldly residence. The death-memorial,
> and all of the ritual objects placed there, lures the soul away from locations
> where it could do harm (the family residence). But the death-memorial is
> also the location where family and friends of the deceased go to assist the
> soul to *si'alig weco*. This term means "beyond the eastern horizon," and
> it is where all O'odham souls reside after death.[4]

Once the dead have completed their journey beyond the eastern horizon,
the living need fear them no longer.

Fear of the dead takes many forms and occurs on many levels. Here
is an example from a second and very different cultural context: the mainstream American health care system.

When Nurse Beamish popped into my office, I assumed it was to report a problem with a patient or a tiff between staff members that the
psychology service might be able to remedy, if we did not, in fact, make
it worse. What concerned her, however, was a recurrent dream. Helen
had been showing up in her dreams lately. This was a long-time friend
who had passed over to the other side a few months previously. Helen
was not in a friendly mood, though. She had been cross with Nurse
Beamish, thereby spoiling her dream, her night's sleep, and even her
next day. I wondered aloud if Helen was an image, a representation.
Nurse Beamish was surprised that I might think such a thing. "She was
Helen!" There was no doubt that it was the real—though deceased—
Helen who had been spoiling her dreams lately. Moreover, Nurse Beamish
was not spooked by these visitations. No, being contacted by a dead

person was not at all strange. After all, Helen did have her rights of visitation.

How's that again? "She made me promise I would burn some letters she left in her bureau drawer with a nice ribbon around them. And I didn't burn them. So she has a right to scold me. She's really being mean, though. I feel like a no-good for letting her down." Helen was always a stubborn person, Nurse Beamish explained, so she probably would continue to make the nurse's life miserable.

We made progress with this dilemma when Nurse Beamish agreed to discuss the whole matter openly with Helen next time around, being sure to explain why she had been hesitating to do what had been promised. I heard no more about the problem from either Nurse Beamish or Helen and therefore entered this episode into my books as a therapeutic triumph (a list that was definitely in need of more entries). Here, then, was Nurse Beamish, a professional health care provider, socialized and educated in mainstream culture, who had readily accepted dreaming as a modality for contact with the dead. Her particular fear of the dead was rational (she hadn't kept her promise) and only put her out of sorts rather than turning her into a quivering mass of protoplasm. That visitations from the dead per se can be regarded as unremarkable events serves to remind us that what Frazer culled from the library shelves can still be observed today.

We now have no fewer than seven reasons for behaving well toward the dead. It is against this background that we begin our considerations of behavior that goes in the opposite direction. Why in heaven would anybody want to treat the dead badly? What circumstances encourage actions that go so much against the grain of many cultural traditions and their moral precepts? And what exactly might be meant by "abuse" of the dead?

IS DEATH A MAN'S WORLD, TOO?

It was a Sunday morning in 1975, and one of the cats had sprawled across the newspaper section I was most interested in reading. There was a second cup of coffee to sip, and the only available section of the paper was the death notices. I wondered again how people managed to die alphabetically. This was certainly a convenience to the editorial assistants charged with the melancholy task of inexorably preparing mortality lists day after day. Bunny, my wife, had a more penetrating observation. She noticed that the deceased men in this edition must have been a deal more distinguished and worthy than their female counterparts. This imbalance occurred in the obituary section where the selected dead are given a longer and more individualized write-up. For the next few days we scanned both sections. Bunny's observations were holding up. "Time for a study!" I decided; Bunny agreed, and student Sara Peyton was invited to read and abstract about four thousand death notices and about five hundred obituaries. These encompassed all such entries appearing in the *Boston Globe* and the *New York Times* in March 1975. (Ms. Peyton had hoped for February.)

The results were clear for both of the big-city newspapers: women were much less likely to be accorded obituaries.[5] Although death itself did not discriminate between genders, the editorial departments certainly did. Obituaries favored men by a four-to-one ratio in both newspapers. Furthermore, only in one day of March's thirty-one did the number of female obituaries equal the number of male in Boston, and this never happened in New York. As fastidious scientists we were not so easily satisfied. Ms. Peyton was given custody of a high-tech measuring device known to researchers as a ruler. The new set of numbers revealed that women received not only fewer but also briefer obituaries. Overall, men were worth about six more lines.

We extracted one more bit of dependable data from the limited information available. Was a photograph of the deceased included in the obituary? In Boston, only about one recently deceased man in fifty received an obituary with a photograph. The odds were certainly against the man who perished within the domain of the *Boston Globe*. The odds for women? Five hundred to one! In New York the newly dead male had about three chances in a hundred for the deluxe illustrated obituary. Women? Only about one chance in a thousand.

As already mentioned, this was way back in 1975, but it was a time when social conscience had been well pricked by disclosures of sexism. Both the governmental and private sectors were proclaiming anew their commitment to equal treatment. It had become increasingly difficult to pretend that inequalities did not exist. On the surface, then, sex discrimination was no longer tolerated by right-thinking Americans. It seemed to us, though, that treatment of the dead involved attitudes and practices so deeply ingrained in our way of life that surface changes might take a longer time to reach the depths. So far as our limited study could take us, it appeared that the sex discrimination endemic throughout life also persisted beyond the grave. Many questions were not addressed by this simple study. Are females also discriminated against throughout the entire process of postdeath activities or only when caught in the coils of mass media? It would also have been interesting to learn how far beyond the grave this discrimination might persist, but our ruler was not long enough.

Other researchers soon took up the cause (some of them with actual budgets). Our basic findings were replicated and extended in other parts of the United States and in an African city. A recent review of the literature finds "little change over time in the recognition of women after death. Consistently fewer obituaries are written about women, fewer obituary lines note the accomplishments of women, and fewer pictures of women appear on the obituary page."[6] Historians Bettie Anne Doebler and Retha M. Warnicke widened the exploration by examining funeral sermons in seventeenth-century England. They discovered a clear pattern of male preference in the relative number of funeral sermons published for women and men and also in the texts, which "helped to perpetuate the sex differences in society." These scholars read something deeper in these findings than simple favoritism for one gender over the other. They note:

> *The Book of Common Prayer* emphasized a human image that was neither distinctly male or female. The generalized service of "The Burial of the Dead" seemed to assume Christ's assertion in Matthew that there would be no sexual distinctions nor beings "given in marriage" in the resurrection. In short, all Christian souls would reside in heaven in a state of love that transcended gender or sexual possessiveness.[7]

Notwithstanding the powerful influence of the Book of Common Prayer, all Christian souls were not being accorded equal treatment and respect. Gender discrimination after death cannot be confined to one time or place. How long this has been going on and what forms it has taken are among the questions that have yet to be answered. We are entitled to wonder, however, why there is such an inclination to show less respect for women in the immediate postdeath period.

Other researchers have documented that gender discrimination persists. The contributions and distinctions made by women throughout their lives remain underreported, underappreciated, and underrewarded. Death seems to become one more opportunity to affirm a cultural value: by and large, men are more important than women. Gender equality has not yet penetrated below ground level.

THE INCONVENIENT DEAD

The dead are at risk for neglect and abuse when they just happen to be inconvenient. This risk occurs many times each day in our health care system, including nursing homes as well as hospitals. To be inconvenient, a person need only become a corpse in the wrong place, at the wrong time, or in the wrong way.

Let us return to Cushing Hospital, the state geriatric facility where a dedicated staff was doing its best to care for too many residents in a place that was crumbling into ruin above, below, and around us (literally so, and with abysmally low budget priority). Most of the residents were in their mideighties and burdened with multiple impairments and life-threatening conditions. Whether they had been in the hospital for five days or five years, almost all would end their lives here. Death was expectable, then. The challenge to the staff was finding a way to provide comfort and, if possible, some semblance of a normal and positive social environment despite the depressing circumstances. Doctors and nurses who required that their patients quickly recover and bounce back to an active life in the community usually bugged out at the first opportunity. The fact that this isolated little fortress of aging and death was located at the fringe of the community and right across from the town dump also failed to inspire much enthusiasm among the go-getters in the health care system. Many of those who did remain in service over the years made their homes in apartments on the hospital's spacious campus, which became a small town of its own.

What might we expect of this little community's dealings with death? Much of the staff had education and training in health care. Almost all were church-going people who had been socialized since childhood into traditional religious ways. They had accepted a responsibility that many others spurned: care for frail and vulnerable elders who had no other place to go. It was also not unusual for staff to become very fond of some of their patients and treat them almost as members of their family. And, of course, they knew their patients would die.

Had I known enough to expect anything when I first set foot into this hospital community, it probably would have included the following: The staff would regard death as a natural occurrence in this situation and therefore would not respond in a highly stressed manner or come completely undone. They would have rituals in place that helped to affirm the value of both the life and the death of the deceased and offered comfort to the survivors. Residents of the facility would also have the opportunity to participate in these rituals, at least those who had known the deceased well. And, finally, there would be an effective informal support network, for example, staff getting together for a drink to share their memories of the deceased and assure one another that they had done their best.

I would have been mistaken, of course, mistaken all the way. It was not unusual for staff to be thrown for a loop when a resident died. There was very little support for staff and none for fellow residents through either formal or informal procedures. (A few might slip away to the chapel to say their personal prayers, but this consolation was seldom available to those who could not ambulate through the lengthy corridors.) Staff were stressed by a death and often had no place to turn. The implicit rule was, "We don't talk about such things." The corollary was, "We don't want to upset the residents by talking about such things." Individuals, then, were locked into their own thoughts and feelings and pressured to deny even these. In place of an affirmative ritual was a code of silence: "Nothing happened, and there is nothing that needs to be said or done." Researchers in other health care systems have made similar observations about the pattern of silence, avoidance, and denial that so often has surrounded death.

The dead suffered as well. Generally they were whisked out of sight as soon as possible. The person who violated the code by dying inappropriately was most at risk. One such perpetrator was a resident of the "best" male ward, that is, the unit for men who were mentally alert and could take care of most of their personal needs. I happened to visit this ward one day just as a melodramatic scene was reaching its conclusion. Even from a distance one could see that the usually placid unit had taken on an urgent character, people moving about at an uncharacteristically hectic pace and without clear direction. At the center of the doings was a physician who had recently joined the staff. She was issuing a barrage of orders in a loud and agitated voice. The other major player had no lines in this scene. He was stretched out on his bed as dead as dead can be.

Other patients and ward staff listened in astonishment as the doctor ordered that the resident's clothes be delivered promptly to another ward. Our mistake! Mr. X was going to be fine. He just needed to be transferred to another ward. Physician and patient departed in a flurry that lacked only blaring sirens. Patients and staff drifted back to their routines. Mum was definitely the word. One of the old New Englanders, however, could not resist nudging the ward clerk: "Hurry, now! Ezra wants his clothes. He has a hot date!" The clerk rolled her eyes and tried to make herself invisible. Everybody on the ward was well aware that the patient was dead regardless of the doctor's charade. The denial had been so ludicrous that staff and residents shared a moment of grim humor. In time, though, this physician would learn how to manage deaths on the ward with more finesse and thereby assure the deceased's exit from society with scarcely a ripple. The only thing really exceptional about this episode was the lack of skill demonstrated in carrying off the charade when a patient had died inconveniently.

Mr. G. and Mr. B.

Consider, if you will, a more protracted sequence of events through which the process of ridding ourselves of the inconsiderate dead became an ordeal for the survivor. On this same open-ward unit, Mr. G. awoke one morning to notice that Mr. B. was not in his bed. Nobody was. Furthermore, the bed had already been made up, even though it was early in the morning. The uneasy feeling already had its grip on Mr. G., but he strolled about the ward and then a little farther, in hopes of seeing his best friend on the ward—actually, the best friend he had left in the world. As the day lengthened it became evident that Mr. B. was no longer among them. Not a word was spoken about Mr. B. and his fate. The ward staff scrupulously avoided the area around Mr. B.'s bed and were poised for flight whenever it seemed that a resident might have a question to ask. What could be more conclusive?

Mr. G. knew the drill. When a resident died, one must behave as though that person had never lived. One suffered, though. One suffered from the loss, from the lack of closure, and from the intensified isolation, feeling more alone than ever. And worse than that. Mr. G. would later tell me that the code of silence around Mr. B. made him realize that the same would be his fate as well. A quiet, reserved man, Mr. G. had to make a great effort to express himself: "Mr. B. was such a wonderful man. He was dignified. Much better than me. And now it's like he never was born. Like he never was anything. . . . That will be me. . . . I'm sorry, I'm sorry [he weeps]. I wish I were dead. I am dead."

Other residents and even some staff members also confided that they were profoundly disturbed when the dead were carted away without a proper farewell. Although they participated in this evasive process themselves, staff often felt it was wrong to treat the dead so coldly. But the anxiety was even more personal. One of them confided to me, "I hope and pray that they won't just shovel me away. It breaks my heart just to think about that."

Back to Mr. G. He resigned himself to his friend's death as best he could. About three months later Mr. G. was on his exercise route through the endless corridors. Turning a blind corner, he literally bumped into Mr. B. It turns out his friend had been sent to the intensive care unit and did recover from a life-threatening emergency. He was now on a ward distant from Mr. G.'s. Although overjoyed to see that his old friend was still among the living, Mr. G. trembled from the shock for several days. He would have been spared both the grieving and the shock had there been a communication network that respected the needs and rights of the residents, but such was not the case.

And this was not the end of Mr. G.'s postmortem encounters with Mr. B. Only a few weeks later he heard via the grapevine that Mr. B. had died again. This was followed after a while by a report that Mr. B. was still alive, though now bedridden. Eventually it became my task to inform Mr. G. that his friend had died for keeps. All through this time, Mr. G., a man with little left to cherish in his life, had been put through an emotional wringer.

At the core of this ordeal was the institution's determination to maintain its own sense of comfort by spiriting away the inconvenient dead without the least attention to spirit. Institutions work hard to maintain "the order of things." The most effective hospital cannot predict all emergencies, mend all frailties, preserve all lives. The hospital must nevertheless preserve its own sense of control and viability. Unexpected or stressful deaths are challenges to the illusion of control. Staff members are pressured to conform to the hospital community's hasty and apparently uncaring disposal of the dead regardless of their personal feelings.

Two other processes are at work. One is the common human response to the presence of a corpse. Awe, fear, wonder, respect, and an indefinable sense of personal involvement often are evoked. Our own respiration and heart rate is likely to change when we encounter a person who no longer breathes or has a heartbeat. Professional experience and familiarity with corpses can reduce, but not completely tame, this response.

The other process is more communal, though also linked to the individual experience of a corpse: *decontamination* of the dead. Hospitals have technical and legal responsibilities in this regard, as do those who provide mortuary services. The corpse, its garments, and its immediate surroundings should be handled in a safe and sanitary manner. An ancient and deeper response lies beneath the utilitarian, however. Many world cultures have taboos against touching a human corpse. Even use of the word *dead* may be proscribed. However, the modern hospital system can be observed using decontamination and distancing rituals that go beyond what is necessary from a medical or legal standpoint.

Is the neglect and abuse perhaps also motivated by the system's covert anger at patients who die in the wrong way, time, or place? We have no dependable evidence on this point, but I have witnessed some staff responses that do raise the question. Dealings with the physical remains must conform with established practices and regulations. The deceased's dignity and status in society lack this protection and are more vulnerable to neglect and abuse.

THE CONVENIENT DEAD

Who, then, are the *convenient* dead? Who are the people who die when, where, and how they should? Mrs. Q. was one such. She became a resident of this facility upon the death of the last family member who could have looked after her. Mrs. Q. seemed a lost soul at first but soon became absorbed into the institution's routines and, as a staff member described her to me, "was always grateful for any little thing you would do for her." After some time she grew weaker, needing more assistance in her daily activities. She was transferred to a ward for the frail and vulnerable. This was a clear signal that Mrs. Q. was heading toward the last stations of her life. An infection brought her to the acute care unit. This was not considered an inexorable step toward death, however, because successful treatments were fairly common. In her case there was a brief reprieve and return to her home ward, but this was followed by renal failure. The prognosis was well established by now. Mrs. Q.'s decline could not be reversed. Accordingly, there was no sense of urgency or conflict on the part of the staff. They had done what they could for Mrs. Q., and all they could do now was to see her through to the end with comfort and dignity.

Up to this point Mrs. Q.'s passage through the institutional labyrinth had been slow and predictable. She had moved through the stations of aging and failing health in accordance with "standard operating procedure." Mrs. Q. completed her life's journey on the same sensible track. Her admission to the intensive care unit signaled her probable demise within a short time. There was still another step or two to go. Mrs. Q. was slipping away into a semicomatose state. She could be roused but soon would slip away again. This further indication that life was also slipping away led to a spatial change as well. Mrs. Q. was placed in a corner of the ward, where her final days would not be subject to view except by those charged with her care.

Even within a unit known to staff as Death Valley, it was useful to reserve a smaller, set-apart sanctum.[8] Just as Death Valley protected the rest of the hospital, so this little corner for the actively dying served to keep death from contaminating the rest of the unit. It was only a day later that the curtains were drawn around Mrs. Q. This signaled that she and Death were seeing each other in private. The staff was saddened by the passing of this gentle old woman. The institution was not convulsed or threatened by her death, however. She had lived and died so conveniently. Every proper and convenient death helps strengthen the illusion that death is obeying protocol, playing by the rules.

People die at home, too. And not only at home. The morning paper today reported several motor vehicle fatalities, the death of a young man who had leaped from a popular lakeside cliff, and at least four fresh homicides. Medical records will indicate that others succumbed to strokes or heart attacks while going about their business or pleasure. As family mem-

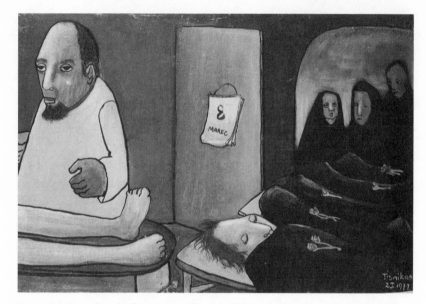

Figure 14 Attending dead women on Slovenia's Women's Day. Joze Tisnikar, the Slovenian artist who created this painting (1971), once had a day job preparing corpses for burial, and he said, "In Slovenia, we celebrate International Women's Day, March 8th. The men congratulate the women, give them flowers, and are generally attentive. Once on that day, when I came in for my shift, I found a number of dead women. I was sad to see the cadavers lying there cold and abandoned on that special day, when all the other women were being given flowers and attention by men. It occurred to me to go into town . . . buy some flowers, and put one on each of them. And that's what I did. You may ask why I did it? There was no one else to give them flowers that day." From Nebojsa Tomasevic, *Tisnikar: Painter of Death* (New York: Two Continents, 1977), fig. 14.

bers, companions, or bystanders, most of us are not as well programmed to deal with inconvenient deaths. This means we are more vulnerable to stressful reactions.

We are also more likely to feel that "something should be done" for the person whose life has ended so abruptly. It would strike us as cold and inappropriate just to pack the body off and go on as though nothing had happened. (In a sense, though, nothing *had* happened.) We would want to "pay our respects" in some way, perhaps by supporting the next of kin and trying to see that the funereal and memorial process does justice to the family's values. We would sense that a failure to behave well toward both the corpse and the image of the deceased would also be a form of neglect and abuse of those who are most grieved by the loss.

Unlike operatives in the health care system, most of us do not have a massive investment in institutional pretense for its own survival. We can be shaken. We can be upset. We can be uncertain about what to do next. In a word, we can be human. Nevertheless, some of us may be so unnerved by the unexpected death that we slip away from the communal concern and try to seal over the place in our psyche where mortality has for a moment penetrated. The dropout from funeral and memorial activities may have a variety of motives for his or her behavior. One of the most powerful motives, though, is the painful reminder of past personal losses suffered and one's own mortality. Those who witness unexpected death in the community cannot disappear into the polished routines of institutional avoidance and neglect.

DEHUMANIZING, PUNISHING, AND SAVAGING THE DEAD

Neglect easily fuzzes over into abuse. And abuse of the dead tends to fuzz over into abuse of the living. Here is a recollection of a hospital experience in one of the world's great cities. What do you see in this episode?

> Old Numero 57 lying crumpled up on his side, his face sticking out over the side of the bed, and towards me. He had died some time during the night, nobody knew when. When the nurses came they received the news of his death indifferently and went about their work. After a long time, an hour or more, two other nurses marched in abreast like soldiers, with a great clumping of sabots, and knotted the corpse up in sheets, but it was not removed until some time later. Meanwhile, in the better light, I had had time for a good look at him. I had seen dead men before, usually people who had died violent deaths. Numero 57's eyes were still open, his mouth still open, his small face contorted in an expression of agony. . . . As I gazed at the tiny screwed-up face it struck me that this disgusting piece of refuse, waiting to be carted away and dumped on a slab in the dissecting room, was an example of "natural" death, one of the things you pray for in the Litany.[9]

Perhaps you react very strongly against the statement that Numero 57 had become a "disgusting piece of refuse." This statement seems to deny Numero 57 his humanity, not even to mention whatever connection any and every person might have to the sacred. Furthermore, you have probably gathered that this hospital served those marginalia of society who could not afford more respectable and effective treatment. It was a huge charity hospital, and this was "How the Poor Die," as the author, George Orwell, entitled this reminiscence. Although we might not condone the characterization of any human corpse as disgusting refuse, it is easy to understand how this impression would fix itself in the mind of a person who was himself suffering from a life-threatening condition in a nearby bed. The author had observed the way Numero 57 was allowed to be exposed in his terminal agony and not considered worth even a passing remark by the indifferent nurses. And the author could well envision the same, if not worse, happening to him. His reflections included this bitter vein of thought:

> There you are then, I thought, that's what is waiting for you, 20, 30, 40 years hence: that is how the lucky ones die, the ones who live to be old. One wants to live, of course, indeed one only stays alive by virtue of the fear of death, but I think now, as I thought then, that it's better to die violently and not too old. . . . Natural death, almost by definition, means something slow, smelly, and painful.[10]

The author was scarred by this experience. Already disenchanted with what he had observed of society as a young journalist, he became even more deeply disturbed by this evidence of dehumanization and indifference to suffering that pursued the unfortunate not only to their death but even beyond. Orwell's grim vision *1984* alarmed the world. As people reflected on where we might all be headed in a future dystopia, they were also indirectly responding to the expression of agony on Numero 57's face. Good can come of this as well. By the time 1984 did roll around, Orwell's native England had become the beacon for the international hospice movement, dedicated to the proposition that natural death does not have to rob people of their dignity and values or be followed by bureaucracy's vicious indifference.

Postmortem Assault as Virtue

At his death Numero 57 had been treated as nonhuman and victimized by a kind of postmortem punishment inflicted without judge, jury, or legal counsel. But history provides us with striking examples in which savage punishment of the dead was ordained by the prevailing justice system. Here we meet up with a rather startling idea: *savaging the dead is good for us*. Mutilating a corpse is an act of virtue. It demonstrates the triumph of good over evil or, more pragmatically, makes it clear whose side one should be on. The conviction that savaging a corpse is a justified, even a required, action must be powerful enough to overcome all the persuasive reasons for respecting the dead. Here is an instructive example of corpse mutilation as a considered and virtuous outcome of the legal process as it operated in England in the year 1326.

> Hugh, you are found traitor, wherefore all the good people of the kingdom, great and small, rich and poor, by common assent do award, That you are found as a thief, and therefore shall be hanged; and are found as a traitor, and therefore shall be drawn and quartered; and for that you have been outlawed by the king, and by common assent, and returned to the court without warrant, you shall be beheaded and for that you abetted and procured discord between the king and queen, and others of the realm, you shall be embowelled, and your bowels burnt. Withdraw, traitor, tyrant and so go take your judgment, attainted wicked traitor.[11]

It was not enough simply to execute Hugh Despenser the Younger. Either hanging or beheading would have accomplished that. Instead his various alleged crimes had each to receive their specific punishments. The imposed sentence established continuity between assault on the living and the dead personage of Hugh Despenser the Younger. Death by hanging is not always instantaneous. There are many reports of the victim suffering a painful and lingering death and even being hoisted up to the gallows for one or more repeats if the first one did not do its job. Presumably in this case Hugh was securely dead before his insides were ripped out. (A century later some priests and suspected antiregime activists were deliberately torn apart as part of a slow, torturous execution.) But for Hugh, the assault that began with hanging would continue until his bowels had been burned as a way of reminding the crowd that the regime is not amused by dissidents.

The purposes of deterrence and retribution were served by the postmortem assault on Hugh and others who were convicted of offenses considered most threatening to the regime. No documents have surfaced to tell us precisely why these indulgences in overkill were considered necessary. We are free to speculate. The following are four possibilities, and perhaps you will come up with others.

So much fury was directed at the culprit (and the cause for which the culprit advocated) that this rage and its underlying anxiety could not be discharged by a quick stroke of the ax. The main event had to be prolonged and provide the opportunity for the satisfying release of anger. An alternative would have been to torture or starve the condemned person until death finally provided release. This alternative was, in fact, practiced occasionally in medieval England and elsewhere. Postmortem assault, then, might be regarded as an act of mercy.

There was a point to be made in reducing the physical remains to a bloody and horrible mess. Actually, two points. First, the corpse would have lost most of its recognizably human characteristics. This could reduce any latent impulse toward compassion. That disfigured and disgusting object is not at all like us, is it? Second, even God might not want Hugh Despenser the Younger now. Many believed that mutilation of the body much endangered one's opportunity for a thriving life in the hereafter (this belief would remain operative five hundred years later when surgeons and their helpful little Igors started to dig up cadavers for postmortem study). Corpse mutilation, then, could be a technique for separating dissidents from their god.

Dissidents and enemies of the state have been known to rally around the body of a fallen leader. In our own time there have been lethal attacks on mourners during the funeral procession or at the burial site. There is that much less opportunity for mourners to demonstrate their support and perhaps fulminate other mischief if the body is massively disfigured and then quickly removed. Make that "spirited away."

Perhaps—just perhaps—a rather different theme was also being expressed through these postmortem assaults. The individual's share of the holy spirit could be thought to reside within the body. This belief has been held in various world cultures. For example, *hara-kiri* is a Japanese term composed of the characters that originally meant "cutting of the stomach." The sacred breath is thereby released through this ritualistic form of suicide. Unfortunately, a person might also be possessed by an evil or demonic spirit. Possession and exorcism were well known in Christian as well as "pagan" lands. Along with retribution and deterrence, then, perhaps such postmortem assaults as ripping out and burning the innards served the beneficial purpose of curing the sinner by expelling the evil spirit within.

Speculation aside, spiked heads were a common sight in often-not-so-merry old England. These heads most often had topped the necks of low-down criminals, but prominent citizens, even nobility, were also eligible for this postmortem exhibition if they sufficiently annoyed the current power brokers. Rulers, as a rule, were even harder on adversaries from inside the regime and liked to make examples of them.

Bloodied History

Outbursts of postmortem assault on one's own neighbors have also occurred repeatedly throughout history. In pre–Civil War Kansas, for example, mobs attacked people known or suspected as abolitionists. These unarmed fellow citizens were beaten and stabbed to death.[12] Their fallen bodies were kicked and mutilated in a blood frenzy. In general, when mobs (including undisciplined armies) abandon themselves to slaughter there is also the distinct possibility that corpses will be mutilated. Ordinary rules of conduct are suspended. Many of the Japanese soldiers who raped and killed civilians in Nanking were model citizens before and after the war.[13] Savage abuse of the dead is not always sanctioned by established authority; it can also be the consequence of a murderous exultation that knows no limits.

Systematic terrorism draws from both official sanction and unmodulated impulse. For example, the sort of atrocities we used to speak of as unspeakable were on occasion committed by Crusaders and Saracens, against each other and against innocent civilians.[14] Disfigurement of the dead was an overflow from bloody acts inflicted on the living. The Crusades and counter-Crusades were officially countenanced ventures. The extremes of violence and desecration, however, were not in accord with the religious and ethical principles that presumably guided all sides in the conflict. Once the gods of war gain sway there is no assurance that even such basic humanitarian values as sparing children and respecting the dead will be honored.

Examples of mutilating the enemy (or simply the other) are depressingly abundant. Vlad the Impaler well earned his sobriquet. Not only potential invaders but even harmless travelers were effectively forewarned as they approached Vlad's turf and saw row after row of the impaled dying and dead.[15] There were nine sacks of severed ears to haul back to Batu the Splendid when Baibar Khan's Mongols slaughtered a large multinational force of defenders.[16] Other armies have selected other body parts as trophies.

We might ask why a particular body part is favored for mutilation or amputation. Again, speculation reigns. Perhaps some body parts are simply easier to hack off and carry along, such as Baibar's cache of ears. Perhaps some are especially persuasive as evidence of the kill. A severed head would be a credible testament to its owner's loss. This practice was often favored when proof was demanded that a particular rival had been eliminated. Soldiers have been known to mutilate the sexual organs of women they have raped, and women have on occasion done the same to the corpses of enemy warriors.

And what do you think about this: when either male or female victors cut off the penis and testicles of their enemies, are they doing so as a symbolic way of destroying the their rival's fertility? Sigmund Freud would probably like the opportunity to answer that question.

Desecrations of the dead often occur within the flow of violence rather than as an independent action. Hussite armies invading Prussia in the fifteenth century entertained themselves by singing a ditty called "We, Warriors of God." Desmond Seward tells us that the catchy verse ended "Slay, slay, slay, slay them every one!"[17] The boom of their war drum was by courtesy of the stretched skin of their deceased "blind and terrible leader," Zizka. Some of the invaders were captured in the forest and burned alive. The following desecration of the remains was but a continuation of the killing frenzy. The Knights Templars of the twelfth century had a code of good behavior to follow, but this did not extend to unbelievers whose remains could be disrespected in whatever manner came to mind. John Wilkes Booth's body was used for target practice, and acid was thrown upon the executed remains of another presidential assassin, Leon Czolgosz.

And—horror within horror—Nazis abused millions of civilians, massacred them, and stole their hair and teeth before destroying their bodies. Hate can be so powerful a force that its violence will not be satisfied with death.

Not all operations performed on the dead are intended as abuse. Headhunters do not necessarily despise their enemies. In fact, they might trade and consort with them on other occasions, even intermarry. The more powerful the adversary, the more valuable the memento. Additionally heads can be precious hand-me-downs to the next generation from one's own ancestors (or even other people's worthy ancestors). These keepsake skulls often served as intermediaries between the world of the living and that of the dead.

Furthermore, saints were often harvested for sanctified body parts (as were the anonymous dead whose parts might be passed off for the real thing), as previously discussed. If we were to view the body of a raided saint, we might be appalled at the disfigurement and come to the mistaken conclusion that here was a reviled person to whom postmortem punishment was justly dealt. Customarily, physical remains attributed to saints (often bones or hair) were sealed in *reliquaries* for their protection. Devotees might have approached these reliquaries (sometimes supplemented by adjacent images of the saint) and uttered prayers in their presence. The magico-spiritual power of saintly remains was impressive enough to overcome the traditional aversion to contact with the dead.[18]

Other cultures have made a more direct use of remains in their rituals. Here is an example as described by Tom F. Driver:

> In the New Guinea highlands, at the death of a man or boy, a close female relative will chop off a piece of a finger or even the whole finger. (This is not done, I think, at the death of a female.) In these instances and many others—think of circumcisions, scarifications, elaborate body decorations—the body is dedicated to the service of display. It is offered as the vehicle of communication.[19]

This part-for-the-whole symbolism is one of the basic principles of folk magic, which, in turn, is often intertwined with religious belief. The severed digit may be particularly suitable as a link to the deceased. It is recognizably human and small, therefore easy to deal with and to include in dance and gesture. Furthermore, when in everyday life we wish to point the way to a destination, a finger comes in mighty handy; so may it be along the path that leads from one life to the next.

In addition to these examples, it is well known that the corpse can have such life-affirming uses as medical education and organ transplantation, sometimes known as organ harvesting. Some people volunteer their physical remains for the benefit of the living. Using is a lot different from abusing. Similar actions can have different meanings. We will dish up some further examples immediately.

RITUALS AND VICTUALS

Cannibalism is one of those topics that most people cannot stomach unless they happen to be ten-year-old horror freaks or the Hannibal Lecter character. Experts on funeral and memorial practices have also been mum on the subject. There are abundant discussions of burial and cremation in their many variations but scarcely a word about cannibalism as a way of exiting the dead. We do meet up with cannibals in fiction, reportage, and scholarly papers. There is little or no attention, however, to the fact that cannibalism is, among other things, a modality of body disposal. We will make a small beginning here, with particular interest in the question of whether or not eating people is wrong, that is, unsanctionable and abusive.

Running Afoul of Cannibalism

A few have studied what most others consider too unpalatable and have offered practical suggestions. We share these observations presented by Phillip J. Clauer. Cannibalism, he finds, is usually caused by overcrowding, excessive heat, excessive light, absence of food or water, unbalanced diets, mixing different types within the population, or abrupt changes in environment or leadership.[20] His suggestions for prevention include finding other ways for the population to discharge their energies, using restraint devices on the most aggressive, and—perhaps best of all— trimming the beaks (use experienced beak-trimmers only).

So much for cannibalism among chickens (although Clauer, poultry extension specialist for the Virginia Cooperative Extension, has a good deal more to say on the subject). Our point here, of course, is simply a reminder that cannibalism occurs in many species, from bugs to primates. The poultry expert warns that "the vicious habit of cannibalism can spread rapidly through the entire flock. . . . Once this habit gets out of hand it is difficult to eliminate." It is alarming and offensive that one chicken might eat another. The fair exit for a fowl is through *our* digestive tract. I don't see any bias or illogic there, do you?

Actually, there might be just a little inconsistency. The megacorporations that "produce" poultry often feed chickens to chickens (or parts thereof, or . . . don't ask!). I once had the good fortune to sit next to a chicken feed representative during the longest three-hour flight in airline history. Upon inquiry, he described the nonlife of the pigeon-holed chickens, who never pranced in a barnyard or clucked sociably with companions. His enthusiasm was reserved for the efficiency of the operation. These producers reduced waste and saved big bucks by feeding processed chicken feathers to those who would in turn bequeath the same to the next generation. The light of a true zealot shined in his eyes as he confided that his outfit was in position to "swallow our rivals and spit them out." (On the return flight my companion du jour was a birdseed merchant, but that's another story.)

A Gathering of Cannibals

We will meet some cannibals now. I have selected a reasonable assortment of people and circumstances to give us a better idea of how and possibly why they have dined on "long pig," as this entrée has at times been known. This is not a general discourse on cannibalism. My focus is on the total context in which cannibalism occurs and its possible connection with exit rituals.

Acts of cannibalism were famous among the gods of antiquity. Zeus swallowed his pregnant wife Metis because he feared she might bear a son who would be more powerful than his own mighty self (surely an example of god-sized male insecurity). It was also actually operating procedure for nervous male deities to eat their male children unless the young scamps managed to get away. The senior generation of gods tended to ingest their male progeny (the females were usually forced into incest). It has not escaped our notice that top gods, whether called Zeus or Kronos, did not simply murder their own through some stock device such as a thunderbolt. They had to eat them alive.

The very first humans, so closely descended from the gods, also had reason for devouring their young.[21] Masye and Masyane acknowledged

Figure 15 Goya's Saturnus gobbles his son (painting ca. 1821–1823).
Reproduced courtesy of the Museo del Prado, Madrid, Spain.

Ohrmazd, Creator of All-That-Is. They promised to be obedient, but you know how that goes. In their defense, it should be said that Ohrmazd had forbidden not only the fruit of one particular tree, but all food and drink. After thirty days they committed the sin of eating, followed by the even more damning sin of lying about their transgressions.

After fifty years Masye and Masyane made another discovery, with the resulting birth of twins. Do you have a bad feeling about that, too? Well justified. Mircea Eliade reports that the twins were just "so delicious that the mother eats one of them, and the father eats the other."[22] A little too late for the twins, an act of divine intervention saves the disappointing human race from extinction. Ohrmazd makes children tasteless; that is, their flavor no longer entices their parents. Masye and Masyane then beget other children who have less flavor than an economy class airline meal, and they live to become ancestors of all the human races. (If we occasionally say and do tasteless things, now we know who to blame.)

As mere mortals we are not in a position to judge the gods. Granted. However, it is difficult not to be influenced by them. There must be something special about human flesh if it is craved by the gods. Furthermore, quite early in the career of *Homo sapiens* our ancestors realized that the gods are ravenous and should be fed because we love and admire them so—or perhaps just because we don't want to be a menu feature. Sacrifice of grain, animals, and fellow humans has long been a custom in many world cultures. The sacrificial rituals often operated on the premise that the gods would actually ingest the offerings, though apparently some believed that the gods could devour with their eyes alone.

Symbolic offerings became more common and human flesh more uncommon as offerings to the gods as societies became larger, more resourceful, and more politically evolved. Anthropologist Marvin Harris tries to explain why societies with a higher level of social organization continued to engage in unrestrained warfare but stopped feeding human flesh to the gods as well as to themselves:

> I think the crux of the matter is the ability of politically evolved societies to integrate vanquished populations into their labor force. . . . Large-scale killing and eating of captives would thwart the governing class's interest in expanding its tax and tribute base. Since captives can produce a surplus, far better to consume the products of their labor than the flesh of their bodies. . . .[23]

Cannibalistic people and their gods, therefore, became limited to band-and-village societies who kill to protect their turf and hunting grounds and find it more cost efficient to eat their enemies than to bring them home as additional mouths that have to be fed.

Gods and Worshipers at the Cannibal Feast, Aztec Style

One of the most notorious indulgences in cannibalism also illustrates how gods and worshipers can share the feast. These actions occurred within a highly developed and complex ritualistic frame. We should not hastily conclude, however, that all or even most cannibalism has occurred as an intrinsic part of ritual exercises. People have eaten people for various reasons, including simply because there was nothing else to eat.

How and why did the Aztecs do it? There were Spanish eyewitnesses to the how. Bernadino de Sahagun described the fate of captives who had been brought to Tenochtitlan for this purpose. They were taken to the sector of the city that was devoted to public ceremonies. The captives, one at a time, were made to climb to the highest level of a flat-topped pyramid. Four priests each seized a limb and bent the victim backward over a stone altar. Another priest tore open the victim's chest

> with a wide-bladed flint knife. And they named the hearts of the captives "precious eagle-cactus fruit." They raised them in dedication to the sun, Xippili, Quauhtleu-anitl. They offered it to him; they nourished him. And when the heart had become an offering . . . they rolled them (the captives) over; they bounced them down. They came breaking to pieces; they came head over heels; they came down headfirst; they came turning over and over. . . . When they had reached the bottom, they cut off their heads and inserted a rod through them, and they carried the bodies to the houses which they called calpulli, where they divided them up in order to eat them.[24]

We get the picture. Add to this picture the dancing and ceremonies that accompanied the great feast. And add the realization that the hearts had been transmuted into the "precious eagle-cactus fruit" for the god's delectation, while all the remaining flesh was intended for the worshipers. An Aztec warrior or priest indulging in this feast would therefore be sharing a meal with the gods, a welcome opportunity to maintain a critical relationship. If I say that about a hundred thousand captives were sacrificed in this manner, I will be within the range estimated by historians, some of whom are still counting skulls and disputing.[25]

But wait—why would the Aztecs have devoured their captives like a less evolved band-and-village society? Harris believes it was basically both a public health and a political policy. Consumption of human flesh provided animal fat and protein for the populace, who, well fed, would be less likely to revolt against the regime. He notes that Aztecs were sometimes reduced to "skimming the greenish scum of waterfly eggs from Lake Texcoco."[26] Freud is supposed to have said, "Sometimes a cigar is just a good smoke." Harris seems to be saying: "And sometimes a human corpse is just a good meal."

He is not alone in that opinion. Derek Denton focuses on an even more specific nutritional advantage of consuming corpses in his book *The Hunger for Salt*. Our bodies require an ever-replenished supply of critical mineral nutrients. The same was true of the sheep who had the dubious honor of participating in his experiments. Denton found that sodium chloride deficiencies lead to a wide range of negative physiological effects and stimulate an intense desire for salt. Denton then examined both historical records and more recent observations from Africa, the Amazon Basin, Australia, New Mexico, New Guinea, and New Zealand. He suggested a link between living in salt-poor jungle environments and the practice of cannibalism. We perhaps should be more appreciative, then, of those salt-intensive supersized fries at our neighborhood fast food pits. Without them, who knows what else might appear on the menu?

Suppose there is something to the dietary explanation. The role that nutritional needs might play in cannibalism is not a possibility to be dismissed out of hand. An obvious question comes to mind, though. Why did the Aztecs and some others need such elaborate rituals if it was just the salt, fat, and protein they were after? And here is an obvious explanation one might offer: rituals, the more imposing and elaborate the better, serve to legitimate cannibalism, to control the aversion and the guilt and the fear attendant on eating one of our own kind. The broader implication is that a core purpose of many, if not all, rituals is to regularize, neutralize, and transform anxiety-producing actions and events. Additionally, preparation-for-war and mortuary rituals might be serving the purpose of laundering other facets of our death-related anxieties.

We do have other explanations to consider, though. There were theories aplenty from the feisty early psychoanalysts. Freud was fascinated by world cultures and the burgeoning field of anthropology. Eating other people could be a passion of the psyche. We incorporate others symbolically as we twist through the conflicts and perils of childhood. The line between symbolic and corporal incorporation can dissolve under intense pressure. Furthermore, all that stuff about gods devouring their children could have been projections of scary family dynamics, one generation or one gender intent on destroying the other through "oral incorporation." (That and castration.)

There is another psychoanalytic track through the wilderness of human emotions and desires. We all have, we don't have, and then again we do have an aggressive instinct (Freud continued to revise his conclusions as he went along). Cannibalism can therefore be seen as one of the more gratifyingly palpable ways of letting loose our personal or communal hounds of hell.

Hold on, though—shouldn't we give more attention to the rituals themselves, the worldviews they represent, and the sociophysical context within which they arise? Yes, we should. Anthropologist Peggy Reeves Sanday is one who has done so. The major Aztec sacrificial rites occurred during ceremonial feasts held in the second, thirteenth, and sixteenth months of the eighteen-month solar year, although it is likely that human flesh was consumed at other times as well. The hearts—a.k.a. the precious eagle-cactus fruit—consecrated for the gods were not simply tasty bits of nutritious flesh. They also preserved and enhanced the established order of things. For example, commoners could become nobles by furnishing nourishment for the gods. Even more significant:

> The whole affair was at once a microcosm of the supernatural order and the material embodiment of political order. . . . The precious eagle-cactus fruit served as a dominant symbol drawing together the cosmological, the sociological, and the biological into one bloody reenactment of the founding of the Aztec universe. . . . Metaphors for sacred and physical being were based on the body and projected onto the screen of cosmology.[27]

For the Aztecs, then, the concept of "the body politic" was living reality, not hollow rhetoric. The ceremonies performed on and about the pyramids were human parallels and tributes to the cosmo-magical events performed by the gods in their own commanding realms.[28] In ways that

made sense to the Aztecs, their dances, ceremonies, orgies, heart har-
vestings, and corpse eating helped the gods keep the cycles of life going.
But why so many sacrifices and so much cannibalism?

Sanday believes the Aztecs were suffering from a bad case of cosmic
anxiety. I am not quite sure about cosmic anxiety, but it sounds like a
miserable thing to have. The expansionist Aztecs had been highly successful and effective conquerors. Now they had to cope with the daunting task of ruling an empire teeming with diverse and rebellion-minded
populations.

And there was something more. A devastating famine had swept the
land not very long before the arrival of Cortés, his conquistadors, and
his priests in 1529. People died everywhere. It was estimated that about
half the population either perished of starvation or straggled out of the
Valley of Mexico. Children were sold by their families for a little food
and then taken away to other regions, where they would become sacrificial and perhaps cannibalistic victims. The mighty empire was shaken
to its foundations. The course of action was obvious: intensify the rituals and offer more sacrifices, and more sacrifices, and more sacrifices. (A
by-product of mass sacrifice and cannibalism, of course, would be more
salt, animal fat, and protein for hungry Aztecs.)

Although the great famine seems to have receded by the time the Spanish arrived, they still bore witness to the continued mass killings. This
brings to mind the Commonwealth of Massachusetts. Many an added
tax was put on the citizens' bill for specified time-limited purposes. I cannot recall the termination of any of the fund-squeezing operations after
the project itself had run its course. Perhaps it was not so different with
the Aztecs. Why stop? Slaughtering all those captives might be just the
thing to prevent the next famine.

Intermission: Some Gnawing Questions

There are more cannibals to meet. First, though, we take a brief working intermission. With the Aztecs still fresh in mind we will consider a
few questions that can be raised about cannibalism in general. The first
pair of questions were posed—and answered to his own satisfaction—
by the leading critic of mainstream anthropological views on cannibalism. W. Arens has in turn been roundly (or is that squarely?) trounced

by his own critics. We do not have to immerse ourselves in this controversy. We should attend, though, to the most salient issues raised by Arens.

How common has cannibalism been throughout human history? Not very, is his answer, as the title of his book suggests: *The Man-Eating Myth*. His position is clear:

> I am dubious about the actual existence of this act as an accepted practice for any time or place. Recourse to cannibalism under survival conditions or as a rare instance of antisocial behavior is not denied for any culture. But whenever it occurs this is considered a regrettable act rather than custom.[29]

Arens then came to his main point. If cannibalism actually has been a very rare phenomenon and never an accepted custom, then how can we account for all the reports that have come to attention since the age of exploration brought adventurers to strange and exotic lands? Arens believes that accusations of cannibalism have served political and racist agendas. Sometimes it has just been a matter of uncritical thinking. People who have strange ways (to our eyes) might do any number of strange things, the more bizarre, the more fabulous, the more fascinating. Often, though, people were branded as cannibals to justify treating them as subhuman. Not only does this contribute to Us feeling superior to Them, but it also liberates us from any lingering moral scruples. It was our duty to invade their lands, exploit their resources, and upturn their established order of life, because, well, they were all pagan savages—were they not?—and it was about time we ended this horrible practice of cannibalism, whether they happened to be cannibals or not.

Give Arens one out of two. He criticized some reports that needed criticism, and he stimulated other anthropologists to enforce higher evidential standards. Nevertheless, there is plenty of solid evidence for cannibalism as an act performed a great many times in a variety of periods and places. Furthermore, cannibalism often enough has been not only culturally sanctioned behavior but also behavior that was crucial for magical, religious, and political purposes. But I, too, think that charges of cannibalism often have been part of a racist and exploitative agenda. Arens is right about that and right to expose and condemn this usage. We should distinguish, though, between biased and undisciplined charges of cannibalism and the patient, skillful, and honest work of the great majority of anthropologists. We would be less than honest ourselves if we were to reject solid evidence of cannibalism because some have made spurious and demeaning accusations in the past.

Is Eating an Abuse? This question and the next pertain directly to the role of ritual in passing through life and death. First, we should consider whether eating people constitutes abuse of the dead. The Aztecs will continue to serve as our example here. Apparently, abuse of the living captives was *not* part of the process. There was no systematic intention to inflict pain and suffering. There was no purpose to be served in shaming and humiliating the captives. Rather, the point was to keep these people alive and lively enough to ascend the pyramid and offer their precious eagle-cactus fruit to the gods. A tortured and starved sacrificial victim would be a disgraceful offering—and also make a less appetizing meal.

On the other hand, though, the victims did experience hardship and stress. There was the trauma of capture, the pangs of separation from their homes and homelands, the stress of the journey to Tenochtitlan and the confinement there. When they realized what fate awaited them, there would also have been anxiety and despair. There was significant harm done to these people while they were alive, even though abuse was not an intrinsic part of the ritualistic process.

But were they abused when dead? This is a more difficult question to answer, because the answer depends so much on our own life-and-death perspectives. *Vegetarians*—let me guess what you think about cannibalism! *Utilitarians and cost-benefit analysts*—how can you not favor a practice that makes use of what would otherwise be discarded? *Cultural pluralists*—should we just shrug our shoulders and murmur "Whatever" and neither approve nor disapprove of cannibalism because all cultures construct their own realities? *Mystics*—are you moved by the simple beauty of incorporating one person into another, especially when this union is hallowed by the soul of a people? *Materialists*—the dead cannot be abused because they are, well, dead, right? *Social scientists*—is cannibalism not the ultimate abuse, because treating the dead as morsels is a colossal display of disrespect for the tradition they represent? *People of faith*—is not the body the temple of the soul and therefore sacred? And do we not place our own souls in jeopardy by committing such a sacrilege? And so on.

Is the Soul Digestible? This unresolved exploration of the abuse issue brings us to the verge of the final question to be considered here: *what becomes of the victim's soul when the body has been dismembered and devoured?* The Aztecs provide a striking example of ceremony and ritual. There is a predictable, replicable, unquestionable sequence of events that are enacted within a cosmic frame of reference. But this impressive ritual is not the victim's ritual. It is the ritual of the Aztec priest and warrior. Discussions of rituals usually focus on participants who are "of the people." In coming-of-age rituals, for example, the youths have been socialized into their roles and expectations since childhood. Although the initiation rites may be harsh and painful, they are meaningful and will bestow a new level of status within one's own community. Being forced to participate in somebody else's rituals is a different story altogether.

The Aztec sacrifice ritual prefaced a feast and orgy. The ritual might have extended to the postmortem careers of the victims. There might have been a reverence shown to the deceased both as fellow humans and as crucial, if involuntary, participants in the ritual. There might have been prayers for the victims' journey to the next life as well as prayers to symbolically wash the blood off the Aztecs' own hands and lips. Might have been. Wasn't.

So I say: *abuse.* The Aztecs were world class in their development and performance of rituals. The contrast between the rituals they performed on their own behalf and the deprivation of memorial and safe conduct rituals for their victims does constitute abuse. This conclusion is not automatically generalized to all acts of cannibalism. For example, in 1972 the members of an amateur rugby team were stranded in a remote area of the Andes when their plane hurtled into a snow-covered mountain. Those who survived the crash found themselves in a subzero environment without medical supplies, food, or access to the outer world. The harrowing story of prayer, effort, death, survival—and cannibalism—is told by Piers Paul Read in his compelling book *Alive.*

It took courage for the survivors to admit that they had resorted to cannibalism. Here were no high rituals, however, and no murders. They had to overcome intense aversions to avail themselves of the only food available. Indeed, the condition of the survivors was only marginally different from those of the deceased. All had been victims of the accident, and all might have ended their lives in the frozen turf. There had been comradeship among them before, not the relationship of captor to captive. Had the accident occurred a little differently, the roles of living and dead might have been reversed.

We do not have direct reports from the Aztecs themselves or from many others who have engaged in cannibalism, but in this case there were reports from those who survived this harrowing experience. Here is what happened after thawing snow had made a number of corpses available for them after a period of near starvation:

> It would have been possible now to avoid eating such things as rotten lungs and putrid intestines of bodies they had cut up weeks before but half the boys continued to do so because they had come to need the stronger taste. It had taken a supreme effort of will for these boys to eat human flesh at all, but once they had started and persevered, appetite had come with the eating, for the instinct to survive was a harsh tyrant which demanded not just that they eat their companions but that they get used to doing so.[30]

Now comes a theme, a revelation that you might have been expecting throughout this chapter. Here it is, coming spontaneously from a normal person of our own time, turned cannibal by the situation. Pedro Algorta was

> a sensitive socialist intellectual—and it was he who had justified eating those first slivers of human flesh by comparing what they were doing to eating the body and blood of Christ in the Holy Eucharist.[31]

We think immediately of the Last Supper. The disciples. Jesus with his presentiment. We can also see Jesus. He is taking a piece of bread. Now he is giving the traditional Jewish blessing for food. And now he divides the bread and offers a share to each companion. "Take it," he says. "This is my body." Jesus drinks from his cup and passes it around the table. He speaks again. "This is my blood, the blood of the covenant, which is to be poured out for many." Thus the Eucharist. Thus a ritual central to the early Christian movement and then the Catholic Church. Thus an interaction between priest and worshiper that evokes the Last Supper. Thus a ritual that is either a symbolic or an actual act of cannibalism, depending on the interpreter.

A thriving ritual is one that is beyond question. The Eucharist certainly can be counted among the thriving rituals. It built upon the existing Jewish tradition of blessing and sharing bread and wine. After the

Last Supper it was transformed into "the most important cult act" in early Christianity, if Eliade is right about that. If we accept this premise, Eliade has more to suggest:

> Jesus' words contain a deeper meaning: the need for his voluntary sacrifice in order to insure the "new covenant." ... This implies the conviction that a new religious life arises only through a sacrificial death: the conception is well known to be archaic and universally disseminated. It is difficult to determine if this ritual communion with his body and his blood was regarded by Jesus as a mystical identification with his person.[32]

Perhaps we trap ourselves in an unproductive semantic puzzle if we insist that the act of eating the bread and sipping the wine is either a physical or a symbolic incorporation of the person of Jesus. Perhaps a fuzzy logic approach would be more in keeping with this compelling but elusive ritualistic act. The freezing and starving Pedro Algorta did not have to reach a firm conclusion about the mysterious inner nature of the Eucharist. All he needed was the flash of revelation that his immediate crisis and that of his companions somehow was connected to an ancient and durable ritual. And when Algorta tasted his first sliver of human flesh he could do so within the protective frame of religious sanction, so powerful a frame that it was available even for those who did not count themselves as practicing Catholics.

Did Algorta and his companions abuse the dead through desperate acts of cannibalism? I think not. Do the faithful abuse Jesus when they take communion? Of course not. If the devoured dead could speak, they could offer their own authoritative opinion, and that might settle the issue. We can only imagine that the rugby team members and pilot who perished in the crash would not have felt abused and might even have felt consoled by having enabled others to survive.

Learning from Other Cannibals

We have a few more things to learn from cannibals before we take their leave. The forms and meanings of anthropophagy are culture-specific, as we will see again in visiting other cannibals as they go about their business within their own distinctive worlds.

Bones in a Cave   Our first visit is to what clichéd rhetoric refers to as the dawn of time. We know a little about how our most distant ancestors lived, and we imagine or invent the rest. We also know something about how they treated their dead, just enough to inspire further speculation. At least some of our distant ancestors buried at least some of their dead with care and respect. Tools and other objects that might be useful in the next life were sometimes buried with them. But did some of our ancestors eat their dead? And, if so, why?

Some anthropologists and paleoarchaeologists believed and some denied that cannibalism was practiced frequently in the old, old days. The balance now has shifted to the believers. Recent discoveries in a French cave provide compelling support for the cannibalistic thesis. A research team directed by Alban Defleur of the Université du Méditerrané at Marseilles examined seventy-eight pieces of broken bone from six or more Neanderthals who evidently had been victims of cannibalism about a hundred thousand years ago.[33] The bones had belonged to children and teens. These remains were much different from the usual finds. All the skulls and limb bones had been broken apart. There were cuts across feet, ankles, and elbows that indicated that tendons had been severed. Marks made by sharp stone flints were found on a skull. The researchers concluded that these unfortunates had been butchered by their comrades, and their bones then opened for marrow and their skulls for brains. The type of violence inflicted on the bones could not have resulted from natural death or animals. Similar finds were made a century ago in Croatia, but the new find appears to be more conclusive.

If cannibalism, then, why? The presence of many deer bone fragments in the same cave and the fact that the human remains were mixed in with those of animals persuaded the researchers that this was *not* an example of funeral rituals. Some band-and-village societies have partaken of selected human remains as a ritual action that is related to the future life of the deceased and, possibly, to the affirmation of group solidarity and viability. The mute remains in this case, though, indicate that humans and animals had been butchered and eaten in the same way, and the bones simply tossed away.

We are left with an apparent contradiction. Some Neanderthals buried their dead with care and most likely with some kind of ceremonial ritual. Others, though, indulged in cannibalism without rituals and with-

out the urgency of starvation. The anthropologists are guessing that Neanderthals were complex and varied people who probably developed different traditions in different regions. There is not much we can say with
confidence about how Neanderthals lived and died. We are left, however, with a cautionary lesson. The act of disposing of a body by passing it through one's digestive system can have more than one meaning.
Anthropophagy was encased within the worldview and ceremonial performances of the Aztecs, but it was a desperate survival measure for the
rugby team. Among Neanderthals, sharing selected remains was a communal ritual that respected the deceased, but others of them devoured
humans and tossed away their bones unceremoniously. Did they *intend*
abuse? Were the victims treated so disrespectfully because they were outsiders? We will probably never know.

Cannibals for Neighbors   I am fortunate in my neighbors; I would like
to think my neighbors are fortunate in me. Perhaps the same cannot be
said for neighbors in Papua New Guinea. Some tribes have eschewed cannibalism and feared their cannibalistic neighbors. Others have engaged
in a limited form of ritualistic cannibalism. Still others have eagerly captured and eaten practically anybody they could get their hands on, demonstrating about as little concern for sacred ritual as the people lined up at
McDonald's. And then there are the Arapesh of the east Sepik area, who
have been reported to exhibit "an amused, faintly condescending interest that is morally neutral in tone . . . and often dismiss the whole matter by pronouncing that those Sepiks are 'another kind of man'; if they
chose to eat each other, that is their business."[34] We see right away, then,
that the same region can be populated by people with a broad range of
practices and attitudes regarding cannibalism.

The specifics of Papua New Guinea anthropophagy have varied con-
siderably. Some informants have told anthropologists that they simply
make use of bodies they encounter here and there: why waste good meat?
This opportunistic cannibalism, then, does not involve sacrificial rites or
slaughter of the innocents. Those so inclined can ponder the question of
whether serving as a meal is more abusive to the dead than their decomposition in the jungle.

The most voracious cannibals were the Mianmin, whose activities seem
to have extended robustly into the twentieth century. They had been encountered by many earlier European visitors but made a particular name

for themselves when they attacked a patrol in 1938 (on the mistaken belief that this was a raiding party from one of their enemies). Reports from other New Guinea peoples, Australian visitors and authorities, and Mianmin informants themselves add up to the picture of people who just enjoy including human flesh in their diet. No associated rituals have become evident, nor were their hunting and trapping expeditions necessarily motivated by rage.[35] They liked their neighbors well enough, but they liked them best as an entrée.

An exception, however. Mianmin cannibalism could at times also have a domestic, even a "romantic," purpose. A raid as recently as 1960 included several murders and resultant acts of cannibalism. Many of the young raiders and the elders who planned the attack were put on trial and pleaded guilty. They were sentenced to death, but consideration of the ethnocultural factors involved resulted in a prison sentence instead. About thirty years later Don Gardner discovered that some of the raiders and even some of the elders were still alive.[36] They confirmed earlier reports that they had not raided just for fresh meat. They were also after young women. Mianmin bachelors needed wives. Incidental to this romantic mission, the raiders tidied things up by killing and eating the husbands, thereby sparing them years of grief and perhaps unpleasant counterraids. Perhaps cannibalism can be channeled to many uses once it has become an intrinsic part of a culture.

There is another facet of New Guinea anthropophagy that deserves more attention than it has received. Alan Rumsey reports that the native people of New Guinea have sometimes believed white men to be cannibals. One of the more spectacular encounters between Europeans and native peoples occurred in the highlands of New Guinea during the 1930s. Neither the visitors nor the residents had laid eyes on each other before. About sixty years later Rumsey listened to Kopia Noma's memory of that extraordinary event, which started with the buzzing and circling of an airplane. He and his comrades

> thought they must be our ghosts—our own ancestors coming back. We dug a hole and jumped in for cover. . . . We felt sure they were going to kill us. People spread the news that these were ghosts. But actually they were Australians. They were wearing what looked to us like women's aprons, so we thought they must be female ghosts. We thought: "These foreigners that have come, they must be cannibals, people who eat other people."[37]

Rumsey offers an observation that applies not only to this "white cannibal" scare but also to much of what we have been exploring throughout this chapter. We are likely to impute all sorts of frightening, disgusting, and bizarre behavior to those we consider others, to those we perceive as fundamentally different from ourselves, perhaps not even human. Cannibalism is one of the most extreme characteristics we might attribute to people who are different from us. In a word, *othering* a person or set of people makes it easier to reject and vilify them, makes it easier to deny our shared humanity. May I add that it is not only the accusation but also the *practice* of cannibalism that is encouraged by othering?

Perhaps we have also discovered in New Guinea further reason to believe that funeral rituals are likely to be denied those who are so different from (and, usually, perceived as inferior to) ourselves that we are obliged to do nothing beyond throwing away their bones.

One Modest Proposal after Another   Otherness turns out to be a crucial element of cannibalism that was practiced around the Arizona–New Mexico border about eight hundred years ago. Anthropologists Christy and Jacqueline Turner describe the victims' condition: scalped, skulls cracked open and roasted, rib cages torn apart, flesh stripped from bones, the cracked bones themselves boiled for their fat.[38] The Turners' reading of these remains aroused fierce indignation as well as the usual academic controversy. Hopi and other descendants of the Anasazi culture have expressed anger at having their ancestors branded as cannibals. But the Turners have a different explanation. They note that the Anasazi were an advanced people who made astronomical observations and cultivated a peaceful and productive way of life. Their culture crumbled, and at least some of their lives were forfeited when they were invaded by a violent people who had been practicing cannibalism in their Mexican territories. The Turners theorize that the Anasazi were cannibalized by the invaders as a terror tactic to subdue opposition. The invaders had no scruples about eating as well as killing the unfortunate "others" who happened to be in their path.

But we come now to examples of cannibalistic othering that, while less bloody, also are less distant from our own cultural heritage. The first is among the most famous examples of dark humor in the catalog of Western civilization. Jonathan Swift wrote in 1729 that he had not the least personal interest in promoting his "modest proposal," seeing that he had no young children by which he might acquire even a single penny. The complete title is: "A Modest Proposal for Preventing the Children of Poor People from Being a Burden to Their Parents or the Country, and for Making Them Beneficial to the Public."[39] Swift's inventive proposal was neither an idle fancy nor his first attempt to solve a pressing problem. His daily walk gave him witness to starving mothers and their children begging for alms on the street. Swift had already made other proposals for improving the economic condition of the Irish, but these were ignored by the British Crown and Parliament.

His proposal was a studious spoof of British "political arithmeticians," who were calculating how many children a "teeming woman" bears within a specified time period as well as the logistics for depopulating Ireland.

> I shall now therefore humbly propose my own thoughts, which I hope will not be liable to the least objection. I have been assured . . . that a young healthy child, well nursed, is at a year old a most delicious, nourishing, and wholesome food, whether *stewed, roasted, baked,* or *boiled,* and I make no doubt that it will equally serve in a *fricassee,* or a *ragout.*[40]

Swift suggested that twenty thousand Irish children be reserved for breeding, while the hundred thousand others should be offered in sale

> to the persons of quality and fortune through the kingdom. . . . I grant this food will be somewhat dear, and therefore, very *proper for landlords,* who, as they have already devoured most of the parents, seem to have the best title to the children.

The "Modest Proposal" offers abundant detail both on the procedure and the benefits of cannibalizing Irish children for the delectation of the lordly and landlordly elite. This scathing attack was too horrifying, too trenchant, and too inspired to ignore. Swift had made his point. For the establishment, the common people were others—others whose lives did not really matter. And since Crown and Parliament did not give a figgy pudding for the lives of Irish children, who cared how they died and what became of their starved and diseased bodies? Why waste good funeral rituals on such nobodies? (Note that Swift recommended the infants be nursed well just prior to their merchandising so they would make a jolly good meal.)

The suffering of a hungry population and its neglect by the powers that be provided the occasion for Swift's biting satire. Another "modest proposal" saw the light of day two and a half centuries later, by "a hungry but upright ordinary person" who "looks like a skinny dog, a walking skeleton wrapped in rags."[41] We are not in Ireland now, but in modern China. *A Modest Proposal to the Impoverished Chinese for a Convenient Solution of Their Predicament* is an element in an imaginative novel by Shen Congwen, a distinguished author who, like Swift, has been a thorn in the side of the establishment.[42] As discussed by Gang Yue, Congwen offers a package of three solutions for the misery of the multitude of the poor.[43] They could become slaves to foreign powers. This would be a woeful kind of life, but at least it would be a life and would contribute to the economic development of the nation. Another solution would be even simpler and more decisive: the poor should just starve themselves to death or, if this does not do the job quickly enough, arrange to get themselves killed. Congwen's skinny dog, walking skeleton spokesperson in the novel argues that encouraging and enabling the poor to die swiftly would "spare philanthropic agencies and government officials the trouble of paying lip-service." It is for the good of the country that the common mass of citizens die young.

> Since Chinese and dogs are not allowed to enter public parks in the international concessions, there is no point in the generous foreign powers advocating the conservation of Chinese cultural relics; their philanthropy may keep some from immediate death, but even the shabby survival of the poor population would strain the limited resources and contaminate the national landscape.[44]

Congwen's third proposal is essentially Swift's plan to sell children as morsels. And, like Swift, he is attentive to the economics. There are just so many poor children in China that the demand for salted and spiced meat would be depressed if all were dumped on the market too precipitously. Rather than inconvenience the flesh merchants, Congwen proposes a carefully monitored infusion of poor children into the food supply. Some children should be allowed to survive to constitute "a sufficient reserve of concubines, maids, and prostitutes for wealthy Chinese."[45]

The modest proposals offered by Swift and Congwen invoke cannibalism as an attention-getting metaphor. Society does not always cherish and protect all its members. The poor tend to be "otherized," if this unattractive term be allowed. We have already had a reminder of "how poor people die," courtesy of George Orwell.[46] Now we have been coerced by Swift and Congwen to acknowledge how the poor often are beaten down by their societies and cast off when no longer capable of menial labor. The children of the poor will either die in short order or replace their parents to be eaten alive by exploitation and deprivation until their juices have dried up and their bones are cracked open.

A CONCLUDING WORD:
DEPRIVATION OF FINAL RITES

Eighteenth-century Ireland and twentieth-century China were nations with rich histories of religion and ritual. Funeral and memorial ceremonies were well established. There were strong expectations for honoring the dead and supporting the survivors. Neither of the modest proposals, however, spares a word about funeral and memorial rituals for the doomed children. There would be none. The children of the poor were not covered by the umbrella of religion, ritual, and conscience. The deprivation of ritual farewells is not among the most obvious features of cannibalism. I have invested all these words, however, in the hope of troubling you a little. Perhaps you would share my concern with the preservation of the tradition of decency and respect that has so often been demonstrated throughout human history upon the death of one of our kind. Strong as this tradition might be, it is not immune from undermining influences, events, and circumstances. More than anything, perhaps, we might concern ourselves with acting upon the principle that every human is one of our kind, and that any person's death is an opportunity to express whatever humanity we possess.

SEVEN

TOO MANY DEAD

The Plague and Other Mass Deaths

Traditional societies often give their all when one of their members has died. The kin and, at times, the entire community devote themselves to seeing that the right things are done in the right way. The rituals can be exacting and time-consuming. Scarce resources, such as the most esteemed foods, may be expended. Other activities are put on hold as the body is carefully prepared and the remains disposed of according to custom. Large, pluralistic, and fast-changing societies such as ours are less inclined to stop everything and give everything when a life has ended. The funereal and mourning process tends to be regarded as an interruption in the flow of our busy lives for all except those few who were very close to the deceased. Nevertheless, many people do "pay their respects" both to the deceased and to the survivors, even if this means travel, effort, expense, and inconvenience. Traditional and contemporary responses to a death usually do have one thing in common that is so obvious it is seldom remarked upon: the dead are most often escorted on their way one at a time. Our rituals are built around the expectation that the focus will be on one dead person. This expectation is challenged occasionally when several related deaths occur. But what happens when there are a great many dead? When there are too many dead? Exploring society's response under this condition might help us to think a little differently about our usual ways of relating to the dead when they present themselves to us one at a time. The Black Death provides us with abundant examples.

"Too many dead." What does that mean? Sometimes we are reacting to an unexpectedly high toll of casualties. Consider the following scenarios:

- Commanding officers had calculated the approximate number of casualties that would occur in achieving an objective in a battle. Injuries and deaths were expected—but not so many. The responsible officers must now find a way to justify and compensate for the "excess casualties."
- Authorities had recognized that a famine was probable. Measures to prevent or mitigate the famine would have diverted funds from projects of higher priority. In fact, a little famine here and there has some political value. The famine and resulting diseases had exceeded estimates, however. The authorities are now uncomfortable because they are being second-guessed and criticized—so somebody will have to be found culpable and dealt with severely.
- City officials had wondered where the municipal budget could be reduced with the least notice and resistance. Easy answer: curtail outpatient medical services for the low-income dwellers of the inner city. The result was a 500 percent increase in sexually transmitted diseases and fatalities when acute infections previously limited to a small area of the city became chronic and more severe infections spread throughout the sprawling urban area. Little thought was given to this prospect, so the public now feels endangered and betrayed by its elected officials.

In these examples the excess loss of life is deplored because it threatens to destabilize the establishment and interfere with operational goals (e.g., military victory, cost savings). Commanders and officials anticipated fatalities ("collateral damage") at an acceptable level. Now, however, there are too many deaths. Perhaps the number of fatalities can be concealed. If not, then a statement of regret and condolence may be issued to the public. The primary concern, though, is for the operational effect of the deaths, not for the loss of individual lives and the emotional impact on the families of the deceased.

Sometimes, though, "too many dead" has a different meaning. The fatalities are not incidental to a military campaign or a political estab-

Figure 16 Death hunts the hunters. From Geiler von Kaisersperg, *Sermones, De arbore humana* (Strassburg: printed by Johann Grüninger, 1514).

lishment indifferent to suffering. A catastrophe strikes in the form of fast-moving natural disasters such as an earthquake (generally the most lethal), volcanic eruption, storm, flood, or fire. A raging epidemic appears as though from nowhere and devastates the population. These deaths occur swiftly. Ordinary life comes apart. Social institutions, such as school and church, and public activities may be interrupted, even suspended. There may be significant problems with clean water, food, shelter, and transportation. Health care providers and facilities are overwhelmed by wave after wave of the seriously ill.

In all of this stress, there is still another problem to be faced: proper, respectful, and hygienic disposal of the corpses. There are too many dead in too short a time for the community to accommodate in its usual manner. Caring for the dead must compete with survival of the living.

WHO'S IN CHARGE—THE LIVING OR THE DEAD?

And there is still another meaning that can be associated with "too many dead." In Western societies it is generally assumed that the living hold sway. The dead should know their place: at a remove, on the sidelines, behind a fence if not a wall. That so many people have lived and died over the millennia is a moderately interesting sidebar, but what does that have to do with us? We do not often see the dead, and when we do it is usually after they have been freshened up by the funerary arts and sciences. As world history goes, North America is still a rather new place that has not yet accumulated the wealth of ghosts, storying, and monuments to the past that characterize other cultures in which the dead seem less remote to the living.

We also expect that the living should decisively outnumber the perished. A thousand people viewing one corpse and one person viewing a thousand corpses—these situations are by no means equivalent.

People often become anxious when just one person of their acquaintance has crossed over unexpectedly. I might think, "Why, I saw Charlie yesterday morning. Yesterday morning!" By implication, Charlie could not and should not have died because he was protected by my having seen him so recently. We are shaken by a single death within our circle. We search uneasily for assurance that Death will not make such an improper move again. Consider, then, how much we may be shaken by loss upon loss, by a landscape in which life itself appears to be wilting and Death riding high. At a "tipping point," as Malcolm Gladwell would say,[1] the number and type of deaths can lead large populations as well as individuals to feel that the too many deaths are prelude to the total destruction of life.

Even young children—the proverbial innocents living in an enchanted and protected domain—may be chanting, "Ashes, ashes. All fall down!" We begin, then, by passing through the gate of time to revisit some of the most terrifying days in human history.

PLAGUE

The word *plague* (from the Latin *plaga,* a forceful blow) has been applied to many contagious diseases but has become associated primarily with the bubonic plague. In its most devastating appearance this pestilence was known as the Black Death. Every major lethal epidemic in the last three hundred years or so has been compared to the plague, and people with a sense of history have an abiding fear that a new form of this disease might yet again emerge and carve an appalling trail of death throughout the global community.

What of the disease itself? How did it spread, how many lives did it end, and what measures were taken to control this horror? What was the world in which the Black Death struck, and what was its impact? And did the memory of this catastrophe die with its survivors, or has the Black Death continued to influence us hundreds of years later? First, the disease itself. We begin with first-person accounts from a devastating return of the plague in the seventeenth century.

The Plague and Its Victims

Florence, 1631. A resplendent and sophisticated city.

A scorpion stung a housemaid just above her knee. At least, that was what seemed to have happened. The wound was a little strange, though, not typical for scorpions. Perhaps it was a carbuncle, the name given to a painful infection under the skin that could become a serious problem if not treated promptly. A deputation of physicians was sent by the Public Health Magistracy. Why such municipal concern for a servant's knee? But Florence was, after all, a cultural center of the seventeenth century, not a superstition-ridden hamlet of the fourteenth. The medical entourage quickly ruled out both scorpion sting and carbuncle. Giulia Calvi, our primary source for the Florentine plague, quotes them as follows:

We concluded that it could not be a carbuncle, as she did not have the symptoms that usually occur: the itching bubbles, like grains of wheat, which produce [fluid] after they break; the deterioration of the skin that sometimes occurs even without the bubbles; and the ulcers that always accompany the scabs.

So that was what the maid's problem was not. What, then, was it?

This scab has a black, ashen color. The bottom is so strongly attached that it is like a nail. Moreover, it is corroding and inflaming the nearby tissues to an extraordinary degree. The ulcer we saw is deep and concave; in fact, it is almost round. The ulcer is neither black nor large, and the inflammation is not very big. It is dry and does not expel any liquid. Thus, the ulcer seems to be a bubo in bad shape.[2]

This careful description brought the physicians to the verge of uttering the most unwelcome of words. They held back, however. The woman had no fever, and the ulcer, as noted, was dry. No doubt she had a serious condition, but one could not say that it was—

But it was. Something as small as a scab could be Death's calling card. The physicians here were hoping otherwise, because they had probably viewed the patient between acute episodes and before more unmistakable signs appeared.

Three points come to our attention through the scab on the servant's knee. First, obscure people had already succumbed to isolated cases of the plague in Florence without their deaths attracting much attention. However, this woman served in the house of a prominent family. If she had the plague, there might be calamitous contagion throughout the higher Florentines. Social status, directly or indirectly, influenced the response to plague right from the diagnostic stage.

Second, fear of the plague had remained so intense through the centuries that physicians and officials remained vigilant even though many years might have passed between major outbreaks. The establishment might have been lax and self-indulgent in other respects, but the prospect of a visit from the plague could never have been ignored, because the peril would have been their own.

And third, victims of the Black Death often could readily be identified by their appearance as the disease took hold. They bore the mark of probable death in the form of buboes and lenticulae, small, reddish spots with a resemblance to freckles. Long before the book and movie, a person with such symptoms was a "dead man walking." Furthermore, the domicile of a plague victim was stigmatized as a house of death. The unfortunates who contracted the plague had to deal not only with their agony and impending loss of life but also with becoming social outcasts.

We learn more from the first-person account of another woman, who survived an attack of the plague during the epidemic of 1630–1633, in which about one Florentine in six, approximately thirteen thousand, died. Although a disease that killed such a high proportion of the local population would be considered an overwhelming catastrophe today, this was actually one of the less severe outbreaks. Other areas throughout Europe, North Africa, and Central Asia had (by estimates) lost from a fourth to two-thirds of their population, and some villages and hamlets had been totally depopulated.

Lisabetta Centenni belonged to a prosperous family and, like many others of that time and place, had a strong faith in the miraculous power of saints. If it was not the power of saints that saved her, it might have been the fact that by this time the upper classes had developed skills in avoiding contagion when given sufficient warning. They cultivated an effective early detection network that usually enabled them to flee the areas that would soon be plague stricken. Calvi estimates that no more than twenty-five of the highly privileged succumbed to the plague that harvested commoners by the thousands.[3] Lisabetta, however, was stricken before word had passed around in what proved to be the start of a three-year bout with the plague in Florence. (Some physicians had accepted bribes to conceal local cases of the plague instead of reporting them immediately as required. Victims and their families often did their best to conceal early signs of the plague as well.)

Lisabetta, required to testify at hearings of the Public Health Magistracy, described her close call:

> I got a terrible fever and horrible headache on 29 August of this year. I became so sick that I couldn't even get out of bed to go to the bathroom. That very day, I felt a great pain between my left leg and my body. I told my husband about it, and we found a hard red swelling there. It hurt more than having a baby. My husband, convinced that it was the plague, was very worried because I was four months pregnant.[4]

Lisabetta's husband, Ottavio, decided against reporting the dread illness to the authorities. He feared (with good reason) that his wife would be taken away to a municipal infirmary and perish as many others did. Instead, Ottavio called in a physician to treat the fever but concealed the bubo. Bloodletting and a dose of syrup did reduce the fever, but the swelling and the pain increased. Ottavio then gave his wife

> a bonnet that had belonged to the blessed Sister Domenica. He said, "This must be your medicine. Place yourself in the hands of the blessed Mother, because I don't know what else to do to save this house from ruin." Faithfully I took it and put it around my neck. I gave myself over to the care of the blessed woman and asked her to cure me of the plague.

Lisabetta now mentions an additional source of terror:

> I got more and more terrified because I heard that two women had died and that *their bodies had been dumped in the fields.* [italics added]

Postmortem abuse has its own chapter in this book. We will have more to say about the Black Death version a little later.

> Finally, about twenty days later, the swelling went down and started to drain. The draining lasted for two months. Then one day I noticed that something the size of my thumb was about to come out. It was hard, and the pain was so bad that I felt as if my insides were going to burst open. It continued to expel the liquid for more than one month, but today, thanks to God, I am totally healed. . . . Because the plague is so lethal and because I kept it hidden, I could have died and infected my family. There are nine of us, and thanks to God we are all still living. My husband, Ottavio, was the only one who knew the whole story, but he dared not tell anyone about it because there are severe punishments for those who do not report cases of the disease. If Your Excellencies had not obliged me to report this miracle, I wouldn't have told anyone about it.

Lisabetta survived, fortunately and perhaps miraculously, but her experiences inform us about death as well as life in the plague years. Her story illustrates three points. First, the sacred dead can save the living. Blessed Sister Domenica resided in a local tomb, where she could be viewed in her remarkable state of preservation. Artifacts associated with Domenica were powerful tools to ward off evil and heal illness. The gen-

eral public was given access to little red crosses and to bread that was
kept in the tomb. Lisabetta had been loaned an actual relic: Domenica's
own bonnet. In more than a figurative sense, the suffering woman wore
her medicine. This "treatment" required belief in effective exchange between living and dead. One treasured and prayed to favorite saints. In
turn, the saints might do something very useful to the worshiper every
now and then.

Second, pregnancy as well as the plague was weighted with beliefs,
meanings, and symbols. Pregnant women were not immune to the plague
in Florence or in other afflicted areas. They were in triple jeopardy from
the plague, complications of pregnancy, and the ignorance that misguided
medical interventions involving the female body. In some cases, such as
Lisabetta's, pregnant, plague-stricken women were seen through their ordeal by a symbolic sisterhood. This included both the women who cared
for other women in their times of need and the healing touch from
Domenica, who herself had been succored through what Calvi characterizes as "a chain of celestial healers." Calvi also observes that for Lisabetta, "the story of the plague was inscribed in the broader context of
hiding the disease, in the sphere of the sacred."[5] The prospect of dying
a shameful death had been transformed through a mysterious covenant
that would surely rescue her soul and perhaps her body as well.

And third, even a privileged person such as Lisabetta had some reason to fear a burial without ritual and without respect (although Ottavio
almost certainly would have managed to have circumvent this practice
through his wealth and influence). Commoners had even more realistic
fears of postmortem abuse. As believing Christians, they had tried to earn
salvation and a chance at heaven. To have their bodies hauled away unceremoniously would be a most inauspicious transition.

The elements we have seen in the death of a servant and the survival
of a woman of the upper class had some local characteristics (e.g.,
Domenica's bonnet) but were by no means restricted to Florence. The
basic pattern obtained through the great plagues of the seventeenth century wherever they occurred. Most of these elements (e.g., social class
differences in diagnosis, care, mortality, and burial) also had come to the
fore in the first "modern" pandemic of the Black Death, in 1348. The
most obvious difference between the earliest and later outbreaks can be
found in public health awareness and somewhat more coordinated and
effective measures. The constant from plague to plague was, of course,

the plague itself (although the disease itself could have mutated from time to time).

The Black Death already had made its name before it struck again in Florence, Milan, and many other places in the seventeenth century. We will see not only how this terror-inspiring name earned its reputation but also how it sent a shiver through the minds and bowels of world civilizations that can still be felt today.

Yersina pestis

Take a bacillus known as *Yersina pestis (Yp)*. Its natural gift is to multiply rapidly and poison the blood of the host organism.[6] Introduce *Yp* into the bloodstream of a rat (or other animal). Now send in the fleas. Most fleas will enjoy their feast and come away none the worse for it. About 12 percent, however, retain *Yp* in their gut. The bacteria grow into a solid mass, blocking passage to the stomach. We now have a fully armed and highly motivated killer: a blocked flea, who hopes vainly that taking in more meals will produce satisfaction. The blocked flea is excited when it discovers such a huge warm-blooded host as a Florentine, Londoner, or Cypriot.

The infected flea sucks the blood of its human host. This action in itself does not usually endanger the host. But we remember that this flea is ravenous, yet has the passage to its stomach blocked by a *Yp* accretion. The flea does not, will not, or cannot stop its feeding. Eventually the blood it has imbibed overfills the gullet, which, in turn, can only contract and expel the excess fluid. And it is precisely here that the Black Death seizes its victim. The regurgitated blood carries the *Yp* infection right back to the sucking wound. Such a tiny breach in the armor. Such a trivial invasion. Such an inconspicuous portal for the entry of Death. (The flea, not the most fastidious of diners, also defecates and thereby introduces more *Yp* into the wound, but I don't think I will mention this.)

The small detachment of *Yp* that enters the human body in this way treks to the lymph glands in the armpit, neck, and groin. Soon there is swelling and intense pain in these areas, either accompanied or soon followed by fever. A swollen area is known as a bubo, from the Greek word for groin. Other skin lesions may also appear, taking the form of carbuncles or *Yp*-filled blisters. Sometimes the bubo will open up after a few weeks, forming a pus-discharging abscess. This may signal the onset of recovery, but by this time the victim may have suffered so much damage from sepsis, exhaustion, and bleeding that the weakened body can no longer sustain itself.

Behavior changes can be dramatic when the disease attacks the nervous system. An ordinarily quiet and sober person may behave as though intoxicated; a victim sunk in passivity may suddenly become manic and try to escape somewhere . . . anywhere. Plague victims often alarmed and confused their family by alternating between stupor and delirium. It was only a few weeks from the encounter with a blocked flea to a ride on the dead cart unless the victim was one of the lucky ones.

What I just described was the usual course of infection and death during the early phases of a plague pandemic. However, the Black Death also took two other routes, and these had different implications for societal response. One of these pathways is thought to have been rare: people nipped by other people's fleas. This form of human-to-human contagion operated only in the presence of an extremely high concentration of Yp in the bloodstream. Much more common and particularly horrifying was the pneumatic form of the plague. Yp floats through the air in droplets from an infected person to any nearby set of lungs.

Scary! A sneeze. A cough. A spit. Invisible stains on objects and clothing? Perhaps that, too. And worse: air-borne plague was even more lethal than the more bubonic form. (It is believed that these variant forms of the plague occurred only after the basic disease had been established through the rat-flea-human cycle.) Medical researcher Graham Twigg notes that the nursery rhyme with the line "a-tishoo, a-tishoo, we all fall down" refers specifically to the pneumatic plague.[7] He also reports that in a Manchurian pneumatic epidemic as recently as 1921, all victims died in less than two days unless given immediate treatment. We can all too clearly imagine the fate of pneumatic plague victims in 1348 and other times when antibiotics and other weapons of modern medicine were not available. A person hale and hearty on rising one morning might be dead within hours, after terrible suffering. Perhaps we can also imagine what it must have been like either to experience this massive onslaught or to witness it in our family, friends, and neighbors.

Twigg offers an interesting challenge to established opinion with his thesis that many of the fatalities attributed to Yp actually were caused by anthrax, a nasty disease that probably could do the work of the Black

Death if given the opportunity. Anthrax anxiety bubbled to the surface in the early years of the twenty-first century when infected mailings claimed several lives and opened a new dimension in terrorist threats.

OTHER VISITATIONS OF THE PLAGUE

Histories of the plague often begin with the pandemic of 1348. But we should not bypass earlier epidemics, even though we have less information about them.

A devastating epidemic struck during the golden age of Greek city-states. Thucydides described the symptoms:

> Many who were in perfect health, all in a moment, and without any apparent reason, were seized with violent heats in the head and with redness and inflammation of the eyes. Internally the throat and the tongue were quickly suffused with blood, and the breath became unnatural and fetid. There followed sneezing and hoarseness; in a short time the disorder, accompanied by a violent cough, reached the chest. . . . An inefficient retching producing violent convulsions attacked most of the sufferers. . . . The body . . . was of a livid colour inclining to red and breaking out in pustules and ulcers. But the internal fever was intense. . . .[8]

The victims usually died within a week or so, felled by the fever, or so Thucydides judged. If they held on a little longer before death, they would suffer other painful symptoms, including "violent ulceration." The disease seized its victims first in the head and worked its way down. Thucydides did not specifically mention the presence of buboes, but he did report that the disease would "leave its mark, attacking the privy parts and the fingers and the toes."[9]

But where were the birds of prey and other animals that were invariably attracted to corpse-strewn fields? It was eerie. All those dead, and no scavengers. Had they tasted the corrupt flesh and either died or hastily retreated?

The sudden and overpowering disease that killed so many Athenians in the year 430 B.C. might have been plague; then again, it might have been typhus or some other condition that remains mysterious. It is certain, however, that this was a clear instance of "too many dead." Proper burial within a ceremonial framework was important to the people of

Athens, who, more than most others, were familiar with proper conduct within a coherent governance. But during this time they did not bury their own dead. There were too many of them, and the living dared not place their own lives at risk.

Another lethal pestilence that might have been a visitation of the Black Death was the plague of Justinian, starting in the Roman Empire in A.D. 540 and spreading throughout the Middle East. The reported death toll was so high that present-day medical historians find it difficult to believe (e.g., ten thousand dying *each day* in Constantinople at the peak of the pandemic). It has been estimated that between 40 and 50 percent of the population had died in the affected regions by the end of the sixth century—and more became victims as repeated outbreaks occurred in the following century. Whatever the actual figure, clearly the populace believed that the end of days was at hand—all would perish. Here there is firmer evidence that the bubonic plague was at least one of the diseases involved. Among the few who survived, their buboes expanded greatly and burst, discharging the pus. Most died and died swiftly. It is likely that other diseases (e.g., smallpox, cholera, dysentery, influenza) took advantage of the weakened condition of the populace and the breakdown of control measures. Again—horror, terror, and societies overwhelmed by both the dying and the dead. People were wrenched from their normal lives to die in a variety of horrible ways and left infected corpses in abundance.

Other lethal pestilences would rage throughout much of the world. These often followed war and famine, as Geoffrey of Monmouth reported of seventh-century Britons, who

> started to quarrel among themselves and to destroy the economy of their homeland by an appalling civil war. There then followed a second disaster: for a grievous and long-remembered famine afflicted the besotted population, and the countryside no longer produced any food at all for human sustenance, always excepting what the huntsman's skill could provide. A pestilent and deadly plague followed this famine and killed off such a vast number of the population that the living could not bury them. The few wretches left alive gathered themselves into bands and emigrated to countries across the sea.[10]

This was probably not the work of *Yp*, but it was obviously a highly lethal contagious disease. Practically any infectious agent can have lethal effects if it attacks a host that has no previous experience with it and therefore no immunity preparation. Whatever the disease or diseases that struck repeatedly through the centuries, they were predictably part of a morbid cycle in which the follies of warfare, banditry, and oppression made easy victims of a large proportion of the population. Stricken and hard-pressed families and communities become less able to function, thereby inviting further disaster.

The violence-famine-pestilence cycles affirmed a sad and familiar theme: the rich get richer, the poor get dead. The cleavage between upper and lower classes (not much then in the middle) became sharper with the differential morbidity and mortality rate. Some of the uppers were inconvenienced by the shortage of laborers and occasional short-lived uprisings. Overall, though, the commoners either were held even more firmly in place or wandered off in arduous emigrations. Another general consequence was the intensification of superstitious, magical, and supernatural modes of thought. There had to be an explanation for these catastrophes. There had to be a way of persuading the powers that be to cease their tormentings.

Debilitating loss and grief were often experienced. It was extremely difficult to go on with the core of their lives destroyed by multiple deaths. Furthermore, their own continued survival was clouded by apprehensions about the next war, the next famine, the next pestilence. And they had brought all this on themselves as a punishment from God, or so the priests insisted. Could things be worse? Yes. The too many dead were their own. They had died, most of them, without the consolation of Christian ritual, and now they had to be returned to earth by whatever crude means were available. Where was the justice? Where was the honor, the dignity? To leave the bodies where they lay would be indecent. To touch them would be to risk infection. Simply to view them was to behold an image of one's own mortal remains at some time perhaps not far distant. Demoralization would be a lame way of describing their response to encountering the corruption of the body unassuaged by a caring society or a diligent clergy.

The Plague of Plagues

Memories and myths arising from severe pestilences of the past suddenly became transformed into present catastrophe in the middle of the fourteenth century. The mood in many places was already tinged with a sense of impending doom. Barbara W. Tuchman's illuminating book *A Distant Mirror* bears the subtitle *The Calamitous 14th Century*. This is no exaggeration. Human violence seemed boundless. The Hundred Years War, bleeding Europe drop by slow drop, was supplemented by vicious banditry in many areas—the common people suffering the most, as usual. Preoccupied with its own fierce infighting and challenges from royal authorities, the church was not in a position to provide much comfort. Furthermore, many serving as priests were illiterate opportunists who did not understand the rites they were performing, let alone possess the higher qualities that one might expect from the clergy.

Meanwhile, Nature seemed in the mood to annihilate the pestiferous human race. Existing agricultural practices could not supply enough food for the burgeoning population. Nature increased all these miseries with an incessant rain that threatened to bring on another universal flood. A relentless freeze gripped some lands. Crops failed almost everywhere. A dependable orchard, for example, would be enveloped in a putrid mist, with all the fruit destroyed. Starving people carried off executed criminals to eat their bodies—and some did the same with their own children. And more: earthquakes of historical magnitude not only produced many casualties but also led others to question both the physical and the spiritual grounds of their existence. One particularly devastating quake in the mountains of China created a lake "more than a hundred leagues in circumference."[11]

These events also left a bad smell. There were many reports of foul vapors arising from fissures caused by earthquakes. Patches of nauseating mist would be dispelled by winds that brought their own foul smell. Meanwhile the stench of human and animal corpses was often upon the land as internecine battles raged and the starving and diseased succumbed. This extraordinary combination of natural catastrophes and human folly brought confusion, sorrow, and misery—and that uncanny sense of foreboding that even greater ordeals were to come.

A greater ordeal was to come from the well-populated East after brewing in more isolated areas such as the Gobi Desert, western Arabia, Kurdistan, and northern India. Influenza, a more familiar contagious disease today, also has its home territory from which new epidemics have arisen (such as the Hong Kong flu, attributed to infected waterfowl). Unlike influenza, though, bubonic plague works in much slower cycles and cruises through its potential victims over a longer period of time once it gets going. Theoretically, then, there is more warning time available to take preventive measures. Global communication and effective public health programs, though, were not available to people experiencing the calamitous fourteenth century.

The plague struck like a thunderbolt. First it emerged in Central Asia, to devastating effect. Memorial stones there dating from 1338 and 1339 specify the plague as the cause of the all too many deaths. It is almost certain that both the bubonic and the pneumatic forms of the plague were at work. And it is conceivable, although not proven, that earthquakes, unsettling weather, and the harvest of corpses attendant upon warfare might have contributed to a wider distribution of infected rats and their fleas as well as unfortunate human hosts. Certainly, the increase in commercial traffic, especially by ship, provided a means for the infected to visit new lands.

There were rumors, of course, circulating in the major European seaports. A terrible disease was ravaging the East. It was said that

> India was depopulated, Tartary, Mesopotamia, Syria, Armenia were covered with dead bodies; the Kurds fled in vain to the mountains. In Caramania and Caesarea none were left alive.[12]

But these were, after all, rumors. And the East was still a vague and mysterious region to most Europeans. There were more than enough immediately pressing concerns than to worry about a remote pestilence.

And then that remarkable human proclivity for folly and violence conspired with a deadly pestilence to assure Europe would also become a killing ground. Is *conspire* too strong a word here? Consider this sequence, if you will:

- The Black Death kills a reported eighty-five thousand Tartars in the Crimea.
- Some Tartars decide that an unpopular minority group—the Christians, in this case—must have been responsible (just as Christians would soon decide about one of their unpopular minority groups—the Jews). There are street brawls (compare to the subsequent Christian actions of burning Jews alive).

- One Tartar dies in a street brawl. This is excuse enough to attack a Genoese trading post and chase their prey to a fortified coastal town (then Caffa, now Feodosia).
- The siege begins. It continues. Caffa holds the fort. The besiegers, fatigued and increasingly hungry, are sitting ducks for the plague. They are ready to pull out and try to escape a full-fledged epidemic in their ranks.
- But first the Tartars would fire a parting shot, something to avenge their own sufferings in front of the walls of a foe who were not cooperative enough to capitulate. Philip Ziegler explains:

> They used their giant catapults to lob over the walls the corpses of the victims in the hope that this would spread the disease within the city. As fast as the rotting bodies arrived in their midst the Genoese carried them through the town and dropped them into the sea. But few places are so vulnerable to disease as a besieged city and it was not long before the plague was as active within the city as without. Such inhabitants as did not rapidly succumb realized that, even if they survived the plague, they would be far too few to resist a fresh Tartar onslaught. They took to the galleys and fled from the Black Sea towards the Mediterranean. With them traveled the plague.[13]

The galleys arrived with crews of the dying and the dead. Other boats of dead merchants and sailors also drifted ashore or disappeared on the seas as time went by. The plague of plagues had reached Europe.

"Conspire" with Death turns out to be an accurate term, then. The plague-afflicted Tartars were out to avenge themselves against their most convenient scapegoats. Frustrated, they assigned their fallen comrades to a sort of postmortem kamikaze mission. The dead would kill. The dead did kill—prolifically. Perhaps lost in this grisly drama is the Tartars' suspension of funeral rites for their own comrades. Flinging corpses into a hostile city is not part of the normal code for honoring the dead and giving them a good send-off to their next lives. Exceptions to standard funeral practice have often occurred in military actions, whether on land or sea. Human ingenuity has no difficulty in rationalizing such practices. Ironically, perhaps, European society would soon be confronted with massive challenges in disposing properly of its own dead as the plague casualties piled up.

Perhaps one vivid description will suffice. Scenes such as the following occurred throughout almost all of Europe except the northernmost realms, where isolation and a determined refusal to admit travelers protected the population. Tuchman is our guide here:

> In the countryside peasants dropped dead on the roads, in the fields, in their houses. Survivors in growing helplessness fell into apathy, leaving ripe wheat uncut and livestock untended. Oxen and asses, sheep and goats, pigs and chickens ran wild and they too, according to local reports, succumbed to the pest. English sheep, bearers of the precious wool, died throughout the country . . . 5,000 dead in one field alone, their bodies so corrupted by the plague that neither beast nor bird would touch them, and spreading an appalling stench. . . . wolves came down to prey upon sheep and then, as if alarmed by some invisible warning, turned and fled back into the wilderness. In remote Dalmatia bolder wolves descended upon a plague-stricken city and attacked human survivors. For want of herdsmen, cattle strayed from place to place and died in hedgerows and ditches. Dogs and cats fell like the rest.[14]

The dead lay where they fell. In larger settlements the dead cart rumbled through the streets. New corpses would usually be lowered into trenches or pits at some distance from town. The mass of deaths had eroded individuality just as it had truncated ceremonial rituals. The traditional practice of attending, preparing, and burying a particular individual had given way to a crude disposal operation that ended in an anonymous grave. The burials were hasty, and the earth coverings sometimes inadequate. Dogs and wolves could easily get at corpses. This, of course, both constituted another insult to the dead and added another source of infection to the living.

Matters were no better in the cities. The cemeteries of Paris, for example, were soon overflowing with bodies. A large garden in rue Saint-Denis was converted to what became the historic cemetery La Trinité. With repeated waves of the Black Death, though, even the new cemetery was not sufficient. Huge pits were dug, some accommodating more than a thousand of the stricken poor. Pressure continued to colonize other areas for gravesites as far as possible from the city. To live in Paris during the plague years was to live with the dead—in the overstocked charnel houses, in the bursting cemeteries, in the anonymous pits, and in the stinking streets.

Florence also suffered greatly during this, its first major visitation from the Black Death. As entire families perished, their bodies were placed to-gether on the same bier:

> Many died daily or nightly in the public streets; of many others, who died at home, the departure was hardly observed by their neighbours, until the stench of their putrefying bodies carried the tidings; and what with their corpses and the corpses of others who died on every hand the whole place was a sepulchre.[15]

As in Paris, long trenches were dug to receive corpses at any hour of the day or night. Boccaccio, safe in his haven away from the city, reported the suspension of "ancient custom" with a "separate resting-place as-signed to each."[16] Astonishingly, officials in Florence and other plague-stricken Italian municipalities were able to keep the government work-ing and thereby limited somewhat the scope of the disaster. How they were able to function while other cities across Europe collapsed under the strain would be worth knowing.

Living with the Dead during the Plague Years

The plague had dire economic consequences. Tuchman has mentioned the inability to harvest crops and the failure of the English wool indus-try. Many other commercial endeavors also were severely affected. The plague affected all spheres of communal life at the time and left ripples well into our own time. Here, though, we focus on the most significant consequences of the encounter with "too many dead."

First we must envision the *necroscape*. Life had always dissolved into death. But this was usually a slow dissolve, counterbalanced by new growth. Now death seemed to have taken the whole world into its dry embrace, from the skeletal crops and fetid stinks to the diseased corpses of humans and beasts. The laughing child, the merry couple, the content elder were very much the exception. Thousands of country towns and villages had been emptied of life. Petrarch, overwhelmed by the desola-tion he saw everywhere, lamented that soon the whole globe would be without inhabitants. *This image of a cold, lifeless earth arose from di-rect experience.* Deadness was also the state of the soul for many indi-viduals who had become numbed by grief upon grief.

Popular science fantasy, with its imaginings of destroyed planets, was anticipated in the fourteenth century by ordinary people whose experiences would no longer be ordinary. Some ecologists, operating from a different set of premises, have also warned that we are conspiring to destroy the life-giving resources of Mother Earth. There had been prophecies of universal doom before the Black Death, but the calamities of the fourteenth century came close enough to these predictions to infiltrate the image of a dead world into humankind's anxiety closet.

Next, we salute the figure that moves slowly but purposely across the necroscape. This is the man who walks hand in hand with Death. This is the man who loads the corpse into the cart and trundles it to the mass grave. This is the man who takes the good shirt off the dead man's body as partial payment, who digs the trench, inters the corpse, and perhaps, just perhaps, pauses to utter a prayer or bawdy jest before covering the remains with a sprinkling of earth. Someone had to take on this dismal work. The tough, the desperate, and the enterprising responded.

There was an odd mixture of unprincipled opportunists who wheedled and stole what they could, the depressed who already felt at one with death, and the pious who believed that every person was owed some decency and respect. There was plenty of business for all of them. In large cities some enriched themselves by proving of service to wealthy families that sought a measure of decency in the proceedings. The reputation of death-handlers, however, was soiled by their identification with the masses of diseased and ravaged corpses. This tainted identity would follow the emerging profession of undertakers, or morticians, into modern times.

The ubiquitous presence of the dead gave rise to heightened imagery of the corpse, the skeleton, and Death himself, who was often portrayed as an emaciated or skeletal fellow. A trio of images became almost inseparable: the dead body, Death in the form of a person, and the living person as somewhat dead or linked with death. Life and death morphed into each other in an exuberant round of variations. The necroscape had made death the imminent concern of the living. Both new and preexistent images and ideas were seized upon and lavishly developed. Some of these themes continued to be expressed long after this visitation from the Black Death and became part of our common heritage.

Memento mori flourished. "Remember, you must die!" was the message of the day. Artists, sculptors, poets, craftsmen, storytellers, and performers became obsessed with death. Both prostitutes and priests, for example, wore death's-head rings.[17] A new theme emerged, first in sepulchral monuments, then in public statuary. The *gisant* and *transi* types of statuary revealed the worm beneath the skull, the corruption inside the facade. The former type presented a likeness of the illustrious dead in their regal or ecclesiastical finery, looking every inch the proud and revered figure. But this representation was compromised by unmistakable signs of emaciation and decay. The more gruesome examples even included the visual confirmation of that phrase so dear to boys of a certain age who are trying to gross out girls who they hope are squeamish: "The worms crawl in, the warms crawl out. . . ." The *transi* style presented a nude or shrouded corpse with a decidedly lifelike appearance. As Kathleen Cohen reports, "Several of these so-called transi images seem to come to life and to stand up, taking all their rotting flesh and worms with them."[18]

Paintings, engravings, and murals disseminated reminders that every mortal, no matter how proud and privileged, faces the prospect of death. Death interrupts the journey of a knight or the pleasures of young lovers. The bishop's sanctity and the lord's wealth do not deter Death from his mission.

It was as though the too many dead had risen and become reanimated through artistic representations in order to deliver an urgent message to the living. But what precisely was this message? What I read in the gripping, exuberant, and bizarre panoply of medieval responses to the plague is both a pro- and an antiestablishment message. The basic message "remember, you must die" was sponsored by the establishment, who not only approved but also paid for those sculptured bishops, princes, and saints with their see-through corrupting innards. And it was certainly the establishment that fostered the dissemination of a new type of literature, the *Ars moriendi,* the tracts offering instruction on the art of dying well. One could hardly expect to die well, though, if one had been living a slothful and sinful existence.

The earliest of these tracts were heavy on illustrations and light on text. Inspecting a surviving tract in Mainz, I could not help but think of comic books, spiced with lurid pictures to get their points across to people with limited or nonexistent reading skills. By both visual image and text, then, the establishment was urging that people devote themselves to the good Christian life, realizing that they will inevitably come to that awful

Figure 17 Three revelers meet three corpses who warn them to repent. From *Horae*
(Westminster: printed by Wynkyn de Worde, 1494).

Figure 18 Victims of the Black Death who were buried alive in 1347 emerge from the grave. From an engraving by A. Aubrey, Germany, 1604.

moment of truth. Eschew vice and blasphemy and waste not your hours in vain and idle pursuits. Think always of your death—and here, in case death has slipped your mind, are also abundant images of skulls and cross-bones, grim reapers, and hourglasses with the sand relentlessly slipping away. The too many deaths had given the church an impressive platform to intimidate the population anew with the misery of damnation and hellfire and the bliss of salvation.

This establishment message sometimes had more than its desired effect. Religious frenzies developed among the susceptible. In their formative phase, these movements were intense, all-consuming, evangelical missions. God was surely punishing us for our sins and failings. Death's bony hand will seize us at any moment, and we will be hurled into the pit of the damned (not a far stretch from what was actually happening).

The flagellants were perhaps the most conspicuous example. Accounts suggest that the original members were both anxious and idealistic people who had become even more unhinged than most by their experiences in the necroscape.[19] They not only agreed with the preachings; they also did something about them. What they did was to punish themselves. They performed an imitation of Christ by relentlessly scourging themselves upon their scarred and bleeding backs with leather whips or bundles of sticks. Processions of two hundred or three hundred flagellants marched through the land. Generally, there were two daily performances for the public and another conducted in privacy. Their self-scourgings were preceded and accompanied by chants and shouts. "Look at us! We are suffering for Christ; we are suffering for you!" At first the people of village, town, and city were receptive, even reverent. Idealistic new members swelled the flagellants' ranks. Here, then, was a vigorous display of willpower, energy, and determination in a time when others were passive and demoralized. True Christians on the march!

But when the flagellant movement turned bad, it turned really bad. They had demonstrated an anticlerical, antiestablishment bias from the beginning. Unprincipled opportunists and outright criminals joined the procession for their own purposes, which included thievery, violence, and rape. Soon they were chasing off priests and assumed such core functions as hearing confession and imposing penance. They attacked churches and disrupted the most sacred of services and rituals, looted valuable objects, and even claimed to have necromantic powers. (And there was a thought to tremble at. What if they *could* raise the too many dead? Is that what we really wanted, or would that be heaping horror on horror?)

And, here again, bad was followed by worse. Having appointed themselves guardians of the faith, the flagellants were ready to smite the foe. That would be the plague-spreaders. Strangers and minorities were everywhere in danger of being accused of intentionally spreading if not instigating the plague (as we have already seen with the unfortunate Christians in the Tartar-ruled Crimea). The flagellants decided that the Jews were at fault. No doubt the Jews had poisoned the wells, they said. Flagellant bands embarked on a campaign of slaughtering the Jewish population in major cities, this conducted with particular fury and thoroughness in the Germanic lands. Jews were murdered by the thousands, and when they attempted to defend themselves in Mainz their own neighbors joined in the carnage.[20]

Many church and civic leaders were appalled and tried to reason with the flagellants, pointing out, for example, that Jews had been dying of the plague just like everybody else. Eventually church authorities banned flagellants, and magistrates erected gallows for them in front of the locked city gates. These were responsible actions to prevent further attacks on the remaining Jews of Europe, but also acts of self-preservation. The flagellants had far exceeded the mark of piety and the guidance of the *Ars moriendi*. Instead of reinforcing Christian values in the face of pestilence, the flagellants were actually doing Death's work and overturning the establishment. In the meantime, though, so many Jews had been slaughtered and their societal connections had been so disrupted that their exiled survivors no longer had an active role in communal medieval life.

Plague → mass death → religious frenzy → slaughter of the innocents. Another melancholy example of human folly and violence adding its own contribution to the already devastated necroscape.

The antiestablishment response took another form that threatened to undermine the structure of society: "If we are equal in death, are we not also equal in life? Should we not have the same rights and privileges? Need one lump of clay bow in submission to another?" People started thinking more seriously about their status in life as death took on the aspect of the leveler or equalizer. Actual rebellions were short-lived, but the ripple effect coursed through generations and across boundaries. Long before Patrick Henry challenged, "Give me liberty or give me death," the dangerous idea that we might be equal both in life and in death had summoned strength from the devastation of the plague years.

It proved more difficult to rebel against another tradition, one in which the dead themselves were positioned as economic adversaries of the living. The living owed debts to the dead, not only emotional but also financial debts that were often specified to the penny. We will consider just one facet of this obligation: *the highway to heaven was a toll road.* Prayers and masses—and even the religious houses that performed these labors—required financial upkeep. The wealthy were at risk of becoming less so as they subsidized dozens, even hundreds or thousands, of masses for their ancestors. On a humbler level but one that could literally take the bread out of their own mouths, commoners also had to pay and pray for the dead. The person stingy or negligent in paying tribute to kin who had passed from this imperfect life was courting damnation. Colin Platt notes that "for the rich and powerful everywhere, a death-bed exchange of the wealth of this world for precisely equal benefits in the next" was a most prudent deal to consummate. A big dealer was Bernard Ezi d'Albret, who with "100,000 masses . . . planned to scale the walls of Heaven."[21]

But now the deaths were too many and too unrelenting. There was little opportunity to go on with life, heal personal and social connections, and accumulate continued resources. Catastrophic in their mode and magnitude, the plague deaths placed a further burden on the existing system of exchange between living and dead.

Another response to the Black Death stood piety and penance on its head. Instead of becoming more virtuous and obedient, many of those who had been spared from the plague, at least for the moment, gave themselves over to drink, lust, greed, violence, and mockery in various combinations. Chroniclers were aghast at this gross misconduct. Boccaccio himself was almost certainly a participant in "lewd and licentious" behavior, albeit in the style of a gentleman, as he penned *Decameron*, although he professed to deplore those who engaged in feasting and drinking to excess, indulging every gratification, indifferent to the suffering of others:

> They wandered day and night from one tavern to another, and feasted without moderation or bounds. They abandoned home and all property like men whose death-knell had already tolled. Amid the general lamentation and woe the influence and authority of every law, human and divine, vanished, and every one acted as he pleased.[22]

The more violent responses to social breakdown and fear of death occurred where famine had driven people to the extremes of desperation. There were scattered reports of cannibalism as well as murder.

The rule-breaking and indulgent type of response to the stress of the plague years have several readily understandable causes. "Live for today, for tomorrow we die" would not have been an unusual thought under the circumstances. Furthermore, dulling one's consciousness with drink would also have had its attraction. For some people, the weakening of social control over lust, gluttony, and public inebriation would have been all the invitation they needed. There was something more, however— what at least one onlooker characterized as "dancing on the grave." All those many dead seemed to arouse in some a manic sense of life. It was as though they said, "You are so dead, and I am so alive!" Lively entertainments and risky behavior confirmed that they were still among the quick. Just being alive could be experienced as a "high." And expecting to die at the same time could also intensify that feeling and give one an exuberance seldom experienced in the midst of a routined, obligated, and sanctioned life.

The mockery topped it all off. I am not speaking of the mass of the unfortunates trapped in the necroscape but of those influential and charismatic people who responded to the plague years by caricaturing the establishment, each other, and even Death himself. Personifications of Death were often grinning cartoonlike beings who deflated human illusions and vanities. Death might even be placed upon a throne to ridicule and chasten monarchs everywhere. Platt selected *King Death* to title his study, subtitled *The Black Death and Its Aftermath in Late-Medieval England*. The cover sports a pair of dancing and perhaps laughing skeletons, appropriate symbols for the way in which human imagination attempted to convert horrors into fantasy, passivity into control. The bizarre images, stories, and songs spawned during the plague years have found receptive minds hundreds of years later (that bony hand arising from the grave and so many other clichés of horror stories and films). The real triumph, though, was that Death had been put to work. Dramatists, poets, and songwriters put words into Death's mouth (or where Death's mouth would have been). Puppet masters pulled the strings for Death's grotesque movements. Artists invented situations and provided costumes.

Death was playing Last Tag!—a frightening game in which just one touch of its skeletal finger could put one out of action forever. So, *we* will make our own rules and make Death play by them. Throughout Europe and perhaps elsewhere games of Tag—You're It! prospered. All had at their core the realization that a lethal touch could turn the living into the dead. Dead Man Arise! was the aptly named English version. Children could try to master the tremendous anxieties of the time in their own way, by *becoming* Death. For a moment they would be the pursuer, the executioner, not the prey. Instead of feeling powerless, they could relish the temporary joy of being It. But what about when they were in the role of victim? The stricken child usually tumbled to the ground (and might even have been covered with leaves, as in Dead Man Arise!).[23]

This provided the opportunity to experience a possibly immunizing episode of thanatomimesis—looking as dead as one could manage while secure in knowing that one would soon pop up as full of life as ever. There was probably also a subtle fantasy at work here that still contributes to death-simulating behavior today, as in the proliferation of rock groups billing themselves as veritable orchestras of the dead (Dies Irae, Dead Milkmen, Megadeth, Grateful Dead, and just plain Death). The secret plan: "If we're already dead, we can't be killed."

Ring-around-a-rosie (also known by several variant names) is one of the hardiest survivors of these Death-taming games. During the years of the plague and its aftermath, it was deadly serious. It was fun. It was comforting. The children would move slowly in a circle, small hands holding small hands. The "rosie" and the "posie" are thought by some historians to have referred to visible marks of the plague, but we do not know this for sure. For whatever reason, they would chant:

> Ring around the rosie
> Pocket full of posie
> Ashes, ashes, all fall down!

And one of the children would fall down, obligingly, perhaps staggering into the center of the circle. The chanting and circle dancing would be repeated again and again, the grave little band of survivors becoming smaller every time. Finally, all would be sprawled on the ground, probably the more antic ones with tongues lolling out of their mouths, or arms and legs extended stiffly from their supine forms, like some animal corpses they had seen. But not to worry! All the dead arise, having completed their own version of a mystical journey through and miraculous escape from the world of the dead.

Dances of Death

The plague did not flare out all at once. It did, however, simmer down in a particular area after the most susceptible members of the population had succumbed. The Black Death would then make itself known in other regions, and there could be repeated visitations after several new generations had become available as potential victims. Nevertheless, there was a collective sigh of relief when the plague seemed to have spent itself.

When so many are dead it can feel strange to be yet among the living. But now there was so much to be done. This included all the arts of survival: the restoration of food production, the replenishment of the species, and the rebuilding of civic competence and confidence. The survivors, though, also had to renegotiate their relationship with the dead and with Death himself. The usual courteous but cautious relationship between living and dead had been fractured and would not easily heal.

Septima etas mūdi   CCLXIII
Imago moztis

Orte nihil melius. vita nil peius iniqua
pma mozs boim. reqes eterna laboꝛ
Zu ferule iugum domno volente relaxas
Uinctoꝛuꝗ graues adunis ceruice catbenas
Enkiumꝗ leuas. ꜩ carceris boftia frangis
Eripis indignis. iufti bona pubus equans
Atꝗ immota manes. nulla exoꝛabiis arte
A pꝛimo pꝛefixa die. tu cuncta quieto
ferre iubes animo. pꝛomiffo fine laboꝛum
Te fine fuppliaum. vit a eft carcer perennis

Figure 19 A dance of the dead. Woodcut by Michael Wolgemut, from Hartmann Schedel, *Liber Chronicarum* (Nuremberg: printed by Anton Koberger, 1493).

A new kind of relationship had to be developed. And, as in relationships among the living, sometimes words are not enough.

The "dance of death" appeared following the plague of plagues. It was also known as the dance of the dead, but even more widely as *Totentanz* and *le danse macabre*. Aries observes that the Maccabees had been revered as patrons of the dead. A derivative—*macchabe*—became a folk expression for the dead body and retains that meaning in French slang. The word *macabre* entered the international vocabulary, then, as another gift of the plague of plagues. Today the term *macabre* is often used when we are faced with a weird, bizarre, threatening, and perverse image, not uncommonly tinged with humor. We might suppose, then, that the dance of death was just another example of nervous parody, trying to rattle the bones of the Grim Reaper. But—not so. Aries offers this encapsulation of the danse macabre:

> . . . an eternal round in which the dead alternate with the living. The dead lead the dance; indeed, they are the only ones dancing. Each couple consists of a naked mummy, rotting, sexless, and highly animated, and a man or woman, dressed according to his or her social condition, and paralyzed by surprise. Death holds out its hand to the person whom it will draw along with it, but who has not yet obeyed the summons. The art lies in the contrast between the rhythm of the dead and the rigidity of the living.

Why this dance?

> The moral purpose was to remind the viewer both of the uncertainty of the hour of death, and of the equality of all people in the face of death. People of all ages and ranks file by in an order which is that of the social hierarchy as it was . . . perceived at the time.[24]

There was no mockery intended in this pure or idealized version of the dance of death. The procession was slow and stately. There was no savage glee on the part of Death and the dead, no terror and frenzy on the part of the living. In this idealized version, the dance of death affirmed the proper order of things—age, rank, title. If anything, Death was rather gentle, and the final passage dignified. (Images of Death as either a Gentle Comforter or a Macabre still come to the surface today, as my studies of contemporary death personifications indicate, but that's another story.)

Aries' account, though, is sanitized. Humor, mockery, and shock value are evident in many of the surviving depictions of the dance of death. Artists in the Totentanz tradition, for example, liked to accompany the dance with a skeletal orchestra whose getup might well be the envy of shock-rock bands today. The dance of death provided the opportunity for people of faith and composure to reconstruct the mortal move in a more humane and acceptable manner. But it also provided the opportunity for anxiety, rage, and rebellion, induced by a variety of motives—including simply the desire to show off one's creative virtuosity.

There were performances of the danse macabre in which participants donned cloaks with skeletal decor (Halloween, before the days of mass marketing and political correctness, provided many examples in this tradition). Mostly, though, the dance of death flourished in the visual arts through woodcuts, tapestries, books of hours, and frescoes on church walls. Perhaps the most influential of the last was the danse macabre painted on the cloister walls of the Innocents, a religious order in Paris. Unfortunately the earliest known versions have been lost to time, though woodcut copies remain of some. These visuals were accompanied by story poems that had achieved a classic status, such as "The Encounter of the Three Living and the Three Dead." Death also became a popular theatrical personage, starring in both moralistic and burlesque productions.

At first, the dance involved just the dead and the living. Soon, though, the latent power of the too many dead morphed into the character of Death himself. The tradition of a gracious and dignified dance procession seems to have dominated in the beginning. Fanciful and bizarre elements became more common later. The morality lesson originally inherent in the dance of death was renewed two centuries after the plague of plagues through Holbein's woodcuts. Little is known about the music that might have accompanied the dance of death. Kathi Meyer-Baer offers a possibility in the form of an old Spanish tune that begins with and repeats such phrases as *"festinamus ad mortem"* (we hasten to death).[25] Meyer-Baer also notes connections between the *danza della morte* and dances of the angels or blessed spirits. The nineteenth-century ghost dance of Native American peoples was also a variant on preexisting circle dance rituals to honor the sun but became a desperate attempt to invoke the protection of ancestral spirits during the genocidal invasion of their lands.[26]

But wasn't there also a very different kind of death-imbued dance—faster, even frenzied? Well, yes, there was. Often confused by later generations with the stately danse macabre were outbreaks of wild and energetic displays known as both Saint John's and Saint Vitus' dance. It may have started in Germany and the Netherlands, but it soon became quite a feature in Italy and France, perhaps elsewhere as well. Here is what we might have been observing—or doing!—had we been in the streets of Aix-la-Chapelle in 1374:

They formed circles hand in hand, and appearing to have lost all control over their senses, continued dancing, regardless of the bystanders, for hours together, in wild delirium, until at length they fell to the ground in a state of exhaustion.

Was this a dance or mass pathology?

They then . . . groaned as if in the agonies of death, until they were swathed in clothes bound tightly round their waists, upon which they again recovered and remained free from complaint until the next attack.[27]

A pathological seizure or fit, evidently. Onlookers apparently were also affected by the noise and disorder, because "following these spasmodic raving [*sic*], bystanders frequently relieved patients by thumping and tramping upon the parts affected." Local authorities also hired additional musicians and instructed them to play faster and faster—the better to exhaust these weird and troubling dancers.

Although the dancers were physically active, their minds seemed far away:

While dancing . . . they were haunted by visions, their fancies conjuring up spirits whose names they shrieked out; and some of them afterward asserted that they felt as if they were immersed in a stream of blood, which caused them to leap so high. Others saw the heavens open and the Saviour enthroned with the Virgin Mary. . . . Indeed we are told that many of the dancers so completely lost their senses as not to be able to take care of themselves; in the extravagance of their actions some ran against buildings or other objects and killed themselves; others rushed into rivers and were drowned.[28]

The dancers exhibited amazing energy and stamina, this being attributed by some to the Evil One. They became sufficiently numerous to take over churches and generally upset the order of things in some villages. Admired and befriended by some and offered exorcism by priests, the dancers eventually came to be disliked by the majority of citizens, who saw them as flagrant nuisances who were liable to "go off" at the slightest provocation. Similar episodes of mass hysteria would continue through at least the sixteenth century. Some casual historians later accepted the story that these dances had started with a wave of tarantula bites, noting the popular lively dance of the same name. The big, hairy, scary-looking tarantula, however, is not much of a biter, while the weight of evidence associates this dance craze with the far more dangerous bite of the blocked flea. More serious historians have also linked these antics to bacchanalian dances of antiquity, whose wild revels may have again come to the fore in this time of heightened death anxiety. (The real Saint Vitus' dancers soon had to compete with pretenders, who enjoyed fooling and milking the crowd: fanaticism and frenzy had become popular entertainment.)

What are we to make of these dances, both stately and frenzied? At the very least, plague survivors demonstrated that they could still move, and to their own rhythms, and with their own living companions. Collectively, the dances tested the possibilities. We pass from this life with dignity and with our place in the order of things assured. There are still rules to follow, a comfort to be sure. Or we escape from the many too many dead by otherworldly visions produced by the physical release of spasmodic dances and perhaps self-imposed starvation as well. The circle dance was around long before the plague years, serving a variety of purposes. Many other responses to the plague years also built upon preexisting models. The Black Death and its associated horrors tested the limits of communal feeling, physical and emotional endurance, and imagination, because ordinary rituals could not suffice for extraordinary events.

The Great Plague of London

The plague has returned many times since its most sweeping attack in the late fourteenth century. Here I will touch on only a few aspects of later epidemics for what they might tell us about the individual and communal response to megadeath. It is true that this version of megadeath emptied rather than destroyed communities. The plague did not blast craters where a cathedral had been. The physical landscape, for the most part, remained intact. This was hardly a saving grace, however. Villages and cities themselves became skeletal. The shell of society stood but with an eerie hollowness inside. Absence became palpable, empty, a mute cry of despair.

Both biblical and modern visions of Armageddon equip the carnage with such violent events as inferno, eruption, storm, flood, quake, and nuclear holocaust. More dramatic? Perhaps. More exciting? Definitely. But for a profound sense of having been stricken and abandoned, of being left adrift in the dead sea of one's own familiar surroundings, the Black Death was perhaps even more insidious and haunting.

Worse yet to the faithful was a terrible fear regarding the fate of the dead—and how that fate might affect their own. So many had died under such repugnant conditions that they went to their graves without absolution for their sins. The unprepared soul would sink to purgatory (a sphere of the afterlife that was on its way to becoming officially sanctioned by the church) or all the way down to the nether regions and total despair. Courageous people could bear the prospect of their own deaths, and a few were eager to trade the corrupt flesh for the robes of immortality. Damnation, though, a failed death—this was harder to bear. And those who had shunned the dying plague victim, who feared infection or just could not bring themselves to witness the suffering—those survivors had reason to fear that their failure to perform their deathbed obligations would be sufficient reason for their own damnation.

Move on to more modern times: to the thriving and desperate metropolis of London, Europe's most populous city in the 1660s. *Thriving* pertains to the bankers, merchant princes, and others who had made their mark. *Desperate* describes many of the commoners, crowded into unhealthy residences, victims of neglect and crime and, to some extent, each other. The plague had never entirely released its hold on the British Isles. Episodes were fresh enough to keep authorities on the alert. Furthermore, enlightened minds had rejected supernatural explanations and were more attentive to the prevention and containment of contagious diseases. Unfortunately, this concern had not resulted in much if any improvement in public sanitation or, as events would soon demonstrate, in fire safety measures.

Eminent Londoners such as Sir Thomas Browne decried the air pollution in which fog grew thick with coal smoke and the "exhalations of common sewers and fetid places, and decoction used by unwholesome and sordid manufactures."[29] At the request of the king, John Evelyn had recently offered a plan to reduce air pollution. Evelyn described his London as

> the suburbs of hell, rather than an assembly of rational creatures. The weary traveler, at many miles' distance, sooner smells than sees the city to which

he repairs. . . . This acrimonious soot . . . ulcerates the lungs, which is a mischief so incurable that it carries away multitudes by languishing and deep consumptions, as the bills of mortality do weekly inform us.[30]

In addition to the severe air pollution, there were no public sewers, and refuse often was dumped illegally into the Thames. Four years after Evelyn's plan was introduced, little if anything had been done to improve the situation. To this everyday misery were added annual epidemics, which, as usual, carried off mostly the very young, the old, the ill, the weak, and the poor. Now came the reports of plague surfacing in Amsterdam. Authorities could and did quarantine ships arriving from that port. Somehow, though, *Yersina pestis* found its way in.

The first plague death in London was reported in December 1664. Londoners knew what they were in for when forty-three died in May. Many packed up and left, but most remained. Braving the danger were many city officials and some physicians and clergy, some of whom became plague victims. The pestilence took advantage of a steaming hot summer, in which pollution from all sources increased. At its peak in the summer, the Black Death was responsible for more than six thousand deaths a week, an astounding number in a population of fewer than half a million, minus those who had fled. About seventy thousand Londoners perished of the plague in 1665. Although this was "only" about a seventh of the population, a smaller toll than the 1348 plague, most of the deaths occurred within just a few months. (About thirty-five thousand died in Amsterdam.) Once again, there were too many dead, and the carts were rolling slowly through the narrow, unpaved streets of London just as they had through so many villages and cities three centuries before.

One response was to conceal the extent of the plague as much as possible. It was bad for business and trade. It was also bad for families who did not want to have their homes identified and quarantined by the authorities. Ordinary self-interest competed with efforts to control the plague. This led to underestimation of plague death in the weekly Bills of Mortality. The more skeptical observers believed the actual toll from the plague was as much as three times higher than indicated in the official reports. Concealment also led to people dying out of view and with little or no care. Although medical remedies of the time were not effective against the bubonic plague, competent nursing and nutrition might have helped more victims to survive. As it was, often it was the stench of decay that alerted the authorities to still another plague death.

And what of the dead themselves? Again, the pits were dug, and the plague victims lowered into their mass graves. Again, many of the deceased were in postmortem jeopardy because they had not been given the opportunity to cleanse their souls and prepare for death. Samuel Pepys, for example, reported having on several occasions "met a dead Corpse, of the plague in a narrow alley."[31] It was not likely that many of these forlorn dead corpses had received the benefit of clergy in their passing. And so, once again, survivors who held their religion dear would be haunted by discomfort, even guilt, at this lapse in performing their obligations.

Authorities came down on the side of prevention rather than tradition, ritual, and solace. Funeral processions were banned. Clergy were pressured to suspend public funerals, and diatribes were directed at those who attended funerals. A little war within a war developed around this issue. Public health officials were incensed that people would contribute to the spread of plague by swarming around funerals, while mourners defied such an outrageous and insensitive abrogation of their traditional rights. Apparently the mourners won. It was important to do the right thing, even if it placed one at heightened risk. The numerous and invisible poor did not have to worry about this predicament: dumping into the plague pits was all the ritual they would receive. Even this would be done in the hours of darkness. The authorities hoped to have all burials carried out as inconspicuously as possible. The dead were too many, though, and the summer nights too short. The plague victims of London had to be buried in the full glare of the brutal sun.

It was a custom in London, as in many other places, to accommodate the dead in their neighborhood churchyard. There were also larger burial grounds operated under parish auspices. Soon the churchyards had accepted all they could hold. Bystanders were alarmed to see the ground risen—body had been placed upon body. A susceptible mind could well imagine the earth ready to open and spew back all its dead. Even a new churchyard was quickly at maximum. Custom now had to give way to necessity. Mass burial pits were dug in church-operated burial grounds. The parish of St. Botoph, for example, consigned 1,114 corpses to their "great pit."[32]

Proper respect for the dead was compromised by another factor in addition to their sheer numbers. The dead had to be buried quickly. Their corpses were regarded as prime sources of contagion. Everybody had to work swiftly, from high authorities to beleaguered grave diggers. Haste did not necessarily make waste, but it did markedly reduce the opportunity to pay last respects and see the departing souls off to their daunting journey with the blessing of ritual.

Custom was further assaulted by the shortage of coffins. Officials again improvised. As early as July it was ruled acceptable to inter bodies protected only by a shroud. (A coffin shortage also developed in the United States and perhaps elsewhere during the killer influenza pandemic of 1918.)[33] The coffin was so much taken for granted by many societies that lack of same intensified the feeling that the world was very much out of tune. And swift, effective burial was handicapped by still another grim element: the custodians of life and death were themselves dying. Churchwardens were especially active in seeing to burials, and they proved especially vulnerable to the plague.

From the Great Plague of London—what lessons? First, we see that awareness of the danger and of the city's own health hazards did not translate into sufficient action. The bubonic plague of 1665 was a pestilence visiting upon pestilence. Reflective people could not help but judge that the lethargic and ambivalent response to well-known public health dangers contributed to the casualties. The people of 1665 should have known better—and did—than the unfortunates of 1348. Inspiring one another to take effective preventive and containment measures was something else, though. It was common in the fourteenth century for people to blame themselves or one another for having invoked the rage and disgust of God by their sinful ways. This was not entirely a misplaced sense of guilt, because human folly (such as that business with the Tartars and the Christian merchants) had indeed contributed to the pandemic. Basically, though, the deadly work was done by the industrious *Yp*, not human imperfection. Seventeenth-century Londoners had at their disposal three hundred years of subsequent history to learn from as well as a more evolved and efficient governmental apparatus. The too many dead were undeniable evidence that the people of London bore a considerable share of guilt for tolerating flagrantly unhealthy conditions and concealing cases. It was not just unfortunate that so many had died; it was also blameworthy.

Second, the risk of infection by contact with plague corpses was more widely appreciated by the populace. This fear altered the relationship between living and dead. The corpse often had been regarded with a sacred awe, this shell left behind by its departed spirit. But now the corpse was also poison. The caring survivor who might have the urge to tend and embrace the body might now also experience disabling panic. The dead person had acquired what today would be called a spoiled identity.

An afterword: the plague had barely ended when a large section of London went up in flames. The Great Fire of London killed people and destroyed some of the seediest and most pestilential areas. (The number of people killed is uncertain because little attempt was made to determine casualties in the slum areas.) This one-two punch—plague and fire—spurred civic action. London would still have its slums and hellholes, but a significant cleanup and regulatory effort created a healthier environment.

There have been many other local visitations of the Black Death that terrorized and decimated populations. Here, in brief, are facets of two episodes that give us something else to think about. Egypt was struck by a devastating epidemic in 1695–1696. The plague arrived in force in Cairo. Many were afflicted; many died. Yet historian Sheldon Watts reports that

> among people of middling rank the decencies of believers were scrupulously maintained. Expanding the Islamic doctrine of good works, family, friends, and neighbors regularly visited plague-afflicted people and assisted in their feeding and bathing.

It is good to hear of such faith, compassion, and courage. But what of the dead?

> Caring family members tidied up the dead, placed them in coffins and brought them to the grave accompanied by large processions of mourners. According to the chronicler, Garbarti, "Many rich men, emirs, great merchants and others, joined in this charitable work and assisted personally with the burial of a great number of plague dead. . . ." In doing what they did, believers accepted that the visitation had been sent by Allah the Merciful to open . . . one of the 360 doorways of Paradise.[34]

Here plague victims were not avoided but given human contact and skills to nurse them back to health if possible, or, if not, they were escorted from this world under the canopy of faith. Whether or not faith can move mountains, it can at times overcome the dread of being with the dying and the dead.

At the Red Dragon Tavern

One evening in the historic old city area of Vienna, I wandered with a companion, not exactly lost but also not exactly knowing where I was, this being not an uncommon state of affairs with me. I discovered a tavern, but I immediately realized that the Red Dragon Tavern had been discovered a great many times before over the years. There were many stalwart feet heading into the tavern and tipsy feet heading out. My attention was captured, though, by a figure who seemed to be not quite of our time. He was also not quite alive, although he was positioned as a patron. "It's Max!" I whispered to my companion. Yes, it was Max.

The plague had returned to Vienna in 1679 as part of its rounds that had included Amsterdam, London, and Cairo, among other places. It was so virulent in Vienna that residents feared total annihilation. But Max Augustin, one of the city's most popular musicians and singers, had his own plan: he would annihilate himself regularly after performing his ballads to appreciative audiences in the Red Dragon. Leaving his workplace early one morning, Max walked a little ways, then toppled over. Hours later he awoke and noticed that he was not in his own bed and, further, that he was not alone. Max had been dumped into a burial pit. Plague victims were his companions, all dead save for himself. He realized that he had been taken for dead when he had passed out dead drunk. One more body for the cart.

A few hours later the cart returned with its next cargo. The workers were astounded to hear themselves being scolded from the open grave. Max demanded rescue—and that they be quick about it. We can only imagine what the cartmen thought when they heard this voice from the dead. Max did persuade them that he was who he was. Who did they expect to sing for them at the Red Dragon tonight if they left him there? And so Max was rescued, survived his close encounter with plague corpses, and lived another quarter of a century.

As I saw him sitting in effigy, a bottle of wine and a glass in front of

him, I could not but think of a song he is said to have composed after
that experience. It begins:

> *Ach du lieber Augustin,*
> *Alles ist hin.*
>
> Oh, you dear Augustin,
> everything is gone.

He catalogs what has been lost and what will be lost:

> *Frau ist weg.*
> *Wein ist weg.*
> *Freud ist weg. . . .*
>
> Wife is gone.
> Wine is gone.
> Joy is gone. . . .

Max continues with the lament that every day was a holiday until the
coming of the plague. Nothing is left but pain and poverty. We poor folk,
we will all be dead soon, and I shall lie with my beloved in my grave.

This sad and tender ballad has probably been performed every day, if
not every hour, since the day it was composed, with the original verse or
with a "happified" version for children in German, English, and other
languages. I think the first time it came to my ears was in a pumped-up,
overly cheerful band arrangement at a local park. Other children started
singing along, "Did you ever see a lassie go this way and that way . . . ?"
Transformed by time and usage, this heritage of the Black Death—created
by a "corpse"—became an enduring favorite of children and beer gardens. Max would have liked that.

"The Scourge That Won't Go Away"

The plague has been the agent of "too many deaths" throughout history.
This force of mortality has repeatedly struck at expanding populations
and, like other diseases, raged with particular virulence among people
already weakened by hunger, deprivation, and other ailments. There is

reason to doubt, however, that the plague can be safely contained within history books.

Edward Marriott reminds us that the plague reasserted itself in Hong Kong in 1894 and again in India in 1994.[35] Occasional outbreaks have also occurred in the United States. Public health authorities remain alert to the danger: physicians are required to report a diagnosis of plague immediately. A few scattered cases of plague have occurred in my home state of Arizona, and prompt diagnosis and treatment have made fatalities even rarer.

The rats of New York City are not featured in tourist inducements, but they have achieved an almost mythic status for their size, might, boldness, and intelligence. It is possible that New Yorkers take somewhat excessive pride in their rats. I have seen rats that looked as large as a mounted police officer's ride when they appeared suddenly on the Boston Commons with their shadows displayed by a full moon. It is likely that other big cities could also make credible claims for their rats. Marriott wants us to know that the danger of plague is still very much with us.

Richard Preston is even more effective in providing nightmare material with *The Demon in the Freezer.* He focuses on smallpox in his all-too-well-documented examination of the bioterrorism potential. However, Preston notes that plague can also be "weaponized," alone or in company with smallpox and anthrax. The irony is not lost on either Preston or his readers: so much effort has been made to rid the world of lethal diseases, and now some medical scientists might be engaged in producing even more powerful versions of the plague and other such diseases.

A FEW CONCLUDING THOUGHTS

When the dead become too numerous, the conditions of life are profoundly affected. The dead are the ones most obviously affected. They tend to lose their individuality, then their humanity. Affection and respect for the deceased person are deprived of their traditional modes of expression. Pragmatic thinking may urge one to conceal the cause of the death and to avoid contagion by avoiding the body and its effects. Furthermore, avoidance often has started while the person is still alive, both out of fear of contagion and a sense of helplessness to save him or her.

The sorrow of bereavement and loss is intensified when we feel we have not come through for a person we have loved or even for a person who has not been a close part of our lives but is a fellow citizen, fellow religionist, or, simply, a fellow human.

Hasty mass burials make sense to us as practical measures. Nevertheless, something in us may well insist that we have been guilty of wrongdoing (or wrong-not-doing). This uneasy state of mind has been especially common whenever there is strong belief in the efficacy of prayer, confession, and other ritual. When there are too many dead we struggle to retain our confidence, self-esteem, and communal feeling. We too, then, are affected. Just as the fields of Flanders were deeply scarred by years of World War I trench warfare, so were the minds of the survivors who could not even bury their mutilated or obliterated comrades as the horror swirled around them.[36] Too many dead; too few offered respect.

In all of this we would not want to ignore the obvious fact that these are the newly dead. We are trying to negotiate an acceptable relationship with the dead under crisis conditions for them as well as for ourselves. This is much different from dealing with the well-established dead. The long dead have snipped the phantom umbilical cord that attached them to their former abodes. They are safely away to where they should be, or, if they are not, there will be the devil to pay. Our beliefs and customs may permit us to interact with them and perform acts of remembrance on their behalf. The distinction between the newly and the established dead has been made by virtually every culture that has been fortunate enough to be studied by anthropologists or reasonable facsimiles thereof. The newly dead tend to be less predictable and more dangerous. When the newly dead are so very many, we are in a precarious situation indeed, and even more so when intensified by the absence of consoling ritual.

Throughout this chapter I have mentioned bad situations becoming worse. One more example is now about to occur. I ask you first to consider the possibility of *a connection between absence of funeral ritual and increased violence among the living*. More familiar is the proposition that increased violence tends to deprive the victims or losers of proper ritual. Now take it the other way around, if you will: the inability to perform vital rituals on behalf of the dead may set off a compensatory reaction. This is most likely to occur when society is reeling both from (1) an overwhelming number of deaths that it has (2) seemed powerless to prevent and from (3) the guilt of failing to provide traditional rituals. The sheer magnitude, the sheer force, of death appears irresistible, and we feel so helpless, so passive.

So—let's go out and kill somebody. Fighting pain with pain and death with death was a common response during major visitations of the Black Death. The flagellants bloodied themselves and burned Jews. Elsewhere Christians or other local minorities became the targets. Everywhere the stranger was a candidate for murder as a supposed plague spreader. The chaos produced by pestilence and mass death provided opportunities for people with a predisposition toward violence. Others who were ordinarily obedient to church and state converted penance into brutality and murder. They were ashamed of what they had not done and of what they had witnessed in the abandonment of the dead. In a sense, they had already become outlaws by straying from the path of faith and good works, and they were also at risk for themselves becoming victims who might pass from life without the blessing of ritual and become just one more desecrated corpse. The answer for some was action to break the depression and passivity. Instead of accepting the roles of outlaw and victim, they would change sides. They would do Death's work.

And whoever heard of Death dying?

I am suggesting that deprivation of ritual for the dying and dead can be so unnerving that it breeds or increases violence. Too many have died, and they have died too badly, and their bodies have been too dangerously neglected. Therefore, more must die, and the chosen victims must also be degraded after death. When we lose respect for the physical remains of a fellow human, we—but Richard Glazar is more qualified to speak of this:

> We were taken to a barracks. The whole place stank. Piled about five feet high in a jumbled mass were all the things people could conceivably have brought. Clothes, suitcases, everything stacked in a solid mass.

Yes, Treblinka.

> On top of it, jumping around like demons, people were making bundles and carrying them outside. [The Squad Leader] shouted, and I understood that I was also to pick up clothing. . . . I asked him: "What's going on? Where are the ones who stripped?" And he replied, "Dead! All dead!"[37]

This is an oblique scene: no bodies, just clothing and personal effects. It is mute testimony, though, to what became of millions of men, women, and children during the Holocaust. The dead as well as the living were treated with deliberate intent to deny their humanity. Nazi pseudoscience held that value resided only in "the master race." All others should be treated as an inferior species. This assertion made it easier not only to kill but also to mock and disrespect the bodies. The Nazi apparatus could therefore devote itself to producing corpses. Testimony and documents have provided details of quota systems for transporting and killing. So many needed to be made dead that urgent messages emphasized the need to "increase production" and to do so at less cost.

But all those dead bodies were produced at immense cost to a society that had operated under rule of law and faith in God. Some who participated in or witnessed this process clearly recognized that all they believed in was being destroyed. It was murder, to be sure. It was a form of self-murder as well. Those who fell victim to Yp and were deprived of ritual comfort and protection at their deaths were thought to be in jeopardy for their uncleansed souls. What would the faithful throughout the ages have thought, then, of humans who attempted to replace rituals of encompassing compassion with the cold precision of killing machines? Into what void had they hurled themselves when they forfeited their own humanity by abusing and mocking the many too many dead?

EIGHT

DOWN TO EARTH
AND UP IN FLAMES

A person has died. Now what? In most societies on most occasions, there will be both a symbolic and a practical response. The symbolic response might be as elaborate as a Hmung ritual or as tellingly direct as an Amish funeral.[1] *A marimba band might be included in the funeral procession, and women closely related to the deceased might be expected to chant and lament ever more intensely as the ritual proceeds, as in Guatemala. Or a solemn silence might be maintained except for recitation of a prayer or a reading of a scriptural passage, as in traditional Church of England services.*[2] *Whatever the symbolic and emotional response, however, something has to be done with the body. Burial and cremation have been the most common choices through the centuries. Both procedures might be carried out, as when cremains are placed in an urn and buried. Circumstances sometimes dictate the choice, as when victims of a deadly epidemic are hastily burned to avoid contamination. Most often, though, the choice of lowering the dead into the earth or offering them to the sky has much to do with a society's conception of life, death, and relationship to the gods. Status and power dynamics within the society also exercise significant influence. And, if we listen carefully, the arrangements also whisper to us about hopes, fears, and fantasies that are lodged deeply within the human breast.*

A BURNING ISSUE

Church burial grounds . . . town graveyards . . . "memorial gardens." In their various forms, cemeteries have been so familiar a part of the landscape that it has often been assumed simply that dead people get buried. More specifically, dead people get buried looking as lifelike as possible. Almost all corpses are embalmed in the United States. Cosmetic art is often applied by professional funeralists to reduce signs of the illness or trauma associated with the death. Care is also given to dressing the deceased either in a stylized respectable outfit or, under pressure from a new generation, in comfortable clothes for the journey. The coffin— airtight, waterproof, vacuum sealed—is designed to preserve the image of the living person as long as possible. Just because a person is dead doesn't mean a person has to *look* dead.

Cremation still strikes some people as being new, improper, profane, and dangerous. Actually, cremation has solid credentials both in history and the current scene. The word itself was acquired from the Latin *cremare,* "to burn," but the practice existed long before the Roman Empire assembled itself. Cremation was practiced in eastern and northern Europe during the Stone Age, and even more widespread evidence has been discovered from the Bronze Age. It has been suggested by E. G. James that these early cremations were associated with cults of the dead.[3] This is a plausible if unconfirmed idea. Fire was exciting. Fire was powerful. Fire purified. Fire was magic. Fire was a gift from the gods. The mystery of life, the mystery of death, the mystery of fire!

My own primitive experiences included a wild evening around a bonfire in the depths of Detroit, in the company of other excited fifth-graders. We were only roasting small potatoes and were only small potatoes ourselves, but the air was full of magic and expectation: we were somehow on the threshold of the sacred and the forbidden. This is perhaps not the best evidence for James's theory, but the child within me readily consents. Prometheus and the cruel gods who punished him for his theft of the divine flame might also agree.

Cremation and inhumation often were combined. Babylonians, for example, wrapped the corpse in combustible material, encased it in clay, then burned it on a brick platform. The ashes were then bottled, along with small objects that might be useful in the next life.[4] Urns have also

Figure 20 Cremation performed in open air by Tolkotin Indians in Oregon, as depicted in J. W. Powell, *First Annual Report of the Bureau of Ethnology, 1879–80* (1881), reprinted in Stephen Prothero, *Purified by Fire: A History of Cremation in America* (Berkeley: University of California Press, 2001).

been discovered in widespread burial grounds dating back to approximately 1500 B.C.

Greek warriors (and probably others) cremated their fallen comrades so their bodies would not be mutilated by the enemy. Assigning a body to the flames could be a demonstration of respect, then, as well as a hygienic procedure or a magico-religious act.

Still another meaning could be associated with cremation. Siddhartha Gautama looked askance at the way people defiled and misinterpreted life. He meditated. He learned. He taught. When his moment came to die, the Buddha asked for the simplest of ceremonies.[5] His followers should not become overly attached to his earthly personality or heap distracting rituals on the natural act of his passing toward the next rebirth. But he might as well have spoken to the wind:

> After seven days of ceremonial homage, an iron sarcophagus, filled with oil, was placed on the funeral pyre, made of many kinds of fragrant wood. When the fire had died down, only the bones were left. For seven days, the closely guarded bones were honored with dance and song and music, and with garlands and perfumes. . . . That the Buddha was cremated indicates not that this is universal practice among Buddhists but rather his status

as a great man. At that time in India, as now, not all dead bodies were cremated; those of children, and of holy men, and of the very poor . . . are buried or even left in a charnel field to be devoured by beasts and birds of prey.[6]

Here was a striking example of public need triumphing over personal resolve. The irony is obvious. One facet of Buddha's greatness was his insight into the essence of being and his dismissal of distractions and vanities. Most of his followers had trouble with that. *They* needed expensive and elaborate ritual even if he did not.

For an illuminating example of what can happen when the deceased-to-be and society agree on a fiery send-off, we visit the Norse as one era is about to end and another to begin.

The Ship of Flames

The Iron and Bronze Ages had passed. Who cared! It was silver now, the stuff of riches and, therefore, of power. Viking society prospered. Military superiority was complemented by a richness of invention and virtuoso craftsmanship. More than a thousand years later, museums would treasure the creativity that transformed silver into beguiling jewelry and fabric into masterpieces of design. And then silver, too, passed, the mines all too quickly exhausted. The Vikings had to expend extra effort to meet emerging military and commercial rivals; after many years of painful experience, other peoples had learned how to deal with their longboats, precision archery, and fluted swords. What would prove to be the most consequential threat was starting to surface in small but unsettling ways: these foreigners with their upstart God, who was called Jesus the Christ.

In the middle of the tenth century, though, the Viking spirit still reigned in the northern realms of Europe. A significant death was a significant opportunity to display this spirit. James Reston, Jr., guides us through the funeral of a Viking chief.[7] The elaborate rituals begin with an unusually long wake. The watchers remain with the body for almost two weeks. The basic purpose of a wake, of course, is inherent in the name: let's make sure this person is really and truly dead and (at the same time) take precautions to ward off opportunistic evil spirits. In this case the time is also well used by having the chief sit or, rather, lie, for the fitting of his burial gown. This elaborate item might have become the prize of any museum in the future, but it was designed to soon perish.

Well, the chief is dead. Time to move on to the big show. Viking legends feature a god of surpassing beauty. Worshipers in another part of the world called him Apollo. He was Baldur to the Scandinavians. A rival god had murdered Baldur with a mistletoe dart (yes, mistletoe!). Everybody who had a heart was heartbroken. So bereft was Nanna, his wife, that she died of sorrow. The mourners placed Nanna next to Baldur on a longboat, conducted their funeral rites, then set the boat afire and gave it a push out to sea—and to eternity. This legend has a part two. Baldur rejuvenates, and from this time forward the mistletoe serves as the symbol of love—but suspend it overhead and never, ever let it touch the ground.

It is this story that will be reenacted in the chief's funeral. With just a bit of cautionary revision. The chief's widow does not die of grief, nor does she yearn to perish on a fiery longboat. Nevertheless, the show must go on. What to do? The widow gathers up the chief's slave girls. "Who would like to be Nanna? Who wants to travel with the chief to the land of the kind gods?" Many, perhaps all, are willing. This is not only a personal honor but also assures that the surrogate wife's family will be raised to a higher status in society. Her sacrifice will free all her family from bondage for generations to come. One of the slaves is selected and prepared for her starring role.

Meanwhile skilled hands have fashioned a magnificent ship, and other participants and resources have been readied for the event. The corpse is carried aboard on a plank cushioned by Oriental carpets. With his brocaded mantle, gold buttons, and sable cap, the chief is splendid enough for any company. His body is placed inside a tent on the deck. Ale, bread, fruit, and meat from freshly slaughtered animals are provided, along with a stringed instrument.

A grim old woman called the Angel of Death brings the slave girl to the boat. In Scandinavian lore both the messenger of death and the executioner were women. Unlike in contemporary American attitudes,[8] for the Vikings it was the woman who personified death. She instructs the slave girl to tell her chief that she has done this out of love for him. Men now gather around the young woman and lift her skyward three times so she can see the land of the dead.

As the Arabian diplomat Ibn Fahlan watched this ritual, somewhat aghast, his guide whispered to him: "The first time they lifted her she said: 'Look there! I see my father and mother.' The second time: 'Look! All my dead relatives are sitting there.' And the third time, 'I see my master sitting in Paradise, and Paradise is beautiful and green. . . . He calls me.'"[9]

These preliminaries completed, it is time for action. The young woman is given a hen. She hacks off its head and places it with the other provisions for the voyage. Next she passes her golden arm rings and anklets to Death's daughters, sings, and imbibes a cup of ale as a farewell toast to her friends. After quaffing another cup, which leaves her appearing somewhat dazed, she enters the tent. The men now do two things they do well. First, they beat their sticks against their shields, the same fearsome sounds that often preceded a Viking assault. Then six men enter the tent and the young woman. These carnal acts supposedly bring them no pleasure: it is their duty to prepare her for her new role as surrogate wife. The rapists are simply enacting the role of surrogate husbands.

The young woman now lies down next to the corpse. The Angel of Death slips a noose around her neck. A signal is given, and the old woman plunges a dagger into her heart while the men pull on the noose. She is now ready for her voyage to the enticing land of the dead. And here comes the next chief, a close kinsman of the deceased.

He stood stark naked and held a torch in one hand, his other hand over his anus. His nakedness symbolized his inheritance of eminent status. . . . The hand on his anus was to protect him from a suspicion of unmanly man love, for there was nothing more degrading in the Viking code than for a man to be taken sexually from behind. . . . He put the first fire to the wood, and others followed his lead. . . . Then the burning ship was launched as a strong wind caught the sail. "Out of love for him, his Lord has sent the wind, so that it will take him quickly," Fahlan's interpreter whispered. "We burn him in a moment, and he enters Paradise at once."[10]

Finally, a mound is constructed on the shore, and there is placed a birch tablet on which the name of the illustrious leader is written.

This spectacle incorporated many of the elements one would expect of a grand send-off. It was:

- *Distinctive.* Few Viking funerals were so elaborate.
- *Expensive.* A glorious ship was constructed and decorated only to be consumed by flames.
- *Participatory.* Many people had specified roles in the endeavor, and everybody who was anybody attended.
- *Invocative.* The tragic but triumphant love-death scenario reenacted by the funeral rites brought a legendary event back to living reality, thereby reaffirming Viking faith and tradition.
- *Sacrificial.* Blood offerings are impressive. The gods like them, and the people are impressed with what they have done. In this case the sacrifice was framed as a companion voyager, but sacrifice it was nevertheless. (History yields many other examples of a deceased ruler taking companions—sometimes by the score—to the tomb.)
- *Transformational.* Before their own eyes, the Vikings could behold the mysterious event taking place. A ship laden with two corpses, provisions, and fineries—and a moment later replaced by a flaming torch carried by a sacred wind to the land of the dead. Flames make for a persuasive passage from the mundane to the sacred.
- *Transcendental.* A ritual so elaborate and powerful must surely have validity. After all that effort, there certainly had to be an afterlife, just as the Vikings had imagined since there had been Vikings.
- *Preservational.* The torch in the hand of the naked man had the dual purpose of lighting the fire and confirming his own succession to leadership. The ritual, therefore, not only provided a glowing send-off to the deceased chief but also reaffirmed belief in an afterlife and helped the survivors to avoid a bitter and bloody campaign to determine who would be the next leader.

These are just some of the elements that occur to me as I imagine myself observing—from a safe distance—the funeral of a tenth-century Viking chief. Perhaps you will have noticed additional elements and implications. But perhaps you are wondering instead what would happen when a powerful Viking woman died. Queen Sigrid the Strong-Minded certainly qualified. She was at least the equal and more often the superior of anybody else around. Reston notes that Queen Sigrid could make her own choice. Yes, she could be cremated in glorious fashion, but she could also decide to descend into the fertile earth.

Each option had its own sacred auspice. The more spectacular the bonfire, the higher the smoke would rise and therefore the greater ascent she would achieve into the upper regions of heaven. That is what happened to Odin, so it could happen for her as well. But she could decide to emulate Frey instead. His body was planted in the earth, and the yield was bountiful harvests and the blessings of peace. (Was this the origin of the expression "Thank God, it's Friday"? This day of the week was, in fact, named for the beloved Swedish deity.)

Sigrid decided to descend to the chamber of Frey, not in the least daunted by reports of his enormous phallus. She wore her finest gown and reclined on a feather bed. Vikings being Vikings, Sigrid also required a ship, even though she was taking the underland rather than the over-sea route to the next life. Like the craft that carried the Viking chief on the sacred winds of fire, Sigrid's vessel was well stocked with provisions and also with an elegant grooming table complete with reindeer-antler combs, Italian glass beads, peacock feathers, needles, thread, and fine cloth. Unlike the impetuous chief, she was in no particular hurry to reach her destination. It might take all winter, but so what? She enjoyed the snow and had four sleds aboard, carved in exuberant animal shapes featuring serpentine designs. A luxury wagon was also on board with representations of her favorite cats, their silver-beaded eyes lighting the way ahead. Sigrid also had her slave girl aboard and a sack of hashish to help pass those longer winter evenings. The dozen horses that were sacrificed on departure were all stallions, perhaps a mordant comment by the famously "strong-minded" queen.

The old Viking religion that Christian missionaries were already calling pagan offered such options as up in flames or down to earth and instant teleportation to heaven or a more leisurely cruise. Perhaps more significant, though, was the active role of women in Viking life and lore. It would be another three hundred years or so before the cult of Mary arose in Europe, and a millennium later the Catholic Church would still not hear of female priests. Furthermore, the Viking spirit included a sinewy sense of independence. Individuals could and did speak their minds; many key decisions were made following debate and voting. Royalty and the priesthood had their influence, to be sure, but Vikings liked to make up their own minds rather than automatically submit to authority.

Another point was so much taken for granted at the time that it might have slipped notice: the dead would not stray far from the homeland, either ascending to our sky or descending into our earth. The sense of place was very much a part of religious feeling. Detachment from the land of our gods and ancestors would become a more common circumstance as commerce, invasion, and migration increased. Accommodations would be made, but nothing was as good as joining one's own people and gods in the homeland.

Save That Body for the Next Life

Christianity was an expansionist force as the first millennium gave way to the second. For some time it was by no means certain that Christianity would survive against its powerful rivals or make much headway against firmly entrenched local customs. The Vikings were a tough nut to crack. Even when they converted to the new religion, they did not completely dismiss the good old dependable gods of the past. Who would you want on your side in battle? The fascinating but enigmatic foreigner or the brawny warrior gods who had already led you to so many victories?

The new death-related doctrines were especially puzzling to the Vikings. No more cremations? A long wait between death and admission to heaven? No sacrifices? No valuable objects to accompany the deceased spirit? In practice, the Vikings often combined what they liked best of the old and the new ways. But why were these intense strangers so dead set against cremation?

Cremation was common when Christianity emerged.[11] The Romans were doing it, perhaps having picked up this practice from the Greek culture they admired and envied. The Hebrews were exceptions in this regard, however. There was something disgraceful, humiliating, about cremation. Only criminals deserved this treatment. On rare occasions bodies might have to be reduced to bones and ashes to avoid mutilation by enemies such as the Philistines. The feeling that cremation shows disrespect to the deceased and their families might well have been carried over to early Christianity as it shaped itself from Judaism.

The first few Christian generations followed local custom in some regards. Being Christian did not necessarily mean that one had to do everything differently. Irion notes, for example, that Coptic Christians in Egypt continued to mummify, while those who still resided in Jewish communities retained burial or sepulture. Nevertheless, resistance to cremation gradually became part of the Christian creed. Irion suggests that this resistance might have come from

> the precedent of Jesus' burial in the tomb of Joseph of Arimathea according to the custom of the Jewish people. Perhaps the expectation of "rising with Christ" produced a desire to imitate the mode of his burial. Emphasis upon the Christian hope for the resurrection may also have caused the preference for burial over cremation. Although Christians did not suppose that destruction of the body by fire would preclude resurrection, the symbolism of the body at rest in the grave may have been a significant context for belief in the resurrection.[12]

Roman contemporaries chided Christians for supposing that the body remains intact in earth burial. In retrospect it might also seem inconsistent that a faith that has disparaged the material life and turned its eyes toward eternity would be so concerned about preservation of the physical shell. Apparently these two themes—attachment to the physical and longing for a spiritual life beyond—have had an uneasy but stimulating coexistence since the beginning. It was the idea of resurrection in the flesh that brought both abundant new converts and derision to the new religion.

But perhaps Irion hits upon the prime reason for Christian resistance to cremation when he suggests that

> early Christian resistance to cremation was stimulated more by strong reaction against the pagan protagonists of cremation than by reasons against the practice inherent in the Christian faith. The mode of burial became one of the significant marks that distinguished the Christian from the pagan in these centuries.[13]

There has been a lot of time for second thoughts on the subject. One influential reappraisal occurred in the middle of the seventeenth century when Thomas Browne analyzed "sepulchrall urnes lately found in Norfolk." The discovery of Roman cremains excited great interest. Browne showed his independence of mind when he suggested that there was nothing to condemn in this ritual:

> That they washed their bones with wine and milk, that the mother wrapt them in Linnen, and dryed them in her bosome, the first fostering part,

and place of their nourishment, that they opened their eyes toward heaven, before they kindled the fire . . . were no improper Ceremonies.[14]

The Catholic Church now does permit cremation but prefers whole body burial. The National Conference of Catholic Bishops recommends that cremation, if chosen, should occur after the funeral so the body can be present at the Mass. It is recognized that special circumstances might make this procedure impossible. In any event, "the cremated remains of a body should be treated with the same respect given to the corporeal remains of a human body."[15] Respect for the dead remains a cardinal principle whatever the mode chosen for body disposal.

Sati: The Woman Who Will Burn Herself Alive

A young peasant woman who was inspired by God to lead soldiers to victory. An elderly leader of the Knights Templar who would not make a false confession. A philosopher-scientist who would not exchange dogma for truth. Joan of Arc, Jacques de Molay, and Giordano Bruno are among those who have been burned alive by the Catholic Church because they would not say what the establishment wanted to hear. Captives were also burned alive in the pagan world, and mass incineration was the fate of some Jews during the plague years. In all these instances the emphasis was on punishment and deterrence. These deaths were intended to be extraordinary and horrifying. Even in a brutal society people did not expect to be burned alive. What, then, are we to make of the practice of widow burning? Why would the immolation of a living person, no criminal, no heretic, become an expected, even an obligatory, action? To India, then, and with Catherine Weinberger-Thomas as our expert guide.[16]

Widow burning is known outside the Hindu world as *sati* (also as *suttee* and other variants). Actually this word refers not to the ritual but to the woman who will die in the flames. *Sati* also denotes a virtuous wife. There was an original Sati who committed suicide at her father's home in defense of her husband, Mahadeva's, honor. This episode in Hindu mythology set the standards by which a devotee is judged. This type of suicide is admired rather than considered sinful. Sanskrit does not offer a precise descriptive name for the ritual. One of the more common terms is *sahagamana*—the "going with." The emphasis is on the woman as a companion, following her husband into death. This is a less alarming image than that of "burning a wife alive."

Suicides by the widows of tribal chieftains were observed by Alexander the Great's army. It is not known how much earlier the practice might have originated, but it was observed again to be well established from the sixth century A.D. and thereafter. Rulers from outside the Hindu tradition (Islamic in the seventeenth century, English in the eighteenth) would later condemn the practice but take few measures to put a halt to it. Early in the nineteenth century, however, both Hindu reformists and colonial officials became active in opposition.[17]

It was not only widow burning that was now becoming unacceptable to influential people. Infanticide was also rife, and pregnant woman were also being put to death. Perhaps tradition had to be respected when the wife of an influential man decided to "go with him." But the practice, once pretty much limited to the elite, was becoming more common. Furthermore, the authorities were especially concerned about involuntary self-immolation. Widows were sometimes forced to join their husbands on the funeral pyre instead of coming forth of their own will. This, by any name, was murder, and the government could rightfully intervene. The practice has become illegal, although occasional violations of the law have been reported. It is not to be confused with traditional cremation, in which a corpse is reduced to ashes and bones, often to be added to the gray, muddy flow of the Ganges, the holy river that "takes all living things in its embrace."[18]

How was the rite of widow burning performed? Here is an eyewitness report by a Dutch traveler in 1770, as shared by Weinberger-Thomas. The preliminaries had been completed, including the washing of her husband's body. The widow, about thirty, sat near the body, brushing away the flies with a branch. She maintained a calm, meditative expression while the women around "spoke continually of the happiness she was about to enjoy, with her husband, in a future life." Her friends embraced her from time to time. The widow was then led to the Ganges, her clothes removed and replaced with a wrapping of red silk and cotton gingham. To a male relative she gave the jewel that signified her marriage. She recited prayers while scooping water from the Ganges, and her other ornaments were then removed and chaplets of white flowers put on her neck and hands. Her forehead was then marked with clay in the same manner as that of her husband. It was now time for the transformation.

> She then took her last farewell of her friends . . . and was conducted by two of her female relations to the pile. . . . She then took some boiled rice, rolled in a ball, and put it into the mouth of the deceased, laying several other balls of rice under the pile. Two brahmins next led her three times around it, while she threw parched rice among the bystanders, who gathered it up with eagerness. The last time that she went round, she set a little earthen burning lamp at each of the four corners. The whole of this was done during an incessant clamor of cymbals and drums, and amidst the shouts of the brahmins, of their relations. After having thus walked three times round the pile, she mounted courageously upon it, laid herself down upon the right side next to the body which she embraced with both her arms; a piece of white cotton was spread over them both; they were bound together over the arms, and middle, with two easy bandages, and a quantity of firewood, straw, and rosin was laid upon them. In the last place, her nearest relation, to whom she had given her nose-jewel, came with a burning torch, and set the straw on fire, and in a moment the whole was in flame. The noise of the drums was redoubled, and the shouts of the spectators were more loud and incessant than ever, so that the shrieks of the unfortunate woman, had she uttered any, could not possibly have been heard, but I was astonished by the woman's tranquility.[19]

The witness also had something else to think about: the women who were present, and who all, sooner or later, would have to undergo the same fate if they survived their husbands, appeared to rejoice at the sacrifice and enter a state of exultation.

Outsiders to Hindu faith and customs (such as myself) are not likely to understand all the meanings and implications of this ritual. We can recognize, however, that it represents core values and beliefs that have sustained Hindus through the trials of life and death over many centuries. Again, outsiders are not likely to condone a practice that appears to sacrifice a person's life so needlessly (to say nothing of depriving children of a mother, siblings of a sister, and so forth). Capital punishment for convicted murderers is a divisive issue in the United States and condemned by many other nations. And yet here a woman died, not because she was a ruthless killer, but because she was a devoted wife.

But what was the alternative? Women were less than men, and widows much less than wives. The widow lost much of her status in society and was likely to lose much of her economic support as well. Surviving one's husband often became a kind of shadowy half life. Moreover, if this was a widow who was expected to "go with" but did not, then she would also bear the stigma of an insufficiently devoted wife. Again, Weinberger-Thomas on this cruel tradition:

> An object of universal repugnance, the widow must lead a life of asceticism and self-mortification. Her head is shaved, and she is deprived of every finery, every pleasure, and every comfort. . . . Because she is a bearer of misfortune, she must avoid appearing in public for the rest of her days; her impurity, rather than being intermittent as in the case of other women, is permanent. . . . The widow is excluded from domestic festivities, even from the wedding of her own children. . . . She is subject to humiliation, insult and abuse. She is beaten and made to subsist on leftovers. . . .[20]

Societal support, the persuasion of ritual, and a few minutes in a hellish inferno might seem preferable to a life of misery. Nevertheless, we can only be amazed by the courage of the women who voluntarily approached the pyre.

The sati, then, the woman who will burn herself alive, is several beings at the same time: the personification of a legendary goddess, an obedient wife, and the victim of a culture in which to be a female is to be property.

Cremation Today

Attitudes toward cremation have become more favorable in Western nations in recent years. There was some precedent. For example, the corpse of English poet Percy Bysshe Shelley was cremated on a driftwood pyre after he lost his life while sailing in a storm. This action showed no lack of respect. Fellow poet Lord Byron even reached into the flames to rescue Shelley's heart (which later was buried with his widow). Henry Laurens, a prominent South Carolina merchant and scholar, is thought to have been the first person cremated in the new nation of the United States in 1792. Interestingly, Laurens made this unusual choice after

> his daughter had been pronounced dead after being stricken with smallpox and was close to being interred when she suddenly sprang back to life.

Laurens directed in his will that his corpse should be burned, and he threatened to withhold his considerable estate if his kin insisted on burial.[21]

There was considerable resistance for many years: it was not traditional in most Western societies; deprived the soul of the body it might want later to rejoin; might be painful to the deceased (like autopsies); and made it difficult to think of the departed as sleeping comfortably in the resting place. Nevertheless, cremation eventually became an accepted option in mainstream society. Convenience was one of the reasons.

Selecting between whole body burial and cremation often hinges on practical rather than religious considerations. Arizona is a handy example. Most of my fellow "Zonians" brought their bodies here from someplace else, and many choose to send their remains "back home" for burial someday. They are not too keen on spending more money than necessary on last things. Why go to the expense and trouble of embalming the body and shipping a coffin two thousand or three thousand miles when a tidy little urn could be sent instead? This alternative seems easier for almost everybody. If there is a family cemetery plot in Illinois or Minnesota, the cremains can be laid to rest there. Cremation has even more appeal to people who are not only concerned about expenditures but also not inclined to "stir up a lot of fuss and feathers." Members of memorial societies often have this orientation, but so do many others who think of death as a natural event that should be looked after in a simple and direct way. (It is possible, of course, to combine urn burial with elaborate funeral and memorial services.)

Other considerations also lead some people to choose cremation. People who are attached to a particular land—or sea—scape might prefer to sprinkle themselves over their favorite locale rather than reside under a stone. More than one person has had his ashes distributed over a baseball field that had been his "field of dreams." It is no longer unusual for a terminally ill person to make specific requests for dispersal of the ashes. Postmortem mishaps do occur, however. Actor Howard Morse, at the time featured in a popular television series, required the emotional support of two colleagues (Sid Caesar and Mel Brooks) as he tried to carry out his late father's instructions to spread his ashes on the Hudson River. Unfortunately, an unexpected gust of wind came up just at that moment and blew the ashes back on him. When he could find voice, the loving son is reported to have blurted out: "Am I supposed to take my father to the dry cleaners now?" Chances are his father had a sense of humor.

Growing concern for the environment has also encouraged the choice of cremation. In some areas cemetery space has become tight. People might prefer that available land be put to other use, such as parks and greenways. Furthermore, not a few people consider cemeteries to be creepy and depressing (some definitely are—after years of neglect). "I wouldn't want to be caught dead there!" is a sentiment that often is shared by relatives who also dread cemetery visits.

What about religion? Few people cite religious belief as the primary reason for selecting cremation. Practical considerations such as economics and convenience are more often noted.

Here is an oddity, though. Bring a chair or stool and clamber up to the top shelf of your local mortuary's special little closet. Along with the dust you are likely also to find ashes (in boxes or urns). Wherever their spirits may be, it is on these dark shelves that their cremains sit and sit. Interrogate the cremains. Try to discover why they languish here instead of completing their journey. I tried that once. Actually, it was one of my students who responded to the challenge. Arizona, temporarily short of real scandals at the time, was entertaining a mild flap about cremains. Funeral directors asked for permission to rid themselves of cremains that, apparently abandoned by their rightful owners, were taking up valuable shelf space; the public was moderately aghast at this insensitivity. Professors know everything, of course, so I was invited to look into the matter. The funeral directors who populated the state board were open to whatever it might take to identify the source of the problem and whatever corrective measures might be indicated.

So it was that just a few days later an energetic and resourceful Arizona State University graduate student inspected a large collection of shelved cremains. The outcomes of her investigation:

- Many of the cremains were to have been released at specified locations, but the individual charged with this responsibility just couldn't bring himself to perform this task. It made him nervous. A steadier hand took over and saw that the deeds were done.

- The tagging and filing system had not kept up with the increasing supply of cremains. The graduate student set up a new system.
- Some next of kin did not fully realize that the cremains were theirs to claim and were not supposed to remain indefinitely with the funeral director. More attention was thereafter given to informing family members of their rights and responsibilities in this matter.
- The funeral director was lonely. The graduate student married him.

Meanwhile, I had cherished my own hypotheses about the unclaimed cremains, dealing with subtle psychological and cultural issues. No evidence was found to support any of these interesting ideas.

The lesson to be drawn from this exercise is obvious: it's good to have bright graduate students!

Throughout North America most cremains are either delivered to the cemetery (41 percent) or taken home (36 percent), where they will have various dispositions: kept at home, buried elsewhere, placed in a columbarium, or scattered. Funeral directors scatter about 18 percent of the cremains at the family's request. And some cremains, as noted, stay on the shelf until, after a period of time, the funeral director has the discretion of disposing of or continuing to keep them.

How much the cremation option has increased in popularity can be gleaned from the historical record as compiled by the Cremation Association of North America. In 1885, there were only 47 known cremations in the United States. By 1900 the number had risen to 2,414. The percentage of cremations to total deaths remained low for many years, even though the number of cremations increased along with the nation's population. In 1960, for example, there were 60,987 cremations, but this represented only 3.56 percent of the deaths in the United States. Leap ahead to 1985. More than two million Americans died that year. Nearly 14 percent (289,091) had chosen cremation. Within that quarter century (1960–1985), the preference for cremation increased fourfold.

The most recent data indicate that cremations are becoming even more common in the United States. In 1999 there were 2,345,702 deaths in the country. Cremation had now become the choice of one out of four families (25.39 percent). Statisticians estimate that by 2010, cremations will account for about 36 percent of the final disposals. Where is cremation most often the choice? Currently it is the most common choice in Hawaii, Washington, Nevada, Oregon, and Montana. It is much less common in southern states, especially Alabama, Mississippi, West Virginia, Tennessee, and Kentucky.

Increasing longevity in the United States means that most deaths occur in later adulthood. Cremations follow suit; among those cremated, the average age at death is about seventy. Caucasians predominate (88 percent) in choosing cremation, but it is also selected by African Americans, Asians, and Hispanics. Some people do not report a religious affiliation. Among those who do, we find Protestant (58 percent), Catholic (26 percent), Buddhist (11 percent), Jewish (3 percent), and Hindu (2 percent) representation. Cremation seems to accord with the preferences of people from a variety of backgrounds.

Japan has become the world leader in cremations: 98.42 percent. This is not entirely an Asian phenomenon, however. Three out of every four deaths are cremated in the Czech Republic and Peru and nearly as many in Denmark and Great Britain. By contrast, cremations are uncommon (between 4 and 5 percent) in Ireland and Italy and even more so in Ghana (2 percent). There is no doubt that cultural factors have much to do with the choice. The Scandinavian nations, for example, include high rates of cremation in Denmark and Sweden, but rates are about three times lower in Finland and Norway. No Viking chief immolations have been reported lately.[22]

We will warm ourselves before the crematory fires again as this chapter ends and yet again in the chapter "Journey of the Dead."

EARTH, THAT NOURISHED THEE, SHALL CLAIM THY GROWTH

> To him who in the love of nature holds
> Communion with her visible forms, she speaks
> A various language . . .

So begins a meditation written in 1812 that conquered its century and endured to that vanishing point in the next century when even the most renowned poems failed to get aboard new generations. William Cullen

Bryant called his poem "Thanatopsis."[23] A fitting title, to be sure: the poem was all about viewing death.

Bryant expresses a love for nature but admits he is disturbed by thoughts of the "breathless darkness, and the narrow house." How should he—or anybody—reconcile to this prospect?

> Earth, that nourished thee, shall claim
> thy growth, to be resolved to earth again,
> And, lost each human trace, surrendering up
> Thine individual being . . . a brother to the insensible rock.

Having figured this out at age seventeen, Bryant went on to a long and distinguished literary life, although the teen meditation on death remained his number-one calling card. It is futile and foolish to be unsettled by our fate. Trust nature. Trust Mother Earth:

> So live, that when thy summons comes to join
> The innumerable caravan, which moves
> To that mysterious realm, where each shall take
> His chamber in the silent halls of death,
> Thou go not, like the quarry-slave at night,
> Scourged to his dungeon, but, sustained and soothed
> By an unfaltering trust, approach thy grave
> Like one who wraps the drapery of his couch
> About him, and lies down to pleasant dreams.

Earth. Nature. Soothed. Trust. A couch. Pleasant dreams. Bryant offers an enticing succession of images. But this is not the only way in which people have regarded descent into the earth. Erich Neumann, a psychoanalyst with a Jungian turn of mind and a historical perspective, was drawn to contemplation of the Terrible Mother. This, he tells us, is an *archetype,* an image buried in the collective unconscious of all humankind. More than that, the Terrible Mother is itself a symbol for the unconscious.

And the dark side of the Terrible Mother takes the form of monsters, whether in Egypt or India, Mexico or Etruria, Bali or Rome. In the myths and tales of all peoples, ages, and countries—and even in the nightmares of our own nights—witches and vampires, ghouls and specters, assail us, all terrifyingly alike. . . . Just as world, life, nature, and soul have been experienced as a generative and nourishing, protecting and warming Femininity, so their opposites are also perceived in the image of the Feminine; death and destruction, danger and distress, hunger and nakedness, appear as helplessness in the presence of the Dark and Terrible Mother.[24]

Stand back, please: Neumann is just warming up. Here is his version of the welcoming earth serenaded by William Cullen Bryant:

> Thus the womb of the earth becomes the deadly devouring maw of the underworld, and beside the fecundated womb and the protecting cave of earth and mountain gapes the abyss of hell, the dark hole of the depths, the devouring womb of the grave and of death, of darkness without light, of nothingness. For this woman who generates life and all living things on earth is the same who takes them back into herself. . . . This Terrible Mother is the hungry earth, which devours its own children and fattens on their corpses; it is the tiger and the vulture, the vulture and the coffin, the flesh-eating sarcophagus voraciously licking up the blood seed of men and beasts and, once fecundated and sated, casting it out again in new birth, hurling it to death, and over and over again to death.[25]

I think we get the picture.

Neumann offers us a gallery of examples of goddesses of the dead from a variety of world cultures. These include Kali, a fearful embodiment of the Feminine who appeared early in the history of India. She and her later embodiments such as Durga lust for blood sacrifices, the better to generate fertility. The fierce force of these female deities cannot be resisted by mortals. In action they are pure energy directed to either destruction or fertility. Neumann's depiction of the Terrible Mother is plenty bizarre and about as politically incorrect as one can get. Nevertheless, his examples are not invented.

We might grumble that such a deity as Ereshkigal, queen of the Sumerian underworld, will never win Miss Congeniality. But she always wins—using her other name, Innanna, the goddess of sex. Hathor, for another example, was a murderous, blood-drinking Nubian war goddess but also the cow of plenty, who nourished the gods and assured their fertility. Working the night shift, she also guided souls to Osiris, the judge of the dead.[26]

We pause for a moment, say, on a peaceful expanse of well-tended lawn with paths leisurely wandering this way and that. Sculptures in stone invite attention. A small bird poses on a handsomely weathered grave marker. Not far off is an attractive pond that invites a circumnavigational stroll. How bad can death be?

What we perceive, though, what lulls and perhaps even tempts us, is the congenial face of the Terrible Mother, if we tumble to the Neumann version. Just let the ground suddenly gape open next to our feet, and let the fetid stink of decay rise around us, and let the grass turn bloodred. Death no longer seems like such a walk in the park.

Allow our own dark side a moment's liberty, and we might discover other images as well. Why have men so often treated women so very badly? Why so much verbal and physical abuse of sexual partners? Why such ambivalence toward the women men love? Many possible reasons, of course. But perhaps one of the most primitive and powerful is the enduring ancient feeling that it is the woman who both gives life and takes it away. The woman not only has that mysterious passage from which a new life emerges but is also—somehow—guardian of that other passage through which we exit from life. Furthermore, we can hardly set one foot in front of another along the anthropologist's trail without discovering how widespread is the belief that females are regularly "contaminated" and are ever a menace to contaminate others. The menstrual cycle with its bleeding provides a physical foundation for this belief, but why should the fear of the "contaminating woman" have become so strongly entrenched in world folklore? Could this have anything to do with the uncomfortably close relationship between sex and death, fertility and destruction? With the awesome power therein concentrated? With blood, as ever, a visible lubricant between the living and the dead?

Just asking.

Into the Ground:
Why and Why Not?

We have viewed images of earth burial that are consoling and appalling but are nevertheless joined together at the hip bone. Both speak of abandoning the surface of things with its celestial canopy and descending into that-from-which-we-came. We have been but dust with borrowed breath of divinity, but clay in the Maker's hands. Christianity is even more rigorous in this regard than many older religions in which the departed could be bundled into their graves with familiar tools and symbols. The Order for the Burial of the Dead (undated) often includes the reminder:

> We brought nothing into this world, and it is certain, we can carry nothing out. The Lord gave, and the Lord hath taken away; blessed be the name of the Lord.

This proposition is stark but not transparent. We had nothing. Now we have a lot. And then we're back to nothing again. It would be challenging enough if the message were to end here. We really don't amount to very much, do we? We just come and go and that's that. This sounds less like a salvational religion than a somber Middle Eastern philosophy of illusion and vanity or a Greek atomist's depiction of a random, meaningless universe.

Perhaps one can follow Omar Khayyam's advice:

> Take the cash and let the credit go
> Nor heed the rumble of a distant drum[27]

Or perhaps one can bury mortal thoughts in the shallow trenches of everyday life until the grave is ready. Work, fight, sleep, reproduce after our kind, but don't think too much about what sense any of it makes. For much later generations: absorb and be absorbed by television, entertainment, and sports. The better—and therefore more difficult—trick is to live a balanced and meaningful life while moving along with "the innumerable caravan" to "the devouring womb of the grave and of death."

All of this would be challenge enough, but we are also enjoined to praise the name of the Lord. We are supposed to thank the Lord for this little prank? Creating us from dry dust, giving us breath, life, and hope, and then abandoning us "to be resolved to earth again"? But, wait, wait, wait! That's really not all there is, Peggy. The earth is only a way station, a stopover. We descend into the grave only to arise to a new life. The Lord does work in mysterious ways. And so does the earth. Let's consider, then, some of the reasons that people have either welcomed or feared ground burial. These reasons come from many levels of human thought and feeling and usually involve a mixture of the practical and the symbolic, the transcendental and the, well, down to earth. And, people being people, the same facet can strike us as both comforting and disturbing.

There's a Place for Us

Throughout life we feel more comfortable when we are secure in our place. This includes our physical space, which is also closely entwined with our relational and status space. The expression itself, "my place," reveals the desire for possession. "I want to sit in my own place at the table!" is a demand I have heard from a three-year-old when visitors have crowded around, and also from a ninety-one-year-old in a congregate living facility when a newcomer has landed in "her" chair. We want our own room, our own office, our own private corner where we can hang out the DO NOT DISTURB sign. As subgroup members, we don't want "those" people moving into "our" spaces. One word reminds us of this stubborn practice: *segregation*. Batman, a recent calendar cat,

> loves to sleep at the window. If the other cats try to usurp his place, he lies on top of them until they move out of the way.[28]

Batman's approach is as effective as and more peaceful than the ways in which gangs, corporations, and nations try to settle turf disputes. Other felines just get sat upon and can go find their own windows. Human conflict resolution strategies all too often have deposited corpses on the disputed space.

"My place" is a concept that has migrated from the physical to the symbolic, as in "I'm Number One" or "Serve the elders first," and so on. To be ousted from one's place is often felt as catastrophic. It is especially distressing to be denied admission to or be ejected from the inner circle, the communal space inhabited by our people.

The grave is a safe place from this perspective. We are within the protective, the magical, the sacred circle. We are with our own. Look, our people have taken care to bring us to this place. Our own little room has been prepared according to custom. All is as it should be. The prospect of residing in the right place with the right people may not dull the sting of death, but it does purify the needle.

People who know they do not have long to live often wish to return home for their final days—and the years after the final days. The important events, the powerful rituals of bonding and separation, should "take place" according to societal custom and personal feeling. Weddings and funerals do have something in common and are best conducted in places saturated with meaning.[29]

The intensity of feelings and the complexity of emotions connected with death and place demonstrate themselves in many ways. For instance, people made homeless by war and famine seek asylum elsewhere. However, this means abandoning their dead—the venerated ancestors. This broken connection is unsettling. Furthermore, what will happen when the displaced themselves die? Must they be covered by alien soil? Depending on circumstances, displaced people may start a new or an "extended" sacred place or continue to seek ways to return the dead to their native land. Millions of people have been forced to leave their homelands during natural and man-made catastrophes since the mid-nineteenth century. And, in so doing, they have left behind their ancestors and reduced their own opportunities to rest with them.

Also, a person who dies away from home may be considered at risk because the soul is lost, confused, and vulnerable to evil influence. A proper burial both launches the spirit securely on its next journey and safeguards the community from disgruntled ghosts.

And finally, the kin of the deceased cannot really move ahead with their lives until the remains are brought home where they belong. Efforts to recover family members missing in action may persist for years and draw upon all available resources. An Eskimo youth fought the museum and governmental bureaucracy passionately until they agreed to return his father's body from their anthropological archives.[30] The increasingly effective movement to return ancestral remains to Native American homelands is still another example. This is part of the larger phenomenon of corpse shifting. Remains that have been turned up by archaeologists once fell under the rule of "finders keepers." Now more obligation is felt to return these remains to where they belong. The task is often difficult because political and national boundaries and even the makeup of succeeding generations continue to change.

Unfortunately, the aching need to bury our own can be manipulated by the ruthless and greedy. An example from the present day:

> If Khasman Okhayeva ever wants to see her nephew Ruslan again, she will have to pay up. The Russian officer who is holding Ruslan's body at a federal military base outside Chechnya's capital, Grozny, has set a

price of $1,000, plus a $200 gold necklace, for his return. This is the going rate in Chechnya these days for corpses, but it is prohibitive for Okhayeva, a Chechen refugee who supports five children by working at a street market.[31]

Treating the dead as commodities was not just the practice of mummy merchants and grave robbers of the past; it has become a business again, even when impoverished and grieving families are involved.

Affirm, Educate, Inspire!

Another good down-to-earth reason for burial is the opportunity to perform a valuable service for the living, not only now, but also in generations to come. We are assuming a few things here: (1) burial grounds will properly reflect society's values and customs; (2) they will be maintained as such indefinitely; (3) a core of continuity will exist between society as it has been and society as it will be. And, by the way, we assume that society agrees in the first place on what values should be advanced and perpetuated by means of burial grounds.

An instructive example comes to us from the cemetery wars that flourished between France and the United Kingdom in the mid-nineteenth century. These wars did not actually occur on the burial grounds, and no body count resulted. However, there was a spirited clash of ideas and values. The question "What kind of cemeteries should we develop?" could be answered adequately only if the parties involved could agree on the answer to "What kind of people are we, anyhow?"

The French had already established several examples of the refined cemetery, the repository not only of deceased citizens but also of artistic sensitivities and noble ambitions. Père-la-Chaise was the model to emulate. But why should only Parisians enjoy such postmortem indulgence? Why not also the Brits, Irish, Scots, and Welsh? Père-la-Chaise was sentiment objectified by drooping willows and ornate sculptures. How tasteful, classical, poetical, and eloquent!

Even within France, however, some demurred. Praised lavishly by some, this cemetery was also derided as a pagan assemblage, a naive and excessive display that had little relevance either to religious belief or the hard facts of death. Conflicting opinions were expressed over and again as other nations sought to upgrade their cemeteries. This endeavor was complicated by the concurrent emergence of social conscience regarding the poor and disabled. Beautify our city and display our burgeoning power! Sounds good. But there are so many of those . . . those *other* people, and they die, too. In fact, they die a lot more readily than we do. The poor also deserve dignified Christian treatment at their death. Class distinctions should not pursue them to the grave. This was pretty re-markable thinking for its time—for any time, actually.

Tradition did not give way easily, though. J. C. Loudon, the distin-guished author of *On the Lay Out, Planting and Managing of Ceme-teries and on the Improvement of Churchyards,* was among those who were determined that cemeteries affirm the equality of all souls at death. Nevertheless, he proposed that temporary cemeteries be established in workhouse gardens. When the graves have been well filled, it's back to growing posies and veggies again. Critics were not lacking: how forward-looking and Christian was this, to convert workhouse paupers into ma-nure? Loudon did win many converts, though, to his basic concept that a burial ground should not affront community sensibilities. Pleasing de-signs and uplifting sculptures would dispel horrific midnight visions. Or so went the theory.

It was Loudon also who articulated the idea of the cemetery as in-struction. Instruction in what?

> To the local resident poor, uncultivated by reading, the churchyard is their book of history, their biography, their instructor in architecture and sculp-ture, their model of taste, and an important source of moral improvement.[32]

Cemeteries could also offer instruction in landscape gardening, ar-boriculture, and botany, and inspiration for neatness and order in gen-eral. Ramshackle graveyards only made people shudder. Proper ceme-teries could raise the level of culture and teach the industrious values that were making the nation great. Furthermore, the handsome stones and their fine shapings and decorations were silent preachers. Stone and virtue are enduring. The beautiful is the true. (The decomposing are safely out of sight.)

Nevertheless, Victorian society continued to struggle with its own emerging and conflicting values (e.g., enfranchised authority vs. science and opportunism; ambition vs. humanity), and the design of each new cemetery would have to pass through an antiphonal chorus of dissenting voices.

The United States was in a slightly different situation. Although much was owed to English tradition, a diversity of other customs and belief systems also came to our shores. The same basic issues had to be considered as population increase required more cemeteries and the public came to expect better as well. But the weight of the past did not sit so heavily—and the pace of expansion and industrialization was even dizzier than in the Old Country. The United States was still trying to discover itself, and it had to do so on the run.

The Yankee City series of studies did much to illuminate life and death in the United States in the 1940s. "Yankee City" was later identified as Newburyport, Massachusetts, after lead investigator W. Lloyd Warner had tried to keep it incognito in his own version of a witness protection program. What particularly interests us here is the way in which the dead represent the living. This phenomenon, of course, depends upon the existence of communal places for the dead.

Warner reminds us that sacred symbols express our hopes and fears. These symbols are essentially evocative and expressive rather than logical. They are shaped by mythic beliefs whose power does not depend on their status as fact or fantasy. Our deepest responses to life and death are of this nature, and their "ultimate meaning lies beyond ordinary experience."[33] The dead in their cemeteries inhabit a kind of sacred space. To say they are only symbolic members of the community is not to deny them influence and power. Symbolism can be one of the most potent of forces.

And so off we go to a Yankee City cemetery with Warner as our observant guide. He sees cemeteries in general as collective representations of the community's basic ideas about itself. It also provides visible symbols that help the living to contemplate their own separate destinies.

> The cemetery and its gravestones are the hard, enduring signs which anchor each man's projections of his innermost fantasies and private fears about the certainty of his own death—and the uncertainty of his ultimate future—on an external symbolic object made safe by tradition and the sanctions of religion.[34]

In other words, the cemetery affirms, educates, and inspires us to feel as safe as possible with our own mortality in our own town. Hastily, we add, if the cemetery "works," that is. Not every effort at affirmation, education, and inspiration does work.

Here, Warner points out that the sacred dead and the secular world of the living are both set apart and joined by clear physical boundaries marked by walls, fences, and hedges. There is also another kind of separating and joining, however—the spiritual. The living come and go as they perform ceremonies for the dead. Rituals of consecration are among the most important of these ceremonies. These rituals make something special of what would otherwise be ordinary land: the earth here becomes sacred because we wish it so. The dead are almost continuously separated from the living by funerals, and yet these rites

> occur with such continuing frequency that they maintain a constant stream of ritual connection between the dead and the living. Once a year the cult of the dead in the Memorial Day rites for the whole community strengthens and re-expresses what the chain of separate funerals accomplishes throughout the year.[35]

With the funeral we have a subtle transformation from time to space or place. The deceased have punched out their time clocks (or been punched out by them). They are no longer on standard time, daylight savings time, or any other schedule devised by humans. The funeral process marks the exit from a time-bound existence and therefore suggests that eternity is the next stop. Whatever else might come after time, the physical remains are now encapsulated in space and with rather more gravity than astronauts experience. (In the following section, however, we will remind ourselves that time is not quite at the standstill suggested by rites and beliefs.)

Warner speaks of the Yankee City cemetery as the final stop on "the conveyor belt of social time." An apt metaphor in a busy industrial city. Our place in the community is always changing, like it or not. What is expected of us, what we expect of ourselves, what opportunities are opening, what opportunities are closing . . . along the conveyor belt we move. Warner discreetly neglects to discuss the "finished product," except to mention that we are ceremonially dumped into a new set of meanings when we are set to earth.

We should take a moment to reflect, though. The Conveyor Belt That Ate America assembled a standard product, piece by piece. Mister Ford rather expected that both this item and the next would finish up as a

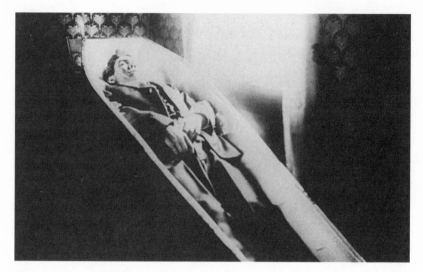

Figure 21 Deceased displayed in a mummy coffin, June 30, 1914. From James K. Crissman, *Death and Dying in Central Appalachia: Changing Attitudes and Practices* (Urbana: University of Illinois Press, 1994).

Figure 22 Headstone with lamb on infant's grave. From Crissman, *Death and Dying in Central Appalachia.*

Figure 23 Plain fieldstone used as grave marker. From Crissman, *Death and Dying in Central Appalachia.*

Figure 24 Metal grave marker in the shape of a mummy's coffin, Tennessee, 1827. From Crissman, *Death and Dying in Central Appalachia.*

Model T (black, of course). People are not nearly that standardized. Often we wonder how our children will turn out, and we might not be sure how we are turning out either. This is where individual character and universal fate diverge. The "finished product" coming off the disassembly line at the Yankee City cemetery might be an aged person who has lived all the life that was within him or her. But it might be a child whose character was still under construction or an adult who was engaged in a process of reconstruction. The conveyor belt and the grave do not much care, but we certainly do.

Back to Warner. The cemetery serves the living by helping to keep the dead real. Emphasis is on the particular dead, but Death itself is also respected. In a death-evading society, the cemetery keeps us tuned to reality just by being there. The most modern cemetery at the time of Warner's studies was "Elm Highlands," as he called it. This was actually established in the nineteenth century and was among the first generation of "garden cemeteries." But it was not only conceived as a garden; it was also a city unto itself. This thought is expressed in a hymn written for its consecration:

> With flowery grass and shadowy tree,
> The City of Our Dead to be.

So—garden and city. That is a long way from a simple town graveyard. Warner puts this endeavor into sociological perspective:

> It is a miniature, symbolic replica of the gardenlike dwelling area of a better-class suburb, or an elaboration of the formal gardens of aristocratic families. It is a symbolic city built in the form of a garden of the dead.[36]

One other point: "garden" is primarily a feminine image in Western culture, according to Warner. It symbolizes life, vitality, growth, and fertility. But it also is host to the processes involved in the perpetual cycling of death and life. Where have all the flowers gone? They flourish, wilt, decay, and arise to greet the next spring.

What does Elm Highlands teach us, then? That the dead live as we do (or would like to) in a replica of the living world. That it is the depot where we leave the conveyor belt and transfer to eternity. That it is where the living and the dead touch and separate. And that it is where, underneath all the rites, beliefs, sculptings, and shapings, Mother Earth does her quiet and relentless work in her own mysterious way, just as our most distant ancestors intuited.

One more brief visit, if you will. Hilton Head Island was occupied for about three thousand years by Native American peoples before the Europeans arrived in force and drove them away. The largest of the coastal islands between Florida and New Jersey, Hilton Head supported a few families who raised indigo, in demand for its deep blue color.[37] Black families farmed in this isolated area after the Civil War. Affluent northerners eventually purchased much of the land for recreational and commercial development. The black population declined to about three hundred, a tenth of its previous level.

Where do cemeteries come into all of this? The black settlers had their roots in West Africa. There, graveyards were not only sacred but also eventful places. People absolutely had to be buried on their home ground. The rites had to be faithfully performed for the good of both the departed and the survivors. Actually, not all of the departed does depart. The soul moves on, but the spirit remains in the vicinity—as friend or enemy. Graveyards must be maintained in proper order and, at all costs, protected. This orientation toward the dead was transplanted to their new homeland on Hilton Head Island.

Fortunately for some and unfortunately for others, the cemeteries are located on prime waterfront property. Developers hunger to acquire this land. This is a source of continuing concern for the black community. It is one thing to be dead, another to be dead and gone. Disturbing the remains would be an unthinkable act of sacrilege, worse than vandalizing a church because irreparable. Already there is a serious problem. A large tract has been developed with luxurious homes, golf courses, tennis courts, and other amenities. A dock and a ferry provide transportation to another island—Sea Pines Plantation, as it is now called, whose access is controlled by security guards. Nonresidents must pay an entry fee.

Black families find it painful to contend with the security guards and the gates when they want to visit their kin at Braddock Point Cemetery. There is anger at the indignity and barrier to this very personal form of religious practice.

As one approaches the cemetery at the far end of Sea Pines, the reality of it is shocking and frightening. A luxury condo has been built in a position to block its residents' view of the graves; marked and unmarked burial sites lay right outside its walls. . . . From within the cemetery itself, villas now block the vista of Calibogue Sound that the original founders had planned as the view "over to Africa across the water" as a comfort for the lonely souls.[38]

It was a good thing to be buried near the water with an open spiritual vista to the homeland. Now the cemetery no longer exists as originally constituted. The physical landscape surrounding the cemetery has been altered, and barriers to access exist. Furthermore, the sacred place has been violated by the influx of other people who have no connection with the living history and values of those who lie under the earth and their kin who visit. Affirming, educating, and inspiring may be significant purposes of the cemetery, but how can these be accomplished when time and change conspire against it?

Time and change have altered the relationship between the living and the dead in other ways as well. Perhaps one example will suffice. Back to France for a moment, but this time back a little further, to the middle of the eighteenth century. Everyday life has been changing rapidly and will crumble even faster when, in a few years, the French Revolution sweeps away the old order. Life in the cemetery is changing, too.[39] For many years the cemetery has been a good place to meet our friends. It is a public space, and the living are the public, are they not? The taverns there are not half bad. Music is bound to be playing somewhere on the cemetery's premises, and where there is music there is dancing. And where there's dancing there may be . . . well, later when the shadows lengthen, there are so many beguiling little places where two strangers can become much better acquainted. If we have work rather than play on our agenda, the cemetery might still be the place. There we can graze our cattle, thresh our wheat, dry our clothes, sell our merchandise. All this noise and activity is quite normal, quite acceptable. The dead never complain.

The Parisians seldom complain about the dead, either. That fashionable lady writing love letters to several of her admirers does not turn up her nose at the stench escaping from the nearby charnel house with its excess occupancy. Her companion meanwhile is browsing through a new collection of dresses and ribbons. Across the cemetery we can hear the lively bidding at the chickens and pigs auction. Other types of flesh are for sale as well. Prostitution and its faithful companion, theft, are also trades that flourish at graveside. Criminals and other fugitives take up residence in cozy spaces atop the ossuaries. Whatever and whomever you are looking for, the cemetery is a promising place to try.

Cemeteries were for the dead, of course, but even more so for the living. The dead reminded the quick that one should make hay while the sun shines and, at the rising of the moon, love.

Some of the pious insisted that Saint Vitus was outraged by seeing Christians dancing in a graveyard and put them under a spell: "Now you will have to dance forever!" This is a good story but not good history. Saint Vitus' dance had broken out hundreds of years before, as we've seen, and faded away with the disappearance of the Black Death. The actual story has more to do with the rise of a prosperous middle class, whose solid homes and materialistic tastes led to a more orderly kind of city. Cemeteries were demarcated from the community by forbidding walls. The authorities became more vigilant in discouraging frivolous and disrespectful behavior on the premises. Cemeteries were becoming more dignified but also more isolated from the boisterous flow of city life.

Death was now contained within the cemetery. This was just how the bourgeoisie liked it. Where was life, then? Public squares started to appear, flanked by galleries of merchants. Shopping had arrived! Ready to browse, purchase, meet a friend, or just see what's happening around town? Stroll to the plaza and leave the dead where they lie.

At one point in time-space, then, the cemetery not only affirmed, educated, and inspired, but also entertained. Even death itself changes, though, with the character and conditions of life. Soon enough the walls that would grow around cemeteries would also grow stronger within the minds of the living. *I am here. Death is there. Let's keep it that way.*

It's Nasty Down There

We have been considering some of the reasons that favor burial. We have also seen that the "resting places" of the dead are also vulnerable to insecurity as circumstances change among the living. Nevertheless, it is good for the dead to have a place of their own and even better when they can comfort and instruct the living. There are also reasons not to be enthused about burial, however. These reasons can be summarized in the shudder, "It's nasty down there!"

All too often, graveyards have been sorely neglected. Mother Earth appreciates loving attention. A splendid garden can deteriorate all too soon with neglect. "If you don't want it, I'll take it back!" Nature seems to say. Cemeteries also deteriorate when untended or exploited. In fact, cemeteries can themselves become killers. Just as an expertly designed and tended garden cemetery can help the community to feel better about mortal matters, so there can be anguish when the graveyard has become a hazard and a horror.

> And who would lay
> His body in the city burial-place.
> To be thrown up again by some rude sexton,
> And yield its narrow house another tenant,
> Ere the moist flesh had mingled with the dust,
> Ere the tenacious hair had left his scalp,
> Exposed to insult lewd, and wantonness?

H. K. White, a gentleman of the early nineteenth century, penned this rhetorical question and also provided a firm answer:

> No, I will lay me in the village ground;
> There are the dead respected.[40]

One of the many blights of modernization was the increasing urban density among the dead as well as the living. People who lived in rural areas often lived frugal and difficult lives. They did not have that much to lose when they sought opportunities in the city. But they did have a sense of belonging—they were somebody to their families, neighbors, and local church. Despite all the hardships, they were decent Christian men and women who could hope for salvation like anybody else. The prospect of death in the city, though, undermined confidence and mocked hopes. Bad enough it was to be buried among strangers. But to have one's mortal remains dumped into those hellish pits?

Intense aversion to burial arose in many countries as urban centers became more populous, congested, and chaotic. Public health measures generally lagged far behind the need. We are taking London as our specimen city and George Alfred Walker as our guide, but similar problems existed elsewhere as well. Walker's *Gatherings from Graveyards Particularly Those of London* was primarily a call for reform. Through his efforts and those of other vigorous reformers, substantial improvements were made, although with many a lag and gap.

Walker was outraged that *consecrated grounds, resting places,* and *sanctuaries* had become hollow and misleading terms. Christian faith and human dignity seemed to look in the other direction while graveyards became ever more odious and dangerous. Everybody was aware of the problem—how could they not be?—but few were concerned. Walker was trying to ring the alarm bell. Where did his fellow Londoners suppose that deadly contagions were so regularly bred and disseminated? The grave itself, so neglected and abused, was reaching out to claim new victims. We should learn from the ancients who took effective, practical measures in disposing of their dead. The laxity and indifference of recent years had invited repeated epidemics and tainted the overall quality of the city.

Had we the time and inclination, Walker would take us into London's every district, every churchyard, every space into which human remains had been carelessly stuffed, often by (who can blame them?) inebriated workmen. He describes the conditions in vivid detail, but I'm guessing you might as soon not be assailed by much of this gruesome material. Suffice it to say that the mortal remains were treated with gross disrespect even if they were deposited in such sacred soil as St. Gile's Church Yard or in vaults beneath Whitechapel Church. Coffins often were broken, and body heaped upon tangled body. Everywhere the stench was overpowering. Furthermore, no special measures were taken for victims of contagious diseases. Indeed, the conditions of their burial—often shallow and open to assault from animals—could hardly have been more conducive to furthering epidemics.

Insult and injury go hand in hand. We probably cannot avoid a few examples if we are to understand the situation that prevailed all too often in London and other burgeoning cities. We are standing—uncomfortably—in the burial ground that adjoins Whitechapel Church. It abuts

> upon one of the greatest thoroughfares in London, and is placed in the centre of a densely populated neighbourhood; its appearance altogether is extremely disgusting, and I have no doubt whatever, that the putrefactive process which is here very rapidly going on, must, in a great measure, be the cause of producing, certainly of increasing, the numerous diseases by which the lower order of the inhabitants of this parish have so frequently

been visited. The ground is so densely crowded as to present one entire mass of human bones and putrefaction.

These remains of what once were gay, perhaps virtuous and eminent, people are treated with ruthless indifference. They are exhumed by shovelfulls, and disgustingly exposed to the passer-by—to the jeers or contempt of the profane or brutal. It appears almost impossible to dig a grave in this ground without coming into contact with some recent interment, and the grave digger's pick is often forced through the lid of a coffin when least expected, from which so dreadful an effluvium is emitted. . . . most of the graves are very shallow . . . within a foot and a half of the surface.[41]

Conditions were even worse in other sectors of the same churchyard. Pits ten feet deep were filled to within a few inches of the top with only a slight covering of earth: one could hardly say these people were even buried. Some family graves were completely exposed, and some coffins "literally cut in two." A few paces away there was a separate area, the "poor ground," and here the dead lay as shallow and as thickly packed as in the churchyard proper.

Consider that burial ground sites such as these were to be found throughout the city. *Was not Death burying the city rather than otherwise?* Londoners tried mightily to avoid noticing the blight, but surely few were comforted by the image of "resting in peace" in "consecrated ground." Consider also that when Walker published this book the nation was still convulsed from encounters with grave-robbing and corpse-selling scandals. And consider also that bodies often were ejected from their temporary permanence to make room for new arrivals. Thieves did not hesitate to rob the dead of what little they had, whether a ring on a finger or the clothes on their backs. Inhumation within the allowed soil of a churchyard did not protect against these crimes, although vigilant authorities occasionally caught the thief dead-handed.

And worse yet. Walker observes that some burials were premature. The deceased was not quite deceased, but why wait? Better to remove the body and have done with it. There would be frenzied reports of unfortunates being buried alive throughout much of the nineteenth century and well into the twentieth in many countries, including the United Studies. Some of these reports were erroneous, but some were not. Jan Bondeson's historical analysis of live burial reports helps to separate the probably accurate from the almost certainly false. Bondeson comments that

the mid-eighteenth century process of dechristianization of death facilitated
the spread of the fear of premature burial. But both the traditional fear of
hell and the new fear of being buried alive were expressions of a deeper,
underlying fear of death.[42]

Crude disposal of the dead and neglect of graveyards could only intensify such fear. In all probability Walker, a careful observer, was reporting actual examples of live burial. The whole process of medical diagnosis and professional handling of corpses was often left to disinterested
and incompetent persons. The well-trained physician and the skilled mor-
tician were outnumbered by the incompetents. In these circumstances, if
you and I were to hesitate about being buried dead, how would we feel
about being buried alive?

A word of sympathy is in order for the undertakers, grave diggers,
and faithful clergy who had close contact with the dead. It was not unusual for them to fall ill, sometimes violently so, when exposed to noxious gases produced by decomposition. For example, both a grave digger and a man who came to his rescue died immediately when exposed
to foul air in the Aldgate churchyard.[43] It *is* nasty down there, nasty!

It's Spooky Down There
(Too Many Vampires, for One Thing)

Suppose that the burial place is not repulsive. Suppose that common sense
and human feeling have given us a decent abode for the dead. Does this
mean that we can feel safe there? Not necessarily. Fear of graveyards has
been widespread. People courageous in other facets of their lives can feel
distinctly uncomfortable around a cemetery . . . especially if alone . . .
on a dark night with only the occasional rustle of a—*what was that?*
Graveyards still make useful scenes in inventing scary bedtime stories.
Ghosts are often supposed to be on the lurk in graveyards, and when
they are not available observers have been known to make do with *wills-
o'-the-wisp*, pale, luminous phenomena that move in an odd and frightening manner. These might just be gaseous emanations from the decomposition, but try telling that to a person who, after several rounds
at the tavern, is trying a midnight shortcut through the cemetery.

By and large, though, the scariest part about the grave might be our uncertainty about what goes on there. Children will share their own theories with each other, though they often hesitate to upset adults with such talk. One five-year-old confided to me that the dead have to lie there and be patient until their heads are put back on. (She had heard about the burial of a body and assumed the head was kept someplace else.) Another child of the same age had figured out that dead people could play only with one another because their clothes and feet were dirty so they wouldn't be allowed back in the house. A seven-year-old boy was more naturalistic. First thing that happens is getting eaten by worms. The next thing is growing another body. "This one is worm-proof." What the dead do after that is a question he was still working on.

Few people of any age have understood the physical changes that occur at and after death. Buddhist tradition does offer an evocative picture of a person passing through as many as eight stages of experience, depending on that individual's level of spiritual development.[44] The process starts with the onset of miragelike visions while eyesight dims. By the fourth stage the individual no longer breathes and would be considered dead by a Western physician. The final set of stages are mental or spiritual. The most spiritually evolved people will experience the clear light of death. This is a unique form of unconsciousness that persists until death is complete. All of these eventful stages occur, though, before there is a corpse.

Medical science has gradually replaced fears and guesses with solid information,[45] although more remains to be learned. We might begin with the interval between death and burial. Several processes occur both sequentially and simultaneously. The muscles relax at death, starting with those of the heart and other internal organs. This sequence continues with the head, neck, trunk, and extremities. At this point we have *primary flaccidity*. *Rigor mortis* and *livor mortis* then follow. Rigor mortis is the stiffening of muscles. It usually starts between two and six hours of the death. The eyelids, neck, and jaw are the first to be affected. Rigor mortis will spread to the other muscles over the next four to six hours. The rigor mortis process has been related to the cessation of glycogen synthesis, which, in turn, deprives body tissues of adenosine triphosphate (ATP). The muscles contract and remain locked in this position, immobilizing the joints. Rigor mortis occurs more rapidly in cold weather and also when the individual has engaged in strenuous physical activity just prior to death. Infants and young children often have a less perceptible rigor mortis phase because of their limited muscular development. There are occasional adult corpses who also show few if any signs of rigor mortis. Iserson notes that folklore in Britain, the Philippines, and possibly other countries ascribes fearsome supernatural powers to these "limber corpses."

Meanwhile, blood collects in the lower parts of the body after the heart stops beating. The skin becomes pale as the blood drains away. A purple-red discoloration *(postmortem stain)* then appears in those places where blood has pooled inside the body. These pools of blood can shift if the body is moved shortly after death. After a few hours, though, the pooled blood remains in its fixed condition. Livor mortis now exists, and the body starts to cool. This cooling period is known as *algor mortis*. Rigor mortis eventually gives way after a while as the locked muscles relax. This laxity or flaccidity may occur as early as twenty-four hours or as late as eighty-four hours after death.

In the natural order of things, decomposition proceeds rapidly. The description that follows (skip it if you'd rather) assumes that the corpse is visible to observers. However, one of the reasons the grave has so often been considered a spooky place is that most of these changes usually occur when the body is already underground. Fantasies flourish when we are unable or unwilling to see what is really happening. First, then, what is really happening, then the fantasies!

(Warning: gross description begins here.) The overall process of decomposition begins with putrefaction. The skin on the lower abdomen becomes greenish two or three days after death. This discoloration spreads over the rest of the body, accompanied by a putrid odor. The discoloration and smell are produced by sulfurous intestinal gas and the breakdown of red blood cells. Foul-smelling gas continues to be produced by the same intestinal bacteria that digested food throughout the decedent's life. This gas will now bloat the body, darken the skin from green to purple to black, make the tongue and eyes protrude, and do things to the intestines that we would probably rather not think about.

About a week later the discolored skin, interrupted in various places with large blooded blisters, is so loose that the top layer peels off under pressure. Production of foul-smelling gas continues as the internal organs decompose. The uterus and prostate can resist decomposition for as long as a year, enabling pathologists to determine the sex of unidentified remains.

Individual cells break down and die as their inner elements dissolve and they lose both connections with other cells and control over their own boundaries. Enzymes escape, and their destructive acidic action completes the work of necrosis.

This is the general picture. There are exceptions. Some corpses deteriorate so rapidly that the features are obliterated within a few hours. Others are preserved for extended periods of time if environmental conditions protect them from oxygenation and bacterial processes. A natural process known as *saponification* can also occur, although its frequency has not been well established. In saponification, body fat is converted into adipocere, a compound of fatty acids. This gives a reddish tinge to the muscles, occasionally bright enough to give the impression that death has occurred only recently, even though the corpse might be a century old.[46] *(Really gross description has ended.)*

The physical changes after death have the effect of reducing the complex structure of the human frame to organic components that are suitable to participate in the life-unto-death-unto-life cycle. This natural process is aborted, if the term can be applied to death, when the body is (1) embalmed, (2) frozen, (3) mummified, which can involve either of the foregoing, or (4) cremated. With the exception of cremation, however, these variations are not necessarily permanent. Ice melts, mummies can be exposed to the elements, and, despite popular assumptions to the contrary, embalming has its shelf life (or death) as well. Our ancestors understood that the dead resemble the living less and less with passing time. There were expectations for the appearance of a corpse should it be unearthed, especially long after its burial. There were also basic expectations for the corpse's behavior: actually, *no* behavior was the expectation. When these expectations were confounded by the appearance or behavior of the corpse—spooky!

This brings us to the vampire, a creature both living and dead. These scary but compelling entities have starred in literature, drama, cinema, and television ever since Bram Stoker introduced us to Count Dracula.[47] The vampire is as new as the latest Anne Rice novel or *Buffy the Vampire Slayer* episode but also nearly as ancient as earth's experiment with *Homo sapiens*. Vampires, or revenants, were well established in folklore and mythology before Dracula, providing abundant raw material for Stoker's epic. Slavic tradition was especially rich in vampire chronicles, and believers continue to tremble within the ominous shadow of the nocturnal fiend. Expanding our retrospective, we find a plentiful supply of vampirelike creatures in medieval belief. The church set upon a vigorous campaign to separate good and evil as strictly as possible. Both were personified, as in vivid descriptions of angels and devils. O. A. Eaves finds that the incubi and succubi beloved to the medieval imagination were essentially vampires under other names.[48] Vampirish creatures also raised goose bumps much further back, even though given renewed life under Christian auspices.

How much further back? Historians tell us:

> The notion behind vampirism traces way back in time—to man the hunter, who discovered that when blood flowed out of the wounded beast or a fellow human, life, too, drained away. Blood was the source of vitality! Thus men sometimes smeared themselves with blood and sometimes drank it. The idea of drinking blood to renew vitality became transferred from the living to the dead, and thereupon the vampire entered history.[49]

It is the Slavic vampire tradition as harvested by Stoker at the end of the nineteenth century that has most influenced our prevailing image of the vampire. And, therefore, it is the Stokerized Slavic vampire whom we have most reason to examine with the knowledge developed by medical science and enhanced by the observations of cultural historians. Our primary guide here is Paul Barber, whose *Vampires, Burial, and Death* is just the book to curl up with on a dark and stormy night.

Why would so many people believe that vampires are real? "Because they *are* real!" would be a stimulating response. "We don't know everything; we only think we do." Besides, the grave is such a weird and spooky place that almost anything just might happen there. But we have already given ourselves some clues about what does happen there. All those postmortem changes. All those foul-smelling gases, as Walker had also many occasions to notice in his tour of London graveyards. Perhaps they have something to do with the undead?

Barber offers numerous accounts of vampire activity, as did his admirable predecessor Montague Summers.[50] Barber's contribution, however, resides in the connections he makes between the reported supernatural and its roots in the natural process. Here are some of these connections, abstracted from Barber's analyses.

Report: Blood on the corpse's lips. Must have had a big night.

Explanation: Blood migrates to the mouth and nose during decomposition as a result of gas pressure. Also, there is often a gravitational flow of pooled blood into the trachea, seeping out through facial orifices. Probably had a normal night for a normal corpse.

Report: Blood gushed when we plunged the stake into the vampire's heart.

Explanation: Well, what did you expect? Be careful with sharps! Blood coagulates, but it also reliquefies under some conditions and tends to pool in the heart. Blood is also more likely to remain or revert to fluid in sudden death such as accident or murder. It has been popularly supposed that a death by violence can turn the victim into a vampire, but all it does is generate a blooded corpse.

Report: Look at those dirty fingernails! They've grown longer and longer in the grave. O grave, where is thy manicurist?

Explanation: After death the skin shrinks and pulls away from the nails, leaving them more exposed.

Report: But, see—he was trying to claw his way out of the coffin. The body has moved, and dead bodies aren't supposed to do that.

Explanation: Our bodies would move, too, if sufficiently bloated with gas. There have also been credible reports of vampire chickens aloft, and these in twentieth-century America. Turns out that a large number of chickens, infected with a contagious disease, were killed and then buried in shallow graves. After a life of foul captivity, they succeeded in a postmortem ascension. Furthermore, differential muscular relaxation can also alter position in the grave.

Report: There was no rigor to the mortis! Must still be alive, at least part-time.

Explanation: Rigor mortis comes and goes. A stiff is not always so.

Report: It is our own fault sometimes. We do not bury the body deep enough, and so it is vulnerable to evil spirits and becomes a vampire. And here is solid evidence for you: we sought a vampire suspect in his grave, and the grave was—empty!

Explanation: Shallow graves are at risk for losing their tenants.

Floods can evict and marauding animals eat them, sometimes the former leading to the latter. Many graves have been lost to agricultural or commercial development—but sometimes the occupants have been removed to new lodgings by considerate hands. Ask around.

Report: The whole body looked rosy, altogether too healthy for a corpse.

Explanation: See saponification. And see about finding another hobby that doesn't require mucking around in graveyards at midnight.

And so on. Barber puts this all together in an explanation that emphasizes most people's lack of understanding of what naturally occurs with the body after death:

> The people who discover it see only one stage of the process—a hand sticking out of the earth, or a body emerging from the earth, or animals eating the body—and this is then presented as a supernatural event. The hand belongs to a sinner; the body is emerging to attack the living, and the animals are killing a vampire. . . . The evidence, in other words, is first interpreted, then the interpretation is used to eke out the evidence . . . thus the European vampire came into being. Dead bodies do bloat and bleed at the mouth—as our informants tell us—but these functions are seen not as evidence of decomposition but as a consequence of their having sucked blood from the living.[51]

Burial, then, might be less spooky and scary a prospect if we could persuade ourselves that our neighbors will not be vampires and that we ourselves will not terrorize the good citizens of our town when the moon is bloodred and the owl hoots from the forest deep.

UP OR DOWN AND OUT?

In a small alcove in her home reside Grandmother's ashes as well as those of two of her favorite cats, who still serve as faithful companions. Actually, only half of Grandmother's ashes are there. The granddaughter reports that she fulfilled the older woman's wishes by spreading some of her ashes in the European place of her birth, a ruggedly beautiful mountainous area. "I started to spread her ashes on the ground—but they went *up!* Knowing Grandmother, I shouldn't have been surprised!"

Up is usually the more positive direction with us. On a good day we ourselves feel "up." When we have the blues we feel "down," and this can be verified by our gravity-stricken body language. A psychiatrist has even reported that the skyjackers he interviewed were clinically depressed people who had felt they were sinking into the ground and therefore reacted by taking to the sky. We would rather continue to climb higher on the career ladder than be a victim of downsizing. There are a few good things to be said about the other direction. We expect our experts to be well grounded in their specialties. And in our more impulsive moments we may have been told to keep our feet on the ground. Heaven, though, has almost always been up there, and hell, the bottomless pit beneath our feet. These and other associations to up and down may influence our attitudes toward the options of cremation and whole body burial.

There are also the specific associations to flaming farewells and inhumations, some of which have already been mentioned. Fire is (relatively) quick. It is also seems more conclusive. Even wannabe vampires will be hard-pressed to survive. Since the gods reign up there, it is reasonable to assume that rising in flame is the preferred route to heaven. Furthermore, flaming can be regarded as a holy rite of purification. The heavy, corrupt, and now useless physical frame vanishes, liberating the spirit. From the public health standpoint, too, cremation avoids the risk of contamination, especially when contagious diseases are involved. Burning the dead could protect the living. Cremation also offers its own options. We could keep cremains in our homes, bury them in the garden or a cemetery, or place them within a memorial niche, vault, or tomb—or decide where in the wide world it would be most appropriate to return the ashes to nature.

Cremation has another association, however, one that takes a lot of forgetting or denial to overcome. The ovens of Nazi death camps sent millions of people up in smoke—so many, in fact, that the townspeople complained of the pollution. As long as the Nazi horrors are remembered, cremation will be a dark cloud over the human spirit.

There has long been another form of "sky burial," as it is called. The bodies can be left exposed for the services of carrion birds. This does not provide the kind of memory image that most people in Western societies

Figure 25 Vultures picking the bones of the dead, India. The vultures themselves are now endangered by pesticides and other toxic chemicals. Photo by Munir Virani/The Peregrine Fund.

would care to take with them. Sky burial has both a religious and a practical rationale, however. The Parsis, followers of Zoroastrianism, are among the many people who believe that the corpse is contaminated and therefore must be purified. Decomposition should occur through natural means before the essential remains are returned to earth, fire, and water. Vultures have been providing this service since ancient times. But now—where are the vultures? And what can be done with the dead?

The Towers of Silence in Bombay have been the most renowned site for sky burial in India (the practice also occurs in Pakistan and with Buddhists in Tibet). For as long as anybody can remember, the towers have been surmounted by an orderly circle of vultures, who, when not otherwise occupied, resemble stone carvings. Since the 1990s, though, their numbers have been sharply reduced.[52] Vultures have been found dead in trees and other natural habitats. Pesticides have been suspected, especially DDT, possibly ingested from the numerous cattle held sacred. Although the actual cause or causes are still not clear, the consequences could be widespread and severe:

1. Without a sufficiency of vultures, Parsis may have to turn to cremation, as the Hindus do; however, this not only requires a shift in religious practice but also runs into the limited availability and considerable expense of wood for the pyre.

2. Because vultures also have attended to cattle and other animal corpses, this work will now probably fall to wild dogs and other predatory animals that can be more dangerous to the general population.

3. Diseases such as anthrax could be spread through the many cattle corpses that will not be "cleaned" quickly and thoroughly.

4. The Hindu ban on touching the corpses of sacred cattle may come under intense pressure for the last two reasons above.

This emerging situation again reminds us that our relationship to the dead, especially the newly dead, is always conditioned by a variety of circumstances. It is also difficult to avoid the metaphysical irony here. How far have Nature and human nature tilted out of balance when those dedicated and impressive vultures, the uppertakers of the dead, themselves fall victim? Who or what will cleanse their bones?

Ground burial has a more limited set of options to offer. Embalming has been common since the Civil War and has practical value when burial must be delayed either for forensic purposes or to give relatives time to gather. We could choose to do without embalming in many cases, but for that we would have to surrender the illusion that corpses will remain intact indefinitely. We can also choose among various types of caskets and grave markers, although cost factors could make the choice for us.

The person who has passed on might have made the decision easier for the survivors by specifying precisely what should be done. Family, though, still have to reach agreement among themselves about honoring these instructions.

Ground burial has its share of horrors as well, including mass graves of the slaughtered in Poland and Bosnia. These victims did not have the opportunity to "approach thy grave / Like one who wraps the drapery of his couch / About him, and lies down to pleasant dreams." This was savagery that exceeded even the demands of the hungry earth.

Both cremation and burial have the potential for either comforting or disturbing the survivors. What makes the difference?

Ceremonies and Rites

There is no point in asserting that one particular kind of ceremony or rite is most suitable or most consoling. In a pluralistic and ever-changing society we must find our own way to balance between tradition and innovation, belief and agnosticism, elaboration and convenience. Hmung immigrants have been able to preserve the core of their complex and resource-demanding rituals by limiting their permeability by mainstream American practices, but also by making some adjustments.[53] The Amish are notable for remaining an intact traditional society while still effectively connecting with the mainstream United States.[54] Like the Hmung, they are family-oriented, but they engage in much simpler funeral and burial practices. Both approaches comfort their respective people, not because of the particular details, but because each group has evolved practices that accord with their own views of life and death. We might ask ourselves if the send-off rites in mainstream American society are still charged with meaning or are hollow repetitions of outworn creeds.[55] More specifically, we might ask if the growing popularity of cremation is being accompanied by send-off rituals with sufficient resonance and meaning to comfort the survivors.

The Place of the Dead in Our Society

How we conduct the final passage has something to do with the basic place of the dead in our society. We have found that the dead are most likely to be important to the living:[56]

- in past-oriented societies;
- where the dead are close (geographically) to the living;
- where children are highly valued for perpetuating the family soul across the gap created by death;
- where elders have significant power and relatively few attain old age; and
- where there are unifying and transcending cultural themes that can assimilate the funeral and memorialization process into its utilitarian motives.

Looking at the dead in this way, we see that they have become increasingly less important in the United States and other high techno-communicational societies. We still grieve for the people we have loved and lost. For society writ large, however, the dead are being further marginalized (even the famous people nobody has ever heard of anymore). Yes, we make an exception for those whose postmortem voting behavior is still highly valued in certain precincts.

Our Place in Nature and the Cosmos

If the cosmos has been designed for our pleasure or enlightenment . . . If a much better or a much worse existence awaits us after death . . . If we are and will again become dust, specks on a speck called Earth . . . If we are meant to participate in the great dying and rebirthing of life . . . If there is a plan to the cosmos or only an odd and doomed sequence . . .

All these *ifs* bear on the way we regard the meaning of both life and death. Why burn a perfectly good ship if the Viking chief isn't really going anywhere? Why knock ourselves out to purify the dead and ward off evil spirits if these exist only in our inheritance of primitive notions? Why take such a nonchalant, cost-effective attitude toward body disposal if our treatment of the dead really does make a difference to the fate of their souls and our own?

It is tempting to dwell on the particulars of funeral and memorial practices, especially if they are rewardingly bizarre. It is also tempting to offer advice (and why wait until it's asked for?). But perhaps it's wiser to give more consideration to the basic ideas, hopes, wishes, and fears that furnish our minds. What—really—is life? What—really—is death? When we have answered these questions to the best of our abilities, then we might be in a better position either to flare upward in flames or to take our place down where earth performs its deepest mysteries.

NINE

JOURNEY OF THE DEAD

There is the leaving. There is the going toward. There is the arrival. We could be talking about any journey. The journey might be marked by rituals, especially at the points of origin and arrival. These rituals are interesting to anthropologists, who use "rites of passage" as a heuristic concept. The first set of rituals helps us to separate from our people and prepare for the journey. The second set of rituals helps us to become part of those who are waiting on the other side after having met their own tests and challenges. We are pretty much on our own, though, as we move through the dangerous zone between one place and one identity and the next. Perhaps it is a long crossing by stormy sea or uncharted wilderness. Perhaps it is a traditional ordeal through which youths become certified as adults. Or perhaps it is that mysterious after-journey from all that we have known to—what? And perhaps all the journeys we have made during our lives, the great and the small, have been subtle preparations, not merely for the crossing over from life, but for the journey of the dead.

Many people throughout the world still walk to the funeral site, along dusty rural paths or the cobblestoned streets of towns where for centuries their ancestors have lived and died. These processions may be silent or accompanied by traditional music. The corpse may be transported in a wagon or on the shoulders of kinsmen. The sense of participation in a journey from life to death is felt with every step, not smoothed over by a limousine ride that is part of a commercial funeral "package."

Laderman characterizes early-nineteenth-century New England burials in which there was the experience of both journey and arrival:

> The last act of throwing into the grave a branch, straw, or commonly dirt from the earth before leaving the place of interment was a frequent gesture recognizing the finality of the journey. Many services at the burial site concluded with this ritual drama that signified both individual and communal acknowledgment that the deceased would no longer be seen or heard from again, and that the body would be finally returning to earth.

The drama was private as well as public:

> The family relations, friends, and other intimate associates standing beside the grave said any last thoughts or prayers before turning their backs on the dead and returning to the community of the living.

Last journey? Final destination?

> The journey of the lifeless body from the place of expiration to the space of disposal was significant for the family and community members involved. The rites of passage from life to death, deathbed to grave, allowed the survivors an opportunity to pay their last respects and to make certain that collective action repaired the rupture in the social fabric. Throughout the journey participants in the funeral had a number of occasions to ensure that the corpse was safely and appropriately handled until reaching its final destination.[1]

This is apt description and commentary—but let's not be so quick in agreeing that this was truly the final journey and destination. The human imagination has provided a wealth of other possibilities. Separation from the world of the living might simply be the condition for extending the journey of existence to other realms. In this chapter, then, we have our eyes on the after-journey: where the dead go and what they do when they get there. Curiosity would be reason enough for this exploration. There is an even more compelling reason, though: the after-journey and its destination are intimately related to the way we interpret and pursue our everyday lives. Replace one conception of the after-death with another, and we might need to rethink our entire pattern of

Figure 26 Portal of death, depicted on Albert Bartholomé's *Monument aux morts,* 1895, Perè-la-Chaise Cemetery, Paris.

relationships, values, and priorities. Ready or not, then, let's share the journey of the dead.

A RIDE ON THE FERRY

"What's keeping you? Hurry—you're holding us up!"

These are the first words known to have been spoken by Charon, the ferryman of the dead. Actually, this display of impatience was expressed by the character of Charon in Euripides' *Alcestis* (fifth century B.C.).[2] The ferryman had already been hinted at long before in the tales attributed to Homer and several subsequent historian-mythmakers. Somewhere along the way Charon shifted his attitude. At first he gave the journeying dead a hard time. They could not just march into Hades and make themselves at home. The border crossing was difficult for both the living and the dead. Even the distinguished dead had to demonstrate their merits and solicit proper observance of funeral rituals to ease their way.

Other barriers might also be encountered. The resident dead, for example, rose up to confront Odysseus, although he had followed instructions scrupulously. He had navigated to the juncture of the infernal rivers, dug a pit, poured a libation to the gods, promised the dead a sacrifice upon his return, and so forth. All this, and yet up swarmed the souls of the dead with a horrible moaning: unmarried youths, virginal brides, slain warriors with gaping wounds, the aged with years of suffering etched upon them—the whole ghoulish community fluttering about Odysseus to obstruct his crossing. (True, Odysseus did not meet one of the zoning qualifications: he was a living person hoping to receive counsel from the shade of the wise Tiresias. This made him a more accessible witness, however.) The early Hellenic myths suggest that the weary journey from life did not completely guarantee or entitle one to enter the realm of the dead. Metaphorically, on the other shore were the kin and priests who had given their dead what they hoped to be a sufficient ritualistic send-off. The infernal regions had their own rules and rituals, however. Mortals were likely to be caught in the scrimmage between gods of the upper and lower realms, making the difficult afterdeath journey all the more so.[3]

How did it feel to be banished from the living and yet not welcomed among the dead? I wonder, for instance, about the connection between unwanted babies and unwanted souls of the dead. Rites of passage usually assume a cultural and spiritual corridor through which individuals move in accordance with communal expectations and their own qualities. But what of the unfortunates who are not welcomed into this process at the start and those who are denied continuation or completion at the end of their earthly stay? And what are the deeper resonances of the person considered an outsider to communal values and privileges even though existing within the frame? And what circumstances convert an insider into an outsider? Is life forfeit yet death also denied to, say, the traitor, blasphemer, or rival?

I wonder, are the recently deceased always at higher risk than the long dead? Most world cultures assume this to be the case, as indicated by their funereal and mourning practices. The record shows Charon dealing not with the veterans of death, only with the newcomers (or -goers). This common attitude serves to emphasize the importance of the journey. Getting dead is not the same as being dead.

Furthermore, just why has humankind been haunted by the nightmare vision of lost souls? How do we manage to have both fear and compassion for the incompletely dead? It is difficult to decode the moral criteria for entering the land of the dead in ancient times with only fragmentary and sometimes contradictory hints. But more ample information from later societies tends to affirm that failures of mourners in the send-off and postdeath rituals increase the risk of the dead becoming lost and restless souls. Wagner's Flying Dutchman was condemned to sail the seas interminably until redeemed by a woman's pure love. Perhaps that woman's real name is Mother Nature? And perhaps, just perhaps, the nightmare vision of lost souls has its roots in the anxious yearning for a return to security by the infant alone in the dark?

Finally, does death change its character as the journey proceeds? In many band-and-village societies death has been regarded as a raider, an external force that destroys life. One should stay within the protective ring of the compound or vicinity as much as possible. We become more vulnerable not only to death but also to becoming a lost, wandering, and potentially dangerous spirit when we venture beyond the relatively safe limits established by tradition. This, as we have seen, is one of the reasons it is considered important to return the bodies for a proper funeral and disposition within the protective ring. And yet it is death that now seems to offer a haven, melancholy though it might be. What's the lesson here? That it's better to be somewhere—in the circle of the living *or* the dead—than to be a nobody in the middle of nowhere?

Charon became a more definite character when the golden age of Greek drama and poetry polished up the hoary myths and added its own nascent sensibilities. The river, given various names in the past, now was definitively "the Hated," better known as the Styx. If the scene had been the American Southwest, it might instead have been called the Río Morte, an ominous flowing boundary between the lands of the living and the dead. Charon himself was a surly fellow, probably assured of permanent employment and not inclined to take guff from any mere mortal. Even though he no longer guarded Hades, he did require proper deportment and hard, ringing coin before he would boat the travelers to the other side. Greek burial customs included placing a coin in the mouth of the deceased to pay Charon's fare. Perhaps this is the origin of the injunction to "put your money where your mouth is." In any event, for Greeks of the classical era the journey of the dead was a pay-as-you-go proposition.

Dying, being dead, and getting to the appointed land of the dead were serious matters, of course, but the Greek imagination had at least its share of playfulness as well. For example, Menippus, a philosopher, arrived without a coin in hand or mouth. Charon scolded him—he should have known better! Menippus replied, in effect, "If you don't have a coin, you don't have it! What was I supposed to do—not die?" Then the philosopher offered a solution: why didn't Charon simply restore him to life? "Oh, sure!" the ferryman shot back. "Then you can brag about this little trick to all your friends, and they'll think they can try it on me, too!" Charon grudgingly agreed to transport Menippus across the Styx, chalk-

Figure 27 In this Roman-era image, Charon, ferryman of the underworld, accepts a dead person from
Mercury to row across the Styx, back in the good
old days. From Frederick Parkes Weber, *Aspects
of Death and Correlated Aspects of Life in Art,
Epigram and Poetry* (1910; College Park, Md.:
McGrath, 1971), p. 647.

ing this one up as a good deed and a bad debt. To make matters worse,
his philosopher-passenger showed no interest in moaning and groaning
during the passage; instead he cheerfully sang and jested.

Charon himself comes in for a bit of affectionate twitting when nineteenth-century poet Walter Savage Landor imagines him charged with
the task of conveying the beautiful Dirce across the Styx:

> Stand close around, ye Stygian set,
> With Dirce in one boat conveyed,
> Or Charon, seeing, may forget
> That he is old and she a shade.[4]

But what of the destination? What of Hades itself? This was once the
name of a god (also on record as Dis and, later, Pluto). He was the foot-
loose, even wicked, son of Kronos, the god of time (also known as Saturnus, still awaiting our thanks for Saturday nights). One can forgive
Hades if he rebelled against his father, whose dining habits had become
notorious. Hades wanted to escape the "happy meal" fate of most of
Kronos's other children. Kronos might have had his reasons for eating

"Say, Donovan, do we have one with muffled oars?"

Figure 28 Charon tries to rent a rowboat. Reprinted with the permission of Simon & Schuster from *My Crowd*, by Charles Addams. Copyright © 1970 by Charles Addams.

his own children, but Hades/Pluto preferred to steal away with the beautiful Proserpine and enjoy a long honeymoon in the underworld. Eventually the romantic scamp's original name was given to the realm of the dead, and Pluto became his official *nom de deus*.

I find this arrangement at least slightly encouraging. The dread underworld did operate under the auspices of a god—actually a devoted couple who had known terror, flight, and love. More hellish conditions have been experienced on the surface of the earth by the victims of fanatic religious or political persecution. And, according to the more credible reports, Hades was not a cauldron of merciless torment where sinners simmered until the end of time.[5] All that would come later, when Christian concepts of damnation, torment, and redemption came to the fore. Journey's end for most shades was a dreary, enervating subexistence,

equivalent, perhaps, to being trapped in the lower echelons of a bureaucracy or next to the world's most garrulous and boring fellow pas-
senger in a holding pattern over Albany.

Depending on the era, one might have had to pass through a ring of
fire or two and deal with Cerberus, the dog-monster with all three serpentine heads thundering their challenges. But that was just part of the
special effects that were featured in the arrival rituals. How else were the
dead to know they were on the right track, nearing the end of their journey? We are familiar with separation rites in the course of mortal life.
We can only guess about the rites of greeting and incorporation when
the dead finally get to the other side. Granted: a ring of fire and a three-
headed dog-monster did not closely resemble the Chamber of Commerce's welcome wagon committee. But they did get one's attention. And
they did serve notice that the dead really were entering a significant realm,
not just another bump in the road. Perhaps—and this is only perhaps—
it was also a subtle way of "selling" Hades real estate to the new residents. If it was so difficult to get in, why, it must have been a hell of a
place! Chances are that many would have preferred to be safe among
their boring but harmless peers rather than trying to escape the hellish
flames and those three huge toothy snapping mouths. (Did dogs go to a
different underworld and have to face ill-tempered human-monsters with
an excess of screaming and biting heads?)

The perimeter of fire might also be interpreted as prophylactic. Those
shades approaching Hades probably included the worse sort of people
and the worst sort of dyings. Best to purify them before allowing them
to enter the fair city. Perhaps the right sort of person, like the Viking chief
of a later millennium, was sufficiently immolated at the send-off, but even
he might have been contaminated as he continued his passage. The idea
of dangerous contamination during passage is hardly uncommon. "Don't
touch those walls, Al-ah-din!"

The occasional ingenious punishment administered in Hades—
Tartaros sector—was reserved for those who had angered the gods. Probably the best known of these was King Sisyphus. He was condemned to
roll a boulder to the top of a hill, a feat that required him to exert every
ounce of his strength. Once perched on the hill, the boulder did what
many a boulder would—it rolled down again, all the way down. His punishment seems to have exceeded the crime: he had only tried to con his
way out of Hades.[6] More despicable was Tantalus, who offered the gods

a stew composed of his son. He was suspended from a tree, unable to slake his thirst in the nearby lake or appease his hunger with the fruit just beyond his reach. Condemned to perpetual thirst were the Danaides, sisters who had murdered their husbands—with hairpins.

Generally, though, being dead was considered punishment enough. If the perpetrator could not be punished sufficiently in his or her own life, then a curse upon succeeding generations was in order. An afterdeath designed specifically and exclusively for prolonged punishment would be a later innovation.

The journey of the dead did not always conclude in the drearier precincts of Hades. One might even find death something of a vacation.

GOING FIRST CLASS:
AN ISLAND GETAWAY

If a few did suffer enormously in Hades, a select few also enjoyed more of an extended island getaway. Welcome to the Isles of the Blest! These were places of endless delight, landscaped to perfection with the sweet-est-scented blossoms, the purest brooks, and the most succulent fruit, all warmed gently by the sun's beneficent glow. Unfortunately, travel agents would not have been helpful in making arrangements for those seeking these isles. They had to find their own way and overcome hazards of the journey (remember how difficult it was to gain entry even into the more dismal sector of Hades?). Furthermore, they had to be worthy of admission to the Isles of the Blest if they were not to be dumped in the sludge pits along with the greater heap of humanity. Of course, if they had the right stuff, they should have been able to find their way there.

The location of the island paradise was somewhat elusive. Plato decided it should be way up there—fly above the stars and keep going. This, however, was a latter-day philosopher trying to be logically consistent. The soul, liberated from the body, would be purer and stronger, so it should ascend to the realm of the gods. Only coarse and heavy stuff should sink into the ground. Greek mythology and religion had already been around for a long time, though, and adherents to the tradition did not take kindly to such revisions. Whatever you do, when you die, don't ask Plato for directions! Everybody knows that the elite afterlife must be reached through secret passages in the underworld. True, much of what's down there is dank, dark, and stinky. The truly deserving, though, should be able to win their way to the land of perpetual sunshine and delight.

The Greeks were not the only ones to believe that the treasures as well as the horrors at the end of the afterlife journey are to be found deep within the earth. There lie mysterious powers, and there lie the secrets of fertility and renewal. Water, so vital for life, also flows beneath the surface—

> Where Alph, the sacred river, ran
> . . .
> Down to a sunless sea

—in Coleridge's words, as he described the pleasure dome of Kubla Khan.[7] The Chinese seem always to have known that the eternal waters have their source below. Enticing in a number of ancient societies were the images of hidden cavern, underground river, and magical crossing to the land of the blessed.

Are we worthy of entry, though? The specific qualifications seem to have been a matter of opinion. Noble birth and personal courage were positives, yet having favorable connections might have been even more useful. A sponsoring deity or two could help; nor should one dismiss the fickle finger of fate. It also helped to be prepared for the journey, the better to slip past barriers and overcome challenges. Virtue was admired, but good and evil had not yet hardened into place. There was no Saint Peter or, for that matter, pearly gates, to control access through calculation of the sin-faith-repentance quotient.

However one prioritized the qualifications, there was agreement that only the most worthy should be admitted. Pindar, influential poet of the fifth century B.C., set the standards high: one must complete *three* praiseworthy lives to earn the privilege. Of course, one would have to agree with Pindar that we have multiple reincarnations; this was an engaging issue to discuss while the mutton was roasting and the wine cups refilled.

There were others who believed the Isles of the Blest were neither above the sky nor below the earth. Instead, they waited tantalizingly on the far side of the ocean. The necessity for the dead to complete a journey across a daunting body of water was still an important element, as were the hazards that one was likely to encounter. A good heart, intelligence, courage, and a lot of luck were required—as well as a ship well suited for the voyage. We remind ourselves that geographical knowledge and mapmaking had a long way to go. There could be practically any kind of land out there, with any kind of bizarre features and populace. Two millennia later, in the age of the great sailing ships, there were still many uncharted lands and, therefore, many possibilities for amazing discoveries. It also figured that so delectable a destination as an afterdeath resort island would require a long and adventuresome voyage. A hint to the wise: the paradise islands were usually located in the direction of the sun, associated with deity in so many religious belief systems.

Arrival signified more than abundance of delight. The souls who reached the fortunate islands were transformed into a higher, more radiant form of being. They had passed through life and through death. Now they were capable of experiencing existence at a level they could only have imagined while earthbound mortals.

We learn a little more about life in paradise from later sources. By the fourth century B.C. this joyous realm had pretty much broken free of the Homeric tradition and escaped from the depths to the heights. It was still regarded by many as an enchanted island, but a fresh image also came into view: the Elysian fields. In these meadows the fortunate ones danced, sang, and sported. There were competitive but friendly contests for those who were most athletically inclined. Tibullus (ca. 54–19 B.C.) provided further detail. He articulated the wave of nostalgia that was engulfing intellectuals and artists within the Roman Empire. Oh, those good old days! That Golden Age! How unlike the present era of ambition, cruelty, and degradation! Gods and mortals were much closer back then. And people really knew how to live and love. Gentle Venus led them to pleasures in the shady vales. Best of all, people could love freely and suffer no rebuke.

> Illustrations of the Golden Age often showed naked couples dancing, playing or reclining at ease in a meadow. Following that pattern, life in paradise meant leisure and loving in a natural setting. Men and women were naked. Generally paired, they spent their time relaxing in the grass, bathing and swimming, or simply strolling about. For Tibullus, the Golden Age was not just a reality of the distant past. It survived in the beyond in the Elysian fields, the land of the dead.[8]

Tibullus had a special place in his heart for young lovers, and so did the Elysian fields. He wrote:

Troops of young men meet in sport with gentle maidens, and Love never lets his warfare cease. *There are all on whom Death swooped because of love; on their hair are myrtle garlands for all to see.* [italics added][9]

This was more than a generous and sentimental provision on the part of Tibullus. I think he has given us here two themes that would become even more salient through history. First, there is the idea of an afterdeath that makes up for life's deprivations and disappointments. It is not fair that these young lovers did not have the opportunity for consummation during their short lives. Even more painful was their fate if Death swooped upon them *because of love*. This tender affection should be allowed to flourish and grow. The compassion of Venus (Aphrodite) makes it so in the Elysian fields.

More than two thousand years later, gospel songs fervently express the belief that joy and freedom will be experienced after years of stress and sorrow. The compensatory feature of an Elysian-type afterdeath is not necessarily restricted to young lovers. A merciful god might grant what was denied by oppression and cruel fate. The hope for a compensatory afterdeath has also taken other forms. One should be mentioned here because it is of such a different character from those already noted. An example sticks in my mind. Bear with me, if you will. As a teen and young man I supported myself, marginally, in the newspaper trade: reporter, later editor. (I had the prime qualities that publishers were looking for: energy and the willingness to work cheap. Hmmm. Not so much has changed after all.) A freelance photographer whom I knew but slightly popped into the office one day to waste my precious time while I was trying to meet the next deadline (when you are editor of a weekly community newspaper, there is almost never *not* a next deadline scowling impatiently at you). I said something journalistically brilliant, like "How ya doing?"

He responded with a psychotic performance that I would not see rivaled until my internship as a clinical psychology trainee. At first he simply told me he would have some great accident photographs for me tomorrow. How could he be so sure, I wondered out loud. Because he knew just where to go: his favorite traffic circle where vehicles are always smashing into one another. His eyes began to glow, and his rate of speech zoomed into overdrive. He *loved* accidents. But that was nothing, really; snapping accident photos was just a way of marking time until—

Until what? Until when? Until the earth gapes open and the flames arise and all the sinners perish, every one! He was now shouting, with rivulets of sweat streaming down his contorted face. The people he sees around him every day will be screaming in their death agonies and he—why, he will laugh! He will be there snapping his great photos as most of the living are slain and consigned to hell for eternal torment. I don't know if I had ever see a man look so pleased with himself. He confided that the world was overgrown with people who thought they were lording it over him—well, little did they know! Those miserable little sinners were doomed to a horrible death and a worse eternity while he, Mr. Nice-Guy-Chosen-by-GOD, would laugh and laugh.

I had not realized that some people could hardly wait for the end of the world. Condemning others to panic, agony, and horror followed by hellish torture would be retribution for the vile pleasures they had experienced and their lack of appreciation for the true belief and the true believers. No, I did not assume that the next photographer I met would also be a raving psychotic or that everybody who is *Longing for the End* exults in the prospect of humanicide.[10] But I did start to understand that the afterdeath can be seen as a way of making up for whatever life has left unfinished—whether ardent love, the fresh air of freedom, or the raging fires of vengeance.

The other theme introduced by Tibullus into the Elysian fields was quite specific to sexual love. His young lovers had died before consummation. Later we would be served up images of lovers who die *for* consummation. So strong are the yearnings, so profound the passion, that a mere romp in the shady glen would only trivialize their love. The act of dying replaces sexual intercourse. The moment of death is the orgasm of orgasms. Only the depth of eternity is sufficient to contain their pure and noble passion. This theme was celebrated conspicuously in nineteenth-century German literature and drama. We lesser mortals might settle for a companionable long-term relationship with refreshing amorous interludes. The great ones, though, are destined for *Liebestod,* preferably to Wagner's harmonic progressions—yearning always more important than fulfillment.[11]

An Orwellian *1984*-type logic underlies the replacement of sexual fulfillment with death. Sex is acceptable only when encompassed within Love. And Love, boiling with pent-up hormones, seeks so profound a release from its tensions that no simple discharge will suffice. Furthermore, one's basic identity has become centered around the yearning, the quest, the distance between desire and its fulfillment. The tension is unbearable but, oh, so delicious!

Love, then, seeks Death. Death is Love fulfilled, and Love, of course, is greater than Life. Or something like that. The amiably pliant realm of afterdeath experiences seems to have a place for whatever imaginings happen to seize our attention. Tibullus, though, was not endorsing a neurotic sexualized death complex; that would come later. He just felt that love should triumph over death even if we have to create a special realm. The doomed young lovers in *West Side Story*, like Romeo and Juliet before them, would have been very welcome.

JUST LIKE HOME, ONLY BETTER

Greek and Roman mythology have long influenced Western culture. This tradition, however, had no monopoly on either the journey or the destination of the dead. People far distant from the Greco-Roman orbit imagined afterdeath adventures and experiences that had much in common with those we have already considered. The more familiar conceptions we have already visited. I select the Native Australians, often called Aborigines, as the example here because Homer, Plato, and Tibullus knew nothing of their land and their lives.

Priests, temples, and sacrificial altars are not required by a religion that believes in a Great Spirit who provides for and protects people. He selected one of the people to be his teacher among them, and he, in turn, educated the elders so they could guide the children properly.[12] Children should develop their souls through enlightened education so that they can eventually become worthy companions to the Great Spirit. Be kind and generous to others. Live in moderation, never becoming a slave to excessive appetites of any kind. Remember that everybody is part of the Great Spirit and should be treated with respect. Basically: cultivate everything good. After completing their sacred initiation rituals the children are praised and informed that the Great Spirit will welcome them in the Land of Perfect Bliss when the time comes.

The time comes. The soul leaves the body. It seeks rest in its new home. Here begins the adventure—thoroughly cinematic. The ledge is narrow. Below is a dark and deep chasm. On the other side rises an enormous perpendicular wall. So smooth is its surface that no creature can find a climbing grip. Just to increase the peril, one also has to be on the lookout for a boulder that enjoys rolling down on those who dare this journey. Keep walking along the ledge. Don't look down. Beware of the mischievous boulder. (So good-natured is this society's temperament that even those who slip off the edge do not plummet to destruction; instead, they float on the dense darkness until rescued by a more established spirit.)

Nature is sympathetic to the weary pilgrim soul. Trees cast their shadows along the path for protection against the blazing sun. The flowers refresh their fragrance. Nevertheless, the soul is hesitant, afraid to take another step. But then the inner voice speaks up. Do not hesitate. We can do this! All will be well! We will meet Biggarroo, the wombat-snake and great physician. He will make you whole again in body, mind, and soul, prepared to enter the Land of Perfection. And so the soul continues on its journey.

Successful but exhausted and only half conscious, the soul reaches the border of the Perfect Land. There stand two huge crystals. Each has an enormous snake coiled around it. Both serpents offer the same welcoming message in their soft, crooning voices. Which of these is Biggarroo, the healer, and which is the evil serpent, Gonnear? The soul approaches one of the snakes and then, if lucky, has a spiritual awakening, detecting just in time the cruel, deceitful eyes of Gonnear. That was a close one! With more confidence now, the soul walks right into Biggarroo's open jaws and continues to walk deeper into its throat. Hmmm. Very nice in here. A carpet of grass, lovely flowers. Think I'll have myself a nap.

That did the trick! The soul awakens, not only refreshed, but feeling whole again. Walking deeper into Biggarroo, he discovers his mother's footprints on the path. She is safe among the spirits, and he will soon see her again. More eagerly now, he moves along the path. Look at all those people! Some were of his own tribe, but others have come from distant places. Yet—and this is curious—all speak the same language. Everybody is friendly with everybody else. The more intelligent or advanced souls are helping the others. It becomes apparent that the human race develops from stage to stage until perfection. All the loved ones then meet again and live within the Perfect Land. How wonderful!

And yet, there is more to come. The soul is given a magical eye on his forehead that enables him to see through the veil of time. All of history becomes visible, from the impenetrable darkness to the rumbling tremor of creation and the vision of a woman suspended between earth and space.

> As it took definite shape the robes unfolded and fell apart from her body in four portions, opening from the head to the feet like the unfolding of a primrose bud, revealing the bright yellow flowers. She stood disrobed, with her golden hair streaming from the crown of her head to her ankles. With both hands she cast her hair from about her, and immediately the strands took the form of beams streaming forth like the rays of the rising sun.[13]

Early acts of creation are portrayed. The goddess of light then draws her robes around her and retires into the darkness of everlasting night. The soul now learns from Biggarroo that all the human race is intended to be "like unto the Mother Goddess." The soul must still receive the elixir of youth and life. This requires a much longer sleep—a century—and the experience of new visions that take the soul further through time. The great and fantastic reptile monsters appear and vanish. Now come the birds . . . the insects . . . the animals and fishes.

Biggarroo now bids the soul to enter the Land of Perfection. Here all the creatures of the sky, water, and land sing and fly and leap according to their kind. None is enemy to another. Nobody hunts another. Creation lives in joy and harmony. *But not in the same way forever.* Even paradise is subject to change as part of the universal process. The flowers are still blooming, the birds still singing, when a mighty storm arises. So powerful is this cosmic event that it churns the ocean into a colossal wave that surges through the formidable wall protecting the Land of Perfection. Not good! Just when cataclysm seems inevitable, the Great Spirit is approached by the goddess of light and life (robed or naked, we are not told). She asks him to save the Land of Perfection, and he obliges. We can see it in the sky when we gaze at the Milky Way. Thank you, Goddess! Praise be to the Great Spirit! But still one might feel a sense of loss. The Land of Perfection was once here on earth (at least sort of). We could imagine taking that journey ourselves and arriving at a destination both sacred and familiar. Now it is so far away. Perhaps it is even more sacred, having been elevated by the Great Spirit himself. But is it still basically a perfected version of our life on earth? Is it still open to the pilgrim souls of our generation? And, to echo Woody Allen's fret, can somebody please tell us how to get there?

This Native Australian account has both distinctive features and characteristics that are typical of afterdeath stories in many cultures. First, the destination is an improved version of the familiar landscape and people. Just like home, only better. For Native Americans on the Great Plains, it was the return of the bison and substantial freedom from the white invaders before the nineteenth century. Despite all the intricacies in preparing the dead for their journey, the Egyptians also assumed an afterdeath modeled on their familiar way of life.

Second, getting to the destination is risky. The Aborigine version presents the hazards of falling and crushing as well as the unspecified but undoubtedly horrific consequences of being swallowed by the wrong snake. Ordeals by fire and drowning, popular in some other stories, are not featured here.

Third, decisions must be made. Whether to go on or turn back is an almost universal decision for the afterdeath pilgrim. There may also be geographical choice-points and, in this case, the issue of discovering whom one can really trust. The answer is also interesting for the Aborigine: one trusts that inner voice, the true soul of the people that will guide us in times of peril. This speaks well for the spiritual integration of the people: We have the wisdom. We know what we're about. Trust us. Trust yourself.

Fourth, strange things happen to mind or spirit. During the afterdeath journey the Aborigine experiences altered states of consciousness. There are episodes of both impaired and enhanced consciousness. New perceptions are granted of the external world and one's own being. One could take the position that all accounts of afterdeath journeys are based on altered states of consciousness. We will discuss this thesis with particular attention to near-death experiences as we go along.[14]

Fifth, spiritual development is required to enter the realm. The Hindu and Buddhist traditions focus more on the journey than the destination. Spiritual enlightenment is the path, and the further we proceed the less we have to ask about the destination. The Aborigine soul also has to transcend its previous limitations to qualify for the Land of Perfection.

Sixth, nature is perfected. The Aborigine Land of Perfection is not all about humans. We do not judge, control, or dispose of other species. We do not transcend or transform nature. We are children of the Great Spirit, one of the many forms in which Nature expresses herself. Visions of the afterdeath vary in their relationship to nature. The Elysian fields displayed nature in attractive aspect, though essentially for the enjoyment of young lovers. By contrast, nature has only a minor role to play in the Judeo-Christian afterlife dramas as well as a number of other religions. The Garden of Eden has its abundant creatures, but after the expulsion of Adam and Eve we hear little more about them, nor do they feature prominently in depictions of heaven. There has been desultory argument about whether animals have souls, but they are generally regarded as subordinates rather than soul brothers to humans. The thrust of salvational religions has been to separate humans from mere animals.

Finally, the afterdeath paradise is located not only within animate nature but also within the flow of the cosmic process. There are obvious similarities between the account given in Genesis and other myths of origin. The end-time scenarios differ, however. The Aborigine conception is naturalism on the grand scale. A cosmic storm will wash away what we know of creation. There are parallels here with Native American scenarios in which even the mountains will one day disappear and everything return to its primal state of nothingness. Christian tradition includes vivid depictions of annihilation by earthquake and inferno, but this catastrophe is punishment by an angry God. The promise of redemption and salvation also is controlled by divine judgment. The Aborigine afterdeath scenario is not framed as sin-punishment-redemption in either its first phase—journey of the individual soul—or the denouement, as the goddess turns off the lights.

I am reluctant to leave the Land of the Perfect. The luxuriant fantasies are warmed by a gentle and companionable outlook on life. Both female and male principles are well represented on the deity level. The Great Spirit is a mentor, not a jealous and vengeful despot. And there is no blood-thirsting savagery among the gods as encountered in some Eastern and African belief systems, though one does have to be careful about which snake to trust.

But there are two more features that stay in the mind. First is the idea of perfection itself, although this is not unique to the Native Australian conception. *The world does not have to be as it is.* Imagination and passion can transform the world into a place where the good endures and all sorrows heal. The spirit we feel inside us must somehow know of such a world. It is our challenge to discover or create it. The impulses that drive artistic creation, practical innovation and invention, scientific discovery, and religious quest find perhaps their most rewarding expression in the pursuit of the perfect.

Second is this little footnote on the otherwise enthralling afterdeath journey. Here we are in the Land of the Perfect. At the risk of immodesty, that probably means that we are perfect, too! One problem, though: it will not last. We will be evicted from the postlife Garden of Eden, though not for an act of transgression. It's just that everything given is taken back; everything solid dissolves; everything brimming with life becomes at one with the dark. *Extinction.* We will need to think about this prospect again. It shadows and often coexists with other views of the afterdeath. We are not ready to focus on extinction, though. There are still other afterdeath journeys to take.

SAILING THROUGH THE SKY:
FOR PHARAOHS ONLY?

Think Egypt and we think death. Think death and we think Egypt. What with mummies, tombs, and pyramids, Egyptian deathlore has proven its fascination in books, museums, films, and fashion trends. This word association has its justifications, but it perpetuates an unbalanced view of Egyptian culture. Life was the foremost concern of these hardy desert dwellers. Survival required communal efforts, individual stamina, and all the ingenuity their best minds could provide. And they needed even more than that. Somehow it all had to make sense: both life and death. There had to be a belief system to guide them through their recurrent encounters with drought, disease, and other hardships.

There was a time before an advanced society constructed pyramids and compiled royal treasures to tempt the tomb robbers. Before astronomers, engineers, and mathematicians developed powerful new tools for thought and action. Before the healing and visual arts were brought to an extraordinary level, and before leaders discovered how to manage sustained and complex projects that required the participation of a great many people. Life—and water—was more precious than any gem. The average life expectancy was about twenty years. Those who survived into their forties or beyond were valuable resources for their know-how.

Death was an insistent part of everyday experience. It could not be glossed over as it has often been in the United States and other Western nations of our time. The buoyant optimism inherent in "progress" could not take a foothold in the eternal sands where the sun ruled both the skies and the earth below, the Nile either bestowed or withheld its precious waters, and the living were all too soon transformed into the dead. The desires and accomplishments of mortals did not seem to make much impression on the controlling forces. This awareness was reaffirmed every time a gust of wind uncovered a shallow grave. A form much like their own would be exhibited to the living: a spontaneous sand mummy preserved by parched sands that inhibited bacterial activity and, therefore, decomposition. The dead did not seem any better off than the living, and the observers were essentially seeing themselves in the grave after being worn down by their hard lives.

And yet—look at these grim, dehydrated replicas of people who once drew breath. They might have a secret message for us. Touched mysteriously by the gods, they have lost the animating principle but have withstood time and change. Of course, there is an afterlife. Everybody in these parts knows that, even the traders and nomads from distant regions. Where? Probably it's way down there in the underworld, as most people say. Could be up in the sky, though, close to the resplendent sun. Then, again, perhaps the body, so nearly intact, is reanimated. By magic? By sympathetic gods? By evil spirits? One way or another, those still-fleshed bodies in the grave must have something to do with our fate after death.

It is reasonably clear that rebirth was one of the prime theories. The bodies were usually buried in a fetal position. They were also provided with beads, knives, and household goods. Somehow, somewhere, the next life would also require domestic activity. For these diligent people, it was probably hard to imagine that a life of ease and plentitude would ever be theirs.

About half a million years go by. The history of *really* ancient Egypt becomes one with the desert. The extraordinary civilization then arises, starting approximately seven thousand years ago. The first dynasties are created about two thousand years later, and early pyramids are erected.[15] The first Pyramid Texts are written about 2500 B.C., and these will still be influential when the Book of the Dead takes shape during the reign of the New Kingdom (ca. 1409–1075 B.C.). Another important set of documents, the Coffin Texts, will appear during the interim. Scholars tell us that "Book of Coming Forth by Day" is the more appropriate translation for what has come to be known as the Book of the Dead.[16] By whatever name, all these papyrus documents were guidebooks for the journey of the dead. We shouldn't leave life without them.

And we shouldn't rush to these guidebooks until we've taken a moment to understand the belief system that generated all those spells, prayers, and precautions. This system would eventually find a place for both the early personifications of multiple gods and magic spells and the later, more abstract conception of one god and one god only, often considered the major precursor to the Judeo-Christian tradition. The Egyptians tended to keep the older stories and beliefs while they added the new. It is not surprising that, thousands of years later, even scholars are often baffled in trying to figure out how all these ideas from various periods worked together. We will see something of this fascinating but somewhat jumbled collection of beliefs and practices as we focus on the journey and destination of the dead.

The "modern" Egypt of five thousand years ago already had an ancient history that included innumerable sunrises, Nile floodings, sproutings and witherings, births and deaths, and on and on with the cycle. These events were transformed into the dramatic legend of Osiris, Isis, and Set (the villain of the piece).

Osiris started out as a king. He was in luck: at that time nobody died, and envy, greed, hatred, and other character flaws were yet to be invented.[17] Osiris himself was a model of virtue among these virtuous people. A wise and loving monarch, he taught the people how to irrigate and raise crops as well as how to get along with the gods (which included his own parents, Geb [earth] and Nut [sky]). The sticky fig in the basket was Set, a wicked brother whose earthly domain was populated only by dunes, scorpions, and rocks. Jealous of Osiris? You bet! Diabolically clever, as wicked brothers usually are, Set first deceived, then murdered Osiris. From that time on Egypt was in big trouble. All the miseries came—drought, famine, theft, violence, and, need we be surprised, death. Bierlein sadly reports:

> Set's kingdom of sand grew until it nearly reached the banks of the Nile. The despair was so great that the people envied the dead.[18]

Isis, Osiris's loving and resourceful wife, succeeded not only in recovering but also in reanimating his body with a kiss. Not to underestimate Set, though. He killed Osiris again, this time slicing his body into fourteen pieces and scattering them in Hither, Thither, and, possibly, Yon. Isis, although vicariously broken up by this turn of events, gathered all the pieces and put them back together again. Peace and prosperity returned to Egypt—but not for long. Envy, greed, and violence now had a place within the hearts of the people. Strife and discord would now be part of the human condition. However, people would never be completely dissipated either. There would always be some goodness in all of us. Osiris himself received what might be regarded as either a promotion or a demotion: he was now and forever King of the Dead and the Great Judge.

And so we come to the new deal. People were now mortal but had the opportunity to become immortal after death. Osiris was at the controls, and this was how it worked:

1. The person consisted of body and spirits, just as everyday life is both practical and sacred at the same time.
2. The body died.
3. There remained the spirits. Every person had three of them— the *ba,* the *ka,* and the *akh.* The ba often stayed close to the mummified body. It liked to take the form of either an actual bird or a human-headed bird. The ba might have been seen perched loyally on the tomb, but it might also have attached itself to statues or other objects or even engaged in celestial travel.
4. The ka was the intimate companion of the person throughout life. One might think of the German doppelgänger,[19] but the ka did not have the more sinister characteristics sometimes attributed to that inner mirror of the outer self. The ka functioned as a life force that continued to protect the person after death, lingering in the vicinity of the grave or tomb. The ka also thanked anyone who left offerings by the tomb. As in many other societies with ancient roots, the dead counted upon the living to keep them going in one way or another.
5. The akh was a more elusive spirit that transfigured into a kind of shimmering ghost or glorified being when the body's own light was extinguished. If the person had lived the good life, there would be a sense of completion, of attainment. In a

sense, the akh was the artistic product of a life that had been lived as it should. Unlike the ba and the ka, the akh was a transformation that had to be achieved.

6. After death, the soul had to find its way through Osiris's realm to immortality. Its qualifications were evaluated rigorously by no fewer than forty-two examiners. These were not ordinary bored and sullen bureaucrats. Originally, they were local demons; later they were enlisted executioner-gods in the service of Osiris. The soul passed this test if the person had committed fewer than half of the sins, a generous criterion, it would seem. The soul was supposed to respond to its interrogation with statements such as these:

> I have not stolen.
> I have not uttered evil words.
> I have not judged too quickly.
> I have not killed man or woman.
> I have not fouled water.

7. Yes, there was a catch. The sin/virtue checklist was just a preliminary. What the soul had become had to be evaluated before final judgment was rendered. Much later in history, the soul of the dying Christian would be the prize of a struggle between angels and demons. Stephen Vincent Benét's "The Devil and Daniel Webster" includes a courtroom scene with a jury of the rascally dead.[20] The ancient Egyptians also had their hopeful demons at the ready and a counsel assigned to defend the dead. But in addition they had a far more efficient and objective system for determining merit. This

final part of the ordeal comprised the weighing of the deceased's heart—regarded as the seat of intelligence and knowledge—against the feather of *maat*, the personification of truth, order, and justice. If the pans of the scale balanced, the dead person would come before Osiris and pass into eternal life in what was visualized as a bigger and better Egypt. If the heart proved heavier, it would be fed to a monster named "the Devourer," and the spirit cast into the darkness.[21]

Lighter is better than heavier because virtuous and warmhearted souls are not burdened with misdeeds and guilt.

This has been but a sketchy description of the complex process that begins at death. We would not want to overlook the unnerving silence, the terrifying darkness, the fear of being seized by demons, and the anxiety of facing such formidable and decisive tests. Were the underworld journey not so dangerous there would not have been the need for the 227 spells found in the papyrus in the pyramid of Wenis and the many other spells that have turned up in other documents. One did not want to be at a loss for words when accosted by horrifying creatures. What made this ordeal all the more difficult is that the same creature could be either deadly enemy or friendly guide, depending on how well one was prepared. A last-minute opportunity to cram for the final exams was offered in the pictorial guide provided on tomb walls for those fortunate enough to have the very best in mortuary arrangements. The snake-demon was an important example of the netherworld inhabitants one was likely to encounter. He represented both the fertile and the life-giving aspects of earth, but also the devouring monster. One would study diligently to learn the spell that repelled the *rrk*-snake (unlike most other serpents, a possessor of nimble feet) and the *Hki*-snake (unfooted but almost as dangerous).

If all went well, the ba and ka achieved reunion in a mystical conjunction with the body. Was the body itself reanimated? Did the mummy stiffly arise, peel off its wrappings, and ask for dinner? This has happened often enough in the popular imagination. It might also have been the expectation or hope of predynastic Egyptians that mummies would walk again. At the pinnacle of ancient Egyptian civilization, however, the body was regarded in a more complex way, whether living or dead. The person was always more than the body. A new form of spiritual alignment would occur after death, and the person of good character would now exist on a higher astral plane.

The Egyptians knew as well as if not better than anybody that life was life and death, death. The underlying reality, though, was a continuity between life and death, a sort of cosmic circle dance in which each invariably morphs into the other. Individuals would die; the fertile earth would replenish—just as decreed.

Are there contradictions here? So it would seem. Bodies should return to earth to participate in the eternal birth-rebirth process. But bodies should also be protected to serve as home base in the ba-ka reunion. Furthermore, the destination is ambiguous if we look at the entire range of

Figure 29 Egyptian funeral boat with shrine.

options conceived by the people of Egypt over so long a span of time. Providing the dead with useful objects and depicting people in everyday situations on tomb murals suggest an afterdeath rather similar to the present life. This would be still another society's version of "just like home, even better." The ideas of reanimation in the flesh and reincarnation have also appeared in Egyptian lore from time to time. These beliefs were common among their neighbors as well. We can also find reference to a continued afterdeath existence in various regions of the underworld. These habitations cover the spectrum from sheer misery to a rather pleasant residency with at least faint resemblance to the Isles of the Blest.

Another variant was described in one of the later guides to a satisfying afterdeath, the Book of Traversing Eternity, circa A.D. 100. The dead do not have to remain underground, nor do they have to travel to some distant and unfamiliar region. Instead, they can return to the realm of the living. They will be welcome to stay as long as they like at sacred places and participate in rites and festivals. But if they also yearn to travel, that, too, is possible.

> The deceased knew that they are secure in an eternal community of celebrants, their existence in the afterlife bound to sacred places and times. They were also supposed to be able to move about freely in the hereafter and to have access to Osiris. . . . the realm of the dead was brought into this life, and this other-worldly Egypt became the "temple of the world" as it came to be viewed in late classical antiquity.[22]

We cannot help but notice that significant differences emerged within the general Egyptian belief system. Scholars have discussed the specific interplay between what was happening in Egyptian life at the time and how mortuary practices and afterdeath beliefs were shaped.[23] Eternity seems to be conditioned by current events.

More complicated yet: a bleak fatalistic outlook was also known among Egyptians as well as their neighbors in the parched and shifting sands that seemed to mock the human desire for permanence. What they had observed with their own eyes was the inexorable transformation of living to dead. As a people, they had inhabited the same area for so very long that the sands of time seemed to be all conquering. This fatalistic attitude endured to become a major—perhaps *the* major—theme in the memorable poetry and storytelling created in the Middle East around the tenth century and thereafter.

I wouldn't presume to sort all of this out. It is clear, however, that several visions of the afterdeath can coexist within the same cultural frame. The journey of the dead, with its associated mortuary practices, is described with a lot more confidence than the destination, and we leave it at that.

But not quite. There is also that glorious vision of the perfected soul sailing across the sky to be with God. This exalted afterdeath journey was at first reserved for the elite. Only pharaohs and their consorts need apply. The sky had become an ocean, the ocean a sky, and the godlike pharaohs soared in splendor to their celestial destiny. The Hollywood celebrities who prove they are stars by stepping into wet cement in front of a movie house should pause for a moment and scan the skies. They just might see the pharaohs who have become real stars.

Royalty had its privileges after death as well as during life. But Egyptian civilization would nurture powerful new ideas: that every soul could seek perfection through a life that is pursued with intelligence, goodwill to others, and a sense of one's place in the cosmos. This would happen in a universe ruled by one god, who, despite taking on so many aspects and personifications, was still one god. Chaos was as real as order, and disaster a possibility, but everyone at least had a chance to sail across the sky with their perfected and certified souls. If we have any doubts about this, just ask the Aborigine's Great Spirit or his mentoring and healing snake.

"LIBERATION THROUGH UNDERSTANDING": THE TIBETAN PASSAGE

The Tibetan Book of the Dead is often considered the Buddhist equivalent of the Egyptian Book of the Dead. W. Y. Evans-Wentz had this in mind when he came up the now standard English title for a document believed to have been written in the eighth century.[24] It is not nearly as ancient as the Egyptian Pyramid Texts and came to prominence only in the fourteenth century, when it was rediscovered. Like the Egyptian writings, the Tibetan is better served with a different title. Asif Agha explains:

> The Tibetan title, *Bardo Thodol,* does not refer to death as such. *Thodol* means "liberation through understanding." *Bardo* means a "between state," an interval or transition between two mental states, whether experienced in life or death. Hence the work's literal title, *Liberation Through Understanding the Between,* alludes to bardo states that may be experienced at any point over the cycle of life, death and rebirth, yet the work overtly describes only the bardo states experienced during death, offering explicit instruction on how to navigate them.[25]

The journey does not begin with death. We are always on our way. We are always on our way not only from one situation to another but also from one self to the next. Permanence and place are misleading concepts if we think life is all about finding our little niche and settling comfortably into it. Similarly, the purpose of life is not to build a bigger house, career, or power base and compile the material trappings of success. Supposing that life and death are separated by a razor's edge is also an illusion. Life melds gradually into death. And death itself is part of the recurring cycle of being and becoming.[26]

Tibetan Buddhism identifies several transitional states, or bardos. Our present life on earth is a bardo of its own. It is part of the larger set of bardos: life; dying and death; after death; and rebirth. Within the bardo of life we have episodes in which our consciousness slips away from its socialized restraints. These are the bardos of everyday life. While falling asleep and again while waking up, our minds are often in a curious place (known to sleep researchers as hypnogogic states). Our thoughts seem to be touching both external reality and inner themes and events without coming down decisively on either side. The dreaming state is another vacation from dealing directly with the external world in our usual rational and problem-solving mode. Other in-between mental states can also be regarded as examples of this bardo (e.g., feeling just a wee bit tipsy or dislodged from our usual focused thought by hunger, sensory deprivation, overstimulation, and so on). There is also a bardo state that is more elevated than ordinary consciousness. Meditation takes us to a zone intermediate between everyday routinized semi-awareness and true enlightenment. We feel as though we are no longer so bound by material constraints but have not yet attained the perfection of spiritual enlightenment.

In life, then, we are often betwixt and between. Same for death. The process of transition moves through living, dying, and what we might call *deathing*. The physical side of life is first to dissolve. The soul loses awareness of the outer world but now experiences a series of internal visions. (This phenomenon of heightened interiority with the removal of external stimulation is precisely what researchers would much later discover in their studies of sensory deprivation.) The person now detaches from earthly concerns and draws the last breath. At this point a physician would be justified in pronouncing death.

The deathing process nevertheless continues. His Holiness, Tenzin Gyatso, the fourteenth Dalai Lama, describes the first stage that follows the death of the body.[27] One experiences not a plunge into darkness but rather the vision of "white moonlight." This is a poetic way of describing what others have characterized as a flooding of vivid light that seems to be coming from everywhere. Other visions and hallucinations then appear until one has moved as far along the passage as his or her level of spiritual development makes possible. Those who have cultivated their souls with dedication throughout their lives are the ones most likely to experience the clear light of death. Through death they are now approaching enlightenment. Lesser souls cannot face this trial by light and will therefore have to go again through the scrimmage of physical desire and delusion at a lower level of existence.[28]

There is no King of the Dead or New Testament God to pass judgment. Instead, each of us, in effect, passes judgment on himself or herself. There is, though, a parallel to heaven and hell. The Bardo Thodol describes both comforting and frightening visions that present themselves to the deathing soul.[29] The postmortem experience begins on a promising note as wise and loving buddhas present themselves during the first seven days.

Only some souls can fully respond; many others are not ready to set aside their shallow and petty ways. These lesser souls will experience a week's worth of terrifying deities.

A taste, then, of what Western religions are apt to categorize as heaven and hell? Yes, but the interpretation has a subtlety of its own. The Bardo Thodol tells us just where these beatific and horrifying visions are coming from: our own minds. We generate our own heavens and hells through the way we have lived our lives, and these come to the fore as we move through the deathing process. The idea that we make our own heaven and hell has not escaped Western minds either. Here, though, this insight is expressed in the sacred writings of Tibetan Buddhism. Those terrifying deities are simply the distortions that weak and anxious souls have made of the beatific buddhas. Again, the courage and discipline developed over the lifetime bardo come into play during the deathing process: we should learn to examine and learn from our experiences rather than fill our minds with terror and other illusions.

There is a possibility of liberation even at this late stage. We can dispel the terror and move toward enlightenment if and only if we recognize that it is our own demons that pursue us. What of those souls who are still in self-imposed torment after encounters with the demonized buddha figures? Now they are really in for it. Agha tells us:

> A mind which has failed to free itself by this point enters the Sidpa Bardo, the third, most desperate stage. Here the mind faces a host of hallucinations, including visions of pursuit by demons and furies, of being devoured, hacked to pieces.[30]

Yet, again, there is still the possibility of liberation. The Tibetan Buddhist universe is not dominated by themes of vengeance and damnation. Life and death are educational experiences. Like the Aborigines and the dynastic Egyptians, we all have the opportunity to perfect our souls, but this is not accomplished quickly or without the most dedicated effort. Therefore, one is not condemned to spend eternity in the horror show known as Sidpa Bardo. After forty-nine weeks, if not before, most souls have experienced as much misery as they can use and are reborn as animals or humans. The slowest of the slow learners will find themselves in another holding camp until such time as other arrangements are made. A bad afterdeath can be bad indeed. However, the worst of the torment does phase away—as is the case with all bardo states—and one is given another chance (and another and another) to approach enlightenment. And there is a significant bonus as well: what the soul has learned through its problematic deathing can be applied during its next incarnation.

For Tibetan Buddhists the journey of the dead is one leg of the longer journey through life and rebirth. "What happens after death?" can be answered with "Another life" in most instances. A season in hell and perhaps a hint of enlightenment alternate with reincarnations. As the soul becomes wiser, it understands there is no transfer of material assets or social distinctions from one incarnation to the next. The soul is on its own and can hope only to cultivate its own resources, detaching from the illusion of a material and stable world.

BUDDHISTS, CHRISTIANS, MUSLIMS, AND ANTHROPOLOGISTS

Everything passes away with time . . . everything. Creation cannot exist without destruction, sound without silence, or life without death. To know how to live, therefore, is to know how to die—a message similar to that delivered by Jeremy Taylor and the *Ars moriendi* movement. Buddhist and Christian thinkers are agreed that one prepares for death through the devotions and practices of a lifetime. One should also see through the illusions (Buddhism) and vanities (Christianity) that distract us from the essentials.

The idea of life as a journey in quest of enlightenment is also central to Islam. Death is not a taboo topic as it has been in some other societies; one should acknowledge and reflect on mortality on appropriate occasions throughout life. The youthful soul is out for pleasure and an easy mark for temptation. With maturity comes awareness of one's failings. It is time to cleave to the path of righteousness. This intention is not easily fulfilled, however. One must call upon God to help in the struggle (jihad) against one's own lower impulses. The fully realized person will go beyond even this attainment. Atoning for sins and coming into harmony with God create an ineffable feeling of peacefulness. Some Muslims believe this state of being can be attained only in the Gardens of Delight after death, but mystics hold that it can be experienced during life's journey by the purest meditation.

Buddhists, Christians, and Muslims all share the basic theme of moving from physical engrossment to spiritual enlightenment throughout a life's journey. One of the differences has already been mentioned: the Buddhist soul is not under the gun of divine judgment and punishment. What becomes of the soul in the afterdeath is the natural consequence of the biography it has written for itself. The Muslim like the Christian (and the dynastic Egyptian) does face postmortem inquiry and judgment. The angels Munkar and Nakir visit the grave and evaluate the soul's strength of belief in Allah. Final judgment is withheld until

> a blast is heard which seizes the remaining souls on earth, and then a second blast is heard which causes all of the souls to be resurrected. At this point, all of humanity is raised up and assembled on a plain. . . . each soul is judged according to its beliefs and actions.[31]

The prophet Muhammad gives each person a book. If it is placed in the right hand, the person knows he or she has passed the Judgment and is in the grace of Allah. Those who receive the book in their left hand are condemned to hell—but some are saved when prophets intercede for them.

> Once the Judgment is over, humanity proceeds to a bridge known as the *Sirat,* and it crosses over to the Hellfire. The ones saved cross it safely to the other side and are greeted by their respective prophets. . . . Those who are condemned are thrust into Hell from the *Sirat.* There are those who will spend only some time in Hellfire as an act of purification. However, according to the Quran, evildoers who did not repent will be condemned forever.[32]

Metaphorically, Islam is the ship that takes one safely to the other side. Charon, the Viking chief, and the gospel choir that sings of crossing over the river might all nod in assent.

In Christianity and Islam, there is another difference from Tibetan Buddhism that we would not want to ignore. Mainstream Christians and Muslims are going someplace (literal or symbolic). The journey ends in arrival. Goal! Touchdown! Home run! After the long and difficult passage, one has crossed the threshold between the temporal and the eternal. Let the festivities (or torments) begin! Again, we speak here of mainstream belief; many adherents of these faiths have their own interpretations of the end state of existence.

Particularly worth our attention here is the assumption that the virtuous dead will *be* there, in whatever there is there at the end. At the end
of the journey there is an abode. A droll testimony to this assumption
comes from the usually solemn man of letters Maurice Maeterlinck:

> If you were not dead, what would you do during eternity? Where would
> you choose to be? Would you look forward to something else? You would
> not be happy; and if you no longer looked forward to anything, would you
> still go on living? What would you wish for? No one, hitherto, has been
> able to give a satisfactory or even a reasonable reply to these questions.[33]

Maeterlinck speaks for many when he expresses puzzlement about
what a person would actually do for ever and ever. (In my own studies
I've found that many people are just as puzzled about what they would
do if they never died in the first place, but that's a different story.)[34] The
point is that several influential world religions provide a destination at
the end of the journey, a "place" (for want of a better word) where one
can praise, learn, love, sport, suffer, or just try to find something to do.

There are replies to Maeterlinck's question, though, and Buddhism
has the answer that is most relevant here. There is no destination, and
we do nothing. Activity, anticipation, and desire belong to a previous
phase of existence. Destination is one of the illusions—and perhaps
journey as well. After everything—including the dyings and the re-
birthings—comes nothing. This is the ultimate liberation: liberation
through understanding.

Nirvana is—well, what precisely is it? Forget precision. Nirvana is not
a place or destination. Not anything upon which we can impose the usual
structure of language and imagery. It is what there is when there is nothing else: no passion, conflict, hope, fear, or regret. This is the state of
being that is beyond states of being. Even to describe it as "nothing" is
to perpetuate an error. Nirvana is beyond our categories, beyond our
ways of thinking. Physicists today are still pondering the meaning of
"nothing" and have been supplying their own interpretations to fill the
void.[35] As I understand it, the present consensus is that nothing is something because everything depends on nothing. This resonates with Buddhist thinking, if not with the way most of us have been taught to think.
The Tibetan Buddhist conception, then, is not for those of us who require a permanent address after we've checked out from our postal zip

code. We can snap a variety of theory modules into our brain-drives, but Buddhism asks us to think differently and, therefore, become different (though the same) persons.

Enter now the anthropologist for a brief but useful visit. The *rites of passage* have become perhaps the signature concept for the whole field since introduced by Arnold van Gennep in 1909.[36] Anthropologists tend to be a little grumpy about this concept because there is a lot more to their field. Nevertheless, with apologies to all anthropologists everywhere, it is still the guiding idea that we find most relevant here.

The theoretical model begins on terra firma. There are zones in which a group of people feel at home. There are other zones which other people cherish as their own. In between these established or claimed zones there is a neutral or ambiguous spatial corridor through which one might pass. Peril increases when we exit from our turf and, again, when we approach the border of a zone to which others might lay claim. Exit is stressful for both the traveler and those who remain behind: rituals of separation are therefore important. Entry into other zones is also stressful: one might be rejected, harmed, even destroyed. Rituals are valuable, then, in gaining access to other areas. This often has included paying as we go. Sometimes I still catch myself pocketing a handful of quarters before going for a drive—a habit developed over years of voyaging on the Massachusetts Turnpike. This is marginally less demanding, though, than the sacrificial rituals that travelers (even proud armies) felt they had to perform when crossing space under the control of a foreign deity. If the destination is another home zone, it is also prudent to perform rites of incorporation. "Welcome. You are now with us and perhaps even of us. This is what we do here, and that is what we don't do. Enjoy—but watch your step!"

Especially dangerous is the transition space between the exit and the entry zones. These often present physical hazards (e.g., deserts and marshes), but also the threat of hostile human or spirit forces. The corridor of passage is not firmly governed by the communal rules protected by the local gods. "Proceed at your own risk" is the warning we should take seriously every time we set out from home base.

A set of terms introduced by van Gennep is helpful:

> I propose to call the rites of separation from a previous world, *preliminal rites*, those executed during the transitional stage, *liminal* (or *threshold*)

rites, and the ceremonies of incorporation into the new world *postliminal rites.*[37]

Van Gennep is speaking of passage both through physical territory and from one social status to another. But there is more, and it is this "more" that has given his approach such heuristic value. The passages all occur within the sphere of the sacred and therefore require magico-religious rituals if travelers are to negotiate the dangers and reach their destination. The journey might require arduous effort across a wilderness or the shorter but perhaps even more intense passage from the parental tent to the tent of one's new husband and relatives.

And, yes, the journey in question might be that from life to death. This connection holds true even when the event does not seem to have direct connection with death. Victor Turner, a distinguished anthropologist who has advanced van Gennep's work, reports many examples of initiation rites in which

> the initiand may be buried, forced to lie motionless in the posture and direction of customary burial, may be stained black, or may be forced to live for a while in the company of masked and monstrous mummers representing . . . the dead.[38]

Fertility rituals often have a touch of death—or even a touch of the dead who offer their potency.[39] Christian pilgrimage was inspired in part by the faith displayed by the early martyrs. These sacrifices were symbolically reenacted by the pilgrims, who had exited from their own lives to participate mystically in the deaths of the hallowed saints.[40] After returning from their hardships, the pilgrims were endowed with an enhanced power of their own to bless others, both the living and the dead.

The journeys of the dead that have been described in this chapter (and those I have not had space to include) can all be interpreted within van Gennep's rites of passage model. The Tibetan Buddhist journey, though, suggests that we might want to bring out a dimension of van Gennep's approach that perhaps does not receive the attention it deserves.

Anthropologists observe and learn from individuals as well as groups, but their usual level of description is the communal, what people do together and by what rules and beliefs. Like experts in other fields, anthropologists tend to favor particular levels of discourse and types of explanation. At a seafood market a particular fish might become dazed and confused from listening to appraisals from an angler, an economist, a game and wildlife manager, an artist, a customer, and, perhaps, another fish. This is by way of suggesting that instead of interpreting the Buddhist conception from the outside, we might listen again to what it has been saying itself all these many years.

Life itself is a journey. A journey within a journey. If we have a "home," it is on the road, on the wayfaring. During this brief life and long journey we stray off the public path repeatedly in bardo states of experience. Observe our own mental operations and see how often we drift from our moorings and are betwixt and between. How we float and flit among possibilities. How we so often exit from our duties in the mundane world to enter other zones, past, future, or indeterminate. How we create our own angels and demons, heavens and hells. Yes, we draw upon available images, but where did those images come from in the first place?

Tibetan Buddhist thought is on to something. External forms such as territorial borders and communal rituals do influence us greatly. These rules and practices, though, had to come from someplace. Perhaps we do not have to look any further than the human mind or spirit. No matter how far we travel, no matter what rituals we perform, no matter what exaltations or terrors we experience along the way, no matter what companions—our journey is enacted within our own *terra spiritus*. There may be precious moments of "harmonic convergence" with a "soul mate" or the *communitas*, but we each have our own path through the imagined cosmos.

What, then, of rites of passage? These naive, ingenious, comforting, and disturbing sequences represent our attempt to function together as a people at points of danger and potential. Once in place they can provide structure and direction. But rites of passage can also be regarded as attempts to externalize and stabilize those free flights of the soul-bird within our unreformed minds. They are a way of persuading ourselves that there really are destinations and reliable rules of the road. Perhaps I am not the only traveler who has not found the available rites of passage to be that persuasive but who nevertheless keeps a pocketful of quarters for Charon and tries to remember what to say to the snake-monster.

TEMPORARY AND VIRTUAL DEATHS

The journey of the dead takes place in our minds and secondarily finds expression in the public sphere. This is the proposition I am taking a little further as this chapter comes to a close. I will open the doors to two corridors that explore different routes.

Near-Death Experiences

Paranormal death experiences is the term Raymond A. Moody now prefers. Too late! His first designation, *near-death experience* (NDE), caught on immediately, and the public is not about to let go. Moody, a psychiatrist and philosopher, listened to many reports and summarized them for us:

> The most common feelings reported in the first few minutes following death are a desperate desire to get back into the body and an intense regret over one's demise. However, once the dying person reaches a certain depth in his experience, he does not want to come back, and he may even resist the return to the body. This is especially the case for those who have gotten so far as to encounter the being of light. . . . As one man put it most emphatically, "I never wanted to leave the presence of this being."[41]

A later, research-based summary by Bruce Greyson identified the most common components.[42] According to his studies, an NDE report is likely to include any or all of the following personal responses:

- I felt as though I were dead.
- I felt at peace; a pleasant experience; no suffering.
- I was separated from my body; I entered a dark region.
- I heard a voice . . . I encountered a kind of presence.
- I could see this spiritual being . . . I spoke with the spirit.
- I reviewed my whole life.
- I saw lights ahead of me . . . lights all around me.
- I actually entered into the light.
- I saw the most beautiful colors.

Greyson does not include three of the most powerful facets of the NDE in this list, but these are mentioned repeatedly by people for whom NDEs have been a turning point in their lives:

- After their NDE, many have gained a renewed appreciation for life and no longer fear death.[43]
- While having their out-of-the-body experience, some could see and hear the people around them (a phenomenon later studied most closely by Michael Sabom and his colleagues.)[44]
- The spirit figure or being of light instructs some people to return to life, saying, for example, "It is not your time yet" or "Your family needs you very much."

Strangely familiar, is it not? (Or familiarly strange.) Sounds much like a journey of the dead scenario, especially as described in Tibetan Buddhism. The instruction to return to life could be interpreted as an "aborted death," if I can use this term. The soul is not ready to be detached from its present bardo state but now has some understanding of what lies beyond. We note also that these components resemble a series of beatific visions. These are not the demonic apparitions that can scare the dead to death. Be assured, though: "bad trips" have also been reported as more people have come forth with their experiences. Positive reports continue to predominate, but nightmare visions also continue to come to light. These have more than a little in common with bad drug trips.

The people who shared their experiences with Moody were not Buddhists (at least, not knowingly so), nor were those involved in most of the subsequent reports that have come to the attention of researchers and scholars. Historians and theologians have enriched the discussion with examples of NDEs from a variety of times and places. Carol Zaleski's *Otherworld Journeys* is one of the most useful of these contributions. She readily establishes the existence of NDE-like reports long before Moody started to collect contemporary cases. She notes at least two similarities: (1) Both the visionaries of the past and the people of today have usually been hesitant to speak of their experiences. To talk about such an exalting experience would be to trivialize it—and how could one expect others to understand? (2) The experiencing-reporting self ascends. For a medieval visionary this might be rising aloft in the company of two angels; for a contemporary person it might be floating above one's own body that has been crushed in a motor vehicle accident or laid open in the operating room. Zaleski reminds us that the soul is *supposed* to rise toward heaven at death.

What, if anything, can be learned from the NDE as an otherworldly journey? Zaleski suggests that these reports are giving us a wake-up call. We have lost the edge of both life and death in our routinizing society; that, at least, is the message I take from her. These revelations come to us one at a time. They get our hearts pumping again, get us to think and feel beyond the narrow confines of everyday life. Unfortunately, perhaps, personal revelations do not necessarily reshape society.

> Those individuals whose understanding has been shaped by an over-whelming visionary experience seem to be isolated from the rest of us who are trying to make sense of things without the aid of direct revelation. . . . [They] still face the problem of finding a community and a context in which to search again for and apply the insights they have received.[45]

There have been numerous attempts to explain NDEs or explain them away. These include, for example, a hallucinatory reenactment of the birth experience ("a light at the end of the tunnel"); changes in brain chemistry during crisis; a temporal lobe reception of spirit messages; G-LOCK, a phenomenon associated with acceleration stress in centrifugal chambers and some aviational situations; and a compensatory and healing interior response when there is nothing a person can do to escape the perceived death threat in external time and space.[46] Interesting theories all, but it is the experience itself that continues to compel attention from most people.

Do NDEs prove survival of death? This is the bigger question, though it is certainly related to speculations about the cause and nature of the phenomenon. The short answer: no. Reports of paranormal or near-death experiences do not pass muster as evidence for survival of death. The long answer is rather too long to unwind here.[47] This conclusion is based on considerations such as the many reports of NDEs by people who were not actually in life-threatening situations and the fact that there has always been an observing self, a split consciousness between the "I" and the "me." "I saw myself dead" gives us a dead "myself" but a lively and perceptive "I." Furthermore, medical case analyses indicate that people who were actually closest to death have been least likely to report a visionary experience. There is also no evidence, and it is difficult to imagine how there could be evidence, linking this experience of "temporary death" with the no-return version.

A Threshold Vision

There might be survival of death, and the experience might be similar to the visionary reports, but the reports themselves just do not suffice as evidence. However, I see no logical or empirical objection to considering another possibility: a *threshold vision*. Here the Buddhist, the vision experiencer, the anthropologist, and the psychologist can stand together at the edge of the known and contemplate what is perhaps the unknowable.

Rites of passage obviously do occur in territorial space. Anthropologists and other observers have also made it clear that sacred and symbolic passages have been devised by societies at all levels of development. Often these passages are from one known (e.g., juvenile) to another known (e.g., adult) status. Even more fascinating are the passages that proceed from the known to the unknown—which is generally furnished with a facade of stories and imagery that take on their own kind of reality. It is not surprising that we construct the passage to the unknown from the materials we have gathered and fabricated from what we do know. Every adult has been a child, for example, so it is not difficult to construct a ritual pathway between these two points. We have to exercise our intuition and invention a lot more strenuously, though, if we are to establish a path from life through death.

How and how well can we envision this phase of the journey, the place of mists and phantoms where the next step may fall away from terra firma, dispatching us where and as who?

And so the threshold visions come. There are enough similarities among visionary reports from many cultures to suggest that they are not entirely concocted of specific cultural elements (at the same time, local ecology and belief systems do contribute to the picture). All societies seem to come up with stories about how the world began and how in the world death barged in. It is an acceptable working assumption that there is also a universal ability to enter into a visionary mode, especially when we are on the edge or threshold of a transfiguring event.

The journey of the dead (I'll take the Buddhist version) and what has come to be known as the near-death experience both seem to be threshold visions. They take us to the opening of the cavern, the first few steps into the tunnel, toward the liberation of the sky. We are on the threshold of the transfiguration. But only the threshold. Some enter deeper than others, and some return with elaborations and improvements on the experiential flash that creative memory concocts on the way back. The vision itself, though, encompasses that liminal zone between one world and the other. We are here and there but mostly in the nowhere in between. We might return with a new perspective on life, but, though we have been at death's door, it is the threshold not the chamber that we have experienced.

That, anyhow, is my story after visiting a few thresholds myself and learning from the experiences of others.

Pearly.Gates.com

I don't know if this is a registered Web site name—if not, you are welcome to appropriate it if you'd like. We have very briefly explored the interior realm of visions. Now, again briefly, we log on to that prolific designer and distributor of digitized visions, the Internet and its kith and kin. With a few taps on the keyboard and clicks of the mouse we can access a cornucopia of death-related sites. If that's not enough, we can pop in a CD-ROM and play a variety of murderous games—die, alien invaders, die! What interests us here, though, is the general conception of a vivid and diverse world that flourishes magnificently despite the fact that it does not exist. Well, not exist in the way that, say, your left shoe exists. You can heft, sniff, and, if the impulse strikes, bite your left shoe. (We have had several furred friends who performed this service for us.) Although seemingly insignificant in the Larger Scheme of Things, your left shoe has a proper existence, occupying its ordained place in the consensual time-space continuum. The Internet cannot say the same for itself. And yet we cannot say it doesn't have its own form of reality. So— what might this have to do with death?

Margaret Wertheim provides some clues in *The Pearly Gates of Cyberspace*. She reminds us that the medieval mind subdivided the universe into terrestrial and celestial space. This accorded with their dualistic view of practically everything. Body and soul each required its own domain. Once set apart, though, it was difficult to understand the connection. The mind-body problem vexed philosophers (who had to be careful to remain within the limits set by theology). And if they were tying themselves into knots trying to unravel the mind-body problem they had created for themselves, how could they reconcile the death of the body with the life of the soul? Oh, it could be done in many ways—but not done very well. The situation became more fraught as cosmology became more scientific and sophisticated. A separate (but connected) realm of spirit started to lose its turf.

Wertheim notes that the angels were demoted as the first step in a process that would culminate in the modern idea of *aliens:*

> What are ET and his ilk, after all, if not incarnated angels—beings from the stars made manifest in flesh? . . . The quintessential angel-aliens are the glowing humanoids of Steven Spielberg's *Close Encounters of the Third Kind,* beings who not only emanate heavenly light but communicate via music, a technological "harmony of the spheres."[48]

Bad as well as good alien-angels now had to take up residence with mortals. Space was being reshaped by science, and the new configuration was less accommodating to heavens and hells. This transformation not only threatened Christian beliefs but also put the kibosh on even more ancient traditions. Pharaohs would no longer sail to the sun, nor Viking chiefs in their flaming longboats. Gods of many cultures were becoming blurred and less tangible for their lack of a readily comprehensible domicile. If gods were in trouble, what about the souls of humble mortal beings? Where would they go after death? Some people would develop a more subtle conception that did not require the assurance of a celestial address. Others have held their grip on the promise that "someday you and I will take our love together to the sky" (from a song that had to be performed at every wedding for several generations). Fast-forward to cyberspace. Here is a parallel universe that borrows what it chooses from the realms of both flesh and spirit. Here the most traditional beliefs and the most luxuriant fantasies not only coexist but also breed. Here the living, the dead, and the undead perform at the bidding of programmers and marketers. And no laborious journeys through life and death. Click, click—you're morphed!

The electronic digitized journey can include all the possibilities imagined in the past and then some. Among the most visionary is robotic expert Hans Moravec.[49] He has suggested that cyberspace will be the cure for mortality. Our minds can be downloaded into computers, and in this form we can live forever. (Unless the Internal Revenue Service catches on to it, this could be even better than it sounds—neither death nor taxes!) But Moravec has his own plan for improving upon digitized immortality. It will take a little doing, of course, but cyberspace technology could be the modality for fulfilling the prophecy of resurrection. All the dead will arise through a mega-simulation exercise. Wertheim adds that "the Book of Revelation promised the joys of eternities to virtuous Christians, but through the power of silicon, Moravec envisages it for us all."[50]

What do you think?

Yes, me too.

"Brother, Sister, have you been saved?" sounds a more resonant chord than "Have you been digitized?" Moravec's scenario (and others of that genre) tiptoes past the question of what it means to be alive. Computer codes and monitor displays do not live forever. They do not for a moment live. A product of human techno-imagination is propagated, but no lives thereby are either engendered or extended. Fun to think about and toy with. But what if somebody actually believes this stuff? Have we become so distanced from both flesh and spirit that we would even consider accepting this fantasy substitute?

Just asking.

ON JOURNEYING

Journeying is a robust idea. It is a little different from getting up and going someplace out of practical necessity. In journeying there is an impulse, a quest, a desire for something beyond what we know and perhaps what we are. With experience often comes the intimation that the journey is the destination. It is also an appealing thought that there will be a going on. Standing or even marching in place is like being a little dead. Moving along with body and soul is more like life, even if death is waiting to cut us off at the pass.

Traditional images of journeying from life through death have grown dusty with neglect since the modern era established itself (with exceptions, of course).

> At the moment when the saint draws his last breath, he has turned his face toward heaven or toward the East. Then his soul embarks upon the journey to heaven, a glorious journey, for there is no chance that the soul of a holy person ends up in some other place.[51]

We have already noted that the direction and location of heaven have become a more problematic issue since the noonday of saints, and devout persons of a later generation have often simmered in anxious doubt on the deathbed. In those days of lustrous faith, however, the soul would begin its journey at the last breath, with a choice of three options: as a small child with an angelic escort, a tiny bird, or a blazing light (think laser beam) streaking nonstop to heaven. We still find journey imagery in Christian accounts of the passage from life to death, but the tradition itself has become fragmented and esoteric.

The reduced salience of Christian postmortem journeys has created openings for other versions, including Buddhist beliefs either in their authentic form or, more often, adapted rather freely according to individual preference. Visions of the NDE type did make strong impressions within Christianity in the past. The journeys took place during states of altered consciousness. The soul would exit its do-nothing body and visit the otherworld. In the earlier years of the Christian era these journeys were usually considered to be "real" (if spiritual) trips to a "real" (if otherworldly) place. By the end of the first millennium some were uncomfortable with this interpretation and suggested that these were dream-trips— a downgrading that was vigorously attacked by those who believed in a literal otherworld and an actual pilgrim soul.

These illuminating and often harrowing personal experiences did gradually become less palatable to the church establishment because of the possible competition with certified dogma. The religious establishment needed its occasional boost through miracles but also had to keep things under control. As visionary experiences became marginalized, so did the inspiration provided by those who had returned with their stories to tell. A person who had been to the other side was certainly a person whose words we wanted to hear. But even this willingness to listen entranced and believe every word also declined over time. Not many were yet questioning the truth of survival after death; however, the personal narratives played to a more mixed reception.

Now personal visionary narratives have returned and again commanded attention. Christian faith, now divided across a wide spectrum of beliefs and practices, has the challenge of either welcoming or rejecting these testimonies. Those who select or create designer religions often seem to be cherishing the vision of voyaging. The Heaven's Gate cult—many of whom were active in the computer field—astonished us not only by their mass suicide but also by their belief that this act would enable them to continue their life's journey on a spaceship courteously waiting for them to board.

The journey idea, though uncomfortable to some who practice well-established religious traditions, is far from inert today, nor do we know what new—and old—forms it might take tomorrow.

TEN

LIVING THROUGH

Should we live for that elusive moment of exhilaration? Or take each moment, no matter how ordinary, as it comes and goes? Perhaps instead we should discipline ourselves to meet expectations and obligations over the long run. Do our lives add up to something, with the best yet to come? Or are we only deceived by such pernicious ideas as continuity, futurity, and meaning? Skepticism itself provides a thread of continuity from ancient times to the present. Societies have sometimes persuaded themselves that life is a brief and brutal exercise that is occasionally transfigured by fleeting episodes of love, beauty, epiphany, achievement, and victory. The exaltation of the moment, though, can threaten the viability of social institutions. Eastern thought warns against becoming too attached to the pursuit of evanescent moments or to the assumption that anything human will endure. "Vanity, vanity, all is vanity," Western thought has often chipped in. Societies have sometimes scorned life in favor of a meaningful passage through death. Believe, obey, follow that path, and we will escape the frying pan of life without being hurled into the fire. Modern societies, though, are more likely to be death-denying than death-haunted. The best way through life, they say, is to avoid reflecting on the death's head in the mirror, which stands in contrast to the dictum that unflinching awareness of our mortality is the only way to keep our feet on the straight and narrow path to our destiny. These conflicting themes are still with us today, but there is also much that is different about the context of our lives and deaths. I con-

clude, then, with an inconclusive but perhaps useful exploration of living through life and death in our own times.

How should we live through? Answers are abundant, rising from the occasionally harmonious but more often cacophonic voices of history. Although differing in significant ways, all the proposed answers invoke a relationship between our lives and our deaths.

- *Reflect at the end of each day about the certain ending of our days.* Only keen and relentless awareness of our mortality can guide us past the temptations and perils on both sides of the grave.
- *Keep the faith.* The hopes that have kept our people going through the centuries are still good enough for us. Live through with the security of received beliefs and customs. This does not necessarily require a state of perpetual gloom about doom. The Creator Spirit, by whatever name, must have had something in mind for us. In god we must trust.
- *Dance in the sunlight while we can.* Folly it is to bury ourselves before the shadows fall. "Gather ye rosebuds . . ." and all of that. Enjoy what we have while we have it and don't borrow trouble from the future.
- *"Live fast and leave a good-looking corpse!"* Go all-out. Dare. Never waste a moment or an opportunity. Make up for finitude with intensity. Never have a normal day or a boring night. The urgency and passion of this approach exceed the genial ease of drifting pleasantly through our days.
- *It doesn't matter much one way or t'other.* Do or don't. Dance or sulk. Nothing means anything. Everything means nothing. There are no directions in space and no destination worth mentioning in a self-destructing universe that doesn't even know we're here and won't miss us when we're gone. Suicide is a logical option, but why even bother? Leave that to the blind mechanism of the universe. Allow ourselves a little satisfaction in the knowledge that we are onto the secret that there is no secret to it all.
- *Live for, as well as with, each other.* Develop a sense of community and compassion. We are all in this together. Do what

Figure 30 *War Refugees* (1976): painting by Joze Tisnikar. A dark, compelling image of people and animals desperately trying to live through one day and hoping for another. From Nebojsa Tomasevic, *Tisnikar: Painter of Death* (New York: Two Continents, 1977), fig. 30.

good we can. Nurture the young. Respect the old. Don't fall for the rhetoric of hatred and divisiveness. Whatever else may befall us as we live through, we have each other.

- *Be careful!* Life is dangerous for everybody everywhere all the time. Don't be lulled by the false sense of security that emanates from the illusions sponsored by society and our own wishful thinking. Live each day as though we might be only a moment away from the edge of survival—because we are.

- *You talking to me?* I can't hear a word you're saying. The noise and the music, the hard work and the harder play, the computer excursions and video escapes (and, OK, a six-pack to wash it all down)—these are what keeps my mind rocking and rolling through life. No place for death here, at least not close up and personal. Death happens mostly to other people—you can look it up! The Me who dies someday is not the I Am who's here today, so forget it!

There's obviously no shortage of answers. Furthermore, there's also no ironclad restriction on our choice. Many of us do keep several answers in our repertoire. Consistency is for bloodless pedants. The rest of us are free to put into play whatever attitude seems to best fit the situation or our mood.

Sometimes, though, we fail to recognize a critical situation until it has leaped upon us. The alarm signals might be difficult to detect or identify, or they might warn of danger from an unexpected source, such as the terrorist attack on the World Trade Center. Familiarity and our own guiding assumptions might dampen response to other sources of danger. We might also be swathed in the pristine belief that we are insulated from the slings and arrows of fate: life-or-death situations happen to other people, almost always those we don't know. Our chances of coping effectively with a critical situation can have as much to do with our own mind-set as with the situation itself.

In the first chapter of this book I touched on the issues of emergency versus routine and real-ization in the terrorist attack on the World Trade Center. We also paused to observe that permanently stunned look on a skull beneath Vienna's St. Stephansdom. Neither life nor death had gone as expected. Perhaps it is time now to consider again the state of mind we bring to critical situations.

BACK TO THE GREAT SWEET MOTHER:
THE DEATH SONG OF INNOCENCE

The hiking tourist blithely ignored warnings from the locals. What kind of story were they trying to palm off on him? A huge and murderous bull roaming the crest of the hill? Bull indeed! But the bull was there, even larger and more menacing than advertised. There was nothing wrong with the hiker's appreciation of immediate danger. He quickly scrambled down the hill. Was the bull thundering after him? Just keep running! Then he stumbled, stumbled and couldn't regain his feet. Something really bad had happened to one of his legs. And something even worse could happen to all of him if he did not keep moving.

Oliver Sacks, M.D., would survive this episode to describe it in *A Leg to Stand On* and also write *Awakenings* and other fascinating books. At the moment, though, his survival was very much in doubt. Getting across a deep stream was a critical point. Although the bull was no longer snorting behind him, he knew he could freeze to death that night if he did not make it to the base of the mountain and find assistance. Notice how neatly he divides his mind into the I and the Me:

> Several times I felt my consciousness ebbing and feared I would faint and drown in the stream; and I ordered myself to hold on, with strong language and threats. "Hold on, you fool! Hold on for dear life! I'll *kill* you if you let go—and don't you forget it!"[1]

He makes it across the stream. Lies there

> shuddering with cold, and pain and shock. I felt exhausted, prostrated, at the end of my strength, and I lay stunned, motionless for a couple of minutes.

And this is where things really get serious. And especially significant for us. Notice that he has again assigned two different roles within his mental theater:

> Then, somehow my exhaustion became a sort of tiredness, an extraordinarily comfortable, delicious languor.
>
> "How nice it is here," I thought to myself. "Why not a little rest—a nap maybe?"

A memory flash exploded in my mind when I first read this passage. More than once I had driven home in the early morning hours after a day's visit with a lady friend who was several hours distant. The road seemed endless. Traffic was light. I was so sleepy. Just for a moment. I could just close my eyes for a moment. That would be OK, wouldn't it? It was with difficulty that the voice of survival barely triumphed over the voice of temptation. For Sacks:

> This soft, insinuating inner voice suddenly woke me, sobered me, and filled me with alarm. It was not a "nice place" to rest and nap. The suggestion was lethal . . . but I was lulled by its soft, seductive tones.
> "No," I said fiercely to myself. This is Death speaking—and in its sweetest, deadliest Siren-voice. Don't listen to it now! You've got to go on whether you like it or not. You can't rest here—you can't rest anywhere.

Sacks credits "this good voice, this life voice" for his survival. He understood that both the voices of tempting Death and urgent Life were his own. In another time and place he might have spoken of angels and demons. Freud would have nodded his approval: Eros had won this round against Thanatos, the twin-headed instincts of life and death perpetually in cunning war against each other.[2] The father of psychoanalysis might also have added that love, sex, and death often make strange bedfellows. In this instance death had appropriated the comforting allure of a lover, or a mother, or both. "No Grim Reaper here, Doc!" the lulling voice seemed to say. "Just come to Momma, Baby!"

Greek mythology carefully distinguishes between death, Thanatos, and sleep, Hypnos. They could seem so much alike—ah, but the difference! Over the centuries many have chosen to ignore this warning. It is still a commonplace in Western culture to speak of the dead as resting, as enjoying their well-earned sleep. This is clearly a thought that comforts the living. It also clearly confuses and sometimes alarms children. Bedtime can be fraught with anxiety for children who have been told that "death is sleep" story: might not sleep also be death? It takes a while for young children to arrive at a firm distinction between sleep and death. We sometimes make this more difficult than necessary. Adult insomnia can also include traces of anxiety from a childhood blurring of sleep and death. I'll just keep that night-light on, if you don't mind. And if death is but peaceful sleep, why should we trouble ourselves to be vigilant, resourceful, and determined about potential life-threatening situations?

Furthermore, death also can disguise itself as sexual union, a consummation devoutly to be desired. That orgasmic episode is overrated. How long does it last, anyway? Consider a far superior option: to exist forever either in the deliciously yearning moment of intimacy before the sexual cataclysm or in the languorous relief afterward, famously known to the French as *le petit mort*. What if this luxurious "little death" were available for an unlimited engagement—what if so-called death is really sexual ecstasy and fulfillment that continue ad infinitum?

Is this a bizarre thought? Sort of. But it is also a thought that has proven itself attractive to some people in every generation. Death is better than sleep. Better than ordinary sex. Better than life, with its numerous frustrations and disappointments. This virtuosic transformation of death from terror to treasure has appeared in numerous cultural settings but perhaps has reached us most often through German literature, song, and drama. The late eighteenth and early nineteenth centuries were a fertile period for this idea. For example, Mathias Claudius penned a narrative poem that was set to music by many composers, most notably by Franz Schubert. "You shall sleep gently in my arms," promises Death to the frightened Maiden.[3] Left unspoken are the specific plans Death has in mind: as father-comforter, lover, or what?

Other wildly popular and influential poems were even more evocative. Foremost was Friedrich von Hardenberg. He was the perfect romantic. He invented a more charismatic name for himself—Novalis—dared to write well beyond the edge of accepted subject matter and style, contracted tuberculosis, and died before age thirty. In the fourth of his *Hymns to the Night*, Novalis depicts his pain as prelude to ecstasy. Soon he will be liberated (i.e., dead) and lie in the very lap of love. He whispers ardently to that all-encompassing night, his words a sensuous conflation of passion for the life that he believes only death can fulfill:

> Suck me toward you, beloved, with all your force
> That I may slumber and love at last.
> I am touched by death's youth-giving flood,
> To balsam and ether is turned my blood.
> I live by day full of courage and trust
> And die every night in holy lust.[4]

One could hardly surpass this exaltation of death, this transfer of love, desire, and comfort from the normal course of life to an imagined realm in which all wishes are fulfilled. Young men thrilled to this message, wrote copycat versions of their own, and came up with their own ways to romance death. For a while it was more exciting to die for—or with—the object of one's desire than to enjoy a direct sexual relationship. What were the passions of the flesh when compared with the heroism of passing through the ring of fire to death and proving one's self deserving of glorious postmortem love? Suicide became an even hotter idea for the young, though, fortunately, the idea itself was satisfying enough for most. This idea was reinforced by Goethe's novella *The Sorrows of Young Werther*, which was swallowed whole by many readers who missed the author's ironic spin on youths captive to their own fantasies.

Worse would follow. Profound yearnings spiced by forbidden relationships could be fulfilled only through borrowed Norse legends and acres of Wagnerian music. All in all, heroic death was the ticket to ride rather than the commuter bus to work and back. Mostly ignored here, too, was the author-composer's game. Wagner, in turn a devotee and then an enemy of Nietzsche, had turned to Norse legends when he decided that the promise of Christianity had come and gone. Life can be redeemed by glorious death—but only until the curtain falls and the weary conductor can at last lay down his baton.

The notion that death is the cure, if not the culmination, of life has received many other memorable expressions.

> I will go back to the great sweet mother,
> Mother and lover of men, the sea.
> I will go down to her, I and none other,
> Close with her, kiss her, and mix her with me.

Mother and lover: what's the difference? Oedipus Schmoedipus! That's Freud's problem. Here expressed is the undisguised desire for intimacy, for more than intimacy, for becoming dissolved in, absorbed by Nature after spending some little time as an eccentric British poet. In this passage from "The Triumph of Time," Algernon Charles Swinburne contrives to have it all.[5] Liberation from the sorrows and vicissitudes of earthly life, of course. But also intoxicating passion:

> Thy sweet hard kisses are strong like wine
> . . .
> My lips will feast on the foam of thy lips

And escape:

> Save me and hide me with all thy waves

And survival through a superbly conscious form of sleep:

> I shall sleep, and move with the moving ships
> . . .
> Alive and aware of thy ways and thee

Ordinary life, then, can but whet our appetite for union with the all-giving and all-taking mother of creation. We scrabble through the limits and imperfections of individual existence in hopes of something much grander and much more satisfying. And here the vintage Christian downgrading of earthly life still exerts its hold, but the redemption has become rather individualistic, sublimated, and dreamlike. We also notice that the principle of femininity, generally kept under wraps in early Christianity, has now come into its own. Nature is a She, and goddesses are making a comeback.

Another version of Swinburne's image of the afterlife penetrated to the core of classic English-language literature. Here we are not at sea but in the garden of Proserpine,[6] the woman-become-goddess

> Who gathers all things mortal
> With cold immortal hands

This realm is bereft of passion. Of hope. Of dread. Of struggle. And yet there is a self, soul, or spirit to experience this absence. It is, after all, a garden, not a wasteland, and a destination, not a void. Not Nirvana or, again, Christian heaven, or Islamic paradise. The garden of Proserpine seems very much like the place our minds drift to as our vital signs fail and even telemarketers can no longer reach us. In Room 225 of the intensive care unit there were past-midnight moments when, staring into the dark, I might have welcomed Swinburne's consolation if I had given myself up to it:

> Here, where the world is quiet;
> Here, where all trouble seems
> Dead winds' and spent waves' riot

In doubtful dreams of dreams;
. . .
A sleepy world of streams.

It is a song of acceptance. We live through until there is no more living to do. Until we have had enough of struggle and strife, enough of ambition, enough of desire, enough of enough. This is good:

> From too much love of living,
> From hope and fear set free,
> We thank with brief thanksgiving
> Whatever gods may be
> That no life lives for ever;
> That dead men rise up never;
> That even the weariest river
> Winds somewhere safe to sea.

Swinburne wrote all this stuff and went on living. Not so Keats. Slowly, painfully dying young of tuberculosis, he hid four or five scraps of paper behind volumes in a bookshelf. It was his "Ode to a Nightingale"— to quite a specific nightingale, whose song had delighted him as the shadows lengthened in the evening.[7] Keats was feeling himself move subtly but relentlessly through life to death. He wanted life, of course. He wanted the sharp excitements, the surprises and delights, the long hours of contemplation. But what life now had on offer to him was a dread prospect. He had observed what had recently befallen so many others:

> Here, where men sit and hear each other groan;
> Where palsy shakes a few, sad, last gray hairs,
> Where youth grows pale, and spectre-thin, and dies;
> Where but to think is to be full of sorrow

He needed to come to terms with the lengthening shadows:

> Darkling I listen; and for many a time
> I have been half in love with easeful Death,
> Called him soft names in many a mused rhyme,
> To take into the air my quiet breath;
> Now more than ever seems it rich to die
> To cease upon the midnight with no pain,

> While thou art pouring forth thy soul abroad
> In such an ecstasy!

Nevertheless, Keats, as he said, was only half in love with easeful Death. Life all too soon becomes pain and despair. Intolerable, yet one must somehow tolerate. But what's next? When the nightingale had taken its song elsewhere Keats was brought back into himself, trapped in a failing body and to wonder just what he had been experiencing:

> Was it a vision, or a waking dream?
> Fled is that music:—Do I wake or sleep?

So many others in both Keats's time and our own would also find themselves tempted by death. The reasons would be varied: a wasting illness, a fear of horrors to come, a failed venture, an imposition of self-respect, a loss of a vital relationship. One might seek temporary oblivion with the juice of the grape or the poppy. Why not go all the way, though? Why not simply cease? Why not take one's own stubborn and useless life? Or find somebody who will perform that service for us?

Many specialists in suicide prevention are convinced that self-murder is frequently thwarted by that inner other voice: the powerful call of life even in the most unfavorable conditions. "I'll *kill* you!" was the paradoxical but effective way in which Oliver Sacks's voice of life threatened his sleepy near surrender to the blandishments of death. A certain prince of Denmark hesitated because nobody knows what might be encountered in the unknown territory beyond this life. Keats was not alone with his doubts about whether death would be a kind of waking, a kind of sleeping, or no kind of anything. Ambivalence in the form of interior dialogue has saved many a life. And often an adroit listener has provided the occasion for the inner debate to come down on the side of life.

Traditional ways of thinking about dying and death, constructing an afterlife, and developing rituals for the final passage continue to have their zones of influence. The more unsettled, speculative, wishful, and individualistic mind-set that we have sampled here has led to a drift away from standard and received customs. Even those who yearn to maintain a clear, unambiguous image of heaven often find it difficult to do so, hence the numerous versions extant and their frequent vagueness and ambiguity.

One of the underlying questions deserves attention here.

Is Death Different from Life?

How and how long we live through depend a lot on where we suppose we will be after the physician pronounces.

As individuals and as a society we often smooth over death. We try to make death seem as lifelike as possible. A nice-looking corpse is conveyed to its resting place in a well-manicured park. Many observers have commented on the proclivity of technologically advanced societies for concealing the deadness of the dead. Foremost among euphemisms is that good old standby "She's only sleeping," a thought reminiscent of the Novalis et alia romancing of death but with the disturbing passion locked away. (Sexualized mingling with Mother Nature, for example, does not seem entirely kosher.)

A Deep, Restful Sleep

Whatever might be gained in the momentary sense of comfort in likening death to sleep is paid for much too dearly. Death is not sleep. Sleep is not death. Impressionable minds (adult as well as juvenile) are not well served by this flawed comparison. Furthermore, this is part of a larger pattern of evasion. When people agree to believe (or to pretend to believe) that death is only a kind of sleep, they are also agreeing to reject their natural curiosities, doubts, and fears. There goes the opportunity for honest and probing discussion about that fact of life we call death. And the evasion does not end with this subject. Children eventually realize that adults are playing a keep-away game with them. Why ask grown-ups anything you really want to know about? They'll probably only tell you a story.

Anxiety about discussing death as death can impair our communication and therefore our relationships. The same is true of any anxiety-arousing subject. We become cautious and stilted because a conversation could veer off to someplace we don't want to go—money . . . sex . . . religion . . . politics . . . death. Children often learn the rules the hard way. Many adults recall that in their own childhood they were shushed or conversation ended when certain topics came up. Alternatively, the tone of the conversation changed markedly. A social worker remembers that the grown-ups would stop breathing for a moment. They'd look at each other, and then look at us with glassy eyes and a completely fakey expression. We [her sister and herself] felt like we were strangers or they were strangers. Whatever they had been talking about must have scared them stiff, and that scared us.

Communication within close interpersonal relationships becomes restricted and distorted when there are emotional land mines one must be careful not to step on. The practice of evading or misrepresenting significant features of reality generates abiding tension and pressure among the very people who should be able to rely on one another for guidance, comfort, and home truths.

Today there is less justification than ever to equate death with sleep. Altered states of consciousness are better, if still imperfectly, understood. Brain death is not sleep. Comatose people are not dead; neither are those whose mental functions have been temporarily inhibited as part of medical treatment. A flat EEG readout does not represent the pattern of either normal or abnormal sleep.

Softly voice the traditional phrase "Rest in peace." Respect time-honored phrases that connect us with religion, poetry, and music ("Sleepers awake!"). Take comfort in the peaceful or serene expression on the face in the coffin. Be tolerant of those who find in the sleep analogy their best and perhaps only way of acknowledging a loss. But death-as-a-kind-of-sleep is simply not a trustworthy proposition to lean upon with all our might and need.

The idea that death is not so different from life often occurs spontaneously to young children as they try to imagine what dead people do all day and night. It is easier to envision the dead doing a little than to envision them doing—and being—nothing. Five- and six-year-olds have told researchers that the dead don't get hungry—except sometimes. They can't see because their eyes are closed, and they don't hear except when there's something really interesting. "Death" is a tough concept for most young children, but "being dead" can be constructed from bits and pieces of their own experience. Usually for the young child, being dead is a diminished form of life. "Dead people are *lonely,*" a four-year-old girl explained to me once. "They have only dead people to talk to, and dead people don't listen, and they don't play, and they miss all the TV shows they liked."

The young child's imagining of death as a reduced life has at least a passing resemblance to views of the afterlife in ancient Mesopotamia and in some African and island cultures. What survives death is a shade, a much diminished residue that becomes increasingly feeble and anonymous. For some peoples the defining moment comes when there is nobody left who knows or remembers the deceased person. The dead cling to a bare pulse of existence through the memory of the living. By implication all the lingering, ebbing dead are extinguished when the last person alive turns the light out before leaving. Death is a life diminished and diminishing.

A Trick of the Mind

There is a trick of the human mind that encourages us to regard death as not so entirely different from life. It is a trick that has been learned within every cultural heritage, discovered by the young and mastered by the adult. How does it work? We are so constituted that we read our own phenomenological and cognitive activity into the subject of our thoughts. In fact, it's hard not to. Our own mental activity imparts life to the subject of its operations. We also tend to impart or attribute human needs, motives, purposes, and logic to whatever comes into our purview. This assimilation of the world to our way of thinking comes most decisively into play when we have few positive cues to guide us and restrain our anthropomorphizing tendencies.

To put it another way: we look at nature and we see ourselves. Floating clouds are shape-shifters that take on one familiar configuration after another. "Verily like a whale." Rock formations were alive with faces long before presidential visages were imposed on Mount Rushmore. "That looks like Uncle Ed with his bald head and long nose." (And even small stones were once treated as cuddly little pets.) The native peoples of Australia and the United States revered certain rocks as petrified gods. Fast-moving streams are live-ly: burbling, chortling. Here there are zestful and prankish spirits in motion, while more powerful gods reside in the mysterious depths of silent rivers. Clocks and cookies attract special attention from infants because they are configured somewhat like the human face, or so researchers believe they have discovered. The broader principle is that from the cradle we are programmed to seek out and respond to the human form, voice, and touch—and will attribute human characteristics to objects that have some resemblance to us.

Animistic thinking was observed frequently by anthropologists as they explored cultures previously unknown beyond their own regions. This way of thinking was also pervasive, though, in the foundations of Western culture. The sky, the waters, the woods, the storms, the caves, the leaping flames—all were endowed with a kind of divinity, and these numerous gods were themselves constructed from the most readily available material: human needs, motives, purposes, fears, and hopes. Animistic thinking has proven hardy. This is a definite boon to the creators of cartoons and the producers of stuffed animals, among others. The ink blots that make up the (in)famous Rorschach test regularly elicit descriptions of people and animals. In fact, a respondent who cannot or will not see human forms in at least a few of these ambiguous visuals is considered to be mentally or emotionally impoverished.

There is a more basic and subtle process at work in all these manifestations. The essential activity of our mind—that it *is* active—equips us well for detecting and interpreting activity in the world. When we draw a blank, though, we just go right ahead and fill it in according to our psychobiological equipment, cultural heritage, and personal makeup. A series of experiments have provided one instructive line of evidence for this proposition.[8] Do you remember the sensory deprivation studies? You would if you had been a participant. You might have been one of the lucky ones in the earlier studies, expected only to enter a cubicle and lie on a bed twenty-four hours a day with but the briefest time-outs for meals and toilet. A U-shaped pillow around your head, a continuous hum of air-conditioning equipment, plastic visors, gloves, and cuffs all contributed to keeping sensory stimulation to the barest minimum. Or you might have participated in one of the later studies in which your eyes and ears were sealed off from stimulation and you were immersed in a dark, quiet, water-filled chamber. There you'd float about long enough to lose orientation for time and space. There would be just you and this amorphous, featureless environment. Nobody to mess with. Nothing to bump into. Nothing to disturb you. Just you with your mind for company.

Many things would happen to your mind, none of them very pleasant. Of most interest here are the hallucinations. Deprived of external stimulation, your mind creates its own. Unfortunately, these are often disturbing. Left to its own devices, the sensorially deprived mind un-leashes visions, phantasms, alarming sequences that seem to obey their own rules, not those of everyday thought and judgment. Give the mind but a blank screen, and it will project the stuff of fantasy and myth, long-ing and horror. Perhaps in this condition we could even reconstruct the most vivid nightmare scenarios of all humankind, should need be.

The sensory deprivation studies have illuminated one facet of our in-clination to generate and project our own mental activity onto the world. Another facet has been known to psychologists for many years. In fact, it was called "the psychologist's fallacy" by William James, the first to describe it clearly.[9] We commit this error when we attribute our own in-terpretation of a situation to another person. Just because we can ana-lyze and construct a plausible version of that person's state of mind does not mean that that is what that person is actually thinking and feeling. This was a timely warning from James to his fellow pioneering psy-chologists, and it remains instructive today. We have a strong predispo-sition to suppose that others think and feel as we do, or how we think we would if they were fortunate enough to have us being them.

It's really hard to think of nothing, though very easy to think of very little. The most adept students of Zen philosophy and practice are de-voted to emptying their minds. By all accounts this is an arduous enter-prise. Many of us can probably reach the point of dispensing with some of the furnishings and knickknacks that knock around in our minds from day to day. It is much more difficult, though, to overcome habits of thought, to disable or transcend our characteristic ways of perceiving and interpreting. Furthermore, if we try really, really hard to get to that pure state of emptiness, we might succeed only in obscuring it through our own arduous efforts.

Take another example from reports of near-death experience. I must have been dead, a person may tell us. Looking down, I could see my body under that SUV or stretched out on the OR table. The body was not re-sponding, not moving. Dead. But, wait! *I* was looking down, and *I* am reporting. The *me* who was dead is an inference drawn by the observer who both survives and remembers (or cocreates) the episode. Again two voices, this time split between perceiver and perceived.

Whatever resonates with death often disturbs us, even though the con-cept of an absolute nothing is elusive. Silence. Dark. Absence. Lack of response. Lack of movement. These situations can bring us close to the thin edge between being and nonbeing. Turn up the music. Keep the TV on. Say something, even if it's stupid. Especially if it's stupid. Light up a cigarette. Populate the silence, the dark, and the absence with our own devices. We continually invest death with life. No wonder death sometimes doesn't seem that different from life! The tricks of our mind enlist the clouds, the rocks, and even death itself for the stories we weave for our children and ourselves.

IS NOTHING NOTHING TO US?

We have been exploring the proposition that death is not that different from life. In so doing we have been confronted with the workings of our own minds and have noted our talent for shaping stories that try to make sense of both life and death. Consider now the person who has been left behind in grief and who cannot help but wonder where the absent companion is when she's not here anymore and how he can possibly go on alone. The sharp divide between here-and-alive and gone-away tears asunder the book of one's life. The story line dissolves; expectations and meanings become disconnected fragments. Philip J. Hilts, trying to cope with his own grief over the death of his wife, articulates this viewpoint while also calling upon the neurosciences for confirmation.

First, the storytelling part:

> Mental life may be imagined as a continuous storytelling—taking bits and fitting them into a running narrative that makes sense of where we have been, what's going on now, and what to do next. . . . The central engines of our mind are bent always and forever on the job of making stories, in large themes and a thousand subthemes simultaneously. The brain's operators within the frontal lobe work together with memory on this. Because it is what we do, and we cannot fail to do it, it is the fundamental bias of the mind. Not ideological or temperamental, it is a biological bias.[10]

Hilts implies that history and culture are little more than the residue of story making. Operating on similar equipment, individuals construct linguistic structures that give shape to their collective experiences and direction to their activities. Some of the most encompassing and influential stories are those we call religion. Perhaps Hilts would agree that his own story is one more example. The entire history of science could be regarded as a procession of stories, most of which have been rejected along the way. Whether we draw upon personal visions, received dogma, or scientific observation, we keep coming up with stories, because story making is what we do. Perhaps the devil makes us do it, but if so, the devil is concealed within our neural wiring.

What happens, then, when nothing happens? Hilts speaks first from his personal experience:

> My wife has died, and I buried her to the words "Out of the low door they stoop into the honeyed corridor, then walk straight through the wall of the dark." My wife has become a memory.[11]

Hilts has given us an evocative phrase. Since the first scribe set down the first Pyramid Text we have indeed been haunted by the image of the departing beloved walking straight through the wall of the dark.

Hilts's interpretation of the storytelling impulse draws upon its assumed basis in the properties and functions of the human nervous system. He begins, though, in the realm of phenomenology:

> We imagine our beloved, and cannot project him or her to become nothingness. Our expectations run on, despite death. And then we find we are mistaken, she is gone. Where there was some light, there is only a blank. Nothing goes forward; all must be revised. A great hole is opened up in our thinking and feeling of the world, a piece of our map of the world is gone.[12]

Many of us know this experience by heart. We have lost a person who was at the center of our life. The everyday world is still buzzing all around us—how strange is now the familiar. We are still here, too, but something—actually, everything—has changed. Perhaps, though, we should add the crucial element of cocreation. Husband and wife had coauthored a story line that was intended to continue throughout their lives. Communication studies have made it clear that our individual expectations are strongly, subtly, and pervasively influenced through both our actual and our symbolic relationships with others. And if many have contributed to an individual's story line, many are also brought up short when the story ends suddenly and too soon.

Separation would be easier to bear if the lost Other were simply someplace else. Our own death would also be a less harrowing process if it, too, were to represent a change in scenery and status rather than oblivion. Death would be taking a form not totally different from life, as we have seen modeled in the religious thought of many world cultures.

There's a catch, though, and here is where Hilts gets down to his main business. The story line concocted by our neurobiological apparatus is credible if and only if we can somewhat finesse our way past the fact of death. Fortunately, according to Hilts, we are well equipped to play this game:

> Belief in an afterlife is almost a necessity of human mentality. It is a deep, biological tendency. We know only life, going forward in the world. . . . Every fiber of our thought leans toward the expectation that we will go on. Death is the sudden breakage of all our long-built-up knowledge that things go on. We cannot picture it; we are incapable of imagining that we are not, that we are not experiencing. Our expectations shoot out into the void without us, and we cannot help but imagine "life" after death.[13]

Although he is taking his stand within the context of modern neuroscience, Hilts's words resonate with world beliefs since ancient times:

> We imagine our bodies going on, but at the same time know they do not, so we imagine some peculiar spirit-replicas of them going on for us. We cannot help it; it is a conclusion that springs directly from the mind's own machinery.[14]

Hilts is offering an explanation for the many forms of immortality that have been conceived over the centuries. Credit or blame "the mind's machinery" for prehistoric man's belief that the dead need tools for the next life, as well as for the subtle and complex ideology of the Egyptians, and for so many other stories in which death turns out to be not completely different from life. *We believe in immortality because we must.*

Nobody Really Believes in His or Her Own Death: Freud Has His Say

Freud was there first. A century before Hilts, Sigmund Freud started his professional life in the laboratory and continued to cherish the belief that the mysteries of the mind could be unveiled by neuroscientific research as well as free associations from his Biedemeier couch. He was also fascinated by early returns from the emerging field of anthropology. His desktop became increasingly populated by miniature figures of gods and demons from exotic world cultures. Freud was out to explain everything that needed explaining and perhaps some things that didn't. For example: why do people fear death? "Because people want to go on living" would seem to be a sufficient answer. This answer could further be enhanced by reference to fear of roasting in hell in punishment for a life of either grand or petty sinning.

The first psychoanalyst, though, was not long taken in by such common misconceptions. Why are people *really* afraid of death? Between toxic puffs on his cigar, Freud would have replied with something like, "They are *not* afraid of death—that's your answer!" This is the way he actually made his point:

> Our own death is indeed quite unimaginable, and whenever we make the attempt to imagine it we can perceive that we really survive as spectators. Hence the psychoanalytic school could venture on the assertion that at bottom nobody believes in his own death, or to put the same thing in a different way, in the unconscious every one of us is convinced of his own immortality.[15]

Freud had to work within the limits of the rapidly developing yet still rudimentary neuroscience of his day. He also had to deal with an enigma of his own creation: a seething and powerful unconscious that, almost by definition, could not be known by the conscious mind, which is constricted by its linear logic, fussy distinctions, and culturally provided blindfolds. Not to worry: Freud was a master at knowing the unknowable. We cannot really comprehend death because

> what we call our "unconscious" (the deepest strata of our minds, made up of instinctual impulses) knows nothing whatever of negatives or denials—contradictions coincide in it—and so it knows nothing whatever about our own death, for to that we can give only a negative purport. It follows that no instinct we possess is ready for a belief in death.[16]

Freud adds another argument to overcome any lingering resistance to his conclusion. We are alive, therefore we have not experienced death. It follows that when we express what seems to be fear of death it is really something else that troubles us. *Thanatophobia,* as Freud called it, should be regarded merely as a presenting symptom. The skilled analyst will light up another stogie and patiently lure the real fear out of hiding. "I'm afraid to die" can be a strategic way of avoiding certain people and situations. It can also be a metaphor for a general sense of impending loss of control and catastrophe. In early psychoanalytic theory there was a presumption that fear of castration was the basic source of anxiety that could not be acknowledged directly. This view came under increasing criticism and was replaced to some extent with the conjecture that thanatophobia can serve as a disguised signal of anxiety over possible loss of security and control from any source.

Hilts tells us that our neural system requires us to imagine that the dead are not so. Freud tells us that we cannot believe in our own death because the deepest levels of the mind operate under a markedly different system (as most thoroughly explored in his *Interpretation of Dreams*). Together they insist that, fundamentally, nothing means nothing to us. We have to make something out of nothing, and so we do.

Both, though, are almost mum on the core emotional issue: we just cannot bear to lose a person we love completely and forever. Even if we could imagine a parent, lover, or child disappearing into the void, we would struggle mightily against this conclusion. ("Resistance," not "denial," to use the psychiatric argot.) But what does this have to do with the supposed impossibility of imagining our own death? Even if I could never conceive of my own cessation, why could I not acknowledge the obvious fact that others die? Neither Hilts nor Freud provide much guidance regarding the relationship among realizing personal death, the death of the Other, and death in general.

The cognitive difficulties in comprehending death may be as formidable as Hilts, Freud, and others have asserted. Perhaps, though, we should not underestimate our ability to hold dissonant thoughts in mind. To put it another way, many a person has the ability to conceive alternative scenarios. "Life dissolves with what we call death" can coexist with the passionate wish that "who I love will not, cannot perish." Even if we do comprehend "nothing," we might brush this awkward knowledge aside with the strength of our will to live and to love. *We go on, then, because our minds secrete an illusion of continuity, purpose, and destination that not only propels us through everyday life but also launches us across the great divide. Belief in immortality is, at root, per-*

haps not so different from assuming we will wake up tomorrow morning and find both ourselves and our familiar world present and accounted for. We do not have to erect cosmic propositions but, more simply, only need recognize the impulse to get on with life as best we can and as best the world supports.

The quirks of our neural equipment and the heritage of dogma, custom, and ritual might impel us to suppose that death just cannot be all that different from life—and our keen wish that this be so often takes over when Nothing occasionally stares back at us from a reflection on a passing train.

But Do We Really Not Know Nothing?

It's for sure a provocative thesis that belief in immortality is based on our inability to imagine our own death, bolstered by our desire for the continuity of life and love. Furthermore, how can we offer a challenge when we are told that this thesis has been established by experts in the heady field of neuroscience? Actually, though, a challenge *is* in order. Hilts and Freud usefully remind us that our efforts to comprehend death are not independent of our "hardware" (neural structures) and "software" (rules of operation within and among various neural networks). This being said, though, we are free to explore alternative interpretations.

Consider first the supposed scientific basis for the converging claims that (1) we cannot fear death because we cannot understand it, and (2) Hilt's assertion that "we cannot help but imagine 'life' after death."

There is no scientific basis. Zippo, *niente.* No findings that come close to passing muster. Not much that even bears directly on the propositions asserted by Freud and Hilts.

Neuroscience has come a long way since Freud's time but still has a long way to go. Hilts, like Freud, does not offer hard data to support the thesis. There's none to be had. Neuroscientists pursue many lines of inquiry. Some of the most exciting studies have focused on connections between neural structures and networks on the one hand and verbal report and experience on the other. Interesting and illuminating stuff! To date, though, Freud's description of unconscious operations has been neither clearly confirmed nor disconfirmed.

Credit Freud with having come up with some fresh observations. He derived his proposition that we have a deeper layer of mental functioning that operates according to its own rules from his pioneering analysis of dreams (both his own and others'). Freud concluded that time, negation, and endings are concepts that do not compute in the unconscious. His source was verbal, not neural. Even the most engrossing reports are but words describing images. Not only are these reports amenable to a variety of interpretations, but also there is no guarantee that what the person has put into words is an accurate description of the dreams. There may be significant omissions, additions, and distortions between the dream and the report. I agree with those who regard dream memories and reports as creative products that include selective elements from the dream experience along with a translating-editing-shaping-integrating process.

Freud's own theory holds that there is a radical difference between dream and waking logic, so we might expect much to be lost in the translation. The speculation that dream elements have resonated with sexual and religious themes in world civilizations since ancient times has had at least the possibility of empirical test through anthropological observations and other sources. But the gap is much greater yet between the verbal report of subjective experience and conclusions about the structure and function of our nervous system. Even Freud, a master of remote inferences, could not rely on verbal reports to prove that our neural organization is incapable of comprehending death. And even recent advances in relating verbal report to concurrent neural activity have not shed much light on the proposition that we are incapable of believing in our own death.[17]

Hilts tries to make the connection from the other direction. What of his assertion that storytelling and the belief in immortality are functions of "the mind's own machinery"? Again, no neuroscience proof is offered, nor has such proof become available during the intervening years. It is human longing and imagination that Hilts discusses, and he does so with sensitivity. Nevertheless, no evidence is offered to document that the mind's machinery is actually tooled in such a way as to propagate stories and immortal visions.

The reverse logic is not convincing. Start with the facts that we do like to make up stories and that we hate it when these stories are interrupted or trumped. It is also clear that we often harbor the notion of an ongoingness of life that will pass safely beyond death. These facts are a long,

long way, however, from supporting the conclusion that, *therefore,* our neural equipment must be made for this very purpose, and that we have always and must always think this way. This is a speculative and rather uncritical inductive generalization that is passed off as though it was a firm logico-deductive conclusion. It would be more consistent with our limited state of knowledge simply to note that we do have the capacity to create memories, expectations, and narratives that range from the tightly factual to the wildly fantastic. That we are compelled to use one kind of story line (e.g., life continues after death) and prohibited from another (e.g., dead is dead) is a proposition that is not required by logic or supported by the great diversity of the stories we come up with in such abundance.

One day perhaps neuroscientists will subject this question to systematic research and come up with the genius methodology required. We can then revisit. For now, though, we are not obliged to accept the proposition that we know nothing and can know nothing about death and therefore must imagine a continuation of life beyond death. These interesting ideas must continue to take their chances in the marketplace without the imprimatur of scientific validation. In the meantime we might reflect on the bias against conscious thought in the position taken by Freud and, to an extent, by Hilts.

Thought that is open to experience, systematic, linguistically sophisticated, disciplined, and yet flexible has been responsible for much of the achievements of civilization. Conscious thought should not be so hastily dismissed. If we only think we comprehend personal death, that should count for something. Furthermore, we are not entirely without experience that provides hints of the elusive condition we call nothing. Perhaps one example will serve to encourage additional review of the glimpses of the void that sometimes comes into our lives.

I was told about a patient on a kidney dialysis unit—a teenager who was a particular favorite of the staff for his outgoing personality and appreciation of their efforts. They were all the more saddened as his physical condition deteriorated. The young man himself became more distant, though still unfailingly obliging and polite. A nurse told me that before dawn one morning she discovered his bed empty. A moment later she also saw the shattered fifth-floor window. The shape of emptiness and absence were there more definitively revealed: the hole in the window preserved the shape of a hurtling body on its desperately brief journey from an intolerable life. We live as people among other people in a world of substance, structure, and ceaseless motion. It is therefore striking when in the midst of so much there opens a rift, there falls a silence, there is suspended over us a pale mist in which time itself must pause. Most of us have been touched by a something that has whispered to us of nothing.

We Know Enough about Nothing to Do Something

It's time now for a closer look at Freud's proposition that we are deceiving ourselves and others when, heart pounding and nerves a-tingle, we think that it's death that has us by the throat. Freud's observations were sometimes right on target: the agitated person in his office described a fear of death that later turned out to have a different source. Many other therapists and counselors have subsequently noticed that an acute death anxiety syndrome often develops during a time of transition and stress and then dissolves rapidly when order is restored to the client's world. A person who is overwhelmed by change, pressure, and uncertainty may feel a terrifying lack of control. This sense of helplessness and lack of structure is also experienced by people who have suffered significant brain trauma. In Kurt Goldstein's words, they suffer from catastrophic anxiety.[18] Fear of death can become a way of labeling and sharing this concern. Some acutely anxious people say they are afraid they are losing their minds; others say they could die at any moment. The good news is that the acute death anxiety can dissolve quickly when the life situation becomes more stable and the person regains confidence in his or her ability to cope. Death served as a metaphor, a proxy, for the confused and menacing state of affairs.

Sometimes, though, our anxiety does swirl around a fear of death. Freud overgeneralized from his clinical observations at an early stage in his career and never quite came around to an official revision, though he did take death as death a lot more seriously later in his long and troubled life.

To insist that death and nothing must be unimaginable is a philosophical sideshow to the gut issue of how we conduct our lives in the shadow of mortality. Where did the concepts of "death" and "nothing" come from, anyhow? If humans were mentally agile enough to come up with these ideas, perhaps we also are competent to do something with them. *Did we imagine something (nothing) that we are incapable of imagining?*

We don't have to know everything about nothing in order to experience a healthy fear of death. And the objection that we cannot be afraid of death because we have never had that experience is an even weaker proposition. Let's dispose of that one first. We are gifted with the ability to become apprehensive about misfortunes that have never happened to us. More young children have been scared of the Closet Monster than have ever been assailed by one. Sometimes we have witnessed or heard about these misfortunes on the part of other people or paid good money to watch them in the movie theater. We're also prolific in anticipating frightening events through the workings of our own creative imaginations. One of my schoolmates in the Bronx would go out of her way to avoid walking across a grate. She had never seen or heard of anybody falling through a closed grate and knew that it couldn't actually happen. Still, one never knows! After we had our little amusement over her silly fears, my buddy and I admitted to each other that we had the same fear but tried not to show it. Actors who have never blown a line may fear that their brains will turn to mush when they step onstage the next time. Our fears may be credible or far-fetched. Whatever, often they are anticipations of dangerous or humiliating things that have never happened to us before. We concoct these fears with the same virtuosity that gives us enhanced memories and enthralling stories.

Our repertoire often includes specific fears of death. The specificity distinguishes these alarm buttons from a more generalized anxiety. Post office employees or mail room clerks might have experienced little or no perturbation about death in daily life. A few days later they might be intensely concerned with the possibility of exposure to anthrax. Perhaps like the rest of us they have difficulty in comprehending the idea of nothing. However, they have no difficulty in recognizing a threat to their continued existence. And here we see plainly how much concrete meaning can be associated with the abstract notions of death and nothing. For example:

- I would never be able to retire with my spouse and do all the things we have been planning for years.
- I would never see my children grow up.

- I would not be there for my parents.
- I would not be able to experience the full course of life from youth to age.

Reflections such as these do not require us to have a profound understanding of death. We do not have to pierce the mystery, if mystery it is. All we need to do is recognize *consequences* of death. Whatever death might "be" (perhaps a contradiction in terms), a very likely consequence of it is that we will not continue to experience and function in the world that has become so familiar to us. Let our neural machinery or unconscious processes entertain the scenario of unending, as Hilts and Freud have averred. We—scanning, learning, coping—have ample reason to believe that our days will in fact come to an end. Our knowledge is based on years of direct observation and plausible logic. Withering replaces blossoming. Unresponsiveness replaces animation. The loss of the qualities we associate with life is evident. Perhaps there are dimensions and meanings of death that transcend these observations. But what we do know of death is the consequences within our own world of experience, and this is plenty enough to command our attention.

Death itself might not be the dread prospect that it has been imagined in some cultural traditions and individual mind-sets. Perhaps when we attribute any descriptor (such as "terrifying") to it we thereby endow death with an insubstantial substance, a mere linguistic construction that has been torn from a supporting network of semantic connections. "Terrifying" becomes a gesture, a shudder, not a descriptor. Suppose that we take seriously the proposition that death is just a way of referring to the cessation of life. From this perspective, death could be regarded as less than nothing, because "nothing" implies a real state of affairs. Even so, "death" still commands attention if it has no credible surplus meanings and is only a reification of a process that has ceased to function. A desire to survive for another day (and then another) is the mark of a healthy creature that has a proper respect for danger.

The possible loss of continuity and futurity makes itself keenly felt. Furthermore, most of us have had personal experiences that contribute to this projection of radical discontinuity. We have moved from one neighborhood, school, or workplace to another, each time losing personal relationships and anchoring points in our life-space (the secret path beyond the meadow; the church where everybody was baptized; the loud, friendly place where we'd all meet after school). We may also have lost several of our cherished future selves (NASCAR driver, rock star, copy-editor).[19] These losses and discontinuities, though, were compensated by new relationships, new environments, and new careers and lifestyles.

The possible compensations of an afterdeath state of being belong to a more speculative realm. A person can regret the loss of this life while also anticipating a more spiritual form of existence after death. Some people come to a point where they feel they have completed a full life and, now weary and frail, are ready for the next. Still others feel secure in their belief in an afterlife but are anxious about what might befall them during their terminal illness or how their funeral arrangements will be conducted. The relationship felt between these two spheres varies from person to person and is subject to change with circumstances. The aged and terminally ill people I have worked with have taught me that serenity and anxiety, faith and doubt, and urgency and transcendence can all coexist in varying configurations. And for every person who withdrew to prepare steadfastly for the last moments, there was another who continued to thrive on activity, continuing to continue. "Death will have to catch me!" said one nonagenarian as she headed toward the "Times Square" area of the geriatric facility, where all the best gossip could be had. People obviously have been finding more than one way to live through their final days.

How we live today has many implications for how we orient ourselves toward death. Here is one revealing example. The concept of a "wrongful death" has become increasingly salient in the business world and the court system. Claims can be made that the surviving family is entitled to financial reimbursement because it lost the earning power of a member who died because of an employer's alleged negligence and failure to maintain required safety standards. Attorneys for the plaintiff may also attempt to include the loss of companionship as a reimbursable item. If the claim is upheld, an awkward question arises: how much is this death worth? Even the most ardent bean-counter is likely to pause before the uncomfortable challenge of translating the value of a human life into a cash settlement. But the pause won't last long, because however difficult a loss of companionship may be to compute, an estimated loss of earnings is not.

Note what has happened here. Death, with all its powerful symbolic and emotional meanings, has been reduced to a particular consequence whose value can be expressed in a number (product of estimated earnings per year × number of years canceled by death). Time is money, and money is an acceptable proxy for life. This way of thinking did not figure prominently in Judaic, Christian, Confucian, Buddhist, or Islamic outlooks on life and death or in the polytheistic religions that arose in many world cultures. Many of us today are also comfortable with the idea of putting a dollar value on life and death. We are probably not surprised, though. The wilderness, thickets, and deserts we have been coping with throughout our lives are composed of layered and overlapping bureaucracies, institutionalized impersonality, and echoing zones of silence where our implorations and laments seemingly are unheard. That we do not rage and rebel against the reduction of death to "a mournful number" is testimony to our acknowledgment that we are living and dying in circumstances that were unknown to most earlier generations.

HOW WE LIVE AND DIE TODAY

Here are just a few facets to remind us of the changed and changing conditions. What follows would be a falsification if applied to the total world population. Many people still suffer deprivation and disease as a result of inadequate economic and health systems, often exacerbated by discrimination and partisan violence. I am speaking at first, then, of the fortunate ones who have access to the resources of a thriving society.

We Are Living Longer

The average life expectancy has increased markedly in developed nations for more than a century. At first the most significant advance was the reduction of the high mortality rates for infants and children. More people are having the opportunity to live into their adult years. A little more slowly, yet impressively, life expectancy has increased for adults as well. There is now a better prospect than ever to have a full course of life to live through. Death is still at the end of the road but less likely to be just around the corner.

Society has the blessing of a larger cadre of experienced people to share their knowledge and transmit culture. Society also has the challenge of accommodating a historically unprecedented proportion of elderly adults while also providing opportunity for younger generations and their own ideas and concerns.

We Are Younger Older

Optimistic medical authorities at the turn of the twentieth century envisioned a time when people would not be old at forty or fifty.[20] Although some people did live vigorously into their eighth decade and beyond, it was more common for adults to shift early from "middle" to "old" age in physical function and appearance. Life was harder and safety nets fewer as compared with the fortunate ones in developed nations today. Retirement rules and benefits emerged from the calculations of clever statisticians who figured that most workers would become unproductive with age in their physically demanding employment and would obligingly die before drawing extensively, if at all, upon their benefits. Old age started to become defined by a number (sixty-five was the winner, of course).

Fear of growing old rivaled concern about being struck down in one's prime. The emphasis on youth and change was already being felt throughout much of society. Bonds of duty and affection were available to some aging adults, but many had reason to fear marginalization and progressive incapacitation. Today's flourishing cosmetic industry and physical fitness programs are among the testimonies to our desire to look and feel young. The theme was already playing generations ago, however, and perhaps with greater urgency because the years of good living seemed so few.[21] In our own time the middle adult years have expanded markedly. People in their sixties and well beyond are continuing with their active lives, making few concessions to age. A couple who would have once been considered aged might well be giving more attention to their travel plans than to last things.

Death can be regarded as a more distant prospect through the long and rewarding years of extended prime time. Again, for the fortunate ones, even the gradual descent into "old age" can be gentler and less traumatic. And, for society at large, what was once the specter of ravaging Death has been downsized to a pale functionary who is stationed far down the road from the vibrant lives we are enjoying here and now. The more horrific images of Death that have been generated over the centuries

Figure 31 Erik Erikson, the psychologist, and his wife, Joan, in 1975: examples of companions who lived through an eventful and long life together. From Walter Kaufmann, *Time Is an Artist* (New York: Reader's Digest Press/McGraw-Hill, 1978).

seem overwrought and melodramatic if its function is simply to turn off the lights after a soul has outworn its body through all the phases of a mortal life course.

We Die Longer

In our great-grandparents' time many deaths were swift, a matter of hours, days, or weeks. Fatal accidents (especially in the workplace) were more common. "Childbirth fever" took the lives of many women. Contagious diseases claimed victims in many households. Infections that would respond to treatment today often proved fatal then. Life-threatening conditions that now can be resolved through surgical procedures were beyond the available medical knowledge and technology. "The crisis" was a familiar phenomenon. The victim of a contagious disease would be close to death's door with high fever, respiratory distress, and other symptoms. Physician and family provided small comforts, prayed, and hoped for the best. Sometimes the person died; sometimes the fever broke and recovery was probable. Either way, the crisis was usually resolved within a few days.

Today many of us have a slower journey between failing health and death. *Dying* is not always the most accurate term. A person can be afflicted with a condition that will probably be the primary cause of death at some point in the future, but he or she can nevertheless remain active and involved in life until then. One can also experience a gradual weakness and limitation of function, as with an accumulation of age-related deficits and chronic conditions. I have known many residents of a geriatric facility who passed away in their sleep without ever having moved through a conspicuous dying process. Many (but not all) people whose vital functions are maintained on a life-support system are often described as having a vegetative form of existence. It is difficult to say they are dying; being suspended someplace between life and death is perhaps closer. It could also be said they are already dead as sentient individuals and probably also as members of society competent to fulfill obligations and make informed decisions.

Even more common today is the situation in which a frail or struggling life is kept going by state-of-the-art medical and nursing care along with the individual's will to survive. Often the person is regarded as being in a life-threatening condition, although there could still be periods of stability or even remission. It could be confusing to apply the term *dying* to both this person and the one who is actually experiencing the end state of a terminal illness. The end state itself, marked by massive failure of vital body systems and functions, can also be extended by medical technology. Both the preterminal and terminal phases now tend to be longer than in years past.

Whatever words we choose to describe the last phases of life, the fact is that more of us will linger rather than rush through these experiences. There are significant implications of this change for patients, families, caregivers, and society. One of the positives is the increased opportunity to affirm and renew core relationships. There is time to share memories, resolve old misunderstandings and grievances, and deal with business matters. An implicit form of "the good death" is shaped by these expectations. The passage is "good" if the dying person has received safe conduct to the place where life ends and death with its mysteries begins. The surviving family members feel they have come through when needed, having participated in care and companionship (perhaps with the guidance of a hospice team). Their faith or philosophy of life has been put to the test and found worthy. Moreover, this companioned, peaceful, and meaningful passage serves as an encouraging model the next time that family, friends, and caregivers face an end-of-life situation.

Unfortunately, this type of passage is not guaranteed, not even with the best of care and intentions. Some terminally ill people suffer from unrelieved pain and other symptoms. Despite valuable progress in symptom control, it is not always possible to achieve the twin goals of freedom from distress and preservation of consciousness and clarity.

For example, Julia Lawton has observed a frequent loss of selfhood among terminally ill patients as their loss of physical function becomes increasingly severe.[22] Family members can feel helpless and even guilty as discomfort and dysfunction come to dominate the situation. Optimal care is also sometimes compromised by health care providers who are either insufficiently trained in palliative methods or reluctant to use them (e.g., withholding effective opiate relief because of unwarranted concern that the dying patient might become addicted). There are also family circumstances that can interfere with loving support. It is not unusual for families to be struggling with other stresses and conflicts at the same time. The "bad" death, then, is one in which the dying person suffers too much

and too long, while family, friends, and caregivers come away with unresolved anxieties and a heightened fear of end-of-life situations. No less
significantly, faith in the value of life and the meaning of death can be
shaken by the long, painful, and unsettling ordeal.

We Are Rethinking Our Route of Passage from Life

Our more lingering passage has intensified issues of end-of-life decision
making. Introduction of the living will document proved to be heuristic
and educational, although the measure itself was limited in its practical
consequences. Soon this gesture toward individual choice received support from court decisions that respected the right to informed consent
in selecting or declining treatment. A groundswell of public support persuaded state legislatures throughout the United States to enact "natural
death" acts that also supported individual choice. The Patients' Self-
Determination Act was still another step in this direction, a federal man-
date requiring medical care facilities to offer decision-making opportunities to their patients. All of these measures and others have their flaws
and loopholes. Health care providers also vary in the diligence with which
they cooperate with the principle of patient self-determination. Nevertheless, there is now a robust new tradition of at least attempting to respect the wishes of patients and families (easier, of course, when they are
in agreement) on the preferred course of medical management near the
end of life. The palliative care movement, so closely associated with hospice programs, remains a bulwark of support for this effort, though not
without its own difficulties.

A tension-ridden distinction has arisen in the medical system as a result of more frequent patient exercise of choice: a life-threatened patient
is a Do Not Resuscitate (DNR) or is not one. (There is no term in general use to designate patients who apparently prefer medical intervention in an emergency situation—e.g., cardiac arrest). The DNRs are the
exceptions and are supposed to be clearly identified as such. These are
the people who have asked their health care providers to restrain themselves from last-minute heroics. They are saying, in effect, that there is
a point beyond which they do not want to contest with death. The emergence of the DNR patient has led to tensions within and among health
care providers and families. Nurses are often the ones who are caught in

the middle. Well informed about the patient's current condition and wishes, the nurse may feel that a patient has been coerced into receiving invasive treatments that undermine what is left of the quality of life without providing any realistic benefit. Some physicians are frustrated by the DNR decision as a barrier to the treatments they believe would still be worth trying. In one of the more electrifying clinical studies in recent years it was found that many physicians actually neglect or override a terminally ill patient's DNR decision.[23] Theoretically, then, we can choose between an exit from life when death beckons or a strenuous battle to perhaps survive for another spin or two on this globe. In practice, though, circumstances beyond our control might actually have the call.

But end-of-life decision making is not restricted to the DNR option. We might decide to end our lives right now. Major social institutions, not least the Catholic Church, have traditionally promulgated negative attitudes toward suicide. Self-murder has been variously characterized as sin, crime, moral weakness, and mental illness. A few culture and situation-specific exceptions exist, for example, the warrior who falls on his sword in lieu of surrender or the stalwart Japanese who affirms his or her honor by ritualistic suicide. Public attitudes toward suicide remained prevailingly negative well into the twentieth century. However, more attention is now given to understanding the desperation that tilts people toward suicide. The international suicide prevention effort has encouraged more compassion and more effective ways of identifying and helping people at high risk. Furthermore, the wall of opposition to suicide has started to give way. Response has been sympathetic, for example, to people who became suicidal as they approached the end phase of a deteriorative condition such as amyotrophic lateral sclerosis (a.k.a. Lou Gehrig's disease).

Physician-assisted death has become a more conspicuous option, although the number of cases reported is very small in proportion to direct suicide. This controversial practice has acquired firm legal support in the Netherlands and has been legalized in Oregon, but in most other places physicians who terminate a patient's life are vulnerable to criminal charges (even though such actions are not common). The controversy extends even to terminology. The most widely used term, *physician-assisted suicide,* is rejected by some experts, such as the Michigan coroner who has certified the deaths of patients last seen by Jack Kevorkian as *homicides.*

As a society we are rethinking our options for the final passage. At one extreme is the determination to call upon all the resources of medical technology despite pain, risk, and expense if there is even a glimmer of hope to prolong life. At the other extreme is the decision to end a life when the future seems unrewarding, even though one may still have considerable time remaining on the clock. Among those who sought the services of Kevorkian, for example, more were depressed than terminally ill.[24] There is a spectrum of choices between these extremes. For example, a person with a life-threatening condition might seek aggressive medical intervention until it becomes clear that these measures will not extend life of a meaningful quality. The endangered person may then choose to receive palliative care in order to experience more comfort and security with the companionship of family and friends. Other decisions include (1) not intervening aggressively when this seems futile; (2) withdrawing some or all life-support measures when existence is at a vegetative level and shows little or no prospect of recovery; and (3) doing something that will probably foreshorten life (such as markedly increasing opiate dosage).

Here I restrain myself from joining in the controversies surrounding these options. The point is that advances in medical technology and changing public attitudes have given us the opportunity and the challenge of deciding among pathways through the final passage (not that nature and circumstance will necessarily comply with our preferences).

Many of us apply an implicit rule in judging such end-of-life decisions as DNR, withdrawal of life support, suicide, and assisted suicide: we try to answer the question "How would *I* feel; what would *I* do if I were in that person's situation?" In recent years it seems that more of us are willing and able to imagine ourselves in such situations.

We Do Not Worship the Same God in the Same Way

There are places in the world where state and church remain tightly intertwined. Differences may exist under the tent between fundamentalists and moderates, but basic beliefs are shared. The Islamic faith remains a major example. The United States is among the many nations in which there is not only distance between church and state but also a plethora of religious orientations. Within each faith there are diverse adherents, ranging from those whose lives are centered on religious practice to those who seldom participate in rituals or consult scripture before making significant decisions. When we come to last things, then, some people bring with them a familiar and secure perspective, while others have little to fall back on. Ability to cope is further compromised by the pervasive influence of a society that has largely denied, compartmentalized, and trivialized death. Clergy as well as the lay public have been subject to this influence. Not alone was the hospital chaplain who confided to me, tears rimming his eyes, that he finds it painful to enact his role with dying people because he has lost his belief in an afterlife.

This situation does not necessarily produce confusion and despair. Some people renew lapsed faith. Others find comfort in one of the numerous alternative configurations of belief that have been constructed from selected elements of various traditional and emerging religions. Still others hew to a lifestyle in which the promises, prohibitions, and rules of religion have been rejected. There are, however, episodes of spiritual doubt and confusion even for those who thought they knew their way. Those firm in their beliefs can also have their anxious moments: Have they lived up to their faith? Will they be saved or damned?

Now add the fact that people of diverse beliefs and practices often encounter one another during the final passage. I have seen hospital staff try to persuade terminally ill people to embrace their own faith, and I have seen staff turn away in discomfort from patients whose ardent faith they did not share. There have also been distressing scenes in which a patient's belief system, unfamiliar to the health care professional, is ridiculed.

Sometimes interactions can bridge or transcend differences in belief systems, as in the following example from a hospice demonstration project in Missoula, Montana. Barbara, a resident of Missoula, had two strong faith orientations within her own worldview: Catholic and Native American. An educator with a national reputation, she lived for seven years after being diagnosed with cancer. Barbara made her end-of-life wishes known through the mainstream medico-legal system, signing a living will and having her doctor write a DNR order. She was devoted to her professional obligations and continued to work until late in her illness. Dissension about treatment options arose within her family, so Barbara chose to stay with a sister who was sympathetic to Barbara's preferences. Mainstream and Native American cultures mingled easily both in her last days and in the events that followed. Palliative medicines were provided, but sweetgrass was also burned to help guide her spirit to the next life. At her funeral and memorial services, there were classical music and Bible reading along with Native American foods and storytelling.[25]

Barbara herself saw to it that her friends from both cultures could participate together in a memorial service meaningful to all. She planned and others made possible a service that included hymns and readings honoring both traditions. A ceremonial potluck meal completed the service. There was respect and understanding where there could have been confusion and conflict. Perhaps most significant, those from both cultures who knew and valued Barbara were able to share their grief and begin their healing together.

We Are Rethinking Our Rituals and Observances

Barbara's bridging of Catholic and Native American belief systems within the context of the often impersonal health care system is but one of many examples of the ongoing process of rethinking our end-of-life rituals and observances. Many of these accommodations are subtle, as when younger and older generations within the same family discover a way to honor both tradition and emerging attitudes and circumstances. We also see more people selecting cremation for practical reasons and still engaging in memorial services and other meaningful symbolic actions. Moreover, a population that has become more familiar with diversity has also become more comfortable with attending funeral and memorial services for people of other faiths and practices.

The impact of the September 11 terrorist attacks on America was felt in many ways throughout the nation and the world. One of the responses might be called "touching base with our home religion." Attendance and participation in church activities increased significantly in the United States in the weeks following the attack. Stunned by the attack and fearful of possible further acts of violence, many people felt the need to return to the religious institutions from which they had strayed over the years. This was perhaps both a quest for affirmation of meaning and structure and a basic need to be with others in a time of danger. Religious expression at public events and in the media correspondingly increased as both country and God came to the fore. Without exception, every public gathering I attended during those weeks started with group singing of—what else?—"God Bless America." As a nation and as individuals we felt a need for the reassurance of shared values and bonding rituals. Two months later, church attendance had declined to its usual level, and patriotism, though still salient, was gradually becoming less dominant.

Spontaneous expressions of grief and compassion appeared not only in the United States but also in other nations where people were shaken by the mass killing of so many who were simply going about their lives and their work. Flowers and messages of condolence were placed in public areas. Those who gathered impromptu as well as at church spoke, read, sang, and prayed. People rose to the occasion with both institutionalized rituals and spontaneous expressions. (After a while, patterns also developed for holding vigils and setting up tribute and message areas: spontaneity itself was becoming somewhat ritualized.)

The focus at first was clearly on the grief experienced by families who had lost somebody in the attacks. The survivors themselves struggled to put into words the trauma and sorrow that had so suddenly ravaged their lives. Interviews with family survivors and the general public expressed the themes of loss, the quest for understanding, and the need to go on somehow with life.

The focus changed. It changed remarkably in just a little over a month, and remarkable also was the lack of critical thinking and analysis about this shift. In short order we were no longer a nation of victims. We were warriors seeking our righteous vengeance. It was war against terrorism. Militant language and images replaced those of grief and sorrow. Psychologists have long known that anger and aggression often provide an effective turnaround of depression, helplessness, and fear. Soon television channels would be dominated by footage of military operations and the commentary of retired officers. We were now dealing death to the fanatics. Our own losses were still fresh and devastating in the hearts of those most nearly concerned, but the government had succeeded in its bid to affirm our communal bonds through war instead of compassion and reflection. The many of us who were uncomfortable with reminders of mortality could now start to put this concern back into our anxiety closet and experience instead the confidence and strength of the warrior.

There were, however, exceptions to this transformation. Police and firefighters had lost their comrades in action. The intensity of this loss perhaps could not be understood by anybody who had not been in a similar situation. They were grieving for their brothers, the men and women who had shared danger with them every day. Two ways were available for expressing their devotion to their comrades that were not readily available to many others who had been bereaved by the terrorist attacks: (1) they could mourn together as well as separately, and (2) they could labor to rescue or at least recover the victims. The police and firefighters who had lost friends at the World Trade Center were joined in the rescue/recovery effort by others who were also moved to participate. The grueling labor in a hazardous situation was certainly directed toward the possibility of rescue while that possibility still seemed to exist. But it was also a way of working out some of the grief through muscular exertion—a variation on the victim-turned-warrior theme.

As hope for rescue gradually ebbed, the most dominant motivation turned into showing respect for both the dead and their families by recovering the bodies for proper burial and funeral services. This would not make up for the loss and the trauma, but it would help comrades and family to begin their own healing. There was little or no precedent for what they were trying to do, nothing on this scale and so close to home. In the absence of established ritual, they developed their own. Wherever human remains were found, all the workers in the area gathered at the spot. Prayers were said, and somebody produced an American flag to place in the rubble. The moral force of God and country was invoked to honor the life and death of a person who might have been a companion or a stranger. Perhaps the most elaborate ritual could have done no more.

The need-driven spontaneous rituals improvised at ground zero occupied the symbolic space vacated by the continual retreat of public rites since the middle of the twentieth century. In the post–World War II era, industrialization and the overall pattern of technological development and social change were not kind to established rituals. The more elaborate and time-consuming rituals seemed especially inimical to productivity and progress. There was still a place for the occasional glittering ritual: the coronation of a monarch with requisite pomp and splendor or the lavish funeral of a celebrity, particularly when there had been a whiff of scandal about the celebrity's life or death. By and large, though, the zeitgeist surged past on its hectic race to what's next, leaving ritual as the province of smaller and smaller enclaves and the occasional public upsurge. This was part of the larger struggle of science and independent thought to break free from what was regarded as the superstitions and shackles of religion. Before long those trying to break away from tradition were introducing their own machined and bureaucratically orchestrated sequences that were themselves a pretty fair imitation of ritual, while some defenders of the faith were modifying their rituals to appeal to those who were tempted to leave the fold.

A lot changed after World War II. Certain horrors had preceded the war and others followed. Shaken in beliefs and confidence, many people throughout the world sought a new or renewed source of strength beyond their all-too-fallible societies. The awkward term *reritualization* had a point to make. In trying to restore order and direction to their lives, people explored religions and creeds previously alien to them or improvised their own rituals. Candlemakers and incense merchants started to thrive. It became almost commonplace to laud ritual as a panacea for our alienated and confused times. I think there was something to this plan.

Some of my friends and some of their friends were engaged in a variety of rituals. These were usually rather simple, inexpensive, and non-life-threatening. The rituals did not always make much sense, but there was no gainsaying how happy the participants felt, at least for the moment. It was a relief to feel connected with other people in a situation not pressured by the competition and task demands that often interfered with communal feeling. We discovered for ourselves that rituals could enhance everyday life.

The reritualists may have overplayed their hand, though. All rituals are not created equal, and all are not enacted with equal power. Furthermore, a little goes a long way in the ritualization of our lives. Not only do some rituals involve drugs, but rituals can also act as drugs. Investing heavily in rituals can dull our minds as effectively as prescription sedatives. Repetition, conformity, and passivity are not conducive to either creative or critical thought. When ritual does call for bursts of passionate action, the target can be displaced and the outcome brutal. Woe to those who happen to be the objects of ritual-frenzied violence. And why continue the difficult quest for meaning when one can so easily succumb to gesture, chant, symbols, and the persuasive company of a thousand other believers? Lapsing into the lockstep of ritual can relieve the individual of anxiety and responsibility—as long as the spell lasts.

Something is thought to happen through ritual. The familiar term *rite of passage* might not apply in a technical sense to every ritualistic process, but it does call attention to what is frequently the crucial element: the transformation. And the transformation itself typically requires a period of heightened danger when we are between social or spiritual harbors. We have moved out of the safety of our previous status and home zone but have not yet reached the other side, where we will have become a somewhat different person in a different world of meaning. We are experiencing the perils of liminality.

The defining moments of our life often involve a risky passage from one sphere of identity to the next. These sometimes occur with and sometimes without benefit of ritual. These transitions and their vulnerabilities are shadowed by the great and still mysterious passage from life. As we have already noted, even the routine surrender of consciousness to sleep has the shape of the final passage, and, indeed, death frequently has been called by this name. "If I die before I wake, I pray the Lord my soul to take" bears testament to our awareness that even the familiar liminalities of everyday life resonate with the voyage through the darkest caverns of the mind and across the silent river with the silent boatman.

Ritual can offer safe conduct through the final episodes of life and at the same time provide a measure of comfort to those who are providing comfort. It almost—almost—goes without saying that these rituals should be meaningful to all involved. An imposed ritual not only can be as oppressive as chemical or physical restraints but also is likely to bar the opportunity for more appropriate and spontaneous interactions. Fie on rituals that are taken off the shelf and serve only to reduce the anxiety of the celebrants! Welcome to rituals that affirm the worth of the life that has been lived and offer the heartfelt affection of the survivors for whatever journey and destination lie ahead! Fie on those who craft a deathbed scene that embeds the dying person within a harshly lit and alienating tangle of equipment! Thanks be to those who never forget that the dying person *is* a person and that people deserve the opportunity for the most natural and authentic leave-taking they can manage!

HARD LIVES, HARD DEATHS

I have been mostly talking about ourselves in this chapter. Chances are that we live in dwellings that have water and electrical power. We do not miss many meals. We are enfranchised to make most of life's decisions for ourselves, including choice of mate and career. At home, in the workplace, and at play we feel relatively safe from violence. When ill we have access to a health care system replete with specialists and state-of-the-art techniques and equipment. Life can and does visit us with misfortune, even tragedy, at times, but we are often able to devote our attention to something other than the struggle for bare survival. Comfort measures are available for us as our lives near their end; we could be among the fortunate ones who have the continued support of family and friends while our physical distress is held to a minimum in our last days.

Not so for many other people. Their hard lives often conclude with a hard death. The mounting death toll from AIDS in sub-Saharan Africa already puts it among the most lethal epidemics in history. The effects are almost certain to be felt in succeeding generations as well. Many women and an increasing number of girls have AIDS, and few have adequate medication. The children of ill, dying, and dead parents are often without reliable food, shelter, and adult guidance and protection. Governments, themselves part of the problem, have been slow and hesitant about responding to the AIDS epidemic; even education about safe sexual practices has run afoul of tradition.

The hard lives and deaths of people in disadvantaged societies would be alarming enough even if AIDS had not become such a menace. An incomplete list of these people's perils includes poor sanitation, hunger sometimes verging into starvation, lack of effective public health programs to prevent and treat illness, and violence both within and between groups, all occurring within a context of deeply rooted fears and hates regarding people with rival territorial claims or religious practices. The concept of "quality of life" is sometimes translated into a list of objective items. Indoor plumbing, yes or no? Assistance programs for disabled and homebound people? Schools with competent teachers and adequate supplies and equipment? Adequate control for pain and symptoms among the terminally ill?

On measures such as these a great many people throughout the world have little in the way of comfort, security, and opportunity. Their very hold on life seems precarious. Yet perhaps any list would miss the point. Perhaps quality of life should be sought elsewhere: in a firm sense of personal and communal identity, in the joy people give each other as lovers, family, and friends, in their pride as skilled warriors in the daily struggle for survival. Perhaps. At best, though, life is hard. Youth, if survived, passes all too soon into a premature aging born of deprivation and stress. There may be a powerful commitment to life for oneself and loved ones. Over the difficult years, however, people experience one grief after another despite all the efforts, all the safeguards, all the prayers, all the rituals. And all too soon comes the time when the sorrows, the pains, and the weariness deep in the bone make death a more reasonable alternative to life. If only. If only the final passage could occur with dignity rather than degradation, serenity rather than agony. If only the funeral and memorial process could offer safe conduct into a better world instead of dismal abandonment. If only there were a thriving clan to remember and honor the memory instead of a shattered family struggling for its own survival in the debris of what was once a vibrant society. If only.

Severely disadvantaged people today include many in traditional societies that have been devastated and demoralized by the cruel edge of political, economic, and technological change. There were hard times before, but the people usually maintained their closely connected territorial and spiritual roots. Now there are more wanderers, forced out of their habitats, sometimes into extremely inhospitable environments. Others have been marginalized in what was formerly their own land. Overall, they are more likely to experience oppression and degradation than the benefits of modernization. Life and death once meant something within the physical and symbolic parameters of a stable community. The teeming cities of desperate people offer little comfort in this life or guidance for the next. Powerful nations are not spared either. Hard life and hard death have become realities for many in Russia and other former member states of the Soviet Union. China, India, and Pakistan are major players on the international scene, but many of their people also struggle for the basics of life. The list could and does go on.

Faith can occasionally rise to the challenge of massive stress and deprivation. Ritual can sometimes keep a people going when other options and resources are lacking. Magic and extremism may be called upon when mainstream custom fails to rally and rescue. I might well become one of those who looks for more intense ceremonies and stronger magic if I were to see devastation all about me in a land without law, justice, sustenance, or hope. We more fortunate ones have the luxury of honing our beliefs and choosing our rituals as but one part of a resource spectrum. For many other people today, as in the past, it is the ability to sustain faith and embrace ritual that offers the most promising way through the miseries of life and the mysteries of death.

EPILOGUE:
THE GHOSTS OF ROOM 225

Nothing in the room seemed familiar. Not the little noises that the room made (all mechanical, no cats purring). Not the shapes of objects dimly perceived (squared off, angular, striking odd postures). Not the bed (where did those side rails come from? What are all those devices snaking in and out?). And certainly not the person in the bed. Who is this alien creature? He is stuck on his back and can't turn over. A comic scene, right? *I* can move and writhe with ease. *He* has feet of stone, can't feel a thing down there. *I* like to wriggle my toes just for the sport of it. *He* has a dead man's fingers, cold and numb. *My* fingers play swiftly and accurately across the computer keyboard (even if I write nonsense, at least I do it quickly). *He* is hooked up to a vital-signs monitor, an IV tree, and a catheter. A catheter! You'd never catch *me* like that.

And he is feeling—well, not very much of anything, and that not very much is difficult to describe. We might say that he feels like one machine among the others in ICU Room 225, connected to the living world by an external source of power. This comparison collapses almost immediately, though. The devices in this room seem to be functioning well and experiencing no doubts, reflections, or anticipations. Smug they would probably feel if they could sense their own functioning. But he doesn't have it that good. His mind is still going through its paces, but it seems to be disconnected from a normal sense of embodiment, while the body itself is abnormally connected to external devices. He is thinking:

> I can think this way or that. I can't think anything into action, though. I can't think my body to stir. I can't make a stir in the world. Is this what people have had in mind down through the centuries when they have spoken of wandering spirits or lost souls? And is this drift of mind from body (or body from mind) perhaps a natural state of being? If so, perhaps it just takes some getting used to.

But that is thinking rather more than feeling. He tries again to think about feeling:

I can only come up with words, and none of these words quite describes the images that form and shift like clouds in a strange sort of motionless motion. Try single adjectives—spacey, floating, hollowed, drowned, or, at very best, idling at the lowest setting.

Still only approximate! So then—become a Zen adept and stop thinking and feeling. Be empty. Go empty. But a Zen adept I'm not. That I'm not. Try something else. "Take each moment as it comes!" There's an appealing philosophy. But what is there to take from or give to this wayward moment that has jumped the time-track, losing its place and mine in the grand sequence of things?

This might be my Forever Moment, but it doesn't feel at all like me. If I could simply absent myself—in a pure act of spiritual suicide or nullification—then perhaps this moment could work after all. It wouldn't be this moment, though, without me, and we've already established that I am not (yet) qualified to evoke the Great Empty through my own doing or nondoing.

He and I try to slip away from anything remotely philosophical. Reality is the handiest escape hatch. Here-and-now reality has its official representation as the hospital clock. Who will approach the bed next and for what purpose? The pale, almost apologetic vampire lady, or the hearty, bustling one who tried to make the blood draw into a merry secret between us? But perhaps it will be a respiratory therapist who, operating on her own clock-within-the-clock, may wander by at any time with an apparently temperamental piece of tubing and a meter I will be enjoined to impress by sucking and blasting air. Pass the test and I will be safe until the next inspection. Fail just once and the tube and the ventilator will be added to the tangle of connections. "Better not speaking than not breathing" is the word, and I cannot disagree. Nevertheless, the prospect of facing the next test and the next gives me a decided interest in coping with immediate realities.

Dealing with the proximal and the practical offers a purposeful exercise of whatever resources I might still have going. There is enough peril in the situation to justify a luxuriant life review: who am I, what have I done, what does it all mean? That sort of thing. Interior dialogue is familiar enough to me, and this can be the right time for it, seeing as how I can't do much of anything else. Somehow, though, the inward path does not beckon as expected. Where is that preterminal recreation of wandering along the streams and byways of memory? Where is escape into the interior landscape when I need it?

Instead I decide to live just a little outside myself. I lure nurses, techs, therapists, doctors, housekeepers, and bringers-of-food into conversation. Invite them to open their lives a bit. See if I can help make our limited interactions personal and distinctive. And perhaps in so doing I may recapture the feeling of still being a person among people, somebody whose nonintellectual answer to all the intellectual questions is simply to live through this moment in this life.

Day and night shifts replace each other in a slow-motion cycle. I settle into the routines. I have either domesticated or been domesticated by what was once the unfamiliar. The recalcitrant ways of my body have become customary and, therefore, less alien. It is as though the humbling force of gravity just happens to be stronger in Room 225. In this cavern, reality is dense, and I am less substantial. Things are starting to sort themselves out, though: I can't do this, this, or this, but I can do that—and, with the occasional complicity of a staff member, I can try doing something just a little beyond that.

The nursing staff flows in and out, with its many faces, shapes, ages, races, and personalities. I come to recognize in all of them an unremitting vigilance beneath their individual ways of performing their responsibilities. Even the several Jennifers are strikingly different, but each has her antennae out. Given the chance, many display antic wit and share off-road stories—but the alertness is always there, the scanning for signs that the situation is (i.e., I am) about to go sour. My admiration for the nurses and techs continues to grow as I see more clearly the tensions they must keep in play: between routine, efficiency, and order on the one hand and crisis detection and response on the other. Everything's just fine; everything can just decide to fall apart at almost any time on the ICU. The more experienced nurses have found ways to draw upon their own values and personalities in their daily dealings with routine and crisis. You can see the younger nurses still trying out ways to bring their best selves into the picture while demonstrating the standardized professionalism required of them. All must decide whether a situation can be handled by the book or calls for independent judgment and innovative response.

I now feel as though I have several worlds or frames of experience going for me, too. There is the person I was. He's on hold. A character in a novel I haven't finished reading (or writing) and don't expect to get back to anytime soon. I am living through something, but it doesn't seem to be that life or that here-and-now. There is also that intense little world-within-a-world of research and writing. I should be feeling anxious and frustrated, perhaps even traumatized, by this interruption in my schedule. For example, there's that book for the University of California Press, so close to completion, and all those other projects. Somehow, though, my customary drive toward completing projects refuses to kick in. What was important, even urgent, a few days ago has slipped off to the periphery.

I search for anger or bitterness. Shouldn't I be railing at the bad hand that Fate has dealt me? (Actually, two bad hands—numb, weak, and nearly residual appendages, a typical feature of acute Guillain-Barré syndrome.) But who's to be angry at and for what? How things are is just how things are. This simple acknowledgment fails to rise to the splendor of fate or destiny. A sense of what Verdi once called "the force of destiny" may loan a resplendent veneer to my circumstances. Struck down by fate, victim of a cosmic drama! No, that doesn't come close to working. Just a flu shot with an extra stinger in its tail. "Fate" has gone down rather smoothly as an answer to the perplexities of existence ever since the narrative voice or voices of Homer started to spin those hoary tales.

If fate has been good enough for so many people, why not pack up my troubles in that old kit bag? But—no go. I like the art and science of explaining—perhaps too much—but I cannot rise to the bait of any namebrand philosophical position at this point. I do not even allow myself the sport of mental flights in appealing directions. Since childhood's hour, I have been fascinated by the place of life in the universe. The universe is really, really big, I gathered, and a kid like myself on his dead-end street in the South Bronx was a really, really small part of the picture. But there also seemed to be even smaller worlds within us and within all the things we can see. I never quite figured all of this out. Now might be the perfect time to think again about the vastness and the finitudes. On the wings of vagrant imagination I can transcend the hypergravity of this body in this bed. I can lose myself in the billions and billions of galaxies and the trillions and trillions of stars that Carl Sagan displayed for us in recent years.[26]

But no go here, either. I'm not feeling very cosmic or transcendental, tempting though these options should be. Instead I find myself living within my skin and just a little beyond—gossiping with the staff and receiving reports from my wife, Bunny, on conditions at home, where one dog and four cats have had their routines disrupted by my absence.

Gradually a coherent sense of situation dawns on me. I have developed a grudging respect for present realities. The here-now of acute Guillain-Barré syndrome and the ICU has its own structure, rules, and sequences as well as its own opportunities for learning and discovering. Somehow my usual orientation toward the future has faded somewhat, and I have also not resorted to reinhabiting the past. A welcome simplification! I can be who I am here and now with whoever happens to set foot in Room 225. Let's just get through another day and night, and we'll let the medical outcomes and great cosmic mysteries take care of themselves.

I awaken! That means I have actually been asleep, not so common an event in the ICU. But I cannot have been asleep for long. Only a little past 1 A.M. Think boring thoughts and perhaps there'll be another round of slumber. These are the slow melting hours that drip from Dali's clock. The more you try to make them pass, the slower they move. A recurring desire torments: how good it would feel if I could wriggle my toes! If I had genuine feet again, it might get me through the night. If I could just wriggle those toes and maybe rotate those ankles a little. Being in bed with somebody who has cold, dead feet is depressing, I must admit. The miracle of the wriggling toes is not to be granted, of course, so I resign myself to another stint of staring the night down.

Then something else awakens within me. A wild horse. It's galloping inside my chest. What energy! What spirit! How the powerful hooves shake the ground. My heart, a wild horse, seems to have a mind of its own, the mind of a trapped creature making the break for freedom. A cold sweat now joins the action. Suddenly my night shift has become more interesting. "Anxiety attack!" I diagnose promptly. I am also quick to accept this diagnosis. A little too quick, though? I seldom have a proper anxiety attack, and I have not been wracked with fear and apprehension since settling into a treatment program and the hospital routine. Then again, I might have been a lot more anxious than I allowed myself to realize. I fool myself just a little: "Sure, you'd like this to be an anxiety attack. Just an anxiety attack. How about pushing that call button?"

Okay, okay. I hear you. It might not be such a bad idea to push the call button. Don't have to. The night nurse enters briskly. She has spotted the accelerated heart rate on the monitor and is also concerned about the rhythm. Tells me she's of a mind to order a cardiac evaluation stat. After that—whatever's necessary. Her worry worries me—but it's also comforting that she would talk her way through the decision-making process with me.

This now seems a good time to review what I've been learning about the syndrome in the past two weeks. The odds of developing Guillain-Barré syndrome (G-BS) in response to a flu shot are mighty small, but it happened. The odds also favor surviving this attack, but that again is statistics, and there is a definite risk of being felled by respiratory or cardiac failure. The course of the syndrome is individual and not fully predictable. It can ring a lot of bells in the autonomic nervous system, and one of those could be the tolling knell.

"What if this is it?" My relatively secure idyll in the ICU has been shattered by the hoofbeats and a general sense of agitation. Perhaps I am now on my way. What is left for me to feel, to think, to say, to do if this is the beginning of that journey envisioned by so many peoples over so many centuries? I have reflected more than once on the launching points for this voyage. I have been with some people who were intensely alive as the moment of death approached and others who slipped into a diminished state of consciousness that gradually crossed the line into death.

I have thought I would want to be present for my death. Here may be my opportunity. I don't know if I am up to it, though. The romantic in me wants this to be what Abraham Maslow described as a "peak experience."[27] The wandering scholar has sought wisdom. The dramatist would appreciate a final scene for affirmation and farewell with the people most dear. However, it doesn't look too good for any of these scenarios. I feel merely like a person who may or may not be on the verge of dying. It doesn't seem horrible, but it is sort of disappointing. I don't know if I can be my best self for the occasion. Evidently, I have been carrying around some expectations that now seem just plain irrelevant.

Morning and the day shift arrive together. I am still the recumbent incumbent in Room 225. The doctors are pretty sure that this nocturnal episode was one of the many pranks engineered by the G-BS. An autoimmune neuromuscular reaction, G-BS often messes with the subcortical centers that control respiration, swallowing, cardiac function, and other vital operations. The anxiety surge, with its cold sweat and runaway galloping, was one such event. My heart itself is OK, but it would be dangerous to have its control toyed with by the syndrome. Add another medication to the mix, then, and continue to keep a sharp eye on cardiovascular activity.

I feel I have learned something from this rehearsal, and perhaps not only about my own way of living through. There is also the feeling of having approached the passage as both more and less than my individual self. The first person who ever died and the person who will be the last of our race to go: unexpectedly and secretly I feel at one with both.

A few more days have passed. I'm hot stuff now. I sit up most of the day and lurch with leaden legs through physical and occupational therapy sessions. I can still do very little but often do that little to soundtracks blaring from my boom box. Therapists and ward staff now join me in tripping the light (or heavy) fantastic to Woody Herman or Duke Ellington as we go through our paces. It's also clear that soon I will be booted out of the hospital and loaded up with rehabilitation exercises for however long it takes to knock around on my own two feet. For now, the tide of life has rolled back to shore while Death mutters and grumbles in the distance.

So it was that during one of my last nights on the ICU we found ourselves talking about ghosts. Especially the ghosts of Room 225, but also those disembodied spirits the night nurse had come across in other ICU settings throughout her many years of service. We had entered into a lengthy conversation after she checked my vitals late in the evening. She exemplified the savvy and level-headedness that enable nurses to cope with situation after demanding situation and find the strength to go it again the next day. When she introduced the subject of ghosts, then, there was nothing wifty-wafty about it, nothing of mix-and-match designer religiosity or shopworn tales featuring clanking chains on dark and stormy nights.

The nurse spoke matter-of-factly about her experiences with patients before and after their deaths. Most often these were people whose world had contracted to a bed in the ICU. They were clinging to life by a thread or two. They might have died yesterday or they might die tomorrow. It was as though they had finished with life but life hadn't finished with them.

Speaking with their faint voices or, more frequently, their eloquent eyes, they had expressed the wish to be free of their failed bodies. "It was so much like labor," she recalled. "A spirit or soul or whatever you want to call it was trying to move on to where it had to go." They were struggling to give birth to their death. This separation of spirit from flesh could occur before or after certifiable death. "You look at some patients and you can see that the essence of their lives has already made off. *They are not dead, but they are lifeless.* You almost have to say they have given up the ghost." Occasionally, though, the spirit is still clenched or blocked for a time after death. It cannot get away or the body will not let go. The body yielding its spirit at the very moment of death is an event that shimmers through the room in a distinctive way, creating a sense of harmonious passage.

She spoke mostly, though, of spirits that had lingered in the room after the perished body had been removed. These were usually patients who had come and gone before she started her shift in this room. She did not actually see them, either in life or after. "I don't see them and they don't say anything, but I just know when they are here. These ghosts, if that's what they are, are dazed and lonely and lost. They don't seem to know they have passed from life. It's as though they are still waiting around, waiting for directions, for instructions." She told me she speaks gently but firmly to them—pretty much the same way she guides her confused living patients through necessary procedures. The spirits generally welcome this reorientation and exit the scene to continue their journey, hopefully on the right path.

I had heard reports like this before, often from health care professionals. The difference this time was the context: evening, an ICU, and the patient in the bed having my own name. The nurse's discourse sounded both credible and incredible at the same time. Listening as a midnight inhabitant of Room 225, I did feel as though this was a boundarying space that could be called liminal, sacred, or both. Here some souls are granted a blessing and return to the lives they have known. Others

Figure 32 *Procession* (1972): painting by Joze Tisnikar. People who have risen from the grave try to find their way back home. From Nebojsa Tomasevic, *Tisnikar: Painter of Death* (New York: Two Continents, 1977), fig. 32.

complete their earth journey and disappear from view through the final passage. Still others remain suspended, belonging not quite to either the world of the living or the world of the dead. This passage could be rationalized within an anthropological framework or sanctified by the passions of faith. The nurse, however, had not tried to support her observations in the courts of empirical science, reason, or faith. She had experienced these contacts, and they seemed real to her. How the presence of departing spirits might fit into anybody's paradigm was an issue she did not feel impelled to resolve. She could not help but be true to her experiences; their ontological status could be left to the ponderings of those so disposed.

The context provided these reports with an aura of credibility. Why not? Why couldn't there be souls in transit? And what better place than an ICU? And what better observer than a level-headed professional who was also a person sensitive to events that have been excluded from society's dominant worldview? Why not?

Besides, the scenario was pleasing. It was enticing to have again the opportunity to contemplate a world of wonders. Collective memory quickly supplied other inducements. The idea of the crossover moment. The idea of a detachable soul or, rather, a body from which the soul could detach itself. The idea of released souls who are unable (or perhaps unwilling) to get on with their journey. The tentative and dangerous status of the newly dead. The passage itself, the vulnerabilities, and the risks. The obligation of priest to guide and of kin to offer safe conduct. All these ideas have been expressed in abundance through belief systems and rituals across cultures, across time. This massive mountain of historical support does not prove that the ghosts of Room 225 exist anywhere other than our receptive and creative imaginations. Yet I hesitated to dismiss this compelling, many-authored story. I had to respect its robust character. Here in a twenty-first-century medical facility, a mature health care professional was persuaded by her own experience of spirit passages that had been the stuff of belief in ancient times. The *sense* that there is a spirit that survives the flesh has itself proven to be a hardy survivor.

At the same time, though, my permeability to the nurse's observations is being challenged by the voice of the inner critic. It said to me, "Dualism is a naive concept, and you know it. Repetition and glorification of a tenuous union between flesh and spirit have not convincingly answered the severe criticisms put forth by scientists, philosophers, and linguists. You'd have to discard or forget much of what you have learned to tumble into the dualistic mode of thought." Liking challenges, I could summon a reply to this criticism, but I had to admit that the dualism underlying many popular conceptions of an afterlife relies more on custom, need, and a leap of faith than upon established fact and tested logic. I did have one rejoinder for the critic: "Can you prove there are no ghosts in Room 225, never have been, and never will be?" The critic replied: "You won't catch me with that all-purpose argument. Can't prove the negative, but—"

I interrupted both of us. "Hold it, please!" If we were going to be reasonable and only reasonable, we would surely misrepresent the quirky flow of ideas, feelings, purposes, actions, and relationships that make up our lives. Ronald Grimes touches on a salient feature of this mix in his comparison of responses to the death of two prominent individuals:

> As the veneration of both Abraham Lincoln and Princess Diana illustrate, it is possible to participate in death rites and to commemorate the dead without necessarily implying belief in their metaphysical persistence. For ritual purposes it is enough that the dead persist in memory, imagination, or in the form of visual icons and that we approach them with empathy or respect. Belief, it seems, is not an absolute requirement.[28]

We are capable of harboring more than one thought and purpose at the same time. These can take the form of what I call primary and fallback orientations. For example, one of the late Ivan Ilych's friends is about to cross the threshold to the room where the open coffin is on display.[29] Peter considers himself to be a sophisticate (primary orientation) who has no use for the mumbo-jumbo of religion. He is stricken by anxiety, though, at the prospect of being exposed to corpse and mourners. Hastily, the nonbeliever makes the sign of the cross before entering (fallback orientation). He is willing to contradict himself to perform this inexpensive act of self-protection just in case there really is a stern God on duty.

Logic demands consistency. Pure, untroubled faith remains confidently within itself. Inflamed fanaticism will consider no alternatives. Most of us, though, have incorporated a variety of values and ways of responding into our repertoire. We also recognize that there are circumstances in which either general rules do not well apply or they enter into conflict with one another. We have to deal with the situation as best we can. In death-related situations this often leads to repeated explorations, testings, and shiftings of response in the effort to find the most effective way of reducing anxiety and living through the threat. The pragmatics of maintaining a sense of security can lead to resourceful and even desperate reconfigurations of beliefs and values. The old bromide that "there are no atheists in foxholes" is patently false but clearly expresses the idea that the immediate situation can scramble our usual attitudinal hierarchy.

Past midnight in Room 225, then, I believe (sort of) and reject (sort of) the idea that ghostly residues of former occupants have emerged, lingered, and moved on to another sphere of existence. I should be ashamed of myself. What a weak position, or lack of position, to take! How will I respect myself in the morning? But it's *not* the cold, clear light of the morning, and that's the point, isn't it? Midnight has its own logic, whether we like it or not. Were I blessed with the wisdom and the strength, I might be able to comprehend the blaze of day and the mystery of night within the same integrated mind-set. I might even be able to comprehend both the heights of joy and the depths of grief to which the human condition is heir. Occasionally I do have at least a touch of this experience, but it is fleeting and I am again back in the scrimmage of everyday life and thought. How ordinary is life! And how extraordinary!

Death educator L. Eugene Thomas wrote about his states of mind during his own terminal illness. He reported:

> Emotional depth charges went off at unexpected intervals. But that is far from being the whole picture. In fact the periods of grief they set off were usually followed by an equally dramatic change in mood. In fact Sue and I found ourselves giggling more than grieving.[30]

The Thomases continued to find humor in the oddities of daily life. Humor has been somewhat neglected in writings about dying, death, grief, and rituals, perhaps because it can seem like a trivial response. In practice, though, humor often provides a welcome balancing measure in grim situations. Death, the antic, pierces "the hollow crown" with a pinprick and the mighty king is dead: so laments Shakespeare's Richard II. The Thomases and many others have discovered that humor can be the pinprick that pierces Death and robs him of his pur-loined finery.

Thomas shares another experience that also strikes me as illuminat-ing. He had been trying to prepare himself for death by discovering or distilling what was truly "authentic" about his life. His frame of refer-ence was not unusual: existentialism had offered an intense and probing focus on death while academic philosophies were studiously engaged with other topics. Thomas observes that

> the existentialists are right about the importance of facing death in lead-ing an "authentic" life. But I suspect they are wrong when they . . . imply that it can become a permanent state. My experience has been that it is a powerful state . . . but not a permanent trait. . . .[31]

From his own experiences and his interviews with religious adepts, Thomas arrived at the conclusion that there are no "permanently en-lightened" or "authentic" people.

> We are all, from moment to moment, in the process of making decisions that are authentic or inauthentic. But one set of authentic decisions doesn't insure that subsequent ones will be such, nor that the creativity unleashed by the facing of one's own mortality at one point in time will become a permanent personal characteristic.[32]

Thomas's observations resonate with my own, and not only in Room 225. Our values may enshrine logical consistency, permanency, and res-olute passage through life on the highest of high roads. Our actual pas-sage is more variable—closer perhaps to a roller-coaster ride on an un-trustworthy apparatus. However, this imperfect traversal of an imperfect world can be splendored by vitality, creativity, courage, humor, good-ness, and intimate sharings. A human kind of life, then, and a human kind of death.

Among the last words written by Thomas is this suggestion for his fel-low death educators: do not coerce. Do not try to impose upon other people the death concepts you favor. Instead

> encourage them to face "little deaths" as honestly, as authentically as one can. In truth, this is what my experience has been all about. The "big" death awareness is really a transient "little death" experience, although at the time it doesn't seem so.[33]

Reading these words after returning home from the hospital, I realized that Thomas has taken us back to the beginning of this book's journey, where we considered bedtime rituals and other separations as forms of practicing for death. How could I not agree with him?

Back home, and grateful. Trying to think again about the grand traditional rituals that have attempted to provide safe conduct from life through death. Trying to think again of the new rituals that are being developed today as replacements or enhancements. But finding my thoughts drawn more to something closer and simpler: the loneliness of the dying person. There are still customs of support and consolation within some sectors of our society. James Crissman, for example, has observed these customs in action in Appalachia.[34] Death is still understood as an intrinsic part of life, and neither the dying nor the grieving are abandoned. Nevertheless, recent studies confirm what we have long known: in hospitals and other care facilities, many dying people are deprived of companionship except for brief servicings by nursing personnel.[35] Never mind powerful rituals of consolation powerfully enacted. Never mind deep spiritual interactions with people who have devoted their lives to the pursuit of enlightenment. How about just a caring person who is willing and able to sit bedside and hold a hand? The issue of reritualization of the passage from life through death deserves more attention than it has received. But I still have to get past the continued neglect of the dying person's basic humanity, the frequent absence of caring people at this of all times.

Thomas had the devoted companionship of his wife through his final illness, as did Sagan, whose universe of billions and billions of galaxies had come down to the cheek pressed to his on what would be his deathbed. Bunny was there for me during the perilous days when we could only wait to discover how much of my life this neuromuscular syndrome intended to take. Even so, blessed by her companionship for most of the day, I experienced the late-late show of aloneness, staring into the dark as so many others had, some of whom may have become the ghosts who were well met by the midnight nurse. The experience was good for me, though not so good that I would care to repeat it anytime soon.

Bunny accompanied me on the homecoming trip. Present and accounted for were Angel, Pumpkin, Serena, and Snowflake, as well as Ulysses, our most ancient of cats, still with us on planet Earth. He had taken up residence almost exclusively in his favorite place on the sofa, but before my hospital interlude I had noticed him occasionally roaming feebly throughout the house at night. I had seen that questing behavior in several of our previous Puss von Wussels (our honorary term for the oldest cat in residence). I settled into bed. A few hours later Bunny told me something that somehow I had already sensed. Ulysses had died almost as soon as I had returned home.

The poem came to me in an instant:

> Where did that cat
> > go
> Now that he's gone?
> > I will go there, too.
> What did he seek
> Moan by moan
> Laboring from room to room?
> > I will seek
> > And you

NOTES

1. John Leslie zestfully expounds the Doom Soon thesis in *The End of the World* (1996) and other writings. Martin Rees (*Before the Beginning*, 1997) is among the stimulating guides to understanding and evaluating the Big Bang theory. This influential theory is still being volley-balled back and forth by ardent proponents and resourceful adversaries.

2. Does everything add up to nothing? The answer—are you ready?—is yes. And also no! Theoretical physicist Henning Genz (1999) examines the cosmic case, and I make a mercifully brief attempt to suggest the relationship between the physicist's "nothing" and the "nothing" that stares us blankly in the face when we try to think about death (Kastenbaum 2000c).

3. A concise and informative history of the journey of life is provided by Thomas Cole in his 1992 book of that title.

4. Émile Durkheim did as much as or more than any other one person to establish the field of sociology. *The Elementary Forms of the Religious Life* (1965) kicked free of tradition and wedged open the door for empirical research and new concepts. His influence is perhaps even stronger in the field of suicide studies. Durkheim's *Suicide* (1951; originally published as *Le suicide*, 1897) continues to generate research and prevention efforts.

5. What is often termed death anxiety in the thanatological literature has two main facets (Kastenbaum 2000c, 2004). A general sense of vulnerability and loss of control can make life miserable for some people even when they are not actually in mortal peril. This condition answers to the name *neurosis* and is almost certainly what Freud intended by his term *thanatophobia*. In contrast, emotionally healthy people experience a functional anxiety surge when they encounter a realistic threat. This emergency response improves the chances of survival. We don't want to be on full alert all the time—that would generate the kind of stress reaction that Selye (see following note) has warned us about; and we don't want to be so smugly wrapped in our illusions of invulnerability that we expose ourselves and others to high-risk situations.

6. Hans Selye was a prodigious bioresearcher who both enriched the scientific un-

derstanding of stress and made this concept more familiar to professionals and the general public. Two of his more accessible books are listed in "Sources Cited."

7. Traumatic grief has emerged as a significant concept in recent years. It usually refers to an exceptionally intense and unremitting response to bereavement, most often when the death was sudden and unexpected. The reference here is to Prigerson and Jacobs 2001.

8. Existential psychoanalyst Avery D. Weisman is a pioneer in providing psychotherapy for people with life-threatening conditions. The reference here is to his book *The Realization of Death* (1974, 4–5).

9. Ibid., 5.

10. Christine Quigley tells us this in *The Corpse: A History* (1996). I haven't heard a convincing explanation for this move. The best one was told me by an enthusiastic guide at the City of Vienna Death Museum (my friend and I had been the only visitors that week, possibly accounting for his zeal). He said it was basically a land-grab operation.

11. Kastenbaum 1996a, 2000a, 2003.

12. Cole (1992) again.

CHAPTER TWO • PRACTICING DEATH

1. The pioneering studies of Sylvia Anthony ([1949] 1972) in England and Maria Nagy ([1949] 1959) demonstrate the ubiquity of death-related curiosity and concern among young children and their eventful progress toward an adult understanding.

2. Mary D. Ainsworth's (1973) classic experiment drew attention to the child's need to remain within "mothering space" even while exploring the environs. Even the most secure infant may at times show fear, even panic, when the comforting person is not in sight: the difference between being gone for a few minutes and gone forever is not yet recognized.

3. *The Rules and Exercises of Holy Dying* is the usual abbreviated title of this opus, though sometimes it is condensed to simply *Holy Dying*. Reprint editions appear and disappear, so happy hunting if the 1977 version is not available at the moment.

4. Taylor 1977, 47–48.

5. Keenan's informative 1997 article invites our attention to continuing shifts in religious conceptions of death within the labyrinth of technology and virtual reality. Will death take on still another face?

6. This quote from Keenan 1997, 14.

7. Hoban 1973, 122. Unfortunately, the novel *Kleinzeit* (the title translates as "small time," but the book was actually published in English) has been out of print for way too long. In it, Russell Hoban gives us an ingenious, harrowing, and darkly humorous updating of the classical journey of the dead.

8. Opie and Opie 1969, 107. *Children's Games in Streets and Playgrounds* is both a delight and an instruction. Hide-and-seek may never seem the same again.

CHAPTER THREE • GOOD DEATH, BAD DEATH (I)

1. Middleton 1996.
2. Ibid., 134.
3. Ibid., 142.
4. Ibid., 144.
5. Counts 1977; Counts and Counts 1985.
6. Counts 1977, 42.
7. Tenzin Gyatso, the Fourteenth Dalai Lama, 1985.
8. Counts 1977, 44.
9. In face-to-face societies nearly all interactions take place between people who are physically present and familiar to one another. Band-and-village cultures predominated throughout the world before the development of cities and nations, and some still struggle to survive today. Foraging-and-collecting bands seldom had more than about fifty members, and two hundred might have been the typical upper limit of those occupying a village, compound, or home zone. A surge in population tended to overload an area, so spin-off bands and villages would form.
10. Plato 1942 (as well as many other editions of *Phaedo*). Socrates' death is also mentioned in several of Plato's Dialogues, but most vividly in *Phaedo*.
11. Ahrensdorf 1995.
12. Plato 1942, 180–182.
13. Ober 1985, 269.
14. Brown 1998, 1999.
15. Brown 1999, 254.
16. Ibid., 4.
17. Mor, Greer, and Kastenbaum 1988.
18. Duclow 1999.
19. Vorgaine 1993.
20. Duclow 1999, 395.
21. Paxton 1990.
22. Ibid., 23.
23. Ibid., 38.
24. Comper [1917] 1977, 56.
25. Ibid., 56.
26. Ibid., 120.
27. Ibid., 132.
28. Ibid., 139.
29. Kastenbaum 2002b.
30. Comper [1917] 1977, 139.
31. John Donne, admired for his generous human spirit as well as his brilliant prose and poetry, was sinking steadily toward death in a bed from which he could hear the tolling of church bells whenever a fellow mortal passed away. He occupied his mind by writing a series of devotions (1624), the most famous of which includes the lines "Ask not for Whom the bell tolls . . ." and ". . . no Man is an island. . . ." The *De-*

votions in their entirety remain a treasure. By the way, John was not yet Donne. He recovered to live another eventful six years.

32. Aries 1981, 108.

33. Binski 1996.

34. Ibid.

35. Guidera 1999.

36. Bland 1986.

37. Ibid., 25. This report comes to us from Robert Carey, "a young kinsman" of the queen.

38. Ibid., 67.

39. Ibid., 53.

40. Stannard 1977, 75.

41. Increase Mather, quoted in ibid., 79.

42. Stannard 1977, 79.

43. McManners 1981.

44. Warton 1826. If you are looking for examples of self-righteous arrogance on the part of a deathbed scene visitor, look no further! (Though, unfortunately, this work is hard to come by. Excerpts are given in my *Psychology of Death* [Kastenbaum 2000c].)

CHAPTER FOUR • GOOD DEATH, BAD DEATH (II)

1. See Nuland's *How We Die* (1994, 254).

2. Larry LeShan, reporting in Bowers et al. 1982, 254.

3. Daniel Sulmasy and Maike Rahn (2001) found that life-threatened hospital patients spent almost nineteen hours a day alone, with most visits being very brief. (Nonwhite patients received fewer total visits.)

4. SUPPORT (Study to Understand Prognoses and Preferences for Outcomes and Risks of Treatment) 1995. Commentaries on this disturbing piece continue to appear in the medical literature.

5. Davis-Floyd 1992. Although mentioned here for its parallels to death rituals, *Birth as an American Rite of Passage* is a closely observed study that deserves attention on its own terms.

6. Kastenbaum 1964. "The Reluctant Therapist" was my attempt to figure out why so few therapists and counselors have made themselves available to work with elderly patients. Status contamination was but one of several factors I observed at the time of that study, and it can still be noticed today, although more clinicians have now stepped up to offer their services.

7. Barney Glaser and Anselm Strauss's *Time for Dying* (1968) was among the handful of books that contributed significant new data and concepts in the early years of the death awareness movement.

8. Sudnow 1967, 96. David Sudnow's *Passing On* is still very much worth reading today. Unfortunately, much of what he observed regarding medicine and society's

response to dying people continues despite the improvements noted through death education and the hospice movement.

9. Ibid., 97.

10. An outstanding book on this topic is Margaret Lock's *Twice Dead: Organ Transplants and the Reinvention of Death* (2002).

11. Walter Whiter [1819] 1977. A rather bold thinker, keeping one foot on the ground and another under it.

12. Dr. Jack Kevorkian published clinical papers on the neglected topic of "the eye in death" in 1957 and 1961. I discuss this work in "Looking Death in the Eye" (2000).

13. See David Clark's concise history (2002a) of the development of the modern hospice movement.

14. See Clark's brief but informative biography (2002b) of Dame Cicely Saunders, founder of the modern hospice movement.

15. Kastenbaum 1975.

16. Ibid.

17. Mount 1997.

18. Weisman 1974.

19. Waugh 1948. Miss Thanatopsis and the other characters also do their thing in the film version of *The Loved One*.

20. Mitford 1963. The author sometimes digresses from the American way of death, but usually to share anecdotes demonstrating that the British have a few odd ways themselves.

21. Harmer 1963. *The High Cost of Dying* was a balanced and scholarly treatment, which, of course, doomed it to finish well behind Waugh's playful novel and Mitford's gleeful exposé in copies sold. (And we're still waiting for the movie version.)

22. Dr. Kenneth V. Iserson provides clear discussions of life support systems, persistent vegetative states, and related conditions in *Dust to Dust* (2001).

23. On "healthy dying," see Kastenbaum 1979.

24. Seligman 1975. *Hopelessness* is a book worth discovering or rediscovering.

25. Kastenbaum and Normand 1990.

26. Quoted in ibid., 210–211.

27. The study is summarized in my *Death, Society, and Human Experience* (7th edition, 2001, 146–147; as well as 8th edition, 2004).

28. See Kellehear's *Dying of Cancer: The Final Year of Life* (1990).

29. Kastenbaum et al. 1981.

30. Ibid.

31. See Lacey Smith's virtuoso exposition *Fools, Martyrs, Traitors: The Story of Martyrdom in the Western World* (1997).

32. See Daniel Leviton's *Horrendous Death, Health, and Well-Being* (1991).

33. In John Keats's "Ode to a Nightingale"—found in many anthologies in addition to the one cited ([1819] 1972)—the young poet describes himself as "half in love with easeful Death" as his body succumbs to tuberculosis.

34. Weisman 1972.

CHAPTER FIVE • CORPSED PERSONS

1. Kolata 2001.

2. On Iceman, see Spindler 1994; on the Ice Maiden, see Benson and Cook 2001.

3. Spindler 1996.

4. Badone 1989, 161.

5. Rufus 1999, 161.

6. From *The Rubaiyat of Omar Khayyam*, in the nineteenth-century translation of Edward Fitzgerald, which brought the philosophy of an eleventh-century Persian mathematician and astronomer to modern readers. The Dover Thrift Edition (1990) will do nicely.

7. Barley 1995, 103.

8. Ibid.

9. Hose and McDougall 1912.

10. This quote and those that immediately follow in this discussion come from ibid., 20–22.

11. Rivers 1914.

12. Badone 1989.

13. Ibid., 135.

14. Ibid., 162.

15. Vulliamy [1926] 1996.

16. Ibid., 43.

17. Ibid.

18. Geary 1994; Kastenbaum 2002a; Williams 1980.

19. Turner 1992.

20. Richardson 1987, 72.

21. See Mary Shelley's *Frankenstein; Or, the Modern Prometheus* (original 1818). An additional source is Leonard Wolf's *The Annotated Frankenstein* (1977).

22. Richardson 1987, 102.

23. Ibid., 89.

24. Ibid., 134.

25. Quoted in ibid., 137.

26. Richardson 1987, 268.

27. Minois 1999; Murray 1998, 2000.

28. Lacey Smith 1997.

29. Murray 1998.

30. Lord Byron, quoted in Gates 1988, 6.

31. Gates 1988, 6.

32. Ibid.

33. See Michael Sappol's *A Traffic of Dead Bodies* (2002, 5–6).

34. Dr. Roy Glover, University of Michigan Medical School Web site.

35. See Dr. Douglas Ubelaker and Henry Scammell's *Bones: A Forensic Detective's Casebook* (1992).

CHAPTER SIX • ABUSING AND EATING THE DEAD

1. The Tohono O'odham have reclaimed their name after being known by mainstream society for many years as the Papago.

2. Kozak 1991, 213.

3. Ibid., 212.

4. Ibid., 212–213.

5. Kastenbaum, Peyton, and Kastenbaum 1977.

6. Moreman 2002.

7. Doebler and Warnicke 1986–1987, 311.

8. Kastenbaum 1967.

9. Orwell [1946] 2002, 1113.

10. Ibid.

11. Quoted in Janofsky 1979, 49.

12. Robinson 1992.

13. Iris Chang 1997.

14. See Desmond Seward's gift to history buffs, *The Monks of War* (1995).

15. See Bram Stoker's *Dracula* in Leonard Wolf's informative *The Annotated Dracula* (1975).

16. Seward 1995.

17. Ibid., 128.

18. Kastenbaum 2002a.

19. Driver 1998.

20. P. J. Clauer, n.d. (See what we've been missing by not reading the *Small Flock Factsheet!*)

21. Eliade 1978.

22. Ibid., 318.

23. Harris 1977, 187.

24. Bernadino de Sahagun, quoted in ibid., 292.

25. Harris 1977.

26. Ibid., 165.

27. Sanday 1986, 173.

28. Davíd Carrasco (1999) supports Sanday's general thesis and also gives particular attention to the role of violence in the Aztec worldview.

29. Arens 1979, 9.

30. Read 1974, 239.

31. Ibid., 238. See also accounts of the Donner Party's ordeal by G. R. Stewart (1992); and W. Mullen and W. Bagley (1997).

32. Eliade 1984, 342.

33. Reported by K. Chang (2000).

34. Gardner 1999.

35. Ibid.

36. Ibid.

37. Kopia Noma, quoted in Rumsey 1999, 108.

38. Turner and Turner 1999.

39. Swift [1729] 1984.

40. Ibid., 494.

41. Congwen, quoted in Yue 1999, 122.

42. Congwen 1984.

43. Yue 1999, 122.

44. Congwen, quoted in ibid., 123.

45. Ibid., 123.

46. Orwell [1946] 2002.

CHAPTER SEVEN • TOO MANY DEAD

1. See Gladwell's popular analysis of how/why things happen when they do: *The Tipping Point* (2002).

2. Quoted in Calvi's detailed examination of a plague visitation in Florence (1989, 72).

3. Ibid., 255.

4. This quote and the ones that immediately follow in this discussion all come from ibid., 237–238.

5. Ibid.

6. Porter 1999.

7. Twigg 1984, 207.

8. Thucydides (ca. 430), quoted in Twigg 1984, 31–32.

9. Ibid., 32.

10. Geoffrey of Monmouth, quoted in Twigg 1984, 40.

11. Tuchman 1978, 101.

12. Ibid., 93.

13. Ziegler 1991, 5.

14. Tuchman 1978, 98.

15. Calvi 1989, 34.

16. Boccaccio [1348–1353] 1955, xxiii–xxiv.

17. Weber 1971. Nothing quite like this collection of death oddments "in art, epigrams, and poetry."

18. Cohen 1989, 273.

19. Tuchman 1978, 114.

20. One of the more remarkable acts of forgiveness and reconciliation occurred in Mainz as its cathedral lay in ruins following Allied World War II bombing raids. Though mindful of the medieval burning of Jews in Mainz and of the far more extensive slaughter of the Holocaust, an aged Jewish artist agreed to design stained glass panels for the restored cathedral. Marc Chagall's radiant panels are pure amazement and inspiration in that ancient city where so much blood has been spilled in ignorance and rage.

21. Platt 1997, 104.

22. Boccaccio [1348–1353] 1955, xxviii.
23. Opie and Opie 1969.
24. Aries 1981, 116.
25. Meyer-Baer 1970.
26. Mooney 1996.
27. Gowen 1907, 2.
28. Ibid., 2–3.
29. Browne, quoted in Porter 1999, 94.
30. Evelyn, quoted in Platt 1997, 77.
31. Pepys, quoted in Porter 1999, 40.
32. Porter 1999, 60.
33. Kolata 2001.
34. Watts 1999, 17–18.
35. Marriott 2002; see also Marriott 2003.
36. Groom 2002.
37. Glazar 1995, 90.

CHAPTER EIGHT • DOWN TO EARTH AND UP IN FLAMES

1. Bliatout 1993; Hostetler 1993.
2. See Habenstein and Lamers 1974 for both the Guatemalan and the Church of England traditions.
3. E. G. James 1957.
4. Irion 1974.
5. Truitner and Truitner 1993.
6. Ling 1988, 24–25.
7. Reston 1998.
8. Kastenbaum, 7th edition, 2001; and 8th edition, 2004.
9. Reston 1998, 67–68.
10. Ibid., 68.
11. Irion 1974.
12. Ibid., 9–10.
13. Ibid., 11.
14. Browne [1658] 1977, 57.
15. National Conference of Catholic Bishops 1997.
16. Weinberger-Thomas 1999.
17. Chaudhari 1989.
18. Endo 1994, 144. The Japanese novelist offers a vivid description of contemporary cremation practices along the Ganges in India.
19. Quoted in Weinberger-Thomas 1999, 99–100.
20. Weinberger-Thomas 1999, 146–147.
21. Prothero 2001, 10.
22. Statistics in this and the preceding four paragraphs are from National Funeral Directors Association 2000.

23. Bryant 1972, 779–780 (poem was written in 1812). (Is there still a public school in which poems like this are memorized?)

24. Neumann 1974, 148–149.

25. Ibid., 149.

26. Westwood 2002.

27. See the eleventh-century work *The Rubaiyat of Omar Khayyam* (Khayyam 1990, 28).

28. Workman Publishing Company 2001. My resident orange cat occasionally knocks this calendar off the desk, possibly not appreciative of competition.

29. Rehm 1994.

30. Harper 1988.

31. Flipov 2001.

32. Loudon, quoted in Morley 1971, 48.

33. Warner 1965, 48.

34. Ibid., 280.

35. Ibid., 281.

36. Ibid., 282.

37. Wright and Hughes 1996.

38. Ibid., 53.

39. Ragon 1983.

40. Quoted in Walker [1839] 1977, 116–117.

41. Walker [1839] 1977, 168.

42. Bondeson 2001, 278.

43. Bondeson 2001.

44. Tenzin Gyatso, the Fourteenth Dalai Lama, 1985.

45. See Iserson 2001 for a review of current knowledge about postmortem physical changes.

46. Evans 1963.

47. See Stoker in Wolf 1975.

48. Eaves 1976.

49. McNally and Florescu 1972, 44.

50. Summers 1929.

51. Barber 1988, 195–196.

52. Bodio 2001.

53. Bliatout 1993.

54. Hostetler 1993; Kraybill 1989.

55. Grimes 2000.

56. Kastenbaum 2001.

CHAPTER NINE • JOURNEY OF THE DEAD

1. Laderman 1996, 36–37.

2. Euripides [5th century B.C.] 1993.

3. Choron 1973; Terpening 1984; Zandee [1960] 1977.

4. Landor 1982.

5. Garland 1985; Knight 1970.

6. Terpening 1984.

7. Coleridge [1816] 1972, 685–686.

8. McDannell and Lang 1988, 125.

9. Tibullus, quoted in ibid., 127.

10. Baumgartner 1999.

11. The most conspicuous example of a "love-death" in music drama occurs in Wagner's *Tristan und Isolde,* where the magnificently clueless lovers are finally united in rather than separated by death. The music is sublime, the message perhaps not all that encouraging.

12. William R. Smith [1930] 1996.

13. Ibid., 179.

14. Zaleski 1987.

15. Hornung 1999.

16. Ikram and Dodson 1998.

17. Bierlein 1994.

18. Ibid., 213.

19. In folklore and fiction, the doppelgänger is a double of the dominant and socially acceptable personality. The Mr. Hyde of Robert Louis Stevenson's Dr. Jekyll is one of the best-known examples. Edgar Allan Poe populated several of his stories with these shadowy and dangerous split-off selves. The early psychoanalysts, of course, feasted on this character.

20. Benét 2000.

21. Ikram and Dodson 1998, 18.

22. Hornung 1999, 52.

23. Eliade 1978; Zandee [1960] 1977.

24. Evans-Wentz [1927] 1960.

25. Agha 2002, 897.

26. Rinpoche 1992.

27. Tenzin Gyatso, the Fourteenth Dalai Lama, 1985.

28. Agha 2002.

29. Thurman 1994.

30. Agha 2002, 897.

31. Hanson 2002, 488.

32. Ibid.

33. Maeterlinck [1909] 1977, 38.

34. Kastenbaum 1996b.

35. Genz 1999.

36. Gennep [1909] 1960.

37. Ibid., 15.

38. Turner 1969, 96.

39. Wilson 1957.

40. Turner 1992.
41. Moody 1975, 11.
42. Greyson 1989.
43. Ring 1980.
44. Sabom 1982.
45. Zaleski 1987, 204.
46. Kastenbaum 2001.
47. Kastenbaum 1995b, 1998a, 1998b.
48. Wertheim 1999, 132–133.
49. Moravec 1988.
50. Wertheim 1999, 21.
51. Spierenburg 1991, 1275.

CHAPTER TEN • LIVING THROUGH

1. This and the following related quotes are from Sacks (1998, 29–30).
2. Freud [1920] 1959. In *The Psychology of Death* (3rd edition, 2000), I've devoted a chapter to evaluating death instinct theory in its own time and ours.
3. Matthias Claudius's lyric is most readily found with recordings of Schubert's famous musical setting (*Der Tod und das Mädchen*, D. 531). A benchmark recording is that by Dietrich Fischer-Dieskau (EMI 2-CD collection CMS 7 6566 2). (Classical recordings often become unavailable because of near chaos in the industry, but Schubert's song can almost always be found in somebody's version.)
4. Novalis, in Kaufmann 1976, 233.
5. Swinburne 1999, 163.
6. Swinburne 1972, 963.
7. Keats [1819] 1972, 769.
8. Schiffman 1982.
9. James [1894] 1950.
10. Hilts 1995, 224–225.
11. Ibid., 221.
12. Ibid., 225.
13. Ibid.
14. Ibid.
15. Freud [1913] 1953, 304–305.
16. Ibid., 305.
17. Significant contributions include Dennett 1991; Penrose 1994; and Restak 1994. A more holistic and, to my mind, even a more heuristic approach is taken by Damasio (1994, 1999).
18. Kurt Goldstein ([1934] 1959) was well ahead of his time in exploring the relationships between basic neurological function and real-life behavior.
19. This is a little test of the copyeditor's sense of humor, and it could, therefore, be a big mistake on my part. (This just in—copyeditor has a sense of humor! There goes another stereotype!)

20. Lorand 1912.

21. I follow the quest for eternal youth through many of its turnings and twist-ings from ancient times to our own in *Dorian, Graying* (1995).

22. Lawton 2000.

23. SUPPORT 1995.

24. Kaplan 2000.

25. Staton, Shuy, and Byock 2001.

26. Sagan 1997.

27. Maslow 1968.

28. Grimes 2000, 280.

29. Tolstoi's *The Death of Ivan Ilych* ([1886] 1960) is as timely now as it was when written.

30. Thomas 2001, 122.

31. Ibid., 124.

32. Ibid.

33. Ibid., 125.

34. Crissman 1994.

35. Sulmasy and Rahn 2001.

SOURCES CITED

Agha, Asif. 2002. Tibetan book of the dead. In R. Kastenbaum, ed., *Macmillan encyclopedia of death and dying*. Vol. 1. New York: Macmillan.

Ahrensdorf, P. J. 1995. *The death of Socrates and the life of philosophy*. Albany: State University of New York Press.

Ainsworth, Mary D. 1973. The development of infant-mother attachment. In B. Caldwell and H. Ricciuti, eds., *Review of child development research*. Vol. 3. Chicago: University of Chicago Press.

Anthony, Sylvia. [1949] 1972. *The discovery of death in childhood and after*. New York: Basic Books.

Arens, William. 1979. *The man-eating myth: Anthropology and anthropophagy*. New York: Oxford University Press.

Aries, Philippe. 1981. *The hour of our death*. New York: Alfred A. Knopf.

Badone, Ellen. 1989. *The appointed hour: Death, worldview, and social change in Brittany*. Berkeley: University of California Press.

Barber, Paul. 1988. *Vampires, burial, and death*. New Haven: Yale University Press.

Barley, Nigel. 1995. *Dancing on the grave*. London: John Murray.

Baumgartner, Frederic J. 1999. *Longing for the end: A history of millennialism in Western civilization*. New York: St. Martin's Press.

Benét, Stephen Vincent. 2000. *The devil and Daniel Webster, and other writings*. New York: Penguin Classics.

Benson, Elizabeth P., and Anita G. Cook. 2001. *Ritual sacrifice in ancient Peru: New discoveries and interpretations*. Austin: University of Texas Press.

Bernstein, Alan E. 1993. *The formation of hell: Death and retribution in the ancient and early Christian worlds*. Ithaca, N.Y.: Cornell University Press.

Bierlein, J. F. 1994. *Parallel myths*. New York: Ballentine Wellstone.

Binski, Paul. 1996. *Medieval death*. Ithaca, N.Y.: Cornell University Press.

Bland, Olivia. 1986. *The royal way of death*. London: Constable.

Bliatout, B. T. 1993. Hmong death customs: Traditional and acculturated. In Donald P. Irish, Kathleen F. Lundquist, and Vivian Jenkins Nelsen, eds., *Ethnic variations in dying, death, and grief*. Washington, D.C.: Taylor & Francis.

Boccaccio, Giovanni. [1348–1353] 1955. *The decameron*. Translated by Frances Winwar. New York: Modern Library.

Bodio, Stephen. 2001. India's disappearing vultures. *Atlantic Monthly* 288, no. 2, September.

Bondeson, Jan. 2001. *Buried alive*. New York: W. W. Norton.

Bowers, M. N., E. N. Jackson, J. A. Knight, and L. LeShan. 1982. *Counseling the dying*. New York: Nelson.

Brickhouse, T. C., and N. Smith. 1994. *Plato's Socrates*. New York: Oxford University Press.

Brown, Raymond E. 1998. *The death of the Messiah*. 2 vols. New York: Doubleday.

———. 1999. *The birth of the Messiah*. Updated edition. New York: Doubleday.

Browne, Thomas. [1658] 1977. *Hydriotaphia, or a discourse of the sepulchrall urnes lately found in Norfolk*. New York: Arno.

Bryant, William Cullen. 1972. Thanatopsis. In Louis Untermeyer, ed., *A treasury of great poems*. New York: Simon & Schuster.

Calvi, G. 1989. *Histories of a plague year*. Berkeley: University of California Press.

Carrasco, Davíd. 1999. *City of sacrifice: The Aztec Empire and the role of violence in civilization*. Boston: Beacon Press.

Chang, Iris. 1997. *The rape of Nanking*. New York: Basic Books.

Chang, K. 2000. Remains of a grisly meal. ABC News Science. www.ABCNEWS.com/ Magellan Geographic, September 30.

Chaudhari, Joyotpaul. 1989. Suttee (Sati). In R. Kastenbaum and B. Kastenbaum, eds., *The encyclopedia of death*. Phoenix: Oryx.

Choron, Jacques. 1973. *Death and Western thought*. New York: Macmillan.

Clark, David. 2002a. Hospice in historical perspective. In Robert Kastenbaum, ed., *Macmillan encyclopedia of death and dying*. Vol. 1. New York: Macmillan.

———. 2002b. Saunders, Cicely. In Robert Kastenbaum, ed., *Macmillan encyclopedia of death and dying*. Vol. 2. New York: Macmillan.

Clauer, Phillip J. n.d. Cannibalism: Prevention and treatment. *Small Flock Factsheet, Number 32*. Virginia Cooperative Extension. www.ext.vt.edu.

Cohen, Kathleen. 1989. Tombs. In R. Kastenbaum and B. Kastenbaum, eds., *Encyclopedia of death*. Phoenix: Arno.

Cole, Thomas R. 1992. *The journey of life*. Cambridge: Cambridge University Press.

Coleridge, Samuel Taylor. [1798] 1970. *The rime of the ancient mariner*. New York: Dover.

———. [1816] 1972. Kubla Khan. In Louis Untermeyer, ed., *A treasury of great poems*. New York: Simon & Schuster.

Comper, Frances M. M., ed. [1917] 1977. *The book of the craft of dying and other early English tracts concerning death*. New York: Arno.

Congwen, S. 1984. *Shen Congwen wenji* (Selected writings by Shen Congwen). Ed. Shao Huaqiang and Ling Yu. 12 vols. Hong Kong and Guangzhou: Sanlian Shudian.

Counts, David. 1977. The good death in Kaliai: Preparations for death in western New Britain. In Richard A. Kalish, ed., *Death and dying: Views from many cultures*. Farmingdale, N.Y.: Baywood.

Counts, Dorothy Ayers, and David Counts. 1985. *Aging and its transformations: Moving toward death in Pacific societies*. Lanham, Md.: University Press of America.

Crissman, James K. 1994. *Death and dying in central Appalachia: Changing attitudes and practices.* Urbana: University of Illinois Press.

Damasio, Antonio R. 1994. *Descartes' error: Emotion, reason, and the human brain.* New York: G. P. Putnam.

———. 1999. *The feeling of what happens: Body and emotion in the making of consciousness.* New York: Harcourt Brace.

Davis-Floyd, Robbie E. 1992. *Birth as an American rite of passage.* Berkeley: University of California Press.

Dennett, Daniel C. 1991. *Consciousness explained.* Boston: Little, Brown.

Denton, Derek. 1982. *The hunger for salt.* New York: Springer-Verlag.

De Wilde, Peter M. 1999. Between life and death: The journey in the Otherworld. In E. E. DuBruck and B. I. Gusick, eds., *Death and dying in the Middle Ages.* New York: Peter Lang.

Doebler, B. A., and R. M. Warnicke. 1986–1987. Sex discrimination after death: A seventeenth-century English study. *Omega, Journal of Death and Dying* 17: 309–320.

Donne, John. [1624] 1975. *Devotions.* Ann Arbor: University of Michigan Press.

Driver, Tom F. 1998. *Liberating rites: Understanding the transformative power of ritual.* Boulder, Colo.: Westview Press.

Duclow, Donald F. 1999. Dying well: The Ars moriendi and the dormition of the Virgin. In Edelgard E. DuBruck and Barbara I. Gusick, eds., *Death and dying in the Middle Ages.* New York: Peter Lang.

Durkheim, Émile. 1951. *Suicide.* New York: Free Press.

———. 1965. *The elementary forms of the religious life.* New York: Free Press.

Eaves, O. A. 1976. Modern vampirism: Its dangers, and how to avoid them. In J. L. Perkowski, ed., *Vampires of the Slavs.* Cambridge: MAL Slavic.

Eliade, Mircea. 1978. *The sacred and the profane: The nature of religion.* Chicago: University of Chicago Press.

———. 1984. *A history of religious ideas.* Vol. 2. Chicago: University of Chicago Press.

Endo, Shusaku. 1994. *Deep river.* New York: New Directions.

Euripides. [5th century B.C.] 1993. *Alcestis.* London: Oxford University Press.

Evans-Wentz, W. Y. [1927] 1960. *The Tibetan book of the dead.* New York: Oxford University Press.

Flipov, David. 2001. Deceased civilians becoming valuable in Chechen conflict. *Arizona Republic,* June 30.

Frazer, J. G. [1933] 1966. *The fear of the dead in primitive religion.* New York: Biblo & Tannen.

Freud, Sigmund. [1900] 1955. *The interpretation of dreams.* New York: Basic Books.

———. [1913] 1953. Thoughts for the times on war and death. In *Collected works.* Vol. 4. London: Hogarth Press.

———. [1920] 1959. *Beyond the pleasure principle.* New York: W. W. Norton.

Gardner, Don. 1999. Anthropophagy, myth, and the subtle ways of ethnocentrism. In L. R. Goldman, ed., *The anthropology of cannibalism.* Westport, Conn.: Bergin & Garvey.

Garland, R. 1985. *The Greek way of death*. Ithaca, N.Y.: Cornell University Press.

Gates, Barbara T. 1988. *Victorian suicide, mad crones, and sad histories*. Princeton, N.J.: Princeton University Press.

Geary, Patrick J. 1994. *Living with the dead in the Middle Ages*. Ithaca, N.Y.: Cornell University Press.

Gennep, Arnold van. [1909] 1960. *The rites of passage*. Chicago: University of Chicago Press.

Genz, Henning. 1999. *Nothingness: The science of empty space*. Reading, Mass.: Helix/Perseus.

Gladwell, Malcolm. 2002. *The tipping point: How little things can make a big difference*. Boston: Back Bay.

Glaser, Barney G., and Anselm Strauss. 1968. *Time for dying*. Chicago: Aldine.

Glazar, Richard. 1995. *Trap with a green fence: Survival in Treblinka*. Chicago: Northwestern University Press.

Glover, Roy. n.d. Plastination Laboratory. www.med.umich.edu/anatomy/plastinate. Accessed in 2002.

Goethe, Johann Wolfgang von. [1774] 1990. *The sorrows of young Werther*. New York: Vintage.

Goldstein, Kurt. [1934] 1959. *The organism: A holistic approach to biology derived from pathological data in man*. New York: American Book.

Goodrich, Thomas. 1998. *War to the knife: Bleeding Kansas 1854–1866*. Mechanicsburg, Pa.: Stackpole.

Gowen, B. S. 1907. Some aspects of pestilences and other epidemics. *American Journal of Psychology* 18: 1–60.

Greyson, Bruce B. 1989. The near-death experience scale. In R. Kastenbaum and B. K. Kastenbaum, eds., *Encyclopedia of death and dying*. Phoenix: Arno.

Grimes, Ronald L. 2000. *Deeply into the bone: Re-inventing rites of passage*. Berkeley: University of California Press.

Groom, Winston. 2002. *A storm in Flanders: The Ypres salient, 1917–1918: Tragedy and triumph on the western front*. New York: Atlantic Monthly Press.

Guidera, Christine. 1999. The role of the Beguines in caring for the ill, the dying, and the dead. In Edelgard E. DuBruck and Barbara J. Gusick, eds., *Death and dying in the Middle Ages*. New York: Peter Lang.

Gyatso, Tenzin, the Fourteenth Dalai Lama. 1985. *Kindness, clarity, and insight*. Ithaca, N.Y.: Snow Lion.

Habenstein, Robert W., and William M. Lamers. 1974. *Funeral customs the world over*. 3rd edition. Milwaukee: National Funeral Directors Association.

Hanson, Hamza Yusuf. 2002. Islam. In R. Kastenbaum, ed., *Macmillan encyclopedia of death and dying*. Vol. 1. New York: Macmillan.

Harmer, Ruth M. 1963. *The high cost of dying*. New York: Crowell-Collier.

Harper, Kenn. 1988. *Give me my father's body: The life of Minik, the New York Eskimo*. Iqualuit, Frobisher Bay: NWT.

Harris, Marvin. 1977. *Cannibals and kings*. New York: Vintage.

Herlihy, David. 1997. *The Black Death and the transformation of the West*. Cambridge, Mass.: Harvard University Press.

Hilts, Philip J. 1995. *Memory's ghost.* New York: Simon & Schuster.

Hoban, Russell. 1973. *Kleinzeit.* London: David Higham.

Hornung, Erik. 1999. *The ancient Egyptian books of the afterlife.* Translated by David Lorton. Ithaca, N.Y.: Cornell University Press.

Hose, Charles, and William McDougall. 1912. *The pagan tribes of Borneo.* London: Macmillan and Co.

Hostetler, John A. 1993. *Amish society.* 4th edition. Baltimore: Johns Hopkins University Press.

Ikram, S., and A. Dodson. 1998. *The mummy in ancient Egypt.* London: Thames & Hudson.

Irion, Paul E. 1974. *Cremation.* Philadelphia: Fortress Press.

Iserson, Kenneth V. 2001. *Death to dust.* 2nd edition. Tucson, Ariz.: Galen Press.

James, E. G. 1957. *Prehistoric religion.* London: Thames & Hudson.

James, William. [1894] 1950. *The principles of psychology.* New York: Dover.

Janofsky, Karl. 1979. Public execution in England in the late Middle Ages: The indignity and dignity of death. *Omega, Journal of Death and Dying* 10: 433–458.

Kantner, J. 1999. Anasazi mutilation and cannibalism in the American Southwest. In Laurence R. Goldman, ed., *The anthropology of cannibalism.* Westport, Conn.: Bergin & Garvey.

Kaplan, Kalman J., ed. 2000. *Right to die versus sacredness of life.* New York: Baywood.

Kastenbaum, Robert. 1964. The reluctant therapist. In R. Kastenbaum, ed., *New thoughts on old age.* New York: Springer.

———. 1967. Multiple perspectives on a geriatric "Death Valley." *Community Mental Health Journal* 3: 21–26.

———. 1975. Toward standards of care for the terminally ill, Part 2: What standards exist today? *Omega, Journal of Death and Dying* 6: 289–290.

———. 1979. "Healthy dying": A paradoxical quest continues. *Journal of Social Issues* 35: 185–206.

———. 1995a. *Dorian, graying: Is youth the only thing worth having?* New York: Baywood.

———. 1995b. *Is there life after death?* London: Prion.

———. 1996a. The cave at the end of the world: How the unknowing studied the unknowable. In Matthew R. Merrens and Gary C. Brannigan, eds., *The developmental psychologists: Research adventures across the life span,* 289–310. New York: McGraw-Hill.

———. 1996b. A world without death? First and second thoughts. *Mortality* 1 (1996): 113–123.

———. 1998a. Near-death reports: Evidence for survival of death? In L. W. Bailey and J. Yates, eds., *The near-death experience reader.* New York: Routledge.

———. 1998b. Temporarily dead. *Readings* 13: 16–21.

———. 2000a. Dr. Paleg's skull: On the geropsychologizing of Robert Kastenbaum. In J. E. Birren and J. J. F. Schroots, eds., *A history of geropsychology in autobiography,* 143–156. Washington, D.C.: American Psychological Association.

———. 2000b. Looking death in the eye: Another challenge from Doctor Kevorkian. *Omega, Journal of Death and Dying* 40: 279–286.

———. 2000c. *The psychology of death.* 3rd edition. New York: Springer.

———. 2001. *Death, society, and human experience.* 7th edition. Boston: Allyn & Bacon.

———. 2002a. Saints, preserved. In R. Kastenbaum, ed., *Macmillan encyclopedia of death and dying.* Vol. 2. New York: Macmillan.

———. 2002b. Seven deadly sins. In R. Kastenbaum, ed., *Macmillan encyclopedia of death and dying.* Vol. 1. New York: Macmillan.

———. 2003. Is death the spice of life? *Illness, Crisis & Loss* 11: 74–89.

———. 2004. *Death, society, and human experience.* 8th edition. Boston: Allyn & Bacon.

Kastenbaum, Robert, and Claudia Normand. 1990. Deathbed scenes as expected by the young and experienced by the old. *Death Studies* 14: 201–218.

Kastenbaum, Robert, Sara Peyton, and Beatrice Kastenbaum. 1977. Sex discrimination after death. *Omega, Journal of Death and Dying* 7: 351–359.

Kastenbaum, R., Theodore X. Barber, S. G. Wilson, B. L. Ryder, and L. B. Hathaway. 1981. *Old, sick, and helpless: Where therapy begins.* Cambridge, Mass.: Ballinger.

Kaufmann, Walter. 1976. *Existentialism, religion, and death.* New York: New American Library.

Keats, John. [1819] 1972. Ode to a nightingale. In Louis Untermeyer, ed., *A treasury of great poems.* New York: Simon & Schuster.

Keenan, William J. K. 1997. Death figures in religious life and components of Marist death culture. *Mortality* 3: 7–26.

Kellehear, Allan. 1990. *Dying of cancer: The final year of life.* London: Harwood.

Kevorkian, Jack. 1957. Rapid and accurate ophthalmoscopic determination of circulatory arrest. *Journal of the American Medical Association* 164: 1660–1662.

———. 1961. The eye in death. *CIBA Clinical Symposia* 13: 51–62.

Khayyam, Omar. [1859] 1990. *The rubaiyat of Omar Khayyam.* Translated by Edward Fitzgerald. New York: Dover.

Knight, W. J. Elysion. 1970. *On ancient Greek and Roman beliefs concerning a life after death.* London: Routledge and Kegan Paul.

Kolata, Gina Bari. 2001. *Flu: The story of the great influenza epidemic of 1918.* New York: Touchstone.

Kozak, David. 1991. Dying badly: Violent death and religious change among the Tohono O'odham. *Omega, Journal of Death and Dying* 23: 207–216.

Kraybill, Donald B. 1989. *The riddle of Amish culture.* Baltimore: Johns Hopkins University Press.

Kübler-Ross, Elisabeth. 1969. *On death and dying.* New York: Macmillan.

Laderman, Gary. 1996. *The sacred remains: American attitudes toward death, 1799–1883.* Ithaca, N.Y.: Cornell University Press.

Landor, William Savage. 1982. *Selected poetry and prose.* London: Carcanet Press.

Lawton, Julia. 2000. *The dying process: Patients' experiences of palliative care.* London: Routledge.

Leslie, John. 1996. *The end of the world.* London: Routledge.

Leviton, Daniel. 1991. *Horrendous death, health, and well-being.* New York: Hemisphere.

Ling, T. O. 1988. *A dictionary of Buddhism.* New York: Charles S. Scribner's Sons.

Lock, Margaret. 2002. *Twice dead: Organ transplants and the reinvention of death.* Berkeley: University of California Press.

Lorand, Arnold. 1912. *Old age deferred.* Philadelphia: F. A. Davis.

Loudon, J. C. 1843. *On the lay out, planting and managing of cemeteries and on the improvement of churchyards.* London: Sign of the Gun.

McDannell, Colleen, and Bernhard Lang. 1988. *Heaven: A history.* New Haven, Conn.: Yale University Press.

McManners, John D. 1981. *Death and the enlightenment: Changing attitudes to death in eighteenth-century France.* New York: Oxford University Press.

McNally, R. T., and R. Florescu. 1972. *In search of Dracula.* Greenwich, Conn.: New York Graphic Society.

Maeterlinck, Maurice. [1909] 1977. *Before the great silence.* New York: Arno.

Marriott, Edward. 2002. *The lost tribe: A harrowing passage into New Guinea's heart of darkness.* New York: Henry Holt.

———. 2003. *Plague: A story of science, rivalry, and the scourge that won't go away.* New York: Metropolitan Books.

Maslow, Abraham H. 1968. *Toward a psychology of being.* New York: Van Nostrand Reinhold.

Meyer-Baer, Kathi. 1970. *Music of the spheres and the dance of death.* Princeton, N.J.: Princeton University Press.

Middleton, John. 1996. Lugbara death. In M. Block and J. Parry, eds., *Death and the regeneration of life.* Cambridge: Cambridge University Press.

Minois, Georges. 1999. *History of suicide: Voluntary death in Western culture.* Baltimore: Johns Hopkins University Press.

Mitford, Jessica. 1963. *The American way of death.* New York: Simon & Schuster.

Moody, Raymond A. 1975. *Life after life.* Atlanta: Mockingbird.

Mooney, John. 1996. *The ghost dance.* North Dighton, Mass.: JG Press.

Mor, Vincent, David S. Greer, and Robert Kastenbaum, eds. 1988. *The hospice experiment.* Baltimore: Johns Hopkins University Press.

Moravec, Hans. 1988. *Mind children: The future of robot and human intelligence.* Cambridge, Mass.: Harvard University Press.

Moreman, Robin. 2002. Gender discrimination after death. In R. Kastenbaum, ed., *Macmillan encyclopedia of death and dying.* Vol. 1. New York: Macmillan.

Morley, John. 1971. *Death, heaven, and the Victorians.* Pittsburgh: Pittsburgh University Press.

Mount, Balfour. 1997. The Royal Victoria Hospital Palliative Care Service: A Canadian experience. In Cicely Saunders and Robert Kastenbaum, eds., *Hospice care on the international scene.* New York: Springer.

Mullen, W., and W. Bagley. 1997. *The Donner Party chronicle: Account of the Dover wagon train 1846–1847.* Lincoln: Nebraska Humanities Committee.

Murray, Alexander. 1998. *Suicide in the Middle Ages.* Vol. 1: *The violent against themselves.* New York: Oxford University Press.

————. 2000. *Suicide in the Middle Ages.* Vol. 2: *The curse on self-murder.* New York: Oxford University Press.

Nagy, Maria H. [1949] 1959. The child's theories concerning death. In Herman Feifel, ed., *The meaning of death.* New York: McGraw-Hill.

National Conference of Catholic Bishops. 1997. Indult on cremation. www.nccbuscc .org/liturgy/current/cremation.htm.

National Funeral Directors Association. 2000. U.S. cremation statistics. www .nfda.org.

Neumann, Erich. 1974. *The great mother: An analysis of the stereotype.* Princeton, N.J.: Princeton University Press.

Nuland, Sherwin B. 1994. *How we die.* New York: Alfred A. Knopf.

Ober, William B. 1985. Did Socrates die of hemlock poisoning? In W. B. Ober, *Boswell's clap and other essays: Medical analysis of literary afflictions.* New York: Harper & Row.

Opie, I., and R. Opie. 1969. *Children's games in street and playground.* London: Oxford University Press.

Orwell, George. [1933] 1983. *Down and out in Paris and London.* San Diego: Harvest.

————. [1946] 2002. How the poor die. In Orwell, *Essays.* New York: Alfred A. Knopf: Everyman's Library.

————. [1949] 1990. *1984.* New York: New American Library.

Paxton, Frederick S. 1990. *Christianizing death: The creation of a ritual process in early medieval Europe.* Ithaca, N.Y.: Cornell University Press.

Penrose, Roger. 1994. *Shadows of the mind.* Oxford: Oxford University Press.

Plato. 1942. *Phaedo.* In Plato, *Five great dialogues.* New York: Walter J. Black.

Platt, Colin. 1997. *King Death: The Black Death and its aftermath in late-medieval England.* Toronto: University of Toronto Press.

Porter, S. 1999. *The great plague.* London: Sutton.

Preston, Richard. 2002. *The demon in the freezer.* New York: Random House.

Prigerson, Holly G., and Selby C. Jacobs. 2001. Traumatic grief as a distinct disorder: a rationale, consensus criteria, and a preliminary empirical test. In Margaret S. Stroebe, Robert O. Hansson, Wolfgang Stroebe, and Henk Schut, eds., *Handbook of bereavement research.* Washington, D.C.: American Psychological Association.

Prothero, Stephen. 2001. *Purified by fire: A history of cremation in America.* Berkeley: University of California Press.

Quigley, Christine. 1996. *The corpse: A history.* Jefferson, N.C.: McFarland.

Ragon, Michel. 1983. *The space of death.* Charlottesville: University of Virginia Press.

Read, Piers Paul. 1974. *Alive: The story of the Andes survivors.* New York: Avon.

Rees, Martin. 1997. *Before the beginning.* Reading, Mass.: Helix/Perseus.

Rehm, Rush. 1994. *Marriage to death: The conflation of wedding and funeral rituals in Greek tragedy.* Princeton, N.J.: Princeton University Press.

Restak, Richard M. 1994. *The modular brain.* New York: Charles Scribner's Sons.

Reston, James, Jr. 1998. *The last apocalypse: Europe at the year 1000.* New York: Doubleday.

Richardson, Ruth. 1987. *Death, dissection, and the destitute*. London: Routledge & Kegan Paul.

Ring, Kenneth. 1980. *Life at death*. New York: Coward, McCann, and Geoghegan.

Rinpoche, Sogyal. 1992. *The Tibetan book of living and dying: Revised and updated edition*. San Francisco: HarperSanFrancisco.

Rivers, William H. R. 1914. *The history of Melanesian society*. 2 vols. Cambridge: Cambridge University Press.

Robinson, John J. 1992. *Dungeon, fire and sword*. New York: M. Evans.

Rufus, Anneli. 1999. *Magnificent corpses*. New York: Marlowe & Company.

Rumsey, Alan. 1999. The white man as cannibal in the New Guinea Highlands. In Laurence R. Goldman, ed., *The anthropology of cannibalism*. Westport, Conn.: Bergin & Garvey.

Sabom, Michael B. 1982. *Recollections of death*. New York: Simon & Schuster.

Sacks, Oliver W. 1998. *A leg to stand on*. New York: Touchstone.

———. 1999. *Awakenings*. New York: Vintage.

Sagan, Carl. 1997. *Billions and billions: Thoughts on life and death at the brink of the millennium*. New York: Ballantine.

Sanday, Peggy Reeves. 1986. *Divine hunger: Cannibalism as a cultural system*. Cambridge: Cambridge University Press.

Sappol, Michael. 2002. *A traffic of dead bodies*. Princeton, N.J.: Princeton University Press.

Schiffman, Harold R. 1982. *Sensation and perception: An integrated approach*. New York: Wiley.

Seligman, Martin. 1975. *Hopelessness: On depression, development, and death*. San Francisco: Freeman.

Selye, Hans. 1976. *Stress in health and disease*. Toronto: Butterworth.

———. 1978. *The stress of life*. New York: McGraw-Hill.

Seward, Desmond. 1995. *The monks of war*. London: Penguin.

Shelley, Mary. [1818] 1977. *Frankenstein; or, the new Prometheus*. In Leonard Wolf, ed., *The annotated Frankenstein*. New York: Clarkson N. Potter.

Smith, Lacey. 1997. *Fools, martyrs, traitors: The story of martyrdom in the Western world*. New York: Alfred A. Knopf.

Smith, William R. [1930] 1996. *Aborigine myths and legends*. New York: Dover.

Spierenburg, Pieter. 1991. *The broken spell: A cultural and anthropological history of preindustrial Europe*. New Brunswick, N.J.: Rutgers University Press.

Spindler, Konrad. 1994. *The man in the ice*. New York: Crown.

———. 1996. *Human mummies*. New York: Springer.

Stannard, David E. 1977. *The Puritan way of death*. New York: Oxford University Press.

Staton, Jana, Roger Shuy, and Ira Byock. 2001. *A few months to live: Different paths to life's end*. Washington, D.C.: Georgetown University Press.

Stevenson, James. 1978. *The catacombs: Life and death in early Christianity*. Nashville, Tenn.: Thomas Nelson.

Stewart, G. R. 1992. *Ordeal by hunger: The story of the Donner Party*. Boston: Houghton Mifflin.

Stoker, Bram. [1897] 1975. *Dracula*. In Leonard Wolf, ed., *The annotated Dracula*. New York: Clarkson N. Potter.

Stone, Irving. 1988. *The trial of Socrates*. Boston: Little, Brown.

Sudnow, David. 1967. *Passing on: The social organization of dying*. Englewood Cliffs, N.J.: Prentice-Hall.

Sulmasy, Daniel P., and Maike Rahn. 2001. I was sick and you came to visit me: Time spent at the bedsides of seriously ill patients with poor prognoses. *American Journal of Medicine* 111: 385–389.

Summers, Montague. 1929. *The vampire: It is kith and kin*. New York: E. P. Dutton.

SUPPORT (Study to Understand Prognoses and Preferences for Outcomes and Risks of Treatment). 1995. A controlled trial to improve care for seriously ill hospital patients. *Journal of the American Medical Association* 274: 1591–1599.

Swift, Jonathan. [1729] 1984. A modest proposal for preventing the children of poor people from being a burden to their parents or the country, and for making them beneficial to the public. In A. Ross and D. Woolley, eds., *Jonathan Swift*. Oxford: Oxford University Press.

Swinburne, Charles Algernon. 1972. The garden of Proserpine. In Louis Untermeyer, ed., *A treasury of great poems*. New York: Simon & Schuster.

———. 1999. *Works of Charles Algernon Swinburne*. Boston: Wordsworth.

Taylor, Jeremy. [1651] 1977. *The rules and exercises of holy dying*. New York: Arno.

Terpening, Ronnie H. 1984. *Charon and the crossing*. Lewisburg, Pa.: Bucknell University Press.

Thomas, L. Eugene. 2001. Personal reflections on terminal illness after twenty years of teaching a death and dying course. *Omega, Journal of Death and Dying* 43: 119–128.

Tolstoi, Leon. [1886] 1960. *The death of Ivan Ilych*. Translated by Maude Aylmes. New York: New American Library.

Truitner, Ken, and Nga Truitner. 1993. Death and dying in Buddhism. In Donald P. Irish, Kathleen F. Lundquist, and Vivian Jenkins Nelson, eds., *Ethnic variations in dying, death, and grief*. Washington, D.C.: Taylor & Francis.

Tuchman, Barbara W. 1978. *A distant mirror: The calamitous 14th century*. New York: Alfred A. Knopf.

Turner, C. G., and J. A. Turner. 1999. *Man corn: Cannibalism and violence in the American Southwest and Mexico*. Salt Lake City: University of Utah Press.

Turner, Victor. 1969. *The ritual process: Structure and anti-structure*. Chicago: Aldine.

———. 1992. Death and the dead in the pilgrimage process. In Edith Turner, ed., *Blazing the trail: Way marks in the exploration of symbols*. Tucson, Ariz.: University of Arizona Press.

Twigg, Graham. 1984. *The Black Death: A biological reappraisal*. London: Batsford Academi & Educational.

Ubelaker, Douglas, and Henry Scammell. 1992. *Bones: A forensic detective's casebook*. New York: M. Evans.

Vorgaine, J. de. 1993. The assumption of the Blessed Virgin Mary. In W. G. Ryan, ed., *The golden legend*. Vol. 2. Princeton, N.J.: Princeton University Press.

Vulliamy, C. E. [1926] 1996. *Immortality: Funerary rites and customs*. London: Senate.

Walker, George A. [1839] 1977. *Gatherings from graveyards particularly those of London*. New York: Arno.

Warner, W. Lloyd. 1965. *The living and the dead: A study of the symbolic life of Americans*. New Haven, Conn.: Yale University Press.

Warton, John. 1826. *Death-bed scenes*. Vols. 1–3. London: John Murray, Albemarle Street.

Watts, Sheldon. 1999. *Epidemics and history: Disease, power, and imperialism*. New Haven, Conn.: Yale University Press.

Waugh, Evelyn. 1948. *The loved one*. Boston: Little, Brown.

Weber, Frederick Parkes. [1910] 1971. *Aspects of death and correlated aspects of life in art, epigram and poetry*. College Park, Md.: McGrath.

Weinberger-Thomas, Catherine. 1999. *Ashes of immortality: Widow-burning in India*. Chicago: University of Chicago Press.

Weisman, Avery D. 1972. *On dying and denying: A psychiatric study of terminality*. New York: Behavioral Publications.

———. 1974. *The realization of death*. New York: Jason Aronson.

Wertheim, Margaret. 1999. *The pearly gates of cyberspace*. New York: W. W. Norton.

Westwood, Jennifer. 2002. Gods and goddesses of death. In R. Kastenbaum, ed., *Macmillan encyclopedia of death and dying*. Vol. 1. New York: Macmillan.

Whiter, Walter. [1819] 1977. *A dissertation on the disorder of death*. New York: Arno.

Williams, Caroline. 1980. *Saints: Their cults and origins*. New York: St. Martin's Press.

Wilson, Monica. 1957. *Rituals of kinship among the Nyakysa*. London: Oxford University Press.

Wolf, Leonard, ed. 1975. *The annotated Dracula*. New York: Clarkson N. Potter.

Workman Publishing Company. 2001. *Page-a-day cat calendar, 2001*. New York: Workman.

Wright, Roberta Hughes, and Wilbur B. Hughes. 1996. *Lay down body: Living history in African American cemeteries*. Detroit: Invisible Ink.

Yue, Gang. 1999. *The mouth that begs: Hunger, cannibalism, and the politics of eating in modern China*. Durham, N.C.: Duke University Press.

Zaleski, Carol. 1987. *Otherworld journeys*. New York: Oxford University Press.

Zandee, J. [1960] 1977. *Death as an enemy*. New York: Arno.

Ziegler, Philip. 1991. *The Black Death*. London: Alan Sutton.

INDEX

Page numbers in italics indicate figures.

abolitionists, attacks on, 195
aborigines. *See* Native Australians
Absalom, 130
abusing and eating the dead, 176–217
Africa, 141, 154, 168, 368, 397
African Americans, 279, 293–94
afterlife, 134, 373
the aged (elderly; old people), 43–44,
  48–49, 102–3, 106, 115–16, 121, 126,
  134, 184–88, 309, 381, 383–86, *385*,
  398; therapists as reluctant to treat,
  418*n6*
aging, premature, 398
Ahitophel (biblical king; 2 Sam. 17), 130
Ahrensdorf, Peter J., 55
Ainsworth, Mary D., 416*n2*
air pollution, in London, 251–52
akh (Egyptian spirit shaped by one's life),
  332–33
akua (Lugbara concept; the home, village
  compound), 45
Algonquian people, 153
algor mortis, 302. *See also* postmortem
  changes
Allah, 341
Allen, Woody, 327
the Almighty, 84
Alph (sacred river), 320
alphabetical dying, 181
altered states of consciousness, 327, 367
ambivalence, death temptation and, 365
The American Way of Death (Mitford),
  114, 419*n20*
amve (Lugbara concept; the outside,
  literally "in the grass"), 45

Anasazi people, 214
anatomists, 161
Anatomy Act (Britain), 162, 164
Angel of Death, 22, 266
angels, 63, 73–74, 76, 78; Islamic, 341,
  362
anger, infernal punishment for sin of, 76
Animal Farm (Orwell), 48
Anthony, Sylvia, 416*n1*
anthrax, 258, 308, 380
anthropologists, 139, 144, 177, 205, 206,
  214, 282, 311, 340, 344–45
anthropophagy, 210–11. *See also*
  cannibalism
anxiety: attacks, 403–4; ritual and,
  95–97
Apocalypse, 78
Apollo, 266
Appalachia, death customs in, 412
appropriate death, 88
Aquinas, St. Thomas, 169
Arapesh people, 212
archetype, 280
Arens, William (cannibalism critic), 205–6
Aries, Philippe, 78
Arizona, Native Americans in, 178–79
Arnold, Matthew, 36
ars moriendi, 32–33, 69–80, 75, 86, 238,
  340
ashes, bottled, 263
assisted suicide, 50, 130
Athens, 53
atomic bomb, 19
Augustine, Max (Viennese entertainer),
  256–57

Augustine of Hippo, 68, 169–70
avoidance rituals, 95–96, 107
awareness of death, living with, 346, 358
Aztecs: cannibalism and sacrifice by, 202–6; worldview of, 421*n*28

ba (Egyptian loyal spirit), 332–34
Babylonians, funeral practices of, 263
bad death, 387–88. *See also* good deaths vs. bad deaths
Badone, Ellen, 151–52
Bagando people, 168–69
Baibar Khan, 196
Baldur (Norse god), 266
band-and-village cultures, 417*n*9
Barber, Paul, 303–5
bardo (phase of being), 337–40, 345
Bardo Thodol (Tibetan Book of the Dead), 331, 337–39
basic security, 112
Batu the Splendid, 196
bed = grave concept, 35
bedtime and bedtime rituals, 26–37, 28, 360
the Beguines, 79–80
Benét, Stephen Vincent, 333
Bentham, Jeremy, 161–62, 165
bereavement and the bereaved, 40
Bernadino of Siena, 79
better death, expectations for, 113–19
Big Bang, 1, 413, 415*n*1
Biggarroo (Native Australian god), 325–26
bills of mortality, 252
Binski, Paul, 78
birth: American practices of, 99; death in, 47; reenactment of experience, 348
Black Death, 14, 218–61, 272; in ancient Greece and Rome, 229–31; bacillus, 227–29; in Florence, 222–27; in London, 250–56; in medieval Europe, 231–36; religious frenzies and persecution during, 240–42; in the U.S., 258; victims buried alive, 240; in Vienna, 256–57. *See also* dances of death
Bland, Olivia, 80
blood, 3, 54–60, 74, 145–57, 195
boardinghouse, murders in, 163–66
Boccacio, Giovanni, plague and, 243
bodies, 12, 18, 78, 195; harvesting, 164; traffic in, 155–67. *See also* corpses

"body politic," 204
Body Providing Bill (Britain), 162
Bondeson, Jan, 298
bones, 15, 17, 145–51, 298. *See also* skeletons; skulls
Book of the Dead (Egyptian), 330–31
Book of the Dead (Tibetan). *See* Bardo Thodol
Book of Traversing Eternity (Egyptian), 335
Booth, John Wilkes, 196
border crossing between life and death, 313
Borneo, 146–51
Braddock Point cemetery, 293–94. *See also* African Americans
brain: death, 367; plastinated, 174
Briar Rose, 65
Brittany, Lower, 151–52
Bronze Age, cremation during, 263
Brooks, Mel, 276
Brother Justin, 37–38
Brown, Father Raymond, 57–58, 61
Browne, Sir Thomas, London plague and, 251, 271
Bryant, William Cullen, 279–80
buboes (plague), 224, 227, 229
Buddha (Siddhartha Gautama), 264–65
Buddhists and Buddhism, 49, 132, 167, 300, 307, 327, 332, 337–42, 344, 347, 349, 350, 352, 381
Bunny (author's wife), 182, 412–13
burial: alive, 240; cremation and, 226–310; gown, 266
Byron, George Gordon (Lord), 171

cadavers, 177. *See also* bodies; corpses
Caesar, Sid, 276
Calvi, Giulia, 222–24, 422*n*2
cannibalism, 198–217; Aztec, 202–6; dietary explanation for, 203; by Donner Party, 421*n*31; in Greek myth, 199–201, 200; and racist agendas, 206; by rugby team, 208–10
capital punishment, 274
cardiac evaluation, 404
cartoons, 20, 114, 127, 317
castration, fear of, 375
catacombs, 15
catapults, plague and, 234
catastrophes, 10, 226

catastrophic anxiety, 379
Catherine of Bologna, 140–42
Catholic Church, 62, 149, 389
cats, 3, 284, 413, 424*n*28
cause-and-effect mechanisms, 5
cause of death, 93; in the Iceman's death, 139–40; in Jesus' death, 60–66
cemeteries, 235–36, 286–95
cere (dying person's parting call), 46
Cerebus (guard dog extraordinaire), 318
ceremonies of incorporation, 344
certification of death, 13, 92
Chagall, Marc, 422*n*20
Champagnat, Marcellin, 36
Charles I (British king), 33, 85–86
Charles II (British king), 82, 88
charnel houses, 151, 158, 235, 294
Charon, 313–17, 316, 317, 345
childbirth, death in, 47
children, 34, 69, 201, 397; as Angel of Death, 22; and bedtime rituals, 25–26, 27–32; curiosity about/fear of death, 360, 366–68, 380, 416*nn*1,2; games and songs of, 13, 31, 39–40, 221–22, 244–45, 416*n*8; graves of, 290
China, poverty in, 216–17
choice, as illusion, 119–20
Christ. *See* Jesus
Christian era, 66–69
Christianity, as expansionary force, 270–72
Christian models of dying and death, 32–37, 75
Church of England, 87, 423*n*2
cinema, as alternative world, 10
city of the dead, 292
Civil War, 293, 308
clans, 6
Clark, David, 419*n*13
Clark University, 44
Claudius, Matthias, 361, 426*n*3
Clauer, Phillip J., on cannibalism among chickens, 198–99, 421*n*20
clinical death, 105
Closet Monster, 380
coffins, 158, 254, 276, 290, 297
Coffin Texts (Egyptian), 330
Cohen, Kathleen, 238
Cole, Thomas, 415*n*3
"collateral damage," 219
coming of age, ritual of, 208

communion, 68, 69. *See also* Holy Communion
communitas, 345
Comper, Frances M. M., 71, 73
Congwen, Shen, 216–17
consecration, rituals of, 289
Constantinople, plague and, 230
consumerism, hospice and, 113
contagion, fear of, 258
"contaminating woman," 258
conveyer belt of social time, cemetery as, 289, 292
Coptic Christians, 270
corpsed persons, 138–75, 188–89, 203
corpses, 3, 18, 92, 101, 103–4, 106, 221, 229, 233, 235, 239, 269, 416*n*10; display of, 290. *See also* vampires
Corpus Domini (church), 141
cosmetic industry, 384
cosmic anxiety, 205
cosmic mysteries, 402
Counts, David R., and Dorothy Ayer Counts, 48
Creator Spirit, 356
cremains, 262, 271, 277. *See also* ashes, bottled
cremation, 264; burial and, 262–310; history of, 261, 307; in India, 423*n*18; today, 275–79, 305, 306; world rates of, 279
Cremation Association of North America, 278
Crissman, James, 290–91, 412
critical situations, 358
Cro-Magnons, 151
crossover moment, 408
crossroads, burial of suicides at, 168–71
crucifixion, 58–62, 78
Crusades, 135
crystal ball, 154
cults, 32, 61, 63; of the dead, 150–51, 263
cultural pluralism, 206
Cushing Hospital, 126, 184–88
cyberspace, 351–52

daily examination of our lives, 34–35, 356
Dalai Lama (His Holiness, Tenzin Gyatso), 338
D'Albret, Bernard Ezi, and masses for the dead, 242

Dali's clock, 403
damnation, 61, 251, 317, 318–19
dances of death, 245–50, 246
danger awareness, 1
danse macabre, 246
danza della morte, 248
Darwin, Charles, 161
David (biblical king), 130
Davis-Floyd, Robbie, 99, 418n5
the dead: contamination from, 41, 188;
  discontented and dangerous, 177–81;
  good treatment of, 176–77; inconvenient, 184–88; journey of, 311–54;
  as killers, 234; knowing their places,
  221; place in society of, 309–10;
  reified, 381
dead cart, 235, 237, 256–57
Dead Man Arise! (children's game), 204
dead man's fingers, 399
deadness, 236
"dead red" (bone tinting), 152–55
death: as different from life, 366–71;
  ideas about, 17, 45–46, 51; images of,
  35–41, 247; as metaphor, 379; personified, 38–39, 220, 237, 247, 260, 360,
  384–86; as unimaginable, 374
Death and the Maiden (Claudius/
  Schubert), 361
death anxiety syndrome, 379, 415n5.
  See also fear of death; thanatophobia
deathbed and deathbed scenes, 43, 51,
  64, 69–70, 73, 75, 77–78, 79, 120–
  23, 133, 242, 396, 418n44; conversion
  on deathbed, 79, 90; Puritan, 89–90;
  of royalty, 80–87; visits to, 418n3
Death, Dissection, and the Destitute
  (Richardson), 156
death education, 94
Death Hunts the Hunters (woodcut), 220
deathing, 99, 338
death instinct theory, 426n2
deathlore, 329
deathniks, 136
The Death of Ivan Ilych (Tolstoi), 409,
  427n29
death's door, 37–38, 313
Death Valley (geriatric hospital unit),
  189
Delaware people, 152
denial, 11–12, 19, 36, 118, 375
Denton, Derek, 202

depopulation, 224, 233
deprivation and disease, 383
deritualization, 94
Despenser, Hugh, the Younger, 193–94
The Devil and Daniel Webster (Benét),
  333
dietary explanation for cannibalism, 203
dignity, death with, 46
disadvantaged societies, 397–98
disasters, 9–11, 13
disengagement, 46, 48, 50
dissection, 156, 159
divine judgment, 31
DOA (dead on arrival) status, 103
dogs, routines and, 3
Domenica, Sister (saint), plague and,
  225–26
Donne, John, 78, 417–18n31
Donner Party, cannibalism by, 421n31
Do Not Resuscitate (DNR) orders, 388,
  391
"doom soon" thesis, 1, 341, 415n1
doppelgängers, 332, 425n19
Dorian, Graying (Kastenbaum), 427n21
Dormition (sleep of the Virgin), 63–64,
  70
Dracula (Stoker), 302, 421n15
dreams, 180–81, 337, 377
Driver, Tom F., 197
Dr. Jekyll and Mr. Hyde (Stevenson),
  425n19
dualism, 71, 408–9
Duclow, Donald F., 63–64
Durkheim, Émile, 6, 415n4
dying, stages of (Kübler-Ross's), 116–18
the dying: becoming a dying person, 101–
  7; voices of, 123–28
the Dying Creature, complaint of, 73–74,
  77–78

earthquakes, vapors and, 232
Eaves, O. A., 303
Edinburgh, anatomists in, 159
Egypt and Egyptians, 255, 329–36, 335,
  377
the elderly. See the aged
Eliade, Mircea, 201
Elizabeth I (British queen), death of, 80–82
Ellington, Duke, 405
Elysian fields, 321–22, 327
embalming, 308

embodiment, sense of, 399
emergency response, 7–8
emptiness, shape of, 378
The Encounter of the Three Living and the Three Dead (woodcut), 246
end of days, 71
end-of-life decision making, 389
Enola Gay (atomic bomber), 19
Erikson, Erik, and Joan Erikson, 385
Eskimo, father's body and, 285
"ethnic cleansing," 131–32
Eucharist, 68, 209. See also communion; Holy Communion
Euripides, 313
euthanasia, 130, 136
evangelists, 66
Evans-Wentz, W. Y., 337
Evelyn, John, on London pollution, 251–52
the Evil One, 74
"excess casualties," 219
exchange society, 145
execution, of Charles I, 85–86
exemplary deaths (of Socrates, Jesus, and Mary), 52–66, 417n10
existentialism, 411, 416n8
exorcism, 194
extinction, 22
eyes: control of, 99; in death, 108–9, 389–90, 419n12

face-to-face societies, 417n9
faith, 398
farewelling, 126, 187
fatal accidents, 386
fatalism and fate, 120, 336, 358, 402
fear of death, 89–91
fear of the dead, 177–79, 181, 374–75, 379–80
Feifel, Herman, 19
fertility rituals, 344
fetal position, 330
final rites, 107
finitiude, 11
fire, fascination with, 263
fire and brimstone, 77
firefighters, 8, 393–94
flagellants and flagellant movement, 240–42, 366
Florence, plague of 1631 in, 222–27, 422n2

force of destiny, 402
"for whom the bell tolls" (Donne's line), 417n31
Frankenstein (Shelley), 158, 420n21
Frazier, Sir James George, 177–78, 180
French Revolution, 36, 294
Freud, Sigmund, 204, 360–62, 373–79, 415n5
Frey (Viking god), 269
funeral boats, 265–69, 335
funeral directors, 114–15, 277–78
funeral rituals, absence of, 259
funerals, 19, 32, 40, 67, 114, 138, 152, 310, 354; plague and, 211; sermons at, 183

Galen, 106
gallows, 157
Ganges, 273, 423n18
"garden cemeteries," 292
Gardens of Delight (Islamic), 340
Gardner, Don, 213
Gatherings from Graveyards (Walker), 296
Geb (earth), 331
Gennep, Arnold van, 343
Gentle Comforter, death as, 247
Genz, Henning, 415n2
Geoffrey of Monmouth, 230
geriatric hospitals: Mr. Carter (patient), 43–44; services in, 20, 43, 116, 184–88, 386
ghosts, 47, 49, 91, 221, 322, 399, 405–10; white men as, 213
gisant (type of memorial sculpture), 238
Gladwell, Malcolm, 221, 422n1
Glazar, Richard, on Holocaust, 260–61
Gobi Desert, 232
God; Lord (Judaic-Christian), 5, 17, 25, 27, 31, 34, 60, 62, 77, 81, 87–88, 169, 368, 392–94
gods (various), 45, 202–6; temporary, 61
Godwin, George, 165
Goethe, Johann Wolfgang von, 362
Golden Age, 321
Golden Legend (de Vorgaine), 63
golden rule, 177
Goldstein, Kurt, 379, 426n18
Gonnear (Native Australian god), 325
good death, types of, 122–31

good deaths vs. bad deaths: in past, 43–92; today, 93–137, 387
"good-looking corpse," 356
"good patient," 100
the Gospels, 57, 59–61, 64, 68
gospel songs, 322
grace, dying in, 81–82
grand send-off, 267–68
Grateful Dead, 244
grave diggers, 254, 299
grave robbers, 159–63
graves and graveyards, 16, 140, 151–52, 159–60; children's graves, 290; grave markers, 290–91; hazards of, 296–99; mass graves, 253–54, 256, 259
Great Fire of London, 255
Great Spirit, 324, 326, 336
Great Sweet Mother, death as, 359, 362. See also Mother Earth; the Terrible Mother
Greece, ancient: city-states of, 229; cremation of warriors in, 264
Greyson, Bruce, 346–47
grief, 12, 87, 133; traumatic, 416n7
Grimes, Ronald, 409
Grim Reaper, 248
Guatemala, funeral rituals in, 262, 423n2
Guidera, Christine, 80
Guillain-Barré syndrome, 402–5
Gyatso, Tenzin. See Dalai Lama

Hades/Pluto, 316, 319. See also underworld
Halloween, 248
hallucinations, 338, 348, 369
Hamlet, 25
Hampole, Richard, 73
Hapsburg Empire, 14
hara-kiri, 194
hard living, hard dying, 396–99
Harmer, Ruth, 115, 419n21
Harris, Marvin, 201, 203
headhunters, 196–97. See also Borneo; Kayan people
headstones. See graves and graveyards
"healthy dying," 113, 118, 419n23
heaven, 89, 135, 363, 365; highway to, 242; teleportation to, 269
hedonic calculus, 162

hell, 341
hemlock, 19. See also Socrates
Herman, Woody, 132, 405
heroic deaths, 129, 167
hide-and-seek, 416n8
High Cost of Dying (Harmer), 115, 419n21
Hilton Head Island, African American cemetery on, 293–94
Hilts, Philip J., 371–77
Hinduism, 167, 272, 274, 327
Hippocrates, 106
Hitler, Adolf, 170
Hki-snake (Egyptian underworld demon), 334
Hmung people, 262
Hoban, Russell, 38, 416n7
Holocaust, 261, 422n20
Holy Communion, 84, 86. See also communion
Holy Dying (Taylor), 32–35, 71, 416n3
holy lust, 361
homicide, 389; at-a-distance, 50–51
Hong Kong: flu, 232; plague, 258
hope, 112
horrendous death, 131
hospice/palliative care movement, 4–5, 29, 88, 93, 96, 109–12, 123–28, 391, 419n14
human heads: dried, 146–50, 147, 148; plastinated, 174
humanicide, 323
hypnogogic states, 373
Hypnos (sleep), 360

the I Am and the Me, 358–59
Ice Maiden and Iceman (Otzi), 139–40, 420n2
ideal death, 52, 64, 131
illusion of continuity, 375
imagined deaths, 120–21
immortals and immortality, 54–55, 376–77
incomplete death, 49
the incorruptibles, 140–42
incubi and succubi, 303. See also vampires
infanticide, 273
infants, 34, 93, 178; graves of, 290
influenza, 139, 232, 254
Innocent III (pope), 140, 142
the Innocents (religious order), 248

insomnia, death and, 360
insubstantial substance, 381
intensive care units (ICU), 189, 363, 399–412
internal dialogue, 363
Internet, 350–52
The Interpretation of Dreams (Freud), 375
Irish children, 215
Isaac, intended sacrifice of, 59
Iserson, Kenneth V., 419n22, 424n45
Isis (Egyptian goddess; Osiris's wife), 331–32
Islam, 341; beliefs about suicide, 167; concept of paradise, 363; doctrine of good works and the afterlife, 255–56; Islamic physicians, 106
Isles of the Blest (in Greek tradition), 319–24, 335

James, E. G., cults of death and, 263
James, William, 370
Japan, cremation in, 279
Jesus, 52, 64, 68–69, 79, 169, 209–10, 242, 265, 271–72, 283; death of, 57–62
Jews and Judaism, 5, 209, 233, 241–42, 271–72, 381, 422n20
Joan of Arc, 272
journey through life and death, 21, 26, 70, 311–51, 415n3. *See also* passage, concept of
Justinian, plague of, 230

ka (Egyptian intimate spirit companion), 332–34
Kali (Hindu female deity), 282
Kaliai (place and people, Papua New Guinea), 48–51, 78, 94, 107
Kayan people, 146–51, 147, 148
Keats, John, 133, 364–65, 419n33
Kellehear, Michael, 124–26
Kevorkian, Jack, 108–9, 389–90, 419n12
Khayyam, Omar, 144, 420n6
kidney dialysis unit, 378
King of the Dead, Osiris as, 332, 338
kinship network, 71
Kleinzeit (Hoban), 38–39, 406, 416n7
Knights Templars, 196, 270
Knox, John, 164
Kozak, David Lee, 178–79

Kronos, 199
Kübler-Ross, Elisabeth, 117, 122–23

Land of Perfection or Perfect Bliss (Native Australian), 324–28
Land of the Dead (Viking), 266–67
Last Judgment, 90
last-minute heroics, 388
Last Supper, 210
last tag (game), 127, 244
last three days of life, 124
last words, 55–56; Jesus', 59–60; King Charles I's, 85–87
Laurens, Henry (first U.S. cremation), 275–76
Lawton, Julia, 387
learned helplessness, 120
leave-taking, 110
lenticulae, plague and, 224
LeShan, Larry, 95
Leslie, John, 415n1
Leviton, Daniel, 131
Liebestod (love-death), 323, 425n11
life expectancy, 383
life review, 400
life support systems, 104, 115, 419n22
"life voice," 362
"limber corpses," 301
liminal (threshold) rites, 343, 406
linguistic structures, 373
"little deaths," 411
Little Red Riding Hood, 28
live burial, 298–99
living and dying today, 383–96
livor mortis, 300. *See also* postmortem changes
Lock, Margaret, 419n10
longevity, 279
The Loved One (Waugh), 114, 419n19
lovers, young, and death, 321–22, 323–24, 425n11
Lugbara people, 44–47
the lustful, punishment of, 76, 77

maat (Egyptian feather of truth, order, and justice), weighing of souls against, 333
macchabe and the macabre, 246–47
Maeterlinck, Maurice, 342
Mainz, cathedral in, 422n20
Maori people, 154

Marists, 3, 36–37, 91
Marriott, Edward, plague and, 258
martyrs and martyrdom, 62, 82, 169, 344, 419*n*31
Mary, Mother of Jesus, 53, 62–66, 78, 249
Maslow, Abraham, 444
mass killing, 393
Masye and Masyane (Greek gods), 199–201
Mather, Cotton, and Increase Mather, 89–90
McManners, John D., 90
medical students, corpses and, 173
memento mori, 237–38
Memorial Day, 289
Menippus, 315
menstrual cycle, 282
mental activity, imparting life and, 368–71
Mesopotamia, 368
the Messiah, 57, 60–61, 64, 70. *See also* Jesus
Metis (wife of Zeus), 199
Meyer-Baer, Kathi, 248
mezuzahs, 5
Mianmin people, 212–13
Middleton, John, 44, 46
miracles, 64, 70
missionaries, 269
Missoula, hospice demonstration project in, 391–92
mistletoe dart, 266
Mitford, Jessica, 114, 419*n*20
modernization, cemeteries and, 296
"A Modest Proposal" (Swift), 214–17
moment of death, 46–47, 51, 406
Moody, Raymond E., 346, 348
Moravec, Hans, 352
Morse, Howard, 276
Mother Earth, 237, 280, 292, 295
Mount, Balfour, 112
mourning garments, 147
Mr. G. and Mr. B. (geriatric patients), 186–88
Mrs. Q. (geriatric patient), 188–90
muffled oars, 317
Muhammad, judgment and, 341
mummies and mummification, 142; coffins, 190, 191
Murray, Alexander, 170
Muslims, 340–41. *See also* Islam

Nader, Ralph, 113
Nagy, Maria, 416*n*1
Nanking, atrocities in, 195
Nanna (Norse god), 266
National Funeral Directors Association, 423*n*22
National Hospice Demonstration Study (NHDS), 62, 124–25
Native Americans, 153–54, 327, 368, 391–92
Native Australians, 324, 328
natural death, 191–92
Nazis, 196, 261, 306
Ndulo people, 154
Neanderthals, 152–53, 210
near-death experiences (NDEs), 346–49, 352
necromantic powers, 241
necroscape, 236, 247
Netherlands, right to die in, 389
neuroscience, 371, 373–78
New Caledonia, 146
New Guinea highlands, 197
New Kingdom (Egypt), 330
newly dead, 46, 259, 308
New Testament, 130, 167, 338
Nietzsche, Friedrich, 362
Nile, precious water of, 330
Nirvana, 342, 363
nothingness, concept of, 15, 370–84, 415*n*2
Nottingham, Catherine (Lady), 81
nova ars moriendi, 136
Novalis (Friedrich von Hardenberg), 361–62
novum ordo defunctorum, 118
Nuland, Sherwin B., 94
Numero 57 (in Orwell), 191
nurses, 95–96, 101, 388–89, 400, 401, 404–8; Nurse Beamish, 180–81
nursing homes, 184
Nut (Egyptian sky god), 331

Ober, William B., 56
obituaries, 181–84
obsecro te (a prayer), 64
obsessive-compulsive sequences, 5–6
Ode to a Nightingale (Keats), 364–65, 419*n*33
Odin (Viking god), 269
odor of sanctity, 141

Odysseus, 313
Oedipus, 362
Ohrmazd, Creator of All-That-Is (Greek god), 201
old age. *See* the aged
Old Testament, 27, 72, 130, 167
ongoingness of life, 8–9, 377
O'odham people. *See* Tohono O'odham people
oral incorporation, 203
Order of the Burial of the Dead, 283
ordo defunctorum, 66–69, 84, 91, 106, 117
Oregon, right to die and, 389
organ harvesting, 197–98
Orwell, George, 48, 192, 217, 323
Osiris (Egyptian king and judge of dead), 281, 331–33, 335
othering, 214, 216–17
Otherworld Journeys (Zaleski), 347–48
out-of-body experiences, 347

pain, 97, 107, 112, 118, 120, 128, 132, 390
Pakistan, 307
palliative care, 112, 387, 389. *See also* hospice/palliative care movement
paradise, 135, 363
paramedics, 8
paranormal death experiences, 346, 348
Paris, 234–38
passage, concept of, 17, 24–25, 91, 94, 106, 165, 387–91, 395, 405, 408. *See also* journey through life and death
Passing On (Sudnow), 418–19n8
Passover, slaughter of lambs for, 58
paternal rejection, 72
path of righteousness, 340
Patients' Self-Determination Act (U.S.), 388
Paxton, Frederic S., 66
peak experience, 404
Pearly.Gates.com (Web site name), 350, 352
Peloponnesian War, 53
Père-la-Chaise cemetery (Paris), 286, 313
persistent vegetative states, 115, 419n22
personhood, 48, 100, 151
pesticides, 307
le petit mort, 361

petrified gods, 371
Phaedo (Socratic dialogue), 53
pharaohs, 311, 336, 351
physician-assisted death, 389
physicians attending to royalty, 82–83
pilgrims and pilgrimages, 141, 155–56
Pindar, 320
plague. *See* Black Death
"plague of plagues," 231–45
plastination, 173–75, *174*
Plato, 53–54, 56–57
Platt, Colin, 242, 244
police, 8
Polynesia, 168
Portal of Death (Paris cemetery), *313*
postmortem assault, 192–95, 225
postmortem changes, 300–2, 424n45
postmortem exam, 44
practicing death, 25–42
prayer, 4–5, 25–26, 28, 31, 33, 37, 64, 66–67, 77–78, 81, 183, 185, 208, 273, 394
precious eagle-cactus fruit (Aztecs), 202, 204
predetermination, Calvinistic, 80
pregnant women, plague and, 226
preliminal rites, 343–44
premature burial, 105, 298
premature death, 180
Preston, Richard, on smallpox, 258
primary flaccidity, 300. *See also* postmortem changes
Procession (Tisnikar painting), 407
prostitutes, cemeteries and, 294
Prothero, Stephen, 264
psychologists, 95
public health, 226, 253, 258
punishing the dead, 191–95
purification rituals, 54, 67, 101
putrefaction, 145. *See also* postmortem changes
Pyramid Texts (Egyptian), 330, 337–39, 372
pyres, 264–65, *264,* 273–75

quality of life, 397
Quigley, Christine, 416n10
Quran (Koran), evildoers and, 341

racist agendas, cannibalism and, 206
rapists, as surrogate husbands, 267

rats, plague and, 227, 233, 258
Read, Piers Paul, 208–10
reality, sense of, 13
realization of death, 10–13, 358
rebirth, 332
reburial, 152
Red Dragon Tavern (Vienna), 256–57
Rees, Martin, 415*n1*
Reeves, Peggy, 204
refigerium interim, 6–9
reincarnation, 320, 325
rejuvenation, 64
relationships, significance of, 125–28, 132
relics, 144
religious frenzies, 240, 242
reluctant therapists, 418*n6*
replica of living world, cemetery as, 292
reritualization and reritualists, 94, 106
respiratory therapist, 400
Reston, James Jr., 265, 268
resurrection, 16
resuscitation, 97, 102
"retribalization," 111
Rice, Anne, 302
Richard II (Shakespeare), 410
Richardson, Ruth, 156
rigor mortis, 300–1. *See also* postmortem changes
ring-around-a-rosie (game), 245
Río Morte, 315
risk-taking behavior, 128
ritual behavior, characteristics of, 98–102
rituals and rites, 1–5, 19, 54; bedtime, 27–32, 91, 231; birth, 99; early Christian, 66–68; of everyday life, 25–42; mortuary, 45, 66; of passage, 314–15, 343, 345, 349, 394
Rivers, W. H. R., 150
River Styx, 68, 315–16, 316
rock groups, death and, 244
Roman Catholic Church, 30, 35, 48
Roman Christians, 67–68
romantic response to death, 152
Romeo and Juliet, 324
Room 225 (of intensive care unit), 363, 399–412
Rorschach test, 369
routines and routinization, 2–3

rrk-snake (Egyptian underworld demon), 334
rugby team, cannibalism by, 208–10
Russia, 398

Sabom, Michael, 347
Sacks, Oliver, 359–60, 365
sacred burial ground, 166
sacred magic, 4
sacrifice, 3, 59, 102, 140, 201–6, 208, 266, 268, 344
safe conduct, 112
Sagan, Carl, 402
sahagamana ("the going with"; Hindu tradition), 273
Saint Augustine, 130
St. Christopher's Hospice (London), 109–10
saints, 68, 140–42, 197, 352
St. Stephansdom (Vienna), 14–15, 17, 358, 416*n10*
Saint Vitus and Saint Vitus' dance, 248
salt, hunger for, 203
salvation, 66, 69, 88, 242, 328
Samson, 160
Sanskrit, 272
saponification, 302
Sappol, Michael, 173
Saracens, 195
Satan, 70
sati. *See* widows, burning of
Saturnus (Goya painting), 200
Saunders, Cicely, 109, 419*n14*
Schubert, Franz, 361, 426*n3*
scryers, 154
self-destructing universe, 356
Selye, Hans, 7, 415*n5*, 415–16*n6*
separation anxiety, 26
serial killers, 163–64
Set (Egyptian god; Osiris's brother), 331–33
Seven Deadly Sins, 74, 76–78, 76, 77
Seward, Desmond, 196, 421*n14*
sex discrimination after death, 182–84. *See also* women
sexual love, afterlife and, 323–24
sexual union, death disguised as, 361
shallow graves, 304, 330
Shelley, Mary Wollstonecraft, 158
Shelley, Percy, 275
ship of flames, 265–66

Siddhartha Gautama. *See* Buddha
Sigrid the Strong-Minded (Viking queen), 268–69
sins and sinners, 72, 74, 76–78, 82, 90, 169–70
Sisyphus (king in Greek myth), 318
skeletons, 16, 237, 246, 247
skulls, 34, 83, 143, 145–52, 154, 197, 212
sky burial, 306–7
slaughter of the innocents, 242
slave girls, sacrifice of, 260
sleep, 26, 28, 73
smallpox, 258
snake-demons of Egyptian underworld, 334
social workers, 366–67
Socrates, 52–57, 64, 417n10
Solomon Islands, cult of dead in, 150
The Sorrows of Young Werther (Goethe), 362
the soul, 22, 54, 77, 83–84, 164, 179, 183, 236, 285, 319, 324–25, 333, 338–39, 396
spirit realm, 46
spiritual development, 300
split consciousness, 348, 425n19
stages of death, Buddhist, 49
stages of dying (Kübler-Ross's), 116–18
standards of care for terminally ill, 110–12
Stannard, David E., 88–89
status contamination, 418n6
stethoscopes, 44
Stevenson, Robert Louis, 425n19
Stoker, Bram, 302, 421n15
storymaking and storytelling, 134, 371–72
strangers and enemies, 48
stress, 7, 12, 94, 179, 243, 387, 398, 415–16n6
Styx. *See* River Styx
sudden and unexpected death, 47
Sudnow, David, 104
suffering, 60–62, 65, 70
suicide, 50, 62, 82, 129–31, 133–34, 166–72, 179, 365; by cop, 169; *hara-kiri*, 194; medically assisted, 389–90; studies of, 415n4
Summers, Montague, 305
superorganism, 6
Supreme Being, 21

Suso, Heinrich, 73
Swift, Jonathan, 214–16
Swinburne, Algernon Charles, 362–64
symbolic offering, 201
symptoms of terminal illness, 121–22

tainted identity, 237
Tantalus, 318
Tartaros sector of Hades, 318
Tartars, plague and, 233–34
Taylor, Jeremy, 340, 416n3
television commentators, 10–11
temptation, 75, 79
Ten Steps of Life, 21
the terminally ill, 4, 96–97, 101, 107, 118, 381, 387
terra spiritus, 345
the Terrible Mother, 280–81
terrorist attack on U.S. (9/11), 7–14, 18, 23, 41, 358, 392–93
thanatology and thanatologists, 19, 415n5
thanatophobia, 375, 415n5. *See also* fear of death
"Thanatopsis" (Bryant), 279–80
Thanatopsis, Miss (in Waugh novel), 419n19
Thanatos (death), 360
theologians, 70
Thomas, L. Eugene, 410–12
Three Revelers Meet Three Corpses (woodcut), 239
threshold vision, 349–50
Thucydides, 229
Tibet, Buddhism and, 307, 337, 339–41, 344, 347
Tibullus, 321–23
time as money, 383
Tiresias, 314
Tisnikar, Joze, *190, 357, 407*
the *Toh* (Bornean spirits), 146–50
Tohono O'odham people, 178–79, 421n1
Tolkotin people, 264
tombs, 152, 329, 334–35
"too many dead," 218–61
Torres Strait Islanders, 154
Totentanz (dance of death), 246
Towers of Silence (Bombay), 307
transfigured death, 133
transi (type of mortuary sculpture), 238

traumatic grief, 416n7
trauma victims, 116
trial by light (Tibetan Buddhism), 338
Tristan und Isolde (Wagner), 425n11
Trobriand Islanders, 144–46
tuberculosis, 133, 419n33
Tuchman, Barbara W., 232, 235
Turner, Christy, and Jacqueline Turner,
214
Turner, Victor, 344
Twice Dead (Lock), 419n10
Twigg, Graham, 288
twins, as unnatural, 50

umbilical cord, phantom, 259
uncharted lands, mapmaking and, 321
underworld, 99, 281, 316–19
unmortal, physicians as, 99
useful dead, 172–75

vampires, 299, 302–5, 400
Venus, 322
victims, U.S. as nation of, 393
Victorian society, 28, 287–88
Vienna, 14–15, 17–18, 23
Vietnam War, 113
Viking cremation and funerals, 265–70,
310
violence, 13, 179, 397; absence of ritual
and, 257; violence-famine-pestilence
cycle, 231
virtual corpsed person, 175
virtual deaths, 346–49
visionary experiences, marginalization
of, 353
visions: beatific and horrific, 339; of the
dead, 141
visitation, 181
Vlad the Impaler, 195–96
the void, 1
Vorgaine, Jacobus de, 63
Vulliamy, C. E., 153–54
vulnerability, 21, 26
vultures, 307–8, 307

wake, functions of, 265
Walker, G. A., cemetery reform and,
296–99
Warner, W. Lloyd, 288–89
warriors of God, 196
Watts, Sheldon, 255
Waugh, Evelyn, 114, 419n19
Weinberger-Thomas, Catherine, 272
Weisman, Avery D., 11, 112, 134, 416n7
Wertheim, Margaret, 351
Westminster Abbey, 170
West New Britain Province, 48
West Side Story (film), 324
White, H. K., 296
Whiter, Rev. Walter, 105, 419n11
"Who I Am" (thought exercise), 18–20
wickol soul (Tohono O'odham tradition),
179
widows, 49; burning of *(sati)*, 272–75;
strangulation of, 51
Wilde, Oscar, 27
wills-o'-the-wisp, 299
will to survive, 386
Winthrop, John, 88–89
wolves, plague and, 235, 394–95
women, 190; obituaries of, 181–84;
status of and discrimination against,
15, 45, 65, 72. *See also* widows
workhouses, 165
World Trade Center, 7, 11, 18, 23, 358,
394
World War I, 143, 152, 259
World War II, 178, 422n20
"worms crawl in, worms crawl out"
(song), 238
worship, 390–92
"wrongful death," 380

Yersina pestis (*Yp*; plague bacillus),
227–29, 252, 261

Zaleski, Carol, 347
Zen masters, 132, 398, 400
Zeus, 199

Text:	10/13.5 Sabon
Display:	Optima
Compositor:	Integrated Composition Systems
Printer and Binder:	Sheridan Books, Inc.